Setting Municipal Priorities, 1986

SETTING MUNICIPAL PRIORITIES, 1986

CHARLES BRECHER

RAYMOND D. HORTON

EDITORS

New York University Press
New York and London
1985

Library of Congress Catalog Card Number: 80-648313
ISBN 0-8147-1081-6 cloth
ISBN 0-8147-1082-4 paper

Clothbound editions of New York University Press
books are Smyth-sewn and printed on
permanent and durable acid-free paper.

Manufactured in the United States of America

CONTENTS

Contributors   ix
List of Tables   xi
Preface   xxi

Introduction
    CHARLES BRECHER AND RAYMOND D. HORTON   1

PART ONE

The Setting

Chapter 1. Local Economy and Local Revenues
    MATTHEW DRENNAN   23
        How Are We Doing?   24
        Economic Performance and Local Revenues   35
        The Outlook   46
Chapter 2. People and Income
    EMANUEL TOBIER WITH WALTER STAFFORD   54
        The Response to Economic Change   55
        Reasons for Slow Income Gains   61
        The Outlook   78

PART TWO

Securing and Managing Resources

Chapter 3. State Aid
    CYNTHIA B. GREEN   87
        New York City's Dependence on State Aid   87
        New York City's State Aid Expectations   91
        The Availability of State Aid   91
        The Outlook for State Aid   100
        Strategies for the City of New York   107
        Conclusion   113
Chapter 4. Federal Aid
    FRED C. DOOLITTLE   118
        Recent Federal Aid Policy   119
        Federal Aid in New York City   126
        Future Options: Ratification or Replacement   134

Chapter 5. Capital Resources
   JAMES M. HARTMAN   139
      The Capital Budgeting Process   140
      Sources of Capital Financing   144
      Investment Priorities   150
      Implementation of the Capital Plan   163
      Conclusion   167
Chapter 6. Human Resources
   RAYMOND D. HORTON   170
      Staffing Policies   171
      Wage Policies   177
      Productivity Policies   185
      Conclusion   194

PART THREE

Delivering Services

Chapter 7. Services to Children
   DAVID TOBIS   207
      Children and Poverty   208
      Public Programs   213
      Future Policy Directions   228
Chapter 8. Education
   ROBERT BERNE   235
      Students, Families, and School Districts   236
      Financing the Public Schools   247
      Public School Performance   261
      Public Funds and Private Schools   267
      Summary   273
Chapter 9. Health
   UNITED HOSPITAL FUND STAFF   277
      The Health Policy Environment   278
      Medicaid   285
      Health and Hospitals Corporation   294
      The Department of Health   307
      Conclusion   312
Chapter 10. Services to the Elderly
   CHARLES BRECHER AND JAMES KNICKMAN   316
      The Elderly Population   318
      Public Programs   324
      Policy Options   339
      Summary   348

Chapter 11. Criminal Justice
   ESTER FUCHS AND JOHN PALMER SMITH   352
      Crime in New York City   353
      Crime and Punishment in New York City   359
      Expenditures for Criminal Justice   367
      Policy Options   374
      Conclusion   378

Chapter 12. Housing
   GEORGE STERNLIEB AND DAVID LISTOKIN   382
      Trends in Housing Supply   385
      Municipal Housing Programs   392
      Housing Futures   397
      Conclusion   409

Chapter 13. Sanitation
   JOHN A. KAISER   412
      Overview of the Department   413
      Refuse Collection   415
      Street Cleaning   427
      Waste Disposal   434
      Conclusion   440

Chapter 14. Mass Transit
   ROSS SANDLER   443
      Dependence on Mass Transit   444
      Recent Mass Transit Policies   452
      Strategies for the Future   456
      Conclusion   463

Index   467

CONTRIBUTORS

PROJECT DIRECTORS

Charles Brecher, Associate Professor, Graduate School of Public Administration, New York University

Raymond D. Horton, Professor, Graduate School of Business, Columbia University

CONTRIBUTORS

Robert Berne, Professor, Graduate School of Public Administration, New York University

Fred C. Doolittle, Public Affairs Analyst, Woodrow Wilson School of Public and International Affairs, Princeton University

Matthew Drennan, Professor, Graduate School of Public Administration, New York University

Ester Fuchs, Assistant Professor, Barnard College, Columbia University

Cynthia B. Green, Research Associate, Citizens Budget Commission

James M. Hartman, President, Citizens Budget Commission

John A. Kaiser, Senior Research Associate, Graduate School of Business, Columbia University

James Knickman, Associate Professor, Graduate School of Public Administration, New York University

David Listokin, Research Professor, Center for Urban Policy Research, Rutgers University

John Palmer Smith, Assistant Professor, Graduate School of Management and Urban Professions, New School for Social Research

Walter Stafford, Fellow in Employment and Economic Development, Community Service Society of New York

George Sternlieb, Director, Center for Urban Policy Research, Rutgers University

Ross Sandler, Senior Attorney, Natural Resources Defense Council

Emanuel Tobier, Professor, Graduate School of Public Administration, New York University

David Tobis, Senior Associate, Welfare Research, Inc.

LIST OF TABLES

1.1   Real Output and Employment, New York City,   25
      1969–84
1.2   Change in Major Sectors of the New York City   26
      Economy, 1969–77 and 1977–84
1.3   Employment in Metropolitan Areas Which In-   29
      clude the 30 Largest Cities, 1977–84
1.4   Employment in 30 Metropolitan Areas in Three   30
      Recent Recessions
1.5   Unemployment in the 30 Largest Cities, 1984   31
1.6   Per Capita Personal Income in Counties Including   32
      30 Largest Cities, 1977–82
1.7   Growth in Consumer Price Index in 20 Large   33
      Metropolitan Areas, 1977–84
1.8   Output and Local Revenues, New York City, 1977   35
      and 1984
1.9   Change in Local Tax Burden, All Governments in   36
      County, for 28 of the 30 Largest Cities, 1977–
      1982
1.10 Local Revenues, New York City and All Govern-   37
      ments in Central County of 20 Largest Cities,
      1982
1.11 Elasticity of Selected Municipal Taxes   39
1.12 New York City Property Tax Rates, Fiscal Years   42
      1982–85
1.13 National Economic Assumptions, 1984–90   46
1.14 Economic Projections for New York City, 1990   47
1.15 Projected Change in New York City Employment   49
      by Major Sector, 1984–90
1.16 City of New York Tax Revenue Forecast, 1984 and   50
      1990

2.1   Population Change in New York City, 1970–84   55
2.2   Change in New York City Population by Age and   56
      Ethnic Group, 1970–80

2.3   Median Family Income, United States, New York   57
      Standard Consolidated Area, and New York City,
      1949–83

2.4   Percentage of Persons and Families below the   58
      Federal Poverty Threshold, United States and
      New York City, 1959, 1969, and 1976–83

2.5   New York City Population by Income and Ethnic   59
      Group, 1980

2.6   New York City Population by Income Group and   62
      Family Type, 1970 and 1980

2.7   Monthly Average Number of Persons Receiving   66
      AFDC and HR Allowances in New York City,
      1969–84

2.8   Relationship between Annualized AFDC Maxi-   67
      mum Payment and Poverty Threshold for Four-
      Person Households in New York City, Selected
      Years 1961–84

2.9   Percentage of Married Couple Families with Two   69
      or More Earners by Income and Ethnic Group,
      1970 and 1980

2.10 Employment-Population Ratio in New York City   70
      by Race, Sex, and Age, 1970–83

2.11 Employment-Population Ratio by Sex and Ethnic   72
      Group, United States and New York City, 1970
      and 1980

2.12 Payroll Employment and Employed Residents,   73
      New York City, 1970–84

2.13 Employment-Population Ratio of New York City   74
      Residents Age 20 to 64 by Education, Sex, and
      Ethnic Group, 1980

2.14 Highest Level of Education of New York City Res-   75
      idents Age 20 to 64 by Sex and Ethnic Group,
      1980

2.15 Percentage of Adults Who Have Completed Four   76
      or More Years of College by Age, Sex, and Ethnic
      Group, United States, Northeast, and New York
      City, 1980

2.16 Earnings of Employed Members of Selected Popu-   77
      lation Subgroups, New York City, 1980

2.17 Summary of New York City Population Projec-   78
      tions, 1980–90

2.18   Projected New York City Population by Age and   80
       Ethnic Group, 1990

3.1   State Aid to the City of New York, Fiscal Years   88
       1975–85
3.2   Planned Revenues, City of New York, Fiscal Years   90
       1985–89
3.3   State of New York General Fund Operating Re-   92
       sults and Aid to Localities, Fiscal Years 1970–79
3.4   Division of New York State General Fund Spend-   95
       ing between Local Aid and Direct Operations,
       Fiscal Years 1983–86
3.5   State of New York General Fund Projected Reve-   101
       nues and Expenditures, Fiscal Years 1986–90
3.6   State of New York General Fund Local Assistance   109
       Appropriations, Fiscal Year 1985
3.7   State of New York General Fund Appropriations   111
       for Aid to Localities, Fiscal Years 1984 and 1985

4.1   Federal Spending and Federal Aid to State and   119
       Local Governments, 1955–78
4.2   Federal Aid in Real Terms, 1978–85   120
4.3   Changes in Block Grant Appropriations, 1981–85   124
4.4   Federal Aid to the City of New York, Fiscal Years   127
       1981–85
4.5   City Agencies in Which Federal Aid is an Impor-   128
       tant Source of Funding, Fiscal Years 1981 and
       1985
4.6   Changes in Federal Aid Spending Proposed by   134
       President Reagan for Fiscal Year 1986
4.7   Proposed Federal Aid Reductions to the City of   135
       New York, Fiscal Year 1986

5.1   City of New York, Actual and Planned Capital   142
       Commitments, Fiscal Years 1977–94
5.2   Funding Sources for the Ten-Year Capital Plan   143
5.3   City of New York Debt Service, Fiscal Years   146
       1976–94
5.4   Planned Capital Commitments by Functional   150
       Area, Fiscal Years 1985–94

5.5 City of New York Planned and Actual Capital Commitments, Fiscal Years 1981–84 — 164

5.6 City of New York Capital Commitments, Actual and Planned, Fiscal Years 1981–94 — 165

6.1 City of New York Expenditures and Employment, Fiscal Years 1970–85 — 172

6.2 Employment by Agency, City of New York, Fiscal Years 1970, 1975, 1980, and 1985 — 174

6.3 Pay Relationships among Selected New York City Municipal Employee Groups, Fiscal Years 1970–84 — 179

6.4 Percentage Change in Real Salaries of Selected Uniformed and Civilian Employees of the City of New York, Selected Periods, 1970–84 — 181

6.5 Productivity and Management Improvements in the City of New York, Fiscal Years 1983–86 — 188

6.6 Residents per Municipal Employee, Selected Years 1970–86 — 195

6.7 Municipal Employment for Common Functions per 10,000 Population in New York City Compared to the Average for All Other Cities Over 1,000,000 Population, 1983 — 196

7.1 Selected Characteristics of Children in New York City, 1980 — 209

7.2 Expenditures for Selected Public Services for Children, 1984 — 212

7.3 Comparison of New York Income Maintenance Benefits for a Family of Four with the Federal Poverty Level and BLS Lower Budget Standard, 1975–84 — 215

7.4 Poverty and Public Assistance Status of New York City Population under Age 65, 1975–82 — 216

7.5 Estimated Need for Day Care in New York City, 1985 — 220

7.6 Discharge Objectives for Children in Foster Care, 1984 — 225

7.7   Trends in Foster Care in New York City, 1981–84   225

8.1   New York City Total and Youth Population by   236
       Race and Ethnic Group, 1970, 1980, and 1990
8.2   New York City Public School Enrollment by Race   237
       and Ethnic Group, 1970–71 to 1983–84
8.3   Median Income, Demographic Characteristics,   240
       and School Enrollment for Community School
       Districts, New York City, 1980
8.4   Poverty Status and Education of Adult Residents   243
       for Community School Districts, New York City,
       1980
8.5   Changes in Median Family Income, Population,   244
       and Public Primary School Enrollment in Com-
       munity School District Groups, 1970 to 1980
8.6   Measures of Inequality for Median Family In-   245
       come, Population, and Public Primary School En-
       rollment among Community School Districts,
       New York City, 1970 and 1980
8.7   Approved Operating Expenses per Pupil and   248
       Price-adjusted Approved Operating Expenses,
       New York City and Rest of New York State, 1966–
       83
8.8   Ratios of Approved Operating Expenses per   249
       Weighted Pupil, with and without Price Adjust-
       ments, in New York City to the Rest of the State,
       1966–83
8.9   Sources of Public School Revenues, New York   251
       City and the Rest of the State, 1966–83
8.10   State Aid and Price-adjusted State Aid per Pupil,   252
       New York City and Rest of the State, 1966–83
8.11   Per Pupil Local School Revenues, New York City   253
       and the Rest of the State, 1966–83
8.12   Local Education Revenue Effort, New York City   254
       and the Rest of the State, 1966–83
8.13   Full Value of Property per Pupil, New York City   257
       and the Rest of the State, 1966–83
8.14   Attendance Rates, New York City and the Rest of   259
       the State, 1965–66 to 1983–84

8.15   Reading Achievement Test Scores in Grades Two   260
       through Nine, New York City, 1977–78 through
       1983–84
8.16   Twelfth Graders as a Proportion of Tenth Graders   263
       Two Years Earlier by Racial and Ethnic Groups,
       New York City Public Schools, Selected Years
8.17   Private School Enrollment, New York City, Se-   265
       lected Years, 1971–72 to 1983–84
8.18   Enrollment in New York City Private Schools by   266
       Racial and Ethnic Status, Selected Years, 1971–72
       to 1983–84
8.19   Family Income of Children Aged Five through 18   269
       by Attendance in Public and Private Schools, New
       York City Residents, 1980

9.1   Health Status Indicators for the United States and   279
       New York City
9.2   General Care Hospitals in New York City, 1973   281
       and 1983
9.3   Expenses per Hospital Admission, New York City   281
       and the United States, 1978–83
9.4   Bottom Line Results of New York City Voluntary   284
       Hospitals, 1975–83
9.5   Projected Medicaid Expenditures, New York City,   286
       Fiscal Years, 1984–88
9.6   Medicaid Expenditures by Eligibility Category,   286
       New York City, 1983
9.7   Medicaid Income Eligibility Standards by Family   291
       Size, New York State, 1973 and 1983
9.8   Role of Municipal Hospitals in the New York City   296
       Hospital System, 1983
9.9   Percentage of All Hospital Care in Local Service   300
       Area Provided by Each Municipal Hospital
9.10   New York City Health and Hospitals Corporation   302
       Operating Budget and Tax Levy Subsidy, Fiscal
       Years 1978–85
9.11   Capital Plan for the New York City Health and   303
       Hospitals Corporation, Fiscal Years 1985–94

10.1   Number of Persons Age 65 and Over, New York   317
       City and United States, 1970–90

10.2   Housing Status of Households with Head Age 65   318
        and Over by Household Type, New York City,
        1980
10.3   Selected Characteristics of Housing Arrangements   320
        of Households with Head Age 65 or Over, New
        York City, 1980
10.4   Elderly Persons with Selected Types of Functional   321
        Disability, New York City, 1980
10.5   New York City Elderly Population by Income,   323
        Disability Status, and Living Arrangements, 1980
10.6   Sources of Care for the Disabled Elderly, 1980   330
10.7   Institutional Long-Term Care Facilities, New York   331
        City, 1983
10.8   Services Provided by Certified Home Health   333
        Agencies, New York City, 1982
10.9   New York City Human Resources Administration   333
        Home Care Activities, 1984
10.10   Weekly Hours of Home Attendant Care Autho-   337
        rized by New York City Human Resources Ad-
        ministration, 1984
10.11   Capacity for Conversion of Beds from Acute Care   339
        to Long-Term Care at New York City Health and
        Hospitals Corporation Hospitals Scheduled for Re-
        construction
10.12   Illustrative Eligibility Categories, Benefit Levels, 347
        and Gross Cost for Long-Term Care Insurance

11.1   Reported Crime in New York City, 1975–84   354
11.2   Per Capita Reported Crime in Major U.S. Cities,   358
        1978–84
11.3   Estimated Outcomes of Felony Arrests in New   360
        York City, 1983
11.4   Probabilities of Being Punished for Felony Of-   366
        fenses
11.5   Expenditures for Criminal Justice Agencies, Fiscal   368
        Year 1984
11.6   Uses of Criminal Justice Funds in New York City,   370
        1978–84
11.7   Sources of Criminal Justice Funds in New York   373
        City, 1978–84

12.1   Change in New York City Housing Supply, 1941–   383
        83
12.2   Permits Issued for New Housing Units, New York   384
        City and the Rest of New York State, 1960–84
12.3   Permits Issued for Publicly Assisted New Housing   387
        Units, New York State and New York City, 1960–
        81
12.4   New Dwelling Units Completed in New York   388
        City, 1921–83
12.5   Permits Issued for New Housing Units by Bor-   390
        ough and Building Type, New York City, 1970–84
12.6   New York Regional Housing and Office Market,   391
        1980–84
12.7   Major New York City Housing Programs   394
12.8   New York City In Rem Housing Inventory and   400
        Management, Fiscal Years 1979–85
12.9   Filings for Conversions from Rental to Ownership,   406
        New York City, 1981–84

13.1   Allocation of Resources in the Sanitation Depart-   414
        ment, Fiscal Years 1974–85
13.2   Refuse Collection Performance Indicators, Fiscal   417
        Years 1974–85
13.3   Street Cleaning Performance Indicators, Fiscal   429
        Years 1974–85

14.1   Hub-Bound Travel on a Fall Weekday, 1982   444
14.2   Total Weekday Usage of Public Transportation in   444
        the Tristate Region, 1970–83
14.3   Revenue Passengers by Public Transportation Sys-   446
        tem, 1970–84
14.4   Number of Persons Entering the Manhattan Cen-   448
        tral Business District Daily by Means of Transpor-
        tation, 1970–82
14.5   Recent Changes in Auto Use to and from Manhat-   449
        tan Compared to Citywide Subway and Bus Use,
        1979–84

14.6 Capacity of River Crossings to Manhattan, 1983   450

14.7 Metropolitan Transportation Authority Capital   452
Needs, 1987–93

14.8 Tristate Region Public Transportation Operating   459
Expenses, Revenues, and Subsidies, 1970–83

PREFACE

The purpose of the Setting Municipal Priorities project is to contribute information and ideas to the policy-making process through the publication of books and the convening of conferences to appraise them. This volume is the seventh in a series focused on New York City and its government.

This volume is published on the eve of a new administration's taking office and is expanded in scope to survey a broad range of issues the next administration will confront. Its expanded scope has meant more work for us, but it also has meant that we have had the opportunity to work with and learn from a larger number of contributors than we have in the past, including first-time contributors and those with whom we have worked before.

No doubt, the complex author-editor relationship was harder for the new contributors to become accustomed to than for the contributors to volumes preceding this. So, our thankful recognition begins with ten new people who authored or coauthored a like number of chapters in this volume: Robert Berne and James Knickman of the New York University Graduate School of Public Administration; Fred Doolittle of Princeton University's Woodrow Wilson School of Public and International Affairs; Ester Fuchs of Barnard College; John Kaiser of Columbia University; Walter Stafford of the Community Service Society; David Listokin and George Sternlieb of the Rutgers University Center for Urban Policy Research; Ross Sandler of the Natural Resources Defense Council; and David Tobis of Welfare Research, Inc. In addition, Bruce Vladeck, a contributor to an earlier volume, persuaded several of his colleagues at the United Hospital Fund to sign on as new recruits.

We are no less indebted to those who have enlarged upon previous contributions. They include Matthew Drennan and Emanuel Tobier of the Graduate School of Public Administration of New York University, Cynthia Green and James Hartman of the Citizens Budget Commission, and John Palmer Smith of the New School for Social Research. This more experienced group evidenced more ingenuity in attempts to evade our editorial strictures than the new contributors, but we enjoyed our renewed collaboration none the less for it. Dick Netzer of the New York University Urban Research Center once again served as consulting editor, a capacity for which he is uniquely qualified and for which we are repeatedly grateful.

This large group of contributors to *Setting Municipal Priorities, 1986* and its coeditors could not have completed the volume without the support of a group of energetic and talented people at the Conservation of Human Resources Project of Columbia University and under the direction of Eli Ginzberg. The Conservation of Human Resources staffers who contributed to this volume include Charles Frederick, Penny Peace, Shoshana Vasheetz, Ellen Levine, and last but not least, Fedor Kabalin. Since preparation of *Setting Municipal Priorities, 1982* when he first appeared as a "night shift" typist, his role has grown steadily beyond that of typist, proof reader, fact checker, copy editor, grammarian, and administrator to include moral support and friendship.

Institutional support for the Setting Municipal Priorities project and for this volume comes from a variety of sources that made the contributions of the individual chapter authors and support staff possible. This volume reflects continued support from the New York Community Trust, Charles H. Revson Foundation, and the Robert Sterling Clark Foundation, new support from the Foundation for Child Development, and indirect support from the Commonwealth Foundation, Robert Wood Johnson Foundation, and United Hospital Fund. Our "home" institutions, the Columbia University Graduate School of Business and the New York University Graduate School of Public Administration, provide the bases from which we direct the Setting Municipal Priorities project.

A manuscript becomes a book because of contributions by those in the publishing business. For the last four years, we have been lucky to have the cooperation of two people at New York University Press who took our manuscripts and converted them into documents suitable for wider circulation. Colin Jones and Despina Papazoglou converted a manuscript received weeks late into a book that met our requirements for timeliness. We are grateful for their tolerance and, as always, skilled production.

Numerous others receive our anonymous thanks for providing information and for commenting on our ideas and drafts. These courtesies and collegial efforts were provided to the editors and contributors by a diverse set of friends and civil servants (not mutually exclusive categories). In a few cases, anonymity was requested, but the list of indirect contributors simply is too long to include in this preface. At the top of this list, were we able to construct it, would be members of the bureaucracy whose performance we study and sometimes evaluate critically. City and State officials occasionally are regarded as a secretive lot bent on withholding information that is a source of their influence within government. This may be an apt characterization for other governments less well known to us, but in New York City the opposite is true. We may not always have friends in the "highest places," but we have many friends and many colleagues in the City and State government who share our belief that policy research from an independent vantage is a public good.

For seven consecutive winters and springs we have devoted much of our time to preparing Setting Municipal Priorities volumes, but our families are our highest priorities in life. In the final analysis, the most important reason we are able to do what we do is that our families understand us. So to Madeline, Sari, and Beth Brecher and to Radley Horton are reserved our deepest thanks.

Charles Brecher
Raymond D. Horton
March 6, 1985

Setting Municipal Priorities, 1986

Introduction

CHARLES BRECHER
RAYMOND D. HORTON

The elected municipal officials who take office in New York City at the beginning of 1986 will deal with a set of issues that have changed markedly over the past four years. Several of the more pressing concerns at the outset of the decade have been handled successfully. Balancing the budget—an overriding objective in earlier years—is now a routine accomplishment; for the past five years the City has recorded surpluses in its operating budget. Moreover, the outlook is for continued stability in the City's finances.

Balancing the budget was assigned high priority because it was essential to obtaining the confidence of investors and securing the capital needed to restore the aging, and too-often decrepit, infrastructure. The city was literally falling apart as highways collapsed, bridge cables snapped, and water mains erupted. Infrastructure investment needs remain enormous, but the City has developed a ten-year plan that will restore much of the capital plant to a reasonable condition and has identified sources with which to finance the plan. Repeated balanced budgets have yielded an investment-grade bond rating, and anticipated bond sales, complemented with other revenue sources, should yield sufficient capital to cope with the difficult problem of upgrading the city's infrastructure.

The costs of eliminating budget deficits often were reductions in the level and quality of basic municipal services. Paring the public payroll by 20 percent to help close budget deficits left service gaps that were not filled with improvements in productivity. As a result, in 1982 the goal of enhancing basic services was moved toward the top of the agenda of the most recent administration. Newly available resources were used to increase the size of the municipal work force on the assumption that more workers could be equated with better services. In several agencies the additional personnel contributed to measurable improvements in services. Refuse collection became more reliable; police patrol cars, fire trucks, and ambulances responded to emergencies more rapidly. But the volume and quality of most municipal services remains well below the public's expectations; service improvement remains an unfinished task to which the next administration should assign high priority.

But the agenda for the next administration includes more than finishing old business. New issues have emerged in the aftermath of the devastating decline in the city's economy during most of the 1970s and as a consequence of the unique character of the more recent local economic recovery. New York has become a city with an unusually large number and share of poor residents, and an improved job market has not proven to be a sure remedy for their plight. The central challenge facing the new administration will be to devise and implement policies that will allow a broader segment of the local population to participate in and benefit from the richness of the local economy.

This volume is devoted to developing a better understanding of the issues confronting the next administration and the policy options available for dealing with them. The book is divided into three parts. The first and shortest section consists of two chapters that describe, respectively, the economic and social setting for the next administration. The middle section considers ways of securing additional resources and of managing them more efficiently. The chapters in the final section analyze specific service functions and identify options for improving each. An overview of the major findings of the chapters provides a basis for linking them to the broader priorities of continuing service improvements and extending the benefits of economic growth to more New Yorkers.

LOCAL ECONOMY AND LOCAL REVENUES

Matthew Drennan places the recent local economic revival in historical and comparative perspective. The city's 7 percent growth in employment between 1977 and 1984 is a welcomed improvement over the 16 percent decline during the prior eight years. But the growth is not better than that achieved by most large cities in the United States in the same period. The city's employment growth was slower than that in 19 of the 30 metropolitan areas containing the nation's largest cities. If the entire New York metropolitan area is taken into account to make the comparison more apt, the local performance rises only to seventeenth place. The economies of most large urban areas are outperforming that of New York City.

The city's economic turnaround has been accompanied by several favorable developments. Inflation has slowed, real per capita income has risen, and the unemployment rate is down. But again, comparative analysis provides a different perspective. In 1984, New York City's unemployment rate was higher than that of 21 of the nation's 30 largest cities; New York City's per capita income was lower than in 15 of the nation's largest urban centers. Perhaps most troublesome is that in 1980 the share of New Yorkers living in poverty was greater than in 17 of the 30 largest cities, and the city's poor population has increased since.

The rebound in the local economy has not been matched with parallel growth in local revenues. While the estimated output of the local economy grew 84 percent between 1977 and 1984, local revenues grew only 58 percent. This had the intended effect of lowering the local tax burden, but the City has not gained in its competition with other cities. In 1984 New Yorkers continued to pay a substantially higher share of their income to local governments than did residents of every other large American urban center. Moreover, the reduced tax burden was achieved largely by freezing the preexisting tax system rather than reforming it. As a result, the property tax fell from accounting for 47 percent of local revenues in 1977 to 37 percent in 1984; in contrast, taxes on sales and personal income rose from 22 to 30 percent. Unsound assessment practices and consumer price increases have combined to transform the local tax system from one which derived the largest share of its revenues from taxes on property owners to one which derives an ever-increasing share from the earnings and purchases of individuals.

The economic outlook is for continued modest growth. Drennan predicts that local output will grow between 1.5 and 1.7 percent annually during the next four years. Employment growth will be slower because of productivity increases, but the net increase in payroll employment between 1984 and 1990 is expected to range between 129,000 and 183,000. Local revenues (excluding intergovernmental aid) will continue to trail economic growth, but they will increase significantly from under $10.8 billion in fiscal year 1984 to about $15 billion in 1990.

PEOPLE AND INCOME

The local economic recovery that began in 1977 has had only a delayed and moderated impact on the population of the city. Emanuel Tobier and Walter Stafford describe the recent trends and examine the reasons for the slow income gains of many New Yorkers in recent years. Despite job growth, the city's population continued to decline into the early 1980s. More recently, the pace of emigration has slowed, and a population of nearly stable size can be expected for the remainder of the decade.

However, the selective emigration of the past has left the city with a population that is poorer than it was at the time of the 1970 census. In that year median family income in New York City was about equal to the national average; steady decline for the next ten years brought the figure to less than 85 percent of the national average, and it has not improved significantly since. The falling average income has been associated with a growing number of families with very low incomes. Between 1970 and 1980 the number of New Yorkers living in poverty increased 25 percent, a staggering increase because the total population fell 11 percent. The city's population living in poverty grew to about 1.6 million or over 23 percent of the total by 1983, the latest year for which figures are available.

The downward shift in the income distribution has been accompanied by a sharp dichotomy between the economic fate of the city's white population and that of its black and Hispanic populations. Dividing the population into four income groups reveals that a clear majority of whites (55 percent) are in the highest group, and only about one quarter of whites are in the two low-income categories of poor and near poor. In contrast, 64 percent of the Hispanics and 54 percent of blacks are poor or near poor; only about one in four blacks and one in five Hispanics are in the top income category in which whites are predominant. This disparity in income distribution contributes to the perception of New York as a city divided racially and economically.

The key to economic success in New York is not a good job; it is two jobs. Fully 70 percent of the married couple families in the highest of the four income groups were two-earner families; for blacks and Hispanics the figures were 88 and 79 percent, respectively. But many New Yorkers have trouble gaining employment. While payroll employment has grown by 239,000 since 1977, the number of employed city residents has increased only 6000. The share of employed adult residents declined during the 1970s, and this appears to be continuing.

These trends have left female-headed, single-parent families in a particularly troubled situation. These families account for about 15 percent of the city's population but 43 percent of its poverty population. Many female-headed families are aided by welfare, but the benefits are insufficient to provide them a living standard even near the federal poverty line.

Tobier and Stafford are not optimistic about the future. Continued economic growth is not likely to abate the incidence of poverty. The trend toward increased numbers of single-parent families and the difficulty many blacks and Hispanics have in securing employment in the local economy may cause an even greater number of New Yorkers to live in poverty by 1990.

STATE AID

One of the reasons for the City's improved financial performance and outlook is significant increases in State aid that are expected to continue for the rest of the decade. In recent years the State has helped the City by providing increased levels of direct aid and by assuming greater responsibility for functions formerly funded by the City such as City University senior colleges, courts, and certain Medicaid services. For the future, the City is depending on increased State aid to the City of $1.3 billion between fiscal years 1985 and 1989.

Cynthia Green's analysis of State aid indicates that the State's ability to fulfill the expectations of the City administration will depend on four factors: the State's own revenue-generating ability, its commitment to increasing local aid at the expense of its own operations, pressures to cut the State's taxes, and efforts to reduce its accumulated deficit. While the State is projecting substantial revenue growth for the future, much of it will be applied to cut taxes. Remaining revenues appear sufficient to meet present commitments for aid to localities, unless direct State operations and tax reductions are greater than the Governor has proposed. These factors point to limited prospects for additional aid beyond that in the City's current plans.

Green believes the City can best pursue the opportunities for added State aid by continuing to advocate greater State participation in the Medicaid and welfare programs under which the City is entitled to receive a larger share of any additional funds. Strong arguments can also be made for more favorable treatment of New York City under education aid and mental-health programs. However, the City should devise a strategy for pursuing additional funds that recognizes that other localities, such as Yonkers and Buffalo, may be favored because their fiscal problems are greater than the City's.

FEDERAL AID

Unlike the State, the federal government cannot be relied on to contribute to the City's future financial health. Federal aid reductions in the beginning of the first term of President Ronald Reagan forced the City to face difficult choices between ratifying or replacing the cuts. The President's 1986 budget proposals indicate he wants a repeat performance. Thus, it is possible that federal policy will result in the withdrawal of funds anticipated by the City and again force the City to decide whether to assume prior federal roles.

Fred C. Doolittle finds that the City's response in the early 1980s was shaped by decisions at the State level as well as at the local level. In general, City officials ratified federal cuts in manpower training and selected social services, were mandated by State actions to partly offset cuts in welfare and Medicaid, and chose to replace other federal aid losses with local revenues in order to sustain a network of day-care and senior-citizen centers.

The full magnitude of the cuts likely to be made during the second Reagan administration still are an unknown, but the President's targets are clear. While programs for the poor are not exempted, his latest proposals would affect broader constituencies. Congress undoubtedly will put its own stamp on the President's proposals, probably softening their impact, but federal-aid reductions appear likely in the next few years. The only consolation is that the City's finances are much improved; it has a greater capacity to replace rather than have to ratify federal reductions.

CAPITAL RESOURCES

The ten-year plan that guides the city's capital investments calls for $26.8 billion to be spent in the next decade, excluding mass transit. James Hartman assesses the proposed uses of these resources and the likelihood that the money can be obtained and spent as intended. He finds that the planned spending will provide adequately for bridges, waste disposal, replacement of vehicles, water-supply systems, water distribution, and street repairs. However, there remain significant unaddressed needs in restoring and replacing aged school buildings and educational facilities, maintaining and replacing old sewers, and restoring the city's large parks. In addition, as discussed in separate chapters, the investment requirements for modernizing the subways and generating new housing are not adequately provided for in the plan.

To finance its capital plan, the City intends to raise most of the money by selling general obligation bonds. To achieve the ten-year target of receiving over $14 billion from the sale of such bonds, the City must raise its annual sales from the fiscal year 1985 total of $1 billion to an annual average of about $1.5 billion in the later years of the plan. In addition, the City is relying on revenue bonds to be issued by a newly created Water and Sewer Authority and other diverse sources, including privately repaid industrial development bonds, to finance the construction of waste disposal plants. Barring substantial changes in the public credit markets, Hartman believes that these funds can be raised without creating a significantly increased debt service burden.

In recent years, as the City accelerated its construction program, it faced difficulty fully implementing the plans. In fiscal years 1981 and 1982 the City fell well below its planned level of capital commitments, and in 1983 it met its objectives only by lowering them. Fortunately, fiscal years 1984 and 1985 have seen substantial improvement in the City's capacity to spend capital resources as planned. However, some agencies face exceptional problems in implementing their capital programs. For political as well as technical reasons the construction of the Sanitation Department's resource recovery plants has fallen behind schedule, and the spending for street and sewer repairs (which often are done together) has been "backloaded" because of difficulties in handling traffic and other problems associated with a major program.

HUMAN RESOURCES

The major use to which the City's financial resources are put is to compensate its more than 250,000 employees. Raymond D. Horton reviews three elements of the City's human resource management—its staffing, pay, and productivity policies. These policies were changed in important ways between 1970 and 1980. Prior to the fiscal crisis, employment and real wages grew, but in ways that disproportionately benefited some agencies (health, welfare, and higher education) and some employees (uniformed police, fire, sanitation, and corrections personnel). In the five years after the fiscal crisis, the level of employment and of real wages fell, and the allocation of employment and of wages also changed. Particularly important was replacement of the wage policy favoring uniformed employees with one that treated all unionized workers alike.

Since 1980, employment and real wages have grown. However, the City's ability to realize productivity gains has declined. Horton sees this as a logical consequence of the City's recent wage and staffing policies. One rationale for the City's expansionary employment policy has been to restore the provision of services to the quality at which they were supplied before the fiscal crisis, which the City measures indirectly by comparing employment levels to those that obtained before the fiscal crisis. While a staff of 251,720 people in 1985 is 14 percent lower than the high in 1974, the population loss since then makes the number of municipal employees per resident nearly comparable. Moreover, when compared to the nation's largest cities, New York has a municipal work force that is 22 percent larger for the functions it performs as compared with the work forces of the other cities.

Horton suggests needed service improvements should be derived primarily from productivity gains rather than expansion of the work force. Controlling the growth of the municipal work force would increase the incentives for managers to perform better and would retain a greater share of the available revenues for other purposes. Part of these resources could be used to improve the quality of the work force through higher pay and more training. Even without enlarging the work force, the City could hire more than 80,000 new workers in the next four years due to attrition. In a metropolitan labor force as large, diverse, and skilled as New York's, there are opportunities to hire and promote a productive cadre of workers. The most immediate productivity gains, however, could come from labor-management initiatives similar to the gainsharing agreement in the Department of Sanitation. Such agreements require City officials and municipal employee union leaders to fashion wage policies that reward increases in productivity.

SERVICES TO CHILDREN

Nowhere is the human toll of the city's past economic decline and service reductions more evident than in the plight of many of its children. At least one-third of the city's children are being raised in families with incomes below the poverty level, and over two-thirds of that group live with only one parent. The more than 550,000 children living in poverty deserve the next administration's highest priority.

David Tobis analyzes four categories of services to children that include income maintenance, day care, family support, and the family substitutes of foster care and adoption. Income maintenance benefits have deteriorated in value over the past decade, and Tobis recommends substantial increases in order to provide families a minimally adequate income with which to raise their children. In 1984 income-maintenance benefits for a dependent family equaled only 87 percent of the poverty level. Closing this gap would be costly, for the program serves approximately 275,000 families and would serve more if benefits rose. But it may be more costly in the long run to continue allowing one-third of the next generation of New Yorkers to be raised by impoverished families.

The City of New York already makes a substantial commitment to publicly supported day care. In fiscal year 1984 about $175 million was spent to provide care to 53,000 children. But the programs do not reach all those in need, and each weekday an estimated 47,000 "latch key" children under age 12 remain home alone after school. Tobis estimates that meeting the needs of these children as well as caring for additional preschool children whose parents seek day care would require additional annual expenditures of over $200 million.

The growing problems of child abuse and teenage pregnancy might be curbed if families received the supportive services their troubled lives require. Earlier intervention with more material assistance could help prevent the disintegration of families, but the City now provides few such services. Tobis recommends the hiring of counselors at day care and income maintenance centers who would comprise an "early warning" system for troubled families and who could authorize the specific services they require. The City will be entering new and largely uncharted waters as it seeks to prevent and reverse the deterioration of families, but the long-run payoffs may be substantial. Under current policies, the number of abused or neglected children exceeded 22,000 in 1984 and was rising; at the same time as many as 20 percent of all poor teenage females (ages 15 to 19) became pregnant, and nearly one-half of that group became children with children.

Nearly 17,000 children are in foster care at an annual cost of over $335 million. The voluntary agencies providing this care are expensive and, until recently, largely unaccountable for their performance. To improve both the efficiency and effectiveness of foster care, Tobis recommends vigorous application of the monitoring standards established by the Board of Estimate. The City's ability to use its financial leverage to upgrade quality is enhanced by the 30 percent decline in the foster care population since 1976, which has left many agencies with slack resources. At annual costs averaging nearly $20,000 per child, the City has a responsibility to put agencies that fail to provide adequate care out of business.

EDUCATION

The City's annual investment of approximately $3400 per pupil in public education ought to make a significant contribution to expanding opportunities for youth. Robert Berne examines the adequacy of this investment and the educational outcomes it produces.

Applying comparable measures of educational spending per pupil, Berne finds that the City has fallen from 15 percent above the rest of the state in 1974 to 4 percent below in the most recent year (1983) for which data are available. When adjustments are made for price and salary differences among school districts and for the disproportionate number of handicapped, bilingual, and other special students in the New York City schools, the City's spending drops to 25 percent below the statewide average. This underinvestment is not due to inadequate local appropriations; the City devotes more of its local tax base to public education than does the average community in the state. Rather, the shortfall results from lower levels of State aid for education. The best policies for increasing educational investments are to shift the State's aid to education to provide a more equitable distribution of funds throughout the state. Provisions in the allocation formulas that channel a disproportionate share of the funds to wealthier districts should be changed to provide New York City and other needy districts in the state with a more equitable portion of State educational aid.

Berne's review of educational performance reveals that schools simply fail to reach a large proportion of children. At least 15 percent of the enrolled students are not in school on a typical day, a figure about twice that in the rest of the state. At least 40 percent of the students starting high school never finish, a record that would not be tolerated by most other communities in the state. Berne also is skeptical of the significance of the recent, and much heralded, improvement in average reading scores for public school children. The test results show that the Board of Education is doing better than it did in earlier years, but the national norms are outdated, and the city's public school students still may be behind that average.

Berne also warns of a potential change in school financing policy that could have a dramatic impact on the city. Federal courts recently have loosened the conditions under which states may provide support for students enrolled in private schools, and within a few

years substantially increased public support for private education
could be a policy adopted in New York State. Is this good or bad
for New York City? Berne's preliminary analysis suggests the fiscal
benefits of lower public-school enrollment could be reduced expenditures, but the impacts include higher private-school tuitions,
more selective and potentially discriminatory admissions policies
at private schools, and relatively large subsidies for middle- and
upper-income families. If federal courts permit it, State and City
officials should proceed cautiously with a program of support for
private schools because the unintended consequences may be profound.

HEALTH

Health care is provided by the private sector and federal, state,
and local governments. The City helps administer and finance the
Medicaid program, operates hospitals, and promotes public health.
These three functions are reviewed by the staff of the United Hospital Fund.

The City's $4.4 billion Medicaid program is, in effect, three
separate programs. It finances comprehensive medical care for poor
families on welfare; it finances long-term care services for many
frail elderly who have exhausted their assets; and it serves as a
catastrophic insurance program for the uninsured poor and near
poor when they are hospitalized. The authors are most concerned
about the more than 900,000 members of poor families, mostly
children, who depend entirely on Medicaid for their medical care.
They often fail to receive preventive services and rely upon multiple
providers who do not know their patients well. To serve this population better with the current investment of nearly $1000 per
person annually, the authors endorse expanded use of Health Maintenance Organizations under Medicaid. But they recognize the limits to the expansion of these new organizations and caution that
other measures are also needed.

The Medicaid program also fails to reach many of the poorer
residents of the city. Since 1970, the number of people receiving
Medicaid has declined 18 percent, despite the previously noted
sharp increase in the size of the poverty population. The decline
can be attributed to limited adjustments in the eligibility criteria

that cut the maximum income, adjusted for inflation, that a recipient was permitted by 46 percent between 1970 and 1983. To rectify the situation, the authors recommend more generous eligibility rules that would make at least all those below the federal poverty standard eligible for Medicaid.

The municipal hospital system operated by the Health and Hospitals Corporation (HHC) has had to provide many services to the poor and near poor that once were financed from other sources. In recent years it has improved the efficiency with which it undertakes these tasks by reducing excess bed capacity, raising occupancy rates, and collecting more revenues from third parties. The authors would like to see municipal leaders move beyond concern for efficiency to improved effectiveness. They recommend changes in the affiliation agreements between municipal hospitals and voluntary teaching institutions that would oblige the latter to become more responsible for maintaining quality standards in the municipal system and more responsive to the primary care needs of the patients.

The municipal Health Department gradually has been relieved of most of its responsibilities to provide services through direct transfers of facilities in HHC as well as by longer-term trends that have shifted patients to other providers. For the future, the Department should concentrate on selecting roles for itself that fit the criteria of treating the community rather than the individual patient. Among the appropriate functions are surveillance and data collection, monitoring standards of care, health education, and advocacy.

SERVICES TO THE ELDERLY

Unlike many other groups in the city, the elderly have fared relatively well in recent years. The major programs providing them with direct benefits are financed by the federal government. They include Social Security, Medicare, and Supplemental Security Income. These programs were enlarged during the 1970s, and it seems they will be continued during the 1980s despite increased federal budgetary pressures. However, the federal efforts leave one important gap in the publicly financed services for the elderly—long-term care for chronic disabilities. Charles Brecher and James

Knickman devote most of their attention to the problems with and potential reforms of long-term care programs.

The authors identify two important problems in the provision of long-term care in New York City—a shortage of nursing home beds and a reliance on often inadequate informal home care arrangements by many frail elderly who do not qualify for Medicaid and who cannot afford formal home care. About 37,600 elderly New Yorkers reside in nursing homes; of this group, about 90 percent have their care paid by Medicaid at an annual cost approaching $1 billion. Several thousand more elderly require nursing home care, but the beds are not available for them. Instead, they wait in general care hospitals or at home under the care of relatives. On most days there are about 2000 patients in hospitals only because they could not be transferred to nursing homes. To alleviate the problem, more facilities should be built, and more public control should be exercised over nursing home admission policy to ensure that those most in need receive priority in obtaining care. The HHC can play a strategic role in implementing this policy by using the funds in its capital budget for reconstruction of three major hospitals to convert underutilized general-care beds to nursing home beds.

An estimated 119,000 elderly New Yorkers live in the community while suffering chronic disabilities. To obtain the help they need to conduct the activities of daily living they rely heavily on friends and relatives; 63 percent rely exclusively on such informal care. These arrangements frequently are unsatisfactory, leaving the frail elderly unattended too often and placing great stress on family members. Both the elderly and their relatives would be served better by a program that helped finance home care, but the Medicaid program does so only for the elderly who impoverish themselves. The "all or nothing" character of Medicaid eligibility forces families to struggle without governmental assistance or to spend all of their elderly relatives' income and assets in order for them to receive home care benefits. Brecher and Knickman believe this dilemma can be avoided by transforming the current financing arrangements for long-term care into an insurance-like program that would provide benefits based on the degree of disability and not on personal income. Their preliminary calculations indicate that this can be accomplished without significant additional expenditures. The evidence is convincing enough to justify experimenting with their proposed model.

CRIMINAL JUSTICE

Administering criminal justice is the responsibility of a number of public agencies, including three local police departments, five separately elected District Attorneys, more than a hundred judges in separate State and City courts, municipal Probation and Corrections Departments, and the State prisons. Together, these agencies spend over $2 billion annually to deter and punish crime.

Ester Fuchs and John Palmer Smith analyze the workings of the criminal justice system in New York City. They deduce from the limited available data that an estimated 1.7 million felonies were committed in 1983, of which about 623,000 were officially reported (which means the public chooses to report less than two of five serious crimes). The police made about 95,000 felony arrests (which means each police officer, on average, makes one every 12 weeks). They estimated that 27 percent of the 95,000 felony arrests resulted in felony indictments (which means that prosecutors allow three of four of those arrested to "walk" or to plea bargain for a misdemeanor). Nearly 22,000 of the felony indictments result in convictions (which means that most of those who are indicted for felonies are found guilty). Roughly one-half of those who are convicted are sentenced to State prisons for terms of at least a year (which means the others either are released on probation or sentenced to City jail for less than a year).

After describing this "leaky" system in New York City, Fuchs and Smith ask, What is the probability that any kind of punishment will be meted out for committing a felony? The answer is three chances in 100. What is the probability of spending any time in jail for a single felony? The answer is two chances in 100. What is the possibility of being imprisoned in a State facility for a term of at least one year? The answer is only one out of 200. However, the odds change for multiple offenders. For example, one who commits as many as 25 felonies in a year would have almost a 50-50 chance of being punished in some form, a one-in-four chance of being sentenced to jail, and a one-in-14 chance of spending time in a State prison. While the data upon which these probabilities are computed are somewhat incomplete, the estimates suggest that the performance of the criminal justice system may not be sufficient to deter many criminals.

The authors analyze alternative strategies for increasing punishment and reducing crime. A popular response, at least among politicians, is to add more police. The authors calculate, on the basis of current productivity and police costs, that increasing the number of arrests to 51 percent of reported felonies would require 126,000 additional police and cost $2.7 billion. A more reasonable strategy, they conclude, would be to allocate more existing police resources to fighting crime and less to the noncrime related functions that the police are asked to perform, largely as a result of the large volume of 911 calls. A primary limitation on the ability of the criminal justice system to punish offenders is a shortage of jail and prison space, not a shortage of arrested or convicted offenders. Therefore, Fuchs and Smith suggest the currently planned expansion of State and City correction facilities be rationed wisely, to increase the probability that multiple offenders are incarcerated.

HOUSING

Historically, the City of New York has played an active role in promoting the development of housing. Public housing in the city predated the federal program, and in subsequent years the City took full advantage of State and federal housing programs. But the withdrawal of the federal support and the City's economic and fiscal difficulties changed the housing market markedly. George Sternlieb and David Listokin trace the decline of housing construction in New York City and demonstrate the need for the next administration to stimulate a revival of local housing construction.

At a high point, in the early 1960s, housing starts in the city averaged over 70,000 annually. The figure fell to an all-time low—below even Great Depression levels—in the 1975–77 period when the annual starts ranged between 3800 and 7600. There has been a modest upturn since 1977, but new construction still averages only about 11,000 units annually or less than one half the rate of the late 1960s and early 1970s. Moreover, the recent construction is heavily concentrated in a few areas of the city. Manhattan and Staten Island accounted for 64 percent of the new units in 1984. The decline has been in both private and publicly assisted construction, but the drop in publicly subsidized housing starts has been exceptional. In the 1970–74 period nearly 116,000 publicly assisted units were started in the city; in the 1975–79 period the figure was under 20,000. A low number of about 5000 units annually have been begun since the early 1980s.

The impact of the decline in housing production was moderated in the 1970s by the sharp population loss in the city. Thus the city was able to accommodate more smaller households with its very limited increases in housing supply. However, with population size stabilizing and the economy growing during the next four years, Sternlieb and Listokin stress the importance of the construction of additional housing to local economic development. If the city cannot house adequately and competitively the work force of its growing corporate headquarters complex, it will begin to lose these jobs and those related to them. This development already is evident in the decline in the city's share of the region's new housing construction from 24 percent in 1980 to 20 percent in 1984 and the simultaneous decline from 44 percent to 20 percent in its share of new office space construction in the region.

At present the City has precious few programs to stimulate housing production. For the poor, the major municipal role is managing *in rem* housing which it acquires from owners who are tax delinquent. This stock includes over 10,000 buildings and nearly 104,000 units, of which about one-half are occupied. However, there are probably many more units which have been effectively abandoned by their owners, for which the City has not taken ownership. The authors believe these units can be made into a useful housing resource, but the City should develop management strategies that build upon its experience and experimentation with various forms of management including direct operation and management by private nonprofit groups.

The major stimulant of new housing construction for the middle class was tax abatement and exemption programs. But these programs were recently reduced in scope because of the perception that they were abused by developers who received subsidies for luxury housing that would have been built and rented in favored neighborhoods even without the subsidy. While not advocating such giveaways, Sternlieb and Listokin recommend that the City continue to subsidize middle-class housing construction in order to generate the added units that are essential to maintaining a healthy job base. New construction adds to the total housing supply, and all residents and potential residents benefit from a growing supply in a tight market.

SANITATION

The municipal Sanitation Department is responsible for collecting refuse, cleaning the streets, and disposing of refuse. John Kaiser assesses its performance in each of these functions and suggests different ways to improve each.

Management of the department's refuse collection and, to a lesser extent, street cleaning services, has improved. Each day municipal sanitationmen collect approximately 14,000 tons of refuse and are responsible for cleaning the city's 6000 miles of streets. Prior to the fiscal crisis, refuse was collected and streets cleaned with a complement of more than 11,500 personnel. In the next six years, this staff fell to 8100. Between 1980 and 1985, it fell to approximately 7500. Yet this smaller staff collects more refuse better and more efficiently.

Kaiser describes the actions that made this improved performance possible. This includes the acquisition of larger trucks, the design of new routes to utilize the new vehicles to better advantage, and the gainsharing agreement whereby sanitationmen receive a productivity bonus in return for reducing manning from three to two per truck.

Having demonstrated that refuse can be collected more efficiently than was dreamed possible a decade ago, sanitation managers now confront a related problem. How can they dispose of refuse when current landfills are full? Projected exhaustion of landfill capacity by the year 2000 means the City needs to build eight resource recovery plants that burn refuse and simultaneously generate energy for sale—one by 1988, three more by 1990, two more by 1993, and the final pair by 1996. There are several obstacles to this plan. One is political. (Who wants a huge incinerator in "their" neighborhood?). Another is environmental. (Who knows for certain how much cancer-causing dioxin these plants will generate?). Finally, there is a financial obstacle. (Are these plants too risky to attract private investment?). Kaiser is optimistic that the Department can meet these challenges.

MASS TRANSIT

No local service is criticized more frequently than mass transit.

The subways often are overcrowded, frequently unreliable, only rarely comfortable, and always require expensive subsidies. Ross Sandler shows that mass transit can and should be more than a necessary evil. The necessity of mass transit for New York City is indisputable. Over 3.1 million people enter the Manhattan central business district each workday, and this number will grow as the local economy grows. Nearly one-third enter in a private vehicle, but the capacity of local bridges, tunnels, and streets is nearly exhausted. The city's economy requires a mass-transit system to sustain it.

Given the necessity of mass transit, Sandler argues that the objectives of the Metropolitan Transportation Authority should be extended beyond the goal of its current five-year, $8.5 billion capital plan to restore the system to good order. For the longer run, the MTA should emulate the development of the Paris Metro since 1963. French planners were not content with simply buying new equipment and modernizing stations; they expanded service within Paris and coordinated Metro, bus, and commuter rail services throughout the metropolitan region. Moreover, like his French mentors, Sandler does not want to gamble that better and expanded service will increase ridership enough to pay for the added costs of the improved system. He would also import the *carte d'orange* concept whereby employers in the Paris region are subject to a payroll tax and, in return, their employees can purchase subsidized monthly passes. The Paris experience indicates that making riders pass holders will increase ridership. On the Metro, 60 percent of the riders possess passes.

Sandler's contribution is not limited to subterranean issues. He also recommends aiding the passengers who ride New York City buses 600 million times a year. Improving this service may be the formal responsibility of the New York City Transit Authority, but the Mayor and Board of Estimate control the streets and could—through regulation—make buses more efficient. Citing a number of successful experiments that have given buses preference over competing vehicles for limited street space, Sandler argues extensions of these special bus lanes—and even special bus streets—are warranted.

The multiple issues, options, and recommendations in these 14 chapters comprise a comprehensive agenda for the next administration. In fact, the resources required to pursue all the desirable actions the authors have identified undoubtedly would exceed what City officials can reasonably expect to receive in revenues over the next four years. In this sense, the authors, and the editors, have failed to set municipal priorities. But it is not the task of analysts to make these choices. Elected officials rightly are responsible for setting municipal priorities, but they can exercise this authority better with the information and ideas that analysis generates.

While not all of the city's needs can be met in the next four years, it seems unavoidable that the next administration extend the municipal agenda beyond the tasks that received highest priority in earlier years. The recovery of the New York City economy, which has continued as long as its 1969–77 decline, provided a foundation for many of the most recent achievements. But the uneven distribution of benefits of this growth also raises an important challenge for the next administration: to fashion municipal policies that will help the growing class of impoverished New Yorkers to share in the work and rewards of the local economy.

In many ways, this new task is more difficult than balancing a budget or developing capital investment plans. Investments in human resources sometimes involve greater risks than investments in physical plant, and the record of the past suggests that the "costs of good intentions" can easily grow beyond locally available revenues. But New Yorkers are venturesome and compassionate. Uncertainties and difficulties are unlikely to deter their support for sensibly designed policies that broaden opportunities for their neighbors and children to partake in all that the city has to offer.

PART ONE

The Setting

1

Local Economy
and
Local Revenues

MATTHEW DRENNAN

Although ten years have passed since New York City's fiscal crisis, those days remain vivid in the memories of many residents and virtually all of their elected officials. Nobody wants to return to a past of sharp economic decline and severe budgetary cutbacks, and all local politicians want to share the credit for avoiding the continuation or repetition of that misfortune. This is clearly a healthy attitude, but it has the ironic effect of setting standards for satisfactory performance on the basis simply of avoiding disaster. In some respects, perception of an economic and fiscal recovery in New York City is distorted by this unusual perspective.

This chapter places the recent turnaround in the city's economy in a broader, comparative perspective. The first section describes local trends and compares New York City's recent performance according to selected economic and fiscal measures with that of other large American cities. The second section focuses more closely on the City of New York's revenue system and the ways in which local tax yields have responded to changed economic trends. The final section presents projections for the local economy and local revenues based on the continuation of current policies.

HOW ARE WE DOING?

To assess dispassionately how New York City is "doing" requires the study of events over a suitable time period for measuring performance. Although the fiscal crisis emerged in 1975, it was not until 1977 that employment in New York City hit bottom, partly because of reductions in municipal employment. From 1975 to 1977, total employment in New York City fell almost 100,000, of which nearly 70,000 was accounted for by government jobs (see Table 1.1). This brought the total job loss from 1969, when city employment was highest, to 1977 to approximately 600,000 or 16 percent. Similarly, local output fell 10 percent in the 1969–77 period.[1] Hence, 1977 is the appropriate year from which to appraise change.

Since 1977, output has expanded at an average annual rate of 2.0 percent. The only year between 1977 and 1984 in which output declined was 1982, during the most severe national recession since the 1930s. This loss was more than made up in 1983 and additional gains were achieved in 1984. Local employment grew 1.1 percent annually from 1977 to 1984, with a slight decline in 1982. Output grew faster than employment during this period because productivity improved.

While growth is evident in many sectors of the local economy, the private commercial sector has lagged behind the nonprofit sector, consisting of government and private nonprofit organizations. The rate of employment increase in the nonprofit sector was more than twice that of the private commercial sector (1.9 versus 0.8 percent annually), and the disparity in output gains was also substantial (2.9 versus 1.8 percent annually). The rapid growth in the area of nonprofit organizations is due primarily to expansion in the fields of health, education, and social services rather than to growth of government. Increases in private employment are concentrated

TABLE 1.1
Real Output and Employment, New York City, 1969–84

Year	Real Output (in billions)			Employment (in thousands)		
	Total	Private Commercial	Nonprofit and Government	Total	Private Commercial	Nonprofit and Government
1969	$94.6	$76.8	$17.8	3,798	2,841	957
1975	80.0	61.0	19.0	3,283	2,348	935
1977	84.8	66.7	18.1	3,187	2,318	869
1978	86.8	67.8	19.0	3,234	2,342	892
1979	87.5	68.3	19.2	3,279	2,379	900
1980	88.1	68.6	19.5	3,302	2,393	909
1981	92.5	72.3	20.2	3,358	2,429	929
1982	91.0	70.5	20.5	3,345	2,398	947
1983	92.7	71.6	21.1	3,356	2,389	967
1984	97.6	75.5	22.1	3,432	2,442	991
Average Annual Percentage Change						
1969–77	−1.4%	−1.8%	0.2%	−2.2%	−2.5%	−1.2%
1977–84	2.0	1.8	2.9	1.1	0.8	1.9

SOURCES: Output data from Drennan–CHR Econometric Model and Data Base. Employment data from U.S. Department of Labor, Bureau of Labor Statistics, *Employment and Earnings, States and Areas*, and *Employment and Earnings* various issues. Nonprofit detailed employment from New York State Department of Labor.

NOTE: Dollar figures are in constant 1983 dollars.

TABLE 1.2

Change in Major Sectors of the New York City Economy,
1969–77 and 1977–84

	Employment (thousands)			Average Annual Percentage Change	
	1969	1977	1984	1969–77	1977–84
Local Sector	1,580	1,273	1,267	− 2.7%	− 0.1%
Export Sectors	2,218	1,914	2,165	− 1.8	+ 1.8
Corporate Complex	1,193	1,089	1,346	− 1.1	+ 3.1
Headquarters	184	135	124	− 3.8	− 1.2
Corporate Services	925	883	1,137	− 0.6	+ 3.7
Ancillary Services	84	71	85	− 2.1	+ 2.6
Goods Production and Distribution	806	575	518	− 4.1	− 1.5
Consumer Services	219	250	301	+ 1.7	+ 2.7
Total	3,798	3,187	3,432	− 2.2%	+ 1.1%

SOURCES: New York State Department of Labor, unpublished data. Headquarters employment is estimated by author.

in finance, communications, and other services; employment in goods production and in transportation, utilities, and trade actually declined. Overall, the nonprofit sector accounted for 122,000 new jobs or 50 percent of the net growth since 1977. As a result of these trends, the nonprofit component of the local economy accounted for nearly three of every ten New York City jobs in 1984.

Another way to view the changes in the New York economy is in terms of export industries and local activities. Export industries are those whose output is sold largely to individuals or firms outside the local area. These activities bring new income into the city's economy. Local industries produce goods or services purchased largely by the area's residents. The size of these activities depends upon the level of income generated by export industries and by the size of the local market.

While all industries serve both local and export markets, most can be categorized as primarily one or the other. It is possible to divide the New York City economy into a local sector and three major groups of export activities: certain consumer services, goods production and distribution, and a corporate headquarters complex.[2] The consumer services group includes two large industries— private health and private education. Those that produce and distribute goods include wholesale trade, water transportation, and four manufacturing industries: apparel, printing and publishing, leather, and miscellaneous manufacturing. Of course, the export industries also serve local demand, and it is not possible to separate an export industry into components that meet either export or local demands.

The corporate headquarters complex is comprised of three parts—headquarters offices, firms servicing headquarters offices, and ancillary services provided to individuals who perform the headquarters and corporate service activities. The headquarters component consists of central administrative offices of manufacturing and mining enterprises, and the offices of insurance carriers. Corporate services are specialized activities required by modern business and nonprofit headquarters, including commercial and investment banking, accounting and auditing, legal and advertising services, computer services, and consulting and transportation services. Ancillary services are those required by personnel working in corporate service firms and headquarters, including hotels, transportation and entertainment.

As is shown in Table 1.2, the recent growth in the city's economy has been led by its corporate headquarters complex. From 1977 to 1984, employment in the corporate headquarters complex expanded 3.1 percent annually, or triple the rate of total employment growth in that recovery period. Within the complex, it was very strong expansion (3.7 percent annually) in the largest part—corporate services—which more than offset the continuing decline in headquarters' employment.

The goods production and distribution export group continued to decline (1.5 percent annually) in the recovery period, albeit at a slower rate than the precipitous drop of 4.1 percent per year during the 1969–77 period. The consumer services export group has expanded at an average annual rate of 2.7 percent since 1977, which is considerably faster than its growth of 1.7 percent annually in the period of employment decline for all other sectors of the city's economy.

Employment in all the export sectors together increased 1.8 percent annually on average in the recovery since 1977. Employment for local production and distribution showed a very slight decrease (0.1 percent annually), in large part reflecting a smaller city population. In the prior period of decline, both the export sector and the local sector had annual average job losses of 1.8 and 2.7 percent, respectively.

These recent trends in employment and output provide a partial answer to the question, "How are we doing?" Compared to earlier years, New York's economy has improved significantly. But, as noted initially, this may not be the most relevant standard for comparison. New York is one of many large cities in the United States, indeed in the world, vying with each other for firms and residents. In this contest, a suitable benchmark for assessing New York City's performance is the behavior of other large cities. While it would be desirable to compare New York to its international as well as its domestic competitors, sufficient data are not available to do so. However, it is possible to compare the recent performance of New York with that of other large American cities. Moreover, data are available relating to multiple criteria. Comparisons can be made with economic indicators relating to employment, income, and inflation.

EMPLOYMENT INDICATORS

Employment expansion in New York City since 1977 has amounted to 237,000 jobs or 7.4 percent. How does that compare with other cities? Employment data are generally available only for metropolitan areas that include both a central city and its surrounding suburbs and satellite cities. Table 1.3 ranks the metropolitan areas which include the nation's 30 largest cities based on their employment growth between 1977 and 1984. The New York metropolitan area was seventeenth, with job expansion of 11.1 percent. If New York City was used in the ranking, the growth in the 1977–84 period, of 7.4 percent, would place it twenty-third. In other words, the New York metropolitan area's performance in terms of employment expansion was below average for large urban areas. Places such as Boston, Washington, D.C., and Nashville grew more rapidly than New York. The places New York outperformed include all the other large areas of the Northeast and North-Central states, some of which suffered employment losses (Detroit, Cleveland, Pittsburgh, and Chicago), as well as Philadelphia, Baltimore, Kansas City, and St. Louis.

In addition to long-run employment growth, the ability of a city's job base to weather national recessions is also important. The changes in employment, from peak to trough, in the last three national recessions are ranked for the same group of 30 metropol-

TABLE 1.3

Employment in Metropolitan Areas Which Include the 30 Largest Cities, 1977–84

Rank	Metropolitan Area	Percentage Change 1977–84	Employment 1977 (thousands)	Employment 1984 (thousands)
1	Phoenix	50.6%	490	738
2	Dallas	38.7	1,197	1,660
3	San Jose	37.8	537	740
4	Atlanta	36.9	823	1,127
5	San Antonio	32.2	345	456
6	Denver	30.6	670	875
7	Houston	29.6	1,174	1,521
8	San Diego	28.8	545	702
9	Seattle	26.6	629	796
10	Jacksonville	21.0	267	323
11	Washington, DC	20.7	1,404	1,695
12	El Paso	19.2	141	168
13	Nashville	19.2	333	397
14	Boston	16.8	1,313	1,534
15	Los Angeles	13.6	3,233	3,674
16	San Francisco	12.4	1,396	1,582
17	New York[a]	11.1	4,418	4,906
18	New Orleans	10.8	455	505
19	Baltimore	10.3	865	954
20	Columbus	9.5	472	517
21	Indianapolis	8.7	486	527
22	Philadelphia	7.7	1,828	1,968
23	St. Louis	5.6	959	1,013
24	Memphis	5.0	340	357
25	Kansas City	4.7	596	624
26	Milwaukee	1.1	630	637
27	Chicago	− 0.4	3,056	3,044
28	Cleveland	− 6.1	881	827
29	Pittsburgh	− 6.2	911	855
30	Detroit	− 8.0	1,729	1,590

SOURCES: U.S. Department of Labor, Bureau of Labor Statistics, *Employment, Hours and Earnings, States and Areas, 1939–82,* and *Employment and Earnings,* various issues in 1984.

a. The New York metropolitan area is defined to include Nassau and Suffolk counties on suburban Long Island. Although Nassau-Suffolk is a separate Standard Metropolitan Statistical Area (SMSA), it is closely tied to the New York metropolitan economy. Its inclusion makes the New York area unit of measurement similar to the metropolitan scope of the units for other areas. If Nassau and Suffolk counties were not included, the New York area alone would rank twentieth with an employment growth of 8.9 percent.

TABLE 1.4

Employment in 30 Metropolitan Areas in Three Recent Recessions

| Metropolitan Area | Change in Employment, Peak to Trough | | | | | |
| | May 1981–Apr 1982 | | Jan–Mar 1980 | | Apr 1973–Jan 1975 | |
	Change	Rank	Change	Rank	Change	Rank
Phoenix	+2.2%	1	−1.1%	25	−5.2%	23
Atlanta	+2.0	2	+1.8	6	−7.2	29
Dallas	+1.4	3	+2.0	4	−1.1	12
Jacksonville	+1.3	4	+1.0	12	−0.9	11
San Antonio	+1.2	5	+1.5	8	+0.5	5
Denver	+1.1	6	+2.0	5	−2.4	13
Boston	+1.0	7	+0.3	16	−5.4	26
San Jose	+0.4	8	+2.6	3	−0.8	9
Columbus	0.0	9	−0.6	23	−4.3	19
New York	−0.1	10	+1.4	9	−6.4	27
San Francisco	−0.3	11	+0.3	17	−0.4	7
San Diego	−0.5	12	−1.2	26	+1.9	3
Honolulu	−0.9	13	−0.4	22	+1.4	4
Seattle	−1.2	14	+0.1	19	+2.2	2
Washington, DC	−1.4	15	+3.7	2	−0.6	8
New Orleans	−1.5	16	+1.8	7	−0.1	6
Houston	−1.6	17	+3.7	1	+7.1	1
Nashville	−1.6	18	−0.3	21	−4.3	21
St. Louis	−1.6	19	+0.6	15	−5.3	25
Los Angeles	−1.8	20	−1.7	28	−3.1	15
Philadelphia	−1.9	21	−0.8	24	−6.4	28
Baltimore	−3.3	22	+1.3	10	−2.6	14
El Paso	−3.5	23	+0.6	13	−0.9	10
Kansas City	−3.6	24	+0.2	18	−4.2	18
Chicago	−3.7	25	+1.2	11	−4.1	17
Indianapolis	−3.8	26	0.0	20	−3.8	16
Memphis	−3.9	27	+0.6	14	−5.3	24
Cleveland	−5.3	28	−1.7	27	−4.4	22
Milwaukee	−5.3	29	−2.1	29	−4.3	20
Detroit	−5.4	30	−3.8	30	−10.2	30

SOURCES: U.S. Department of Labor, Bureau of Labor Statistics, "Lobstat Series Report" (unpublished), October 24, 1983. Seasonally adjusted monthly data used to calculate quarterly averages.

itan areas in Table 1.4. The metropolitan areas are listed from best to worst for the last, and most severe, recession that extended from the third quarter of 1981 to the fourth quarter of 1982. The performance in that recession is varied, from a 2.2 percent employment gain in Phoenix to a 5.4 percent loss in Detroit. New York ranks tenth with a slight (0.1 percent) employment decline. That is close

TABLE 1.5
Unemployment in the 30 Largest Cities, 1984

Rank	City	Unemployment Rate
1	Phoenix	3.2%
2	Boston	3.8
3	Dallas	3.8
4	Nashville	4.1
5	Denver	4.8
6	San Antonio	4.8
7	San Jose	5.1
8	San Diego	5.4
9	Kansas City	5.5
10	Jacksonville	5.6
11	San Francisco	6.0
12	Atlanta	6.3
13	Indianapolis	6.3
14	Houston	6.4
15	Philadelphia	6.9
16	Columbus	7.1
17	Memphis	7.1
18	Milwaukee	7.2
19	Seattle	7.4
20	St. Louis	7.7
21	Baltimore	7.8
22	New York City	7.9
23	Los Angeles	8.0
24	Pittsburgh	8.1
25	Washington	8.3
26	Chicago	8.6
27	New Orleans	9.4
28	El Paso	9.9
29	Cleveland	12.6
30	Detroit	14.8

SOURCE: U.S. Department of Labor, Bureau of Labor Statistics, Local Area Unemployment Statistics, unpublished data for November 1984, except for Detroit which is August 1984. Comparable data for 1977 or other years prior to 1982 are not available.

to its rank (ninth) in the mild 1980 recession, when employment in the New York area grew 1.4 percent. The change in employment in the New York area in those last two recessions represents a dramatic improvement over the change in the 1973–75 recession. In that prefiscal crisis decline, New York ranked twenty-seventh and lost 6.4 percent of its jobs. Thus, in terms of weathering recessions, New York experienced a significant improvement, rising from almost the worst of large areas to ranking within the top third.

TABLE 1.6
Per Capita Personal Income in Counties Including 30 Largest Cities, 1977–82

Rank	City	Percentage Change 1977–82	Per Capita Personal Income 1982	Per Capita Personal Income 1977[a] (1982 $)
1	Boston	+ 10.8%	$11,072	$9,991
2	Washington, DC	+ 10.8	15,064	13,601
3	New York	+ 8.2	12,240	11,315
4	Dallas	+ 7.4	14,701	13,694
5	New Orleans	+ 7.0	11,837	11,065[b]
6	San Jose	+ 6.7	14,998	14,053
7	San Antonio	+ 6.2	10,140	9,548[b]
8	Houston	+ 5.2	14,654	13,924
9	Philadelphia	+ 4.0	10,535	10,131
10	Baltimore	+ 3.7	12,767	12,312
11	Phoenix	+ 3.0	11,086	10,766[b]
12	Pittsburgh	+ 0.8	12,796	12,689
13	Jacksonville	+ 0.6	10,957	10,887[b]
14	Los Angeles	+ 0.6	13,080	13,005
15	Nashville	− 0.4	11,542	11,584[b]
16	Denver	− 0.9	14,557	14,690
17	El Paso	− 1.6	7,832	7,959[b]
18	Atlanta	− 2.2	13,203	13,506
19	Columbus	− 2.5	11,099	11,384[b]
20	Memphis	− 2.7	10,413	10,704[b]
21	St. Louis	− 2.7	14,286	14,687
22	San Francisco	− 3.4	16,126	16,694
23	Milwaukee	− 4.5	12,404	12,993
24	Seattle	− 4.8	14,050	14,763
25	Indianapolis	− 4.9	11,718	12,318[b]
26	Kansas City	− 5.6	11,184	11,848
27	Cleveland	− 7.0	13,215	14,202
28	Chicago	− 7.8	12,897	13,984
29	San Diego	− 10.1	11,638	12,945
30	Detroit	− 11.3	11,558	13,037

SOURCES: U.S. Department of Commerce, Bureau of Economic Analysis, *Local Area Personal Income, 1976–81*, 1983, and "County and Metropolitan Area Personal Income," *Survey of Current Business* (April 1984).

a. Per capita personal income in 1977 has been converted into 1982 dollars using the Consumer Price Index for the corresponding metropolitan area, available from the Bureau of Labor Statistics.

b. No Consumer Price Index was available for these metropolitan areas, so the national Consumer Price Index has been used.

TABLE 1.7

Growth in Consumer Price Index in 20 Large Metropolitan Areas,
1977–84

Rank	Metropolitan Area	Percentage Increase
1	Detroit	62.6%
2	New York	62.9
3	Philadelphia	64.2
4	Boston	66.5
5	Los Angeles	67.1
6	Kansas City	69.6
7	Washington	69.6
8	Baltimore	69.7
9	Pittsburgh	71.2
10	St. Louis	73.3
11	Atlanta	74.3
12	Chicago	74.5
13	Houston	74.8
14	Seattle	76.7
15	San Francisco	77.2
16	Dallas	81.0
17	Milwaukee	83.9
18	Cleveland	84.4
19	Denver	86.1
20	San Diego	87.8

SOURCES: Data for 1977 from U.S. Department of Labor, Bureau of Labor Statistics, *Handbook of Labor Statistics* (Washington, D.C.: United States Government Printing Office, 1980), Table 138. Data for September and October 1984 from Bureau of Labor Statistics "Consumer Price Index," News Release, November 21, 1984, Table 6.

NOTE: Consumer Price Index data are not available for ten of the 30 metropolitan areas with large cities. Areas shown are ranked from "best" (lowest growth) to "worst" (highest growth).

In terms of unemployment among city residents, however, the performance of New York is not as good. New York ranked twenty-second among the 30 largest cities, with an unemployment rate of 7.9 percent in November 1984 (see Table 1.5). Philadelphia and Baltimore fared better than New York, and Boston ranked second with an unemployment rate of 3.8 percent. Among the cities with worse unemployment than New York were Los Angeles (8.0 percent), Washington (8.3 percent) and Chicago (8.6 percent). At the very bottom were Cleveland (12.6 percent) and Detroit (14.8 percent).

INCOME INDICATORS

Not all jobs are equal in terms of the income they provide. This makes income as well as employment an important criterion for assessing urban economic performance. The best available measure of annual income changes for cities is per capita personal income in real terms (i.e., with the effects of inflation removed). From 1977 to 1982, the latest year for which comparative data are available, this measure rose 8.2 percent in New York City. This was relatively rapid growth, placing New York third among the 30 largest cities (see Table 1.6). Indeed, all of the Sun Belt cities ranked lower than New York, and more than half of all the cities had declines in real per capita income since 1977.

One factor behind New York City's relatively strong performance in real income growth is the comparatively low local rate of inflation. If inflation is slower in one region than another, then similar gains in nominal income become greater gains in real or constant dollar income. This differential has played an important role in New York's recent performance. Between 1977 and 1984, the Consumer Price Index increased 62.6 percent in the New York area. This was below the national average of 71.2 percent and below the pace of inflation in 18 of the 20 large metropolitan areas for which data are available (see Table 1.7).

The slower pace of inflation in New York has benefited the city, but differential inflation is part of the economic adjustment process in a largely market economy. That is, high inflation often results from a long-term booming economy and low inflation from a long-term slack economy. The relative performance of New York and other cities seems to be explained by this basic economic process. For example, the area with the lowest inflation rate, Detroit, had a very weak economy during this period. Moreover, New York's recent modest recovery seems to be increasing relative inflation. In the two most recent years, local inflation has been more rapid than the national average. In 1983, the national rate was 3.2 percent; for New York it was 4.7 percent. In 1984, the respective figures were 4.7 and 4.1 percent.[3] Two years cannot be viewed as a firm trend, but recent indicators suggest the different inflation rates are related to the city's longer-term economic condition.

Finally, it should be added that, despite substantial average per capita income growth, a relatively large share of the population of New York City receives an income below the federal poverty level. In 1980, the most recent period for which comparative data are available, fully 20 percent of New York City's residents were in families with incomes below the poverty level. This percentage is lower (i.e., better) in 17 of the 30 largest cities. New York fell between Washington, D.C. (18.6 percent) and Boston (20.2 percent) in the share of its population in poverty. Among the cities with a lower incidence of poverty were not only Sun Belt cities like San Jose (8.2 percent), San Diego (12.4 percent), Houston (12.7 percent), and Dallas (14.2 percent), but older cities like Pittsburgh (16.5 percent), and the Midwestern cities of Columbus (16.5 per- cent) and Indianapolis (11.5 percent).[4]

ECONOMIC PERFORMANCE AND LOCAL REVENUES

Overall, New York City has achieved modest employment growth and above-average income growth. In another time or place, this

TABLE 1.8

Output and Local Revenues, New York City, 1977 and 1984
(millions of dollars)

	1977	1984	Percentage change 1977–84
Total Output in New York City	$55,175	$101,386	83.8%
City of New York Own-Source Revenues	6,817	10,756	57.8%
Property Tax	3,236	3,957	22.3
Personal Taxes	1,494	3,237	116.7
Income	626	1,551	147.8
Sales	868	1,686	94.2
Business Taxes	1,013	1,774	75.1
General corporation	489	851	74.0
Commercial occupancy	203	389	91.6
Utility	100	193	93.0
Financial corporation	145	172	18.6
Unincorporated business	76	169	122.4
All other taxes and fees	1,074	1,788	66.5

SOURCES: City output data from Drennan–CHR Econometric Model; New York City revenues for fiscal years 1977 and 1984 from City of New York, *Comprehensive Annual Report of the Comptroller,* 1977 and 1984 editions.

TABLE 1.9

Change in Local Tax Burden, All Governments in County,
for 28 of the 30 Largest Cities, 1977–1982

Rank	City	Growth in Own-Source Revenues Relative to Growth in Personal Income	1982 Index of County Own-source Revenues (1977 = 100)	1982 Index of County Personal Income (1977 = 100)
1	Boston	.67	105.8	156.9
2	San Jose	.68	129.2	191.3
3	Los Angeles	.69	117.0	170.4
4	San Diego	.82	150.9	183.6
5	New York City	.89	139.1	156.0
6	San Francisco	.90	146.6	163.3
7	Denver	.92	159.0	172.3
8	Dallas	.94	186.3	199.2
9	Seattle	.94	166.2	177.1
10	Jacksonville	.96	162.0	168.8
11	Kansas City	.96	143.0	148.9
12	Indianapolis	.97	145.9	150.9
13	Philadelphia	.98	148.3	150.7
14	Phoenix	.99	195.6	198.4
15	Milwaukee	1.01	155.6	153.7
16	Cleveland	1.02	149.3	146.8
17	El Paso	1.03	181.8	176.0
18	Memphis	1.03	166.1	161.6
19	Houston	1.04	221.2	212.0
20	San Antonio	1.04	193.0	185.6
21	Chicago	1.07	157.4	147.8
22	Columbus	1.07	167.0	156.8
23	Washington, DC	1.07	169.3	158.6
24	Nashville	1.08	176.8	164.0
25	Pittsburgh	1.13	176.7	155.8
26	Atlanta	1.14	190.9	166.9
27	Detroit	1.23	161.3	131.3
28	New Orleans	1.23	209.6	170.6

SOURCES: City own-source revenue data for 1977 are from U.S. Department of Commerce, Bureau of the Census, *1977 Census of Governments, Local Governments in Metropolitan Areas,* Vol. 5 (Washington, D.C.: United States Government Printing Office, 1979). City own-source revenue data for 1982 are from U.S. Department of Commerce, Bureau of the Census, *1982 Census of Governments, Government Finances, Compendium of Government Finances,* Vol. 4, No. 5 (Washington, D.C.: United States Government Printing Office, 1985). Personal income data by county for 1977 are from U.S. Department of Commerce, Bureau of Economic Analysis, *Local Area Personal Income, 1976–81* (Washington, D.C.: United States Government Printing Office, 1983). 1982 personal income data are from *Survey of Current Business,* April 1984.

NOTE: Consistent data for Baltimore and St. Louis are not available.

real economic growth might have been associated with relative growth in local government revenues and with expansion or improvement of municipal services. But since its fiscal crisis, the City of New York has sought to reduce local tax burdens by capturing a smaller share of local income for public services. The underlying assumption has been that lower tax burdens are necessary to make the city a more competitive business location.

Since 1977 municipal decisions on tax policy, or more accurately nondecisions, have resulted in two important changes in the nature of the City's local revenues. First, the aggregate local tax burden has fallen. Between 1977 and 1984, output of the New York City economy grew nearly 84 percent while locally derived revenues increased less than 58 percent (see Table 1.8). As a result, local revenues as a share of economic output fell from 12.4 to 10.6 percent.

TABLE 1.10

Local Revenues, New York City and All Governments in Central County of 20 Largest Cities, 1982

Rank	Central County	Own-source Revenue Per Capita	Own-source Revenue as Percentage of Money Income
1	Bexar (San Antonio)	$419.02	6.8%
2	Marion (Indianapolis)	530.05	6.9
3	Maricopa (Phoenix)	597.47	7.7
4	Franklin (Columbus)	632.13	8.3
5	Baltimore	640.04	10.9
6	Orlean (New Orleans)	640.73	9.9
7	Los Angeles	653.52	7.9
8	Shelby (Memphis)	667.73	10.0
9	Dallas	712.78	8.2
10	San Diego	717.48	9.0
11	Milwaukee	765.68	9.6
12	Cook (Chicago)	774.00	11.0
13	Santa Clara (San Jose)	793.33	8.3
14	Philadelphia	851.09	14.1
15	Harris (Houston)	861.86	9.5
16	Cuyahoga (Cleveland)	875.49	10.8
17	Wayne (Detroit)	879.14	11.5
18	Suffolk (Boston)	1,065.93	16.3
19	San Francisco	1,173.03	12.7
20	New York	1,472.18	20.2

SOURCES: U.S. Department of Commerce, Bureau of the Census, *1982 Census of Governments, Government Finances, Compendium of Government Finances,* Vol. 4, No. 5 (Washington, D.C.: United States Government Printing Office, 1985).

Comparisons of tax levels among urban areas are potentially misleading because local governments perform different functions in different areas. However, with respect to local taxes, it is possible to make a meaningful comparison. All the revenues collected by local governments in the county in which a central city is located can be compared to those collected by the City of New York, because the City performs the combined functions of cities, counties, and units such as school districts in other areas.

This analysis reveals that the reduction in local tax burden in New York City has been greater than in most large cities, but New York has not been leading the way (see Table 1.9). Among 28 large cities, 14 reduced their relative tax burden over the 1977–82 period. (The most recent comparable data are for 1982.) New York ranked fifth in reduced tax burden, behind Boston, San Jose, Los Angeles and San Diego. The greater reductions in Boston and the three large California cities are related to the passage of measures to limit property taxes in the states of Massachusetts and California.

While New York has been reducing its tax burden more rapidly than many large cities, it remains an area with an unusually high tax burden. In 1982, New York City had the highest tax burden among the nation's 20 largest cities (see Table 1.10). Its taxes per capita, $1472, were 25 percent higher than second-place San Francisco and more than double that of middle-ranked San Diego. Local revenues as a share of local money income were 20 percent in New York City, compared to 16.3 percent in second-place Boston and 9.6 percent in middle-ranked Milwaukee. Thus, while the New York City tax burden may be declining, it is still well above those of all other larger American cities.

The second important change in the City's local revenues is a shift in the sources from which they are raised. During the 1977–84 period, property taxes grew more slowly (22 percent) than personal taxes (117 percent) consisting of the sales and income taxes, and than business taxes (75 percent). As a result, the property tax accounted for less than 37 percent of local revenues in 1984, compared to over 47 percent in 1977. In contrast, personal taxes rose from less than 22 percent to almost 30 percent of local revenues.

These substantial changes in the City's revenue system result more from underlying shifts in the economy than from explicit policy decisions by municipal leaders. There have been relatively few

TABLE 1.11
Elasticity of Selected Municipal Taxes

Tax	Elasticity Measure	Base
Property Tax	.67	Market Value Two Years Earlier
Total Personal Taxes	1.94	Total City Value Added
Sales	.98	Total City Value Added
Personal Income	2.30	Total City Value Added
Total Business Taxes	1.18	Private Sector Value Added
General Corporation	2.15	Private Sector Value Added
Commercial Occupancy	1.60	Private Sector Value Added
Utility	1.28	Total City Value Added
Unincorporated Business	2.60	Total City Value Added

SOURCE: Author's calculations. See note 5 for method and data sources.

changes in local taxes since 1977. Property tax rates were virtually stable from 1977 to 1980 and increased modestly in each subsequent year; a temporary personal income tax surcharge was imposed in 1983 and 1984; and corporate income tax rates were lowered in 1977 and 1978. While the personal income tax surcharge accounts for some of the rapid growth in that source, the more significant municipal policy has been essentially to "freeze" the tax system. At the same time, the local economy underwent significant growth and transformation. These economic changes explain most of the differential rates of growth in the tax sources.

Without changes in tax policy, different taxes will grow at different rates because of their varying relationship to economic growth, which economists call "elasticity." An analysis of the elasticity of the major city tax sources provides measures of the different elasticities.[5] The measure shown in Table 1.11 indicates the percentage change in tax revenues that accompanies a percentage change in the economic base. For example, as the local economy grows by 10 percent, the personal income tax grows by 23 percent while the property tax grows by only 7 percent.

The different elasticities are explained by the nature of the individual tax. The high elasticity of the personal income tax is due to its progressive rate structure and the apparent fact that economic growth is disproportionately benefiting higher income individuals who are subject to the higher rates. The high elasticity of the unincorporated business tax is related to the disproportionately rapid growth in sectors such as medical services and legal services, which are characterized by many unincorporated firms. The high elasticity of the corporate income tax is due to relatively rapid growth among the most profitable types of corporations. The commercial occupancy tax has a high elasticity because rents have grown more rapidly than the overall economy.

The unusually low elasticity of the property tax is due to City assessment practices. Both the rate and the base of this tax have grown in recent years. The rate in 1977 was $8.80 per $100 of assessed value, and in 1984 the average rate was $9.21. The market value of property in the city in the same period rose 95 percent, from $81.3 billion to $158.9 billion. If the City regularly and fairly updated its assessments, the combined rate and base growth would have increased taxes from the 1977 figure of $3.4 billion to nearly $7.0 billion in 1984.[6] Instead, the City collected only $3.9 billion in 1984 because assessments were not changed to reflect growth in market value. As a result, the effective tax rate (taxes per $100 of market value) was cut from $4.20 to $2.65.

The transformation of the tax system resulting from the combination of economic change and municipal inaction is undesirable in several respects. While a lower aggregate tax burden has been a desired objective, the shift from property taxes to personal and business taxes raises important issues. In his contribution to an earlier Setting Municipal Priorities volume, Dick Netzer argued that municipal tax policy should seek (1) to reduce the share of revenues derived from business taxes because they distort market forces to favor some types of industries and harm others, and (2) to increase the share of revenues derived from a well-administered property tax that would be economically neutral and affect all types of business fairly. With respect to the property tax, he stated that "The economy will not be harmed if assessments, and hence tax revenues, uniformly track market values."[7] If the City had followed this policy since Netzer made the recommendation, it would have maintained the fiscal year 1982 effective property tax rate of $3.54 (per $100 of market value) and collected an additional $1.4 billion in property-tax revenues in 1984. These funds could have been used to finance service improvements or, if continued reduction in the tax burden were desired, to finance substantial reductions in business or personal taxes.

This failure to utilize properly the property tax has taken place despite, and in some respects because of, a so-called property-tax "reform" enacted by the State legislature in December 1981.[8] The problems which spurred the calls for reform are of two broad types: interclass inequities and intraclass inequities. Interclass inequities arise when different types of property are taxed at different effective rates. Such practices are considered undesirable because they are economically inefficient, providing an indirect subsidy for types of economic activity that are undertaxed and imposing an excess tax burden on types of activity that are overtaxed. If interclass inequities are substantial, they can distort the nature of a city's economy and hinder its growth.

New York City long has been characterized by substantial interclass inequities. The most comprehensive study of the subject, using fiscal year 1979 data, found that the average effective tax rate in the city was $4.16 per $100 of market value, but that one- and two-family homes were taxed only $2.15 per $100 while the average rate for nonresidential property was $5.55 per $100 and for larger residential units $5.19 per $100.[9] Moreover, among different types of nonresidential property there were variations in effective tax rates; notably, property owned by utilities was taxed more heavily than other forms of commercial property.

Intraclass inequities arise when similar types of property are taxed at different rates. Such unequal treatment of individuals or businesses in similar positions violates most norms of fairness and, when such inequitable treatment can be proven, generally provides grounds for reductions of individual or corporate-tax liability. However, such inequities were difficult to prove in the past, and New York City's tax administrators historically created and tolerated significant intraclass inequities. Injustices are evident in all classes of property, but the most fully documented problem plagued homeowners. A study sponsored by the New York Public Interest Research Group (NYPIRG) and released in early 1981 found that two of every three homeowners were assessed inaccurately and therefore subject to incorrect tax liabilities.[10] Most of those overtaxed lived in relatively poor neighborhoods in homes of relatively low value.

Both interclass and intraclass inequities violated the state laws which, before "reform," governed the City's property tax. When the State Court of Appeals ordered the City to obey the laws, considerable controversy arose. Homeowners, who as a group benefited from interclass inequities, successfully opposed the elimi-

TABLE 1.12

New York City Property Tax Rates, Fiscal Years 1982–85

	Fiscal Year			
	1982	1983	1984	1985
One-, Two, and Three-family Homes	$8.95	$8.95	$9.10	$9.10
Other Residential Property	8.95	8.95	9.06	9.15
Utility Property	8.95	9.11	9.24	9.05
All Other	8.95	9.29	9.32	9.45

Source: City of New York, Resolution of the Council Fixing the Tax Rate, annual.

nation of these inequities. The City opposed rapid elimination of intraclass inequities because this would have required it to revise the tax bills of two-thirds of all homeowners and, more importantly, would have forced abrupt upward shifts in some tax bills if the City were not to lose revenues from the downward revisions of owners currently overtaxed. The outcome was a new law that required few significant changes from the inequitable practices of the past and in some respects actually hinders true reform.

The new law legitimized interclass inequities by establishing a classification system of property taxation. All properties are divided into four categories: Class One includes one-, two-, and three-family homes; Class Two covers all other residential property (except hotels and motels); Class Three is utility property; and Class Four involves all other property, including all commercial property. The share of the total property-tax bill to be paid by owners in each category is linked to the share they paid in fiscal year 1982. In effect, the interclass inequities existing in fiscal year 1982 were perpetuated by the new law. However, progress towards eliminating interclass inequity was made possible, if only gradually, by a provision which allows the City Council to alter the share of the tax liability borne by a class by up to 5 percent per year.

In practice, the City Council has not used its authority to eliminate interclass inequities. Instead, the authority to tax different classes of property at different rates has generally worked to worsen interclass inequities. In fiscal year 1982, all properties were subject to a tax of $8.95 per $100 of assessed value. Beginning in fiscal year 1983, the City used its new authority to vary the rates among classes of property. For that year, taxes on both types of residential property were frozen, but significant increases were imposed on utility and other commercial property (see Table 1.12). This had the political appeal of protecting homeowners while generating new revenue from the business community.

In fiscal year 1984, City officials had second thoughts about the impact on economic development of the disparity in tax rates. To help businesses, the greatest increase in that year was imposed on smaller residential properties, and an almost equal increase was imposed on other residential property. The rates on utility and commercial properties also were increased, but by smaller amounts. As a result, disparities among classes remained, but they were smaller than in fiscal year 1983.

In fiscal year 1985, the City reduced the rate on utility property, but increased disparities between residential and other commercial properties. The reduction in the property tax rate of utilities is intended to alleviate the substantial tax on them that resulted from a combination of high property taxes and other taxes on utilities. The intended result was to slow price increases for energy and communications services and thereby make New York City a more competitive business location. Unfortunately, the possible economic gains from lower utility tax rates may be offset by the adverse effects on the local economy of the growing disparity between residential and commercial property taxes. The rate for commercial property was increased from $9.32 to $9.45; the rate for smaller residential property was kept at $9.10, while the new rate for other residential property was increased to $9.15. The greater disparity between residential and commercial uses is a cause for concern among those favoring tax policies that encourage economic development.

Complaints about continued intraclass inequities under the new law have arisen from two sources: small residential property owners, who feel they are overtaxed, and large commercial property and apartment house owners, who feel they are overtaxed. The case for the small residential owners has been made most effectively by the NYPIRG. As noted above, their 1981 study revealed that about one-third or an estimated 172,140 one- and two-family homes were significantly overassessed and hence overtaxed. The excess tax burden averaged $355 annually for these homes. During the winter of 1981, NYPIRG urged and aided many of these homeowners in appealing their tax bill before the New York City Tax Commission. The results were disappointing; in the words of

NYPIRG's leadership, "The Commission simply did not want to hear about or recognize assessment inequality."[11]

The homeowners then took their case to the State legislature and the result was a new bill establishing a special small claims assessment review court empowered to hear such claims beginning in 1982. Faced with the possibility of significant tax revenue losses due to the appeals, the Mayor and the Finance Commissioner sought to have the bill repealed. When this failed, the Finance Commissioner began a program to lower assessments in neighborhoods that were overtaxed. In February and March of 1982, over 50,000 one- and two-family homeowners received tax reductions averaging $188 each. The following year, the Commissioner lowered taxes on an additional 56,000 homes an average of $171 each. This substantial effort still leaves tens of thousands of homeowners with inequitable bills, but it does reflect some effort to deal with the problem by City officials.

Temporarily satisfied with the City's commitment to rectify the worst problems for one- and two-family homeowners, NYPIRG turned its attention to three-family homes. A study released in early 1983 revealed that most of the city's 42,000 three-family homes are overtaxed. These properties are supposed to be assessed on the same basis as one- and two-family homes (all are in Class One under the new classification system), but the three-family homes tend to be assessed much closer to their actual market value than are the other homes. To rectify this problem, NYPIRG has recommended a large-scale program of lowered assessments for three-family homes.[12]

The case that certain large commercial and apartment house properties are being overtaxed was made by the Real Estate Board of New York. They argued that the City's assessment policies placed unfair tax burdens on recently sold buildings.[13] The City's policy was to assess eventually all commercial property at 60 percent of its market value, and market value was based on sales price. The City began to implement this policy by assessing at this level those properties which were recently sold. This meant that buildings that changed hands had their assessments, and hence their tax bills, increased sooner or more markedly than properties that remain with the same owner. This was both unfair and made little economic sense.

In response to the Board's criticisms, the City announced in

October 1983 a new assessment policy for large apartment buildings and commercial property. The new policy seeks to reduce intraclass inequities for commercial property by lowering target assessments from 60 to 45 percent for new and recently sold buildings. For buildings that had not been sold, assessments would be brought closer to the 45 percent target through more frequent assessment based on income data to be provided by owners. If properly implemented, this policy will narrow intraclass inequities.

However, the elimination of intraclass inequities, whether for small residential or large commercial properties, has been hampered by certain provisions of the 1981 State law. Since the law limits the share of tax liability that is borne by each class of property, City officials need to increase one owner's bill to offset the revenue losses from lowering the bill of another owner in the same class. Moreover, the State law limits the magnitude of the increase any owner can experience in a given year. For homeowners, the increase is limited to 6 percent annually and 20 percent over five years. For commercial property, there is no limit on the increase in assessment in a given year, but any assessment increase must be phased in over a five-year period. Thus, effectively, the annual increase is only one-fifth the difference between previous assessments and what the assessor now thinks the property is worth. In light of these restrictions on increases in assessments, the City's desire to avoid decreases in tax bills is more understandable.

In sum, despite passage of a 1981 law that was hailed as "reform," New York City's property tax continues to suffer two major problems. Although interclass inequities violate basic principles of economically sound taxation, they have become a fixed feature of municipal property tax administration. As a result, growth in some sectors of the economy, notably those that require office space and utility services, may be hampered by a tax burden that is larger than that imposed for other uses of land, notably owner-occupied housing. Neither State legislators nor municipal officials have had the political courage to incur the wrath of homeowners in order to rectify this inefficiency.

Intraclass inequities impose unfair tax burdens on some owners while giving unjustified tax relief to others. While created and maintained out of administrative neglect, these inequities cannot now be fully remedied by administrative action because of restrictions related to the combination of statutory limits on the tax lia-

TABLE 1.13

National Economic Assumptions, 1984–90

Year	Percentage Change in Real GNP	Percentage Change in Employment	Percentage Change in GNP per Employee	Unemployment Rate
1984	6.8%	4.5%	2.2%	7.5%
Projected				
1986	3.2	1.2	2.0	6.6
1987	3.2	1.2	2.0	6.6
1988	2.8	1.3	1.5	6.5
1989	2.7	1.4	1.3	6.4
1990	2.8	1.7	1.1	6.3
Average Annual Rate, 1984–90	3.1%	1.6%	1.5%	

SOURCE: Author's projections based upon a number of national forecasting services' outlooks in the winter of 1985.

bility of a given property class and statutory limits on the annual increase in a single owner's assessment. Only overassessments can be eliminated rapidly, but there is little fiscal or political sense in doing so if the foregone revenues cannot be recovered by offsetting increases in the assessments of undertaxed property. Rather than reforming the property tax, the recent State law has made progress towards reform more difficult.

THE OUTLOOK

The outlook for the local economy and for City revenues depends in large part on two factors: the pace of national economic growth and the city's competitive position with respect to other business locations. Both are difficult to project, but some reasonable assumptions provide a basis for analyzing the local outlook.

Table 1.13 summarizes a set of assumptions about the course of the national economy through the 1980s. Between 1984 and 1990, real Gross National Product (GNP) is expected to grow at an average annual rate of 3.1 percent. Due to average productivity gains of 1.5 percent annually, the GNP growth yields a 1.6 percent annual employment increase. Unemployment declines from the 1984 figure of 7.5 percent to 6.3 percent in 1990.

This national outlook is more favorable than the national economic situation between 1977 and 1984. In that period, due to two national recessions, the GNP growth averaged only 2.6 percent annually, and employment grew 1.9 percent annually. (It increased only 1.5 percent annually from 1977 to 1983. The large gain of 4.5 percent occurred in 1984.) The unemployment rate was below 7.0 percent in only the first three of those eight years and was above 9.0 percent in 1982 and 1983. However, in the forecast period 1986–90, the unemployment rate is expected to be in a more favorable range, from 6.9 to 6.4 percent.

It is especially difficult to foresee trends in New York City's competitive position. As noted earlier, over the 1977–84 period costs of business, as reflected in the CPI, grew less rapidly in New York than in the nation as a whole and than in most other large cities in the United States. This suggests an improved competitive position. However, in the two most recent years the pattern was reversed, indicating a possible decline in competitive position. It is not clear what the pattern for the remainder of the decade will be. Therefore, it seems appropriate to make three alternative assumptions. (1) The city's competitive position will follow the earlier trend and continue to improve; that is, regional inflation will be less than national inflation by 0.7 percentage points per year. (2) There will be no change in the city's competitive position; that is, regional inflation and national inflation will be equal. (3) The city's competitive position will deteriorate; that is, regional inflation will exceed national inflation by 0.6 percentage points per year.

TABLE 1.14

Economic Projections for New York City, 1990

	Real Local Output (1983 dollars in billions)	Employment (in thousands)
Actual, 1984	$97.6	3,422
Projected, 1990		
Low	106.7	3,553
Middle	107.4	3,582
High	108.0	3,607
Average Annual Percentage Change, 1984–90		
Low	1.5%	0.6%
Middle	1.6	0.7
High	1.7	0.8

SOURCE: Author's forecast; see text.

These assumptions can be referred to as "high," "middle," and "low," respectively.

The national economic assumptions and the alternative assumptions about local competitiveness provide a basis for econometric projections of output and employment in New York City. The model developed by the author indicates that these assumed conditions will result in real output growth of between 1.7 percent (high) and 1.5 percent (low) annually and employment growth of between 0.8 percent and 0.6 percent annually over the 1984–90 period. The percentage changes in employment are equal to net growth of between 175,000 and 121,000 jobs over the period (see Table 1.14).

Interestingly, even the most favorable assumptions yield projected local economic growth rates that are below the national average and somewhat lower than those of the recovery period of 1977–84. Employment growth in the city averages only 0.8 percent annually compared to the assumed national rate of 1.6 percent. This is consistent with historical relationships between the city and the nation. For example, from 1977 to 1984 national employment expanded 1.9 percent annually compared with city employment growth of 1.1 per year.

More surprising is the projection that even under the most favorable assumptions, the next few years will witness somewhat slower growth than was evident in the city in the 1977–84 period. This is true despite an improved national economy and the assumption of improved local competitiveness. The projected high rate of growth in real output is only 1.7 percent compared to 2.0 percent annually in the earlier period, and the rates of employment growth are 0.8 percent and 1.1 percent, respectively. The middle case projects output growth of 1.6 percent annually and employment growth of 0.7 percent annually. This relative slowing in the city's economic expansion reflects the fact that from 1977 to 1984, the city's economy was emerging from a very steep and long decline, not tied to any one business cycle. This condition left significant slack in the local economy that permitted the quick recovery. Such a recovery situation is almost bound to slow down over the years as the slack disappears. Thus, the 1984–90 projection period, following the long-term low of 1977 by between seven and 13 years, indicates somewhat slower growth than in the initial recovery years.

The modest projected growth in the city's economy can be attributed largely to the continued, but slower, growth prospects for

TABLE 1.15
Projected Change in New York City Employment by Major Sector, 1984–90

	Employment (thousands)			Average Annual Percentage Change	
	1984	1990	Change	1977–84	1984–90
Local Sector	1,267	1,284	+17	−0.1%	+0.2%
Export Sectors	2,165	2,298	+133	+1.8	+1.0
Corporate Complex	1,346	1,463	+117	+3.1	+1.4
Headquarters	124	120	−4	−1.2	−0.6
Corporate Services	1,137	1,248	+111	+3.7	+1.6
Ancillary Services	85	95	+10	+2.6	+1.9
Goods Production and Distribution	518	494	−24	−1.5	−0.8
Consumer Services	301	341	+40	+2.7	+2.1
Total	3,432	3,582	+150	+1.1%	+0.7%

SOURCES: 1984 data from New York State Department of Labor, with headquarters employment estimated by author. Projections for 1990 made by author.

TABLE 1.16

City of New York Tax Revenue Forecast, 1984 and 1990
(millions of dollars)

Tax	Actual 1984	1990 Projections		
		Low	Middle	High
Property	$3,957	$4,810	$4,860	$4,920
Personal Taxes	3,237	4,770	4,820	4,880
Personal Income	1,551	2,580	2,620	2,670
Sales	1,686	2,190	2,200	2,210
Business Taxes	1,774	2,790	2,832	2,884
General Corporation	851	1,370	1,395	1,430
Commercial Occupancy	389	660	667	674
Utility	193	260	263	265
Unincorporated Business	169	320	327	335
Financial Corporation	172	180	180	180
All other fees and taxes	1,788	2,550	2,550	2,550
Total Own-source Revenues	$10,756	$14,920	$15,062	$15,234

SOURCES: Revenues for 1984 from City of New York, *Comprehensive Annual Financial Report of the Comptroller for the Fiscal Year Ended June 30, 1984*. Forecasts from Drennan–CHR Econometric Model.

its corporate complex and its consumer services. As shown in Table 1.15, the corporate complex is expected to grow 1.4 percent annually in the 1984–90 period. However, the strongly expanding sectors of the recent recovery, namely corporate services, ancillary services and consumer services are all expected to have markedly slower growth in the next six years. In contrast, the declining sectors of the recent recovery, namely the local sector, corporate headquarters, and production and distribution of goods, are expected to either show a slight gain (the local sector) or diminished rates of decline. These converging trends among the sectors are reasonable over a longer-term growth period as contrasted with the more divergent trends of the recent recovery.

The employment changes from 1977 to 1984 analyzed here plus the projected changes to 1990 indicate a continuing transformation of the city's economy. The share of city employment in the corporate complex was 34 percent in 1977 but is expected to be almost 41 percent in 1990, mostly due to the relative expansion in corporate services. In contrast, employment in the export sector of goods production and distribution is expected to shrink from 18 percent in 1977 to less than 14 percent in 1990. Thus by 1990, the corporate complex and the consumer services export sectors together will account for half of all employment in New York City.

The continuing transformation of the local economy provides a basis for projecting local revenues. Assuming nothing is done to alter City tax policy, local revenues are projected to grow from $10.8 billion in 1984 to between $14.9 and $15.2 billion in 1990 (see Table 1.16). In the middle case, the growth rate for revenues is 40 percent compared to projected local output growth (both real growth and inflation) of 42 percent. This means that between 1984 and 1990, the share of output captured by local taxes will fall slightly. Similar to the past, business and personal taxes will grow faster than economic output, and property tax growth will lag behind economic growth. As a result, by 1990 the property tax will represent only 32 percent of local revenues and the personal income tax will be 17 percent; their respective shares in 1984 were 37 percent and 14 percent.

In order to slow or halt the shift in revenue sources from property to income taxes, the City will have to make affirmative tax policy decisions. Failure to act will be endorsement of the underlying trends. Local officials have an obligation to raise the basic political issues of whether the public sector should continue to shrink relative to the total economy and whether wage and salary earners should continue to bear an increased share of the tax burden while property owners pay a decreasing share. In addition to the basic values reflected in these decisions, concerns of economic efficiency also play a role. The shift away from reliance on the property tax is undesirable because it makes economically distorting business tax revenues substitute for more economically neutral foregone property tax revenues. An improved assessment system is warranted, regardless of whether more or less taxes are sought in the aggregate, because the additional revenues could be used to finance tax reforms that would eliminate economic disincentives and inequities inherent in the current package of business and personal taxes.

NOTES

1. Output is measured in terms of value added by economic activity in the city. For a

description of the measurement approach, see Matthew Drennan and Georgia Nanopoulos-Stergiou, "The Local Economy and Local Revenues," in Raymond D. Horton and Charles Brecher, eds., *Setting Municipal Priorities, 1980* (Montclair, N.J.: Allanheld, Osmun and Co., 1979), pp. 6–33.

2. For more complete discussion of this approach, see Matthew Drennan, "The Local Economy and Local Revenues," in Charles Brecher and Raymond D. Horton, eds., *Setting Municipal Priorities, 1984* (New York: New York University Press, 1983), pp. 19–44.

3. U.S. Department of Labor, Bureau of Labor Statistics, "Consumer Price Index, December 1984," News Release, January 1985.

4. Figures from U.S. Department of Commerce, Bureau of the Census, *1980 Census of Population, Summary Characteristics for Governmental Units* (Washington, D.C.: United States Government Printing Office, 1982).

5. For the commercial occupancy tax and the unincorporated business tax, the elasticities shown in Table 1.11 are computed as averages of year-to-year elasticity measures, i.e., percentage change in tax revenues divided by percentage change in income base, both deflated. All of the others were computed using multiple regression time series equations in which the variables are in natural log form. The dependent variable is the natural log of the particular tax revenue variable in constant dollars (i.e., with the inflation effect removed). The key independent variable in each equation is the natural log of the appropriate base in constant dollars. With the exception of the property tax (where the appropriate base is deflated market value of real property), the base is either total city value-added or private sector value-added, in millions of 1972 dollars. Those series are from the Drennan-CHR Econometric Model and Data Base, and are equivalent to national income generated in the city. For an explanation of how those value-added series are computed, see Matthew Drennan, *Modeling Metropolitan Economies for Forecasting and Policy Analysis* (New York: New York University Press, 1985), Chapter Two.

The deflator used for all the dollar variables is the GNP Implicit Price Deflator (1972 = 100), published by the U.S. Department of Commerce, "National Income and Product Accounts," *Survey of Current Business,* various issues. In some equations, additional independent variables were included to take into account changes in the tax rate over the period. In the property tax equation, the effective property tax rate was included as a variable. In the personal income tax equation, a dummy variable was used to represent a tax rate increase effective in 1976, and the addition of the surtax in 1983 and 1984. The equations were estimated in log form because then the partial regression coefficient on the value-added variable (or market value of property variable) is the estimated elasticity of the tax.

6. It should be noted that State constitutional limits on the amount of property tax collections and statutory limits on annual assessment increases might have prevented the City from obtaining all these revenues, but the growth would still have been substantial.

7. Dick Netzer, "Taxes," in Charles Brecher and Raymond D. Horton, eds., *Setting Municipal Priorities, 1982* (New York: Russell Sage, 1981), p. 154.

8. This discussion of the property-tax reform bill and its implementation is from Charles Brecher, "Changes in the City Property Tax: The Illusion of Reform," *Citizens Budget Commission Quarterly,* Vol. 3, No. 4 (Fall 1983), pp. 14–16.

9. In fiscal year 1979, the nominal tax rate was $8.75 per $100 of assessed value. The variation in effective tax rates is due to variations in the relationship between assessed value and actual market values. See Graduate School of Public Administration, New York University, *Real Property Tax Policy for New York City,* December 31, 1980.

10. Frank Domurad et al., *City of Unequal Neighbors: A Study of Residential Property Tax Assessments in New York City,* New York Public Interest Research Group, 1981.

11. Frank Domurad and Gene Russianoff, *City of Unequal Neighbors—One Year Later,* New York Public Interest Research Group, 1982, p. 3.

12. See Frank Domurad, Dan Kaplan, and Gene Russianoff, *City of Unequal Neighbors III: A Study of Three-Family Home Property Tax Assessments in New York City*, New York Public Research Center, 1983.

13. *Sudden Peril—The Negative Impact of New York City's Real Property Assessment Policy*, Real Estate Board of New York, April, 1983.

2

People and Income

EMANUEL TOBIER
WITH WALTER STAFFORD

Economic and demographic changes have been closely linked throughout New York City's history. As job opportunities increased, people were attracted to the city and its suburbs. Labor market competition between "locals" and new arrivals from other parts of the world or other parts of the United States has been a constant theme in the city's evolution. But the historic pattern was that virtually all groups—newcomers, long-time city residents, and commuting suburbanites—benefited from the continuing economic growth.[1]

The abrupt turnaround in 1970 of the city's long-term trend of economic growth altered many of these historic patterns and forced New Yorkers to face the consequences of economic decline. These were a substantial loss of population and a worsening of the income of New Yorkers in both absolute and relative senses. Modest economic recovery began in the late 1970s, but underlying social and economic transformations make the character of New York City's future population particularly uncertain. Changing modes of family formation and continued obstacles to effective labor force participation by minority groups may keep a substantial portion of the population in poverty despite renewed economic growth.

This chapter analyzes the changing composition of the city's population in order to provide some insights into the course of future demographic trends. The first section reviews the changes since 1970 in terms of population size, ethnic composition, and income. The next section describes the social and economic forces behind the growing impoverishment of New Yorkers, including new patterns of family formation, labor force participation, and labor market discrimination. The final section presents the outlook for the size, racial composition, and economic status of the population.

THE RESPONSE TO ECONOMIC CHANGE

Economic forces underlie much, but not all, of the city's population dynamics. The sharp decline in the local economy from 1970 to 1977 was followed almost immediately by a sharp drop in the population as aspiring workers came in smaller numbers and ambitious residents left in greater numbers than before. The post-1977 recovery did not reverse these trends but yielded a lagged

TABLE 2.1

Population Change in New York City, 1970–84

(in thousands)

	Population	Average Annual Change from Preceding Date		
		Total	Natural Increase	Net Migration
1970	7,727	—	—	—
1975	7,265	−92	+33	−126
1978	6,948	−106	+29	−135
1980	6,889	−30	+30	−59
1981	6,872	−17	+28	−45
1984	6,950	+26	+35	−9

SOURCES: 1970 and 1980 data from U.S. Bureau of the Census, *Census of Population* (Washington, D.C.: United States Government Printing Office, decennial editions); 1975, 1978, 1981 and 1984 data from U.S. Bureau of the Census, Housing Division, *New York City Housing and Vacancy Survey*; natural increase statistics (excess of births over deaths) are based on unpublished data from New York City Department of Health, Bureau of Health Statistics and Analysis. Note that in order to make the decennial census figures comparable with the housing and vacancy survey data, the census figures used are those for the population in households and not the total population. (The former excludes people living in institutions and group quarters.)

and moderated response. Despite the job increases, more people continue to move out of than into the city; it is primarily natural increase, or the excess of births over deaths, that has kept the city at its current population size during the early 1980s.

These trends are evident in the available population figures, decennial censuses for 1970 and 1980 and additional surveys conducted by the Census Bureau in interim and subsequent years (see Table 2.1). From 1970 to 1978, estimates of the comparably defined population fell from over 7.7 million to slightly under 6.9 million. In this period, the net movement out of the city was nearly 130,000 annually, but natural increase kept the annual loss to about 100,000. Even after its economic recovery began New York City continued to experience net emigration, but the rate fell to about 59,000 annually in the late 1970s and about 9000 annually in the early 1980s. In the most recent period natural increase more than offset the migration losses, and the population grew slightly from 6,872,000 in 1981 to 6,950,000 in 1984.

The pattern of migration, and hence net population change, has varied significantly among ethnic groups. During the 1970s the city's non-Hispanic white population (hereafter, whites) was char-

TABLE 2.2

*Change in New York City Population by Age and Ethnic Group,
1970–80 (in thousands)*

	1970	1980	Percentage Change
Ethnic Group			
White (excluding Hispanic)	4,996	3,686	−25.2
Black (excluding Hispanic)	1,513	1,702	+12.4
Hispanic	1,201	1,429	+19.0
Other	185	275	+48.6
Total	7,895	7,092	−10.2%
Age			
Under 5	616	472	−23.4
5–17	1,616	1,296	−19.0
18–54	3,818	3,623	−5.1
55–64	890	744	−16.4
65 and over	955	957	+0.2

SOURCES: 1970 and 1980 data from U.S. Bureau of the Census, *Census of Population*, Public Use Microdata Sample. Population totals in this table differ from those in Table 2.1 because this table includes all persons.

acterized by a rapid rate of net emigration and fell by over one-quarter (see Table 2.2). In contrast, the non-Hispanic black (hereafter blacks) and Hispanic segments of the population experienced much lower rates of emigration, and their natural increase pushed their numbers up by 12 and 19 percent, respectively. The much smaller category of "others," mostly Asians, increased by nearly 50 percent. As a result, by 1980 only a bare majority (52 percent) of the city's population was white, with the remainder divided among blacks (24 percent), Hispanics (20 percent), and others (4 percent).

The population decline of the 1970s also affected the age composition of the city's residents. The elderly increased as a group because of the large number of adults aging into the over-65 category during the 1970s, despite the quickened rate of emigration among this group.[2] In contrast, the younger segments of the population declined most rapidly because birth rates dropped and because young adults and families with children tended to move in the greatest numbers. As a result, less than one-quarter of the local population was under age 18 in 1980, compared to 28 percent in 1970.

The post-1980 data are not sufficient in detail and reliability to determine if these differential rates of migration and change have been altered by the recent economic recovery, but it seems likely.

TABLE 2.3

Median Family Income, United States, New York Standard Consolidated Area, and New York City, 1949–83

(in 1979 dollars)

	United States	New York Standard Consolidated Area (SCA)	New York City	New York City as Percentage of	
				U.S.	N.Y. SCA
1959	$13,475	$16,452	$14,966	111%	91%
1969	18,804	21,479	18,619	99	87
1979	19,908	21,705	16,818	84	77
1982	17,672	18,567	14,880	84	80
1983	17,994	19,663	15,224	85	77

SOURCES: Current dollar figure in each year converted to constant 1979 dollars by use of the Consumer Price Index (CPI). For New York City, the CPI for the New York, New York–Northeastern New Jersey SMSA was used; for the United States, the national CPI was employed. Current dollar figures for 1959, 1969 and 1979 obtained from the U.S. Census of Population for 1960, 1970 and 1980, *General Social and Economic Characteristics* volume. The 1982 and 1983 figures are unpublished data obtained from the U.S. Bureau of the Census, Income Statistics Branch of the Population Division.

The one ethnic group for which reliable figures can be estimated, whites, seems to have halved its earlier rate of emigration in the 1981–84 period.[3] Thus, the population increase in recent years may be attributed largely to slowed white emigration rather than increased immigration of other ethnic groups.

The city's economic decline not only caused its population to shrink, it also resulted in a poorer population. While the city's growth in the 1960s lagged behind that of the nation, it was still sufficient to raise the real incomes of New Yorkers significantly. Between 1959 and 1969, the real median family income of New York families rose over 24 percent (see Table 2.3). In the next decade it fell nearly 10 percent, while the national average rose 6 percent. As a result, at the end of the 1970s median family income in the city was only 84 percent of the national average. In less than a generation, New York was transformed from a relatively affluent to a relatively poor city.

TABLE 2.4

Percentage of Persons and Families below the Federal Poverty Threshold, United States and New York City, 1959, 1969, and 1976–83

| | New York City | | United States | |
	Persons	Families	Persons	Families
1959	16.0%	N.A.	22.4%	N.A.
1969	12.9	11.5%	11.6	10.7%
1976	17.5	15.5	11.8	9.4
1977	18.5	15.4	11.6	9.3
1978	18.7	16.4	11.4	9.1
1979	19.3	17.1	11.7	9.1
1980	20.9	17.2	13.0	10.3
1981	21.7	19.1	14.0	11.2
1982	24.2	21.6	15.0	12.2
1983	23.4	19.9	15.2	12.3

SOURCES: Data for 1959 and 1969 from U.S. Department of Commerce, Bureau of the Census, 1970 Census of Population, Supplementary Report PC(S1)-105, *Poverty Status in 1969 and 1959 of Persons and Families for States, SMSAs, Central Cities and Counties: 1970 and 1960* (Washington, D.C.: United States Government Printing Office, 1975). National data for 1976–83 from Current Population Reports, *Consumer Income, Characteristics of the Population below the Poverty Level*, Series P-60 (Washington, D.C.: United States Government Printing Office, various issues). Data for 1976–83 for New York City based on tabulations from the annual U.S. Bureau of the Census, Current Population Survey computer tapes.

NOTE: N.A. means not available.

During the 1979–82 period, which included two national recessions, family incomes, in constant dollars, fell in New York City and the nation. However, in 1983 New Yorkers' real incomes rose, perhaps for the first time in 14 years, and their standing relative to the national average also improved slightly. One year does not constitute a trend, but the latest figures suggest that the deterioration of the incomes of New York families may be coming to a halt.

Similar trends are evident in the share of the city's population with incomes below the federal poverty threshold (see Table 2.4). At the start of the 1960s, the rate of poverty in New York City was below the nation's and, in both, the extent of poverty was falling. These positive downward trends persisted through the 1960s, but more slowly in the city than in the nation. By the end of that

TABLE 2.5

New York City Population by Income and Ethnic Group, 1980

	Number (thousands)	Percentage of total	Percentage Change from 1970
All Groups			
Total	6,889	100.0%	− 10.9%
Poor	1,394	20.2	+ 25.5
Near Poor	1,461	21.2	− 9.5
Lower Middle Class	1,258	18.3	− 22.7
Middle Class and Above	2,776	40.3	− 17.8
Whites	3,597	100.0%	− 27.2
Poor	368	10.2	− 12.0
Near Poor	598	16.6	− 20.0
Lower Middle Class	653	18.2	− 37.2
Middle Class and Above	1,978	55.0	− 27.8
Blacks	1,640	100.0%	+ 12.0
Poor	483	29.4	+ 40.4
Near Poor	410	25.0	− 4.6
Lower Middle Class	311	19.0	− 3.7
Middle Class and Above	436	26.6	+ 18.5
Hispanics	1,384	100.0%	+ 14.1
Poor	502	36.3	+ 51.7
Near Poor	381	27.5	− 7.3
Lower Middle Class	239	17.3	+ 0.4
Middle Class and Above	262	18.9	+ 12.4

SOURCES: U.S. Bureau of the Census, Census of Population, Public Use Microdata Sample for 1970 and 1980.

NOTE: The figures for the "other" ethnic group are not shown separately but are included in the total. The total in this table differs from the totals in Tables 2.1 and 2.2 because it excludes unrelated persons sharing a housing unit with families.

decade, the city's poverty rate exceeded the national figure. During the first half of the 1970s, the poverty rate began to rise locally, even though it declined gradually in the nation as a whole. After 1977, despite its economic turnaround, the city's poverty rate persisted in its upward trend. It reached 24 percent of the population by 1982, well above the 1969 figure of 15 percent and the 1977 figure of 18 percent. The nation's poverty rate also grew between 1977 and 1982, but in the latter year was still well below the level in New York City. The city's poverty rate fell slightly between 1982 and 1983 as the national recovery got underway, but the share of the local population in poverty (23 percent) was still well above the national average (15 percent).

It is often believed that the decline in average incomes has been accompanied by a bifurcation in the local income distribution due to greater numbers of both the poor and the rich and smaller numbers of those in the middle. However, analysis of the 1970–80 income shifts indicates this is not the case. All groups except the poor have declined, and the relative growth of the poor has been at the expense of all other segments of the population, not just those in the middle.

These trends are documented in Table 2.5, which classifies the city's population in terms of four income groups: (1) the *poor* are those with household incomes below the federal poverty threshold; (2) the *near poor* are those with incomes between 100 and 200 percent of the poverty level; (3) the *lower middle class* are those with incomes between 200 and 300 percent of the poverty line; and (4) the *middle class and above* are those with incomes at least triple the poverty line. The poverty thresholds vary with family size and, over time, are adjusted for inflation. To illustrate the categories, a family of four with an income below $9862 in 1979 would be in the poor group and above $29,586 would be in the middle class and above group.

The figures reveal a 26 percent increase in the poor group and declines in all other groups. The highest income group declined by 18 percent, a rate above the overall average. As a result, this group as a part of the total population fell from 44 percent in 1970 to 40 percent in 1980. The lower middle class share fell by three percentage points, while the near poor's share remained almost constant.

However, a form of polarization is evident across ethnic groups.

The distribution of whites among income groups differs markedly from that of blacks and Hispanics. A clear majority (55 percent) of whites are in the highest income group, and only about 27 percent of whites are poor or near poor. In contrast, most blacks (54 percent) are poor or near poor, and only 27 percent are among the highest income group. The situation is even worse for Hispanics; 64 percent are poor and near poor, while 19 percent are in the high-income group. In a city where most whites are relatively affluent and most minorities are outside of the middle class, it is not surprising that there is a perception of economic polarization along racial lines.

Moreover, the available evidence, while limited, suggests that this situation has worsened since 1980. Analysis based on national trends and their historic relationship to developments in New York City suggests that the poverty rate among the city's black and Hispanic populations by 1982 had risen to between 35 and 40 percent, and between 40 and 45 percent, respectively.[4] Meanwhile, the city's (mainly white) higher-income households seem to be more than holding their own. The number of households with constant (1983) dollar incomes of $40,000 and over rose by about 10 percent between 1979 and 1983.[5]

Analysis of data from the triennial *Housing and Vacancy Survey* suggests a similar conclusion. Between 1974 and 1980, increases in median household incomes lagged well behind the inflation rate. This gap was greater for renters than homeowners throughout the 1974–80 period. Between 1980 and 1983, as the city's employment recovery continued and inflation abated, real median household incomes rose. But it did so for owners, not renters.[6] The significance of these differences lies in the fact that homeowners disproportionately include higher-income whites, while renters have much lower incomes and are disproportionately black and Hispanic.

REASONS FOR SLOW INCOME GAINS

The dominant trend in the well-being of New York City residents over the past decade and a half has been declining real incomes in a period of economic contraction and a resistance, if not immunity, to improved economic status during the recent recovery. Why was the impact of the decline so severe and the response to recovery so slow? The answer is undoubtedly complex, but two important sets of forces apparently have exerted a strong influence. First, modes of family formation are changing in ways that make it difficult for some to achieve middle-class status through the now conventional means of having two or more earners in a household. Second, obstacles to effective labor force participation, including poor educational preparation and deeply rooted patterns of racial discrimination, keep many others from earning a satisfactory livelihood.

CHANGING FAMILY STRUCTURES

Patterns of family formation and dissolution play a critical role in determining how well individuals live. The family is typically thought of as a unit that provides affective support to its members, a haven in a heartless world. When it works, it is also a highly

TABLE 2.6

New York City Population by Income Group and Family Type, 1970 and 1980

(in thousands)

	Total	Poor	Near Poor	Lower Middle Class	Middle Class and Over
1970					
Families With Children	4,442	716	1,160	1,140	1,426
Female Head, No Husband	821	392	236	117	77
Other	3,621	324	924	1,023	1,349
Families Without Children	2,351	149	268	345	1,589
Nonfamily Households	932	245	187	143	357
Total	7,725	1,110	1,615	1,628	3,372
1980					
Families With Children	3,688	970	900	759	1,059
Female Head, No Husband	1,064	605	254	118	87
Other	2,624	365	646	641	972
Families Without Children	2,044	135	312	316	1,281
Nonfamily Households	1,157	289	248	183	437
Total	6,889	1,394	1,460	1,258	2,777

SOURCE: U.S. Bureau of the Census, *Census of Population*, Public Use Microdata Sample for 1970 and 1980.

effective economic unit. Where it works best is when married couples are part of it. The Survey Research Center's long-term *Panel Study of Income Dynamics* demonstrated quite conclusively that changes in family composition account for much of the change in economic status experienced by individuals. Most affected in a negative manner during a period of time were adult women who remain unmarried heads of their own households, young children, and women who have been divorced or separated.[7] In other words, single adults and single parent families are most likely to be among those at the bottom of the income distribution.

In this context, the trends in New York City have been unfavorable. As shown in Table 2.6, the population groups that have increased in New York City are comprised of persons who are part of single-parent, female-headed families and the group labeled "nonfamily" households containing primarily single individuals. Despite the 11 percent total population decline between 1970 and 1980, the number of individuals in single-parent, female-headed families rose nearly 30 percent; their share of the total population advanced from less than 11 percent to over 15 percent. Unfortunately, this group has a high probability of living in poverty. In 1980, nearly 57 percent of the people in these families lived in poverty, and another 24 percent were near poor; less than one in 12 received middle-class or higher-level incomes. Together, members of single-parent, female-headed families and of nonfamily households accounted for 64 percent of the city's poor in 1980.

While single-parent, female-headed families accounted for only 15 percent of the city's overall population, they accounted for 43 percent of its residents below the poverty level. The feminization of poverty is a national phenomenon, but its pronounced form in New York City is noteworthy. Nationally, in 1980 female-headed families accounted for 17 percent of all families; in New York City, this figure was 34 percent. Nationally, 7 percent of all families were poor and headed by females; in New York City, the comparable figure was 18 percent. The incidence of single-parent families headed by females, poor as well as not, is higher for each racial group in New York City than in the nation as a whole. For example, within the city's Puerto Rican community 41 percent of all families with related children were headed by poor women; the national figure was 29 percent.[8]

The rapid increase in female-headed families is fueled by a complex mix of factors. To begin with, women live longer than men, causing more families to be headed by widows, even quite young ones, than by widowers. A notable rise in marital instability, as reflected in the increase in divorce and separation, and the growing proportion of births out of wedlock, also have contributed to the rapid expansion of such families.

As more women began to work for pay, they became less economically dependent on men. Some women, particularly in working-class families, took jobs to augment family income, while others—in all classes—did so because of factors that underlie the changing status and self-image of women in society, such as higher levels of education. In the same period, marked improvements in and wider utilization of birth-control techniques had the effect, by limiting family size, of allowing women to participate more fully in the labor market.

The expansion of the social welfare sector also helped reduce the economic dependence of women on men. Indeed, one major initial impetus for the creation of the Aid to Families with Dependent Children (AFDC) program in 1935 was the widespread desire to assist women with young children who had either been widowed or deserted by their husbands. Among industrialized countries, the United States lagged in developing such a program on a national scale, and it was enacted only under the direst of economic circumstances. At the time, the group that was intended as the beneficiaries of such a program—single or widowed mothers—was expected to be quite small. And compared with today, it was. In that earlier period, strong social norms militated against divorce and separation. In addition, generalized economic hard times tended to keep otherwise unhappy families together out of necessity. But in time, the mere existence of such a program, because it changed the balance of power between the sexes in marriages where children were involved, encouraged the dissolution of many marriages that might otherwise have continued, however miserably.[9]

The creation and subsequent expansion of the AFDC program did not "cause" the rapid growth in the number of female-headed families that has taken place in recent decades. A more credible view is that AFDC and subsequent social welfare programs, such as Medicaid and Food Stamps, represented society's way of providing women and their children with an acceptable level of support to help them cope with adverse economic circumstances over which they had little control. Simply put, women are not as economically dependent on men as they once were because of rising levels of education, smaller families, and the creation of a social welfare system oriented to the needs of children.

While these trends affect all groups, their impact on black and Hispanic families has been particularly profound. Several factors in addition to historical and contemporary patterns of racial discrimination account for such differences. One is that black and Hispanic women who are family heads have weaker labor market credentials and attachments than similarly situated white women. They tend to have considerably lower levels of schooling, quantitatively and qualitatively. Adding to these disadvantages is the fact that minority females who head families typically have much greater child-caring responsibilities than their white counterparts. Nationally, the average numbers of children in single-parent families headed by females were 1.1, 1.8, and 1.8 for whites, blacks, and Hispanics, respectively; the comparable figures for New York City were 0.9, 1.6, and 1.7. [10]

Finally, families headed by white women typically receive more financial support from the fathers than do black and Hispanic families headed by women. Among families headed by white women, 42 percent received child support payments; the comparable figures for black and Hispanic female-headed families were 16 and 24 percent, respectively. [11] The primary reason for this is not greater empathy on the part of white fathers, but greater resources. It is more than likely that the depressed economic position of black and Hispanic young and middle-aged males serves to undermine their ability psychologically as well as economically to remain heads of families. Thus, the rapid growth in the number of poor black and Hispanic families headed by women is explained not only by the marginal economic status of the mothers, but also by the deteriorating economic status of the fathers.

While the foregoing factors help explain the rapid increase in the number of families headed by females, they do not necessarily account for the increased impoverishment of these families. Between 1970 and 1980, the proportion of the city's single-parent, female-headed families who were living in poverty rose from 43 to 55 percent, with the figures for blacks increasing from 46 to 52 percent and for Hispanics from 55 to 75 percent.

TABLE 2.7

Monthly Average Number of Persons Receiving AFDC and HR
Allowances in New York City, 1969–84
(in thousands)

Year	Total	AFDC	Home Relief
1969	911.1	756.9	154.2
1970	963.9	813.2	150.7
1971	1,039.2	888.2	151.0
1972	1,051.4	910.8	140.6
1973	1,002.7	873.0	129.7
1974	950.4	837.5	112.9
1975	984.9	848.0	138.9
1976	993.7	841.9	151.8
1977	961.9	831.0	130.9
1978	920.1	795.7	124.4
1979	887.2	767.4	119.8
1980	879.0	763.2	115.8
1981	871.6	760.0	111.6
1982	859.2	735.7	123.5
1983	889.0	741.0	148.0
1984	918.7	756.1	162.5

SOURCES: 1969–82 data from New York State Department of Social Services, *Statistical Supplement to Annual Report for 1982*; 1983 data from *Social Statistics*, December 1983, Table 6; 1984 data are from City of New York, Human Resources Administration (unpublished).

A major factor behind the deteriorating position of families that already were disadvantaged is the restrictions in public assistance programs. Enrollment in the AFDC program in New York City was nearly equal in 1969 and 1984, although the population in the city's poor, female-headed households with children rose by 72 percent between 1969 and 1979 and has increased further since (see Table 2.7). The number of people on Home Relief, which primarily serves single, non-elderly adults rose by 5 percent between 1969 and 1984, well below the growth in the number of poor persons in this category.

The AFDC program was expanded in the early 1970s. But with the exception of a single year, the trend in AFDC participation was persistently downward between 1972 and 1982, even though the poverty population was steadily expanding. The number of persons on AFDC increased between 1982 and 1984, however, by 3 percent. The Home Relief caseload, however, contracted sharply between 1969 and 1974. Its trend then became irregular: rising

TABLE 2.8

Relationship between Annualized AFDC Maximum Payment and Poverty Threshold for Four-Person Households in New York City, Selected Years 1961–84

	Annual Maximum Payment	Poverty Threshold	Annual Maximum as Percentage of Poverty Threshold
1961	$1,656	$3,054	54%
1969	3,612	3,721	97
1974	4,584	5,038	91
1981	6,180	9,287	67
1984	6,804	10,200	67

SOURCES: 1961 and 1969 data computed from C. Peter Rydell et al., *Welfare Caseload Dynamics in New York City* (New York: The New York City Rand Institute, October 1974), Table 7.9; July 1974 data (unpublished) from Office of Policy and Economic Research, City of New York Human Resources Administration; July 1981 data from U.S. Department of Health and Human Services, Social Security Administration, Office of Policy, *Quarterly Public Assistance Statistics,* various issues. 1984 poverty threshold from "Notes and Brief Reports: The 1984 Federal Poverty Income Guidelines," *Social Security Bulletin,* Vol. 47, No. 7 (July 1984), Table 2; information on poverty thresholds in earlier years from Bureau of the Census, *Current Population Reports,* Series P-60, No. 68, and subsequent applicable reports.

between 1975 and 1976 and falling through 1981. But it has been sharply upward, 46 percent, in the last three years.

The chief reason for the pronounced divergence between the population on welfare and the population in poverty is the drastic change during the 1970s in the relationship between the poverty threshold, as defined by the federal government and the State-defined eligibility levels for public assistance. For example, between 1969 and 1984 (see Table 2.8), the poverty threshold in current dollars for a four-person family rose by 174 percent, from $3721 to $10,200. In 1969, the maximum income limit for welfare eligibility for such a family was $3612 in New York City, or 97 percent of that year's poverty threshold. This income limit was adjusted upward 27 percent between 1969 and 1974, but it dropped to 91 percent of the 1974 poverty line because it lagged behind the inflation rate. In 1974, however, the State capped the maximum income limit and did not increase it again until 1981, when the basic grant was raised, and not again until 1984, when the shelter allowance was increased. Because of this cap, by 1981 a four-person family whose income was as little as 67 percent of the prevailing poverty threshold would not qualify for welfare. The increase in

1984, which is confined to the shelter allowance, kept the percentage at approximately that level. If the maximum income limit had been adjusted in accordance with the poverty threshold, New York City's welfare population would have risen sharply between 1969 and 1984, perhaps by as much as 40 percent, instead of growing a mere 2 percent.

Those who were, in effect, removed from or kept off the public-assistance rolls by the process just described were typically the working poor. But even families without any earned income found themselves with drastically reduced benefits as inflation eroded the value of their public-assistance grants. Even after the legislated increases in the basic grant in 1981 and 1984, the AFDC allowance for a four-person family was still worth only 69 percent of what it had been in 1969 in real purchasing power. However, the increased availability and substantial value of noncash benefit programs, such as Food Stamps and Medicaid, have partly offset erosion in the living standards of families either totally reliant on AFDC or who fall below the poverty level. [12] Minuscule in 1969, the Food Stamp program added approximately $2100 to the annual purchasing power of a family of four on public assistance in early 1985. [13]

While single-parent, female-headed families grew in numbers and became increasingly impoverished, other types of households, though less numerous, also faced obstacles to retaining their economic status. For example, the proportion of married-couple families with children who were either poor or near poor rose from 34 to 39 percent between 1970 and 1980. Those who suffered least appear to be families without children. These families comprised about 30 percent of the city's population in 1970 and 1980 (refer to Table 2.6). They are overwhelmingly in the middle class or above (63 percent) and comprise 46 percent of the population in that income category.

Families consisting of two parents with children were not a majority in the city in 1970 and comprised just 38 percent of the total in 1980. They were disproportionately in the near-poor and lower middle-class groups, comprising 49 percent of the group in these two income categories. Over 37 percent were middle class or above, and 14 percent lived in poverty. The distinctive nature of New York City's family composition and income structure is perhaps aptly summarized in the observation that only 972,000 residents, or 14

TABLE 2.9

Percentage of Married Couple Families with Two or More Earners by Income and Ethnic Group, 1970 and 1980

| | 1970 | | | | | | | 1980 | | | | | |
	Total	White	Black	Puerto Rican	Other Hispanic	Other	Total	White	Black	Puerto Rican	Other Hispanic	Other
Poor	12%	16%	12%	7%	20%	18%	14%	13%	17%	10%	15%	31%
Near Poor	26	25	31	20	33	44	36	29	40	67	44	59
Lower Middle Class	43	36	56	52	63	51	51	39	68	58	65	59
Middle Class and Above	64	59	84	74	73	65	70	64	88	79	79	68
All Groups	45	46	51	32	51	50	51	48	61	49	53	59

SOURCE: U.S. Bureau of the Census, Census of Population, Public Use Microdata Sample for 1970 and 1980.

TABLE 2.10

Employment-Population Ratio in New York City by Race, Sex, and Age, 1970–83
(percentage of population employed)

	Total	Whites				Blacks and Other Races			
		Total	Men 20 and over	Women 20 and over	Both Sexes 16–19	Total	Men 20 and over	Women 20 and over	Both Sexes 16–19
1970	54%	53%	74%	38%	33%	58%	81%	49%	23%
1971	53	52	73	38	29	55	77	47	21
1972	51	51	73	36	32	51	73	44	11
1973	51	52	74	37	30	51	71	42	16
1974	51	51	72	37	30	51	72	43	17
1975	49	49	69	36	28	48	65	44	14
1976	48	49	68	36	26	47	64	43	14
1977	49	49	67	37	28	48	66	45	12
1978	50	50	68	39	39	50	68	46	17
1979	51	51	69	40	28	50	66	47	16
1980	52	52	N.A.	N.A.	N.A.	50	N.A.	N.A.	N.A.
1981	51	51	N.A.	N.A.	26	50	N.A.	N.A.	13
1982	50	50	N.A.	N.A.	24	50	N.A.	N.A.	12
1983	49	49	66	39	23	48	63	46	12

SOURCE: U.S. Department of Labor, Bureau of Labor Statistics, *Geographic Profile of Employment and Unemployment* (Washington, D.C.: United States Government Printing Office, annual issues).

NOTE: N.A. means not available.

percent of the total population, are members of families with incomes in the range of the middle class or higher and comprised of two parents and their children.

Moreover, among two-parent families the achievement of high-income status is heavily dependent upon having two earners in the family. Fully 70 percent of all two-parent families in the highest income group have two workers; even among those in the lower-middle class, more than one-half have two earners (see Table 2.9). Having two earners is especially important in achieving middle-class status for minority groups. Among black, two-parent families in the highest income category, 88 percent had two earners, and among Hispanics the figure was 79 percent. For all ethnic groups, the share of married couples with two earners has been growing, with the overall figure increasing from 45 to 51 percent during the 1970s.

OBSTACLES TO WORK

Although public assistance and other welfare programs play an important role in determining the well-being of some groups of New Yorkers, the more important source of income for most local residents is employment. A major factor in the deteriorating income position of New Yorkers is the decline in the share of the working population. From 1970 to 1983, the employment-to-population ratio (that is, the share of the adult population that is employed) fell from 54 percent to 49 percent. While there was some improvement in this measure from 1976 to 1980, the more recent trend has been a decline despite economic growth (See Table 2.10).

However, there have been significant differences in the trends in employment opportunities for different groups in the population. Teenagers, especially minority teenagers, had sharply reduced work opportunities. Over the 1970–83 period, the employment-to-population ratio for white teenagers fell from 33 to 23 percent; for black teenagers it fell from 23 to 12 percent. Both black and white adult males experienced employment-to-population ratio declines, but the drop from 81 to 63 percent was especially sharp for black males. The employment-to-population ratios for women were relatively stable. Throughout the period, slightly under 40 percent of

TABLE 2.11

Employment-Population Ratio by Sex and Ethnic Group,
United States and New York City, 1970 and 1980
(percentage of population employed)

	United States		New York City	
	1970	1980	1970	1980
Total Males	70.8%	68.5%	70.7%	64.2%
White	71.8	70.0	71.4	66.6
Black	62.8	55.8	67.4	56.6
Asians	64.6	70.3	N.A.	71.7
Hispanics	71.4	69.6	71.4	63.2
Puerto Rican	68.5	60.0	67.8	57.8
Other Hispanic	71.9	71.0	77.9	70.2
Total Females	39.1	46.6	40.3	43.5
White	38.6	46.6	40.4	44.0
Black	43.7	46.6	43.9	46.3
Asians	42.5	33.8	N.A	55.8
Hispanics	36.1	44.4	33.8	36.1
Puerto Rican	29.4	34.8	26.8	29.7
Other Hispanic	37.2	45.9	47.4	45.2

SOURCES: National data from U.S. Bureau of the Census, Census of Population, *General Social and Economic Characteristics* volumes, decennial editions; New York City data from U.S. Bureau of the Census, Census of Population, Public Use Microdata Sample for 1970 and 1980. In the national data, Hispanics may be of any race and thus there is some relatively minor double counting involved. In the New York City data, however, the ethnic groups are mutually exclusive.

NOTE: N.A. means not available.

white women worked, and between 43 and 49 percent of minority women worked.

These trends in employment-to-population ratios are unique to New York and do not conform to national patterns (see Table 2.11). Between 1970 and 1980, the local rate for males fell much more rapidly than the national average and for each ethnic group. In 1970 the national and local rates for males were nearly equal, but the city's figure dropped to 94 percent of the national average in 1980. Among women, the local rate exceeded the national figure in 1970, but its slow growth during the past decade left it only 93 percent of the national average in 1980. This trend prevailed among women in all ethnic groups.

Why is only a smaller proportion of New York City residents able to find work? The answer is not simply that there are fewer jobs, because the recent job growth has not significantly increased the

TABLE 2.12

Payroll Employment and Employed Residents,
New York City, 1970–84

	Payroll Employment	Employed Residents	Employed Residents as Percentage of Payroll Employment
	(in thousands)		
1970	3,746	3,143	84%
1977	3,182	2,726	86
1978	3,188	2,762	87
1979	3,237	2,773	86
1980	3,298	2,781	84
1981	3,357	2,794	83
1982	3,345	2,772	83
1983	3,356	2,730	81
1984	3,432	2,768	81

SOURCES: 1970–82 payroll employment from U.S. Department of Labor, Bureau of Labor Statistics, *Employment and Earnings, States and Areas* (Washington, D.C.: United States Government Printing Office, 1984). The 1983 and 1984 payroll employment from New York State Department of Labor, *Employment Review* (January 1985). Employed residents data from U.S. Department of Labor, Bureau of Labor Statistics, Middle Atlantic Region Office, *News* (January 9, 1985), Table 1.

number of employed residents. As shown on Table 2.12, the number of employed residents has grown much less rapidly than the number of payroll jobs since 1978. Between 1978 and 1984, the 233,000 increase in jobs was accompanied by only a 6000 increase in employed residents. Most of the new jobs went to nonresidents.

These figures suggest that New York City residents are at a competitive disadvantage in securing locally generated jobs. Two important factors help explain this relative disadvantage: education and racial discrimination.

Education. As Table 2.13 shows, education makes a difference in the likelihood of employment. Among all adults 20 to 64 years of age in the city, the employment-to-population ratio increases from 51 for those with less than a complete high-school education to 83 for those with at least a four-year college education. Similar patterns are evident within each sex and ethnic group.

Because education is so important, part of the difficulties many city residents face in securing employment can be related to the low educational attainment of the black and Hispanic populations relative to the local white population. (However, at any given level of education the employment-to-population ratio is lower for blacks

TABLE 2.13

Employment-Population Ratio of New York City Residents
Age 20 to 64 by Education, Sex, and Ethnic Group, 1980
(percentage of employed population)

		Highest Level of Education			
	Total	Less than High School	High School Graduate	Some College	College Graduate
Males	77%	69%	80%	77%	88%
White	82	74	83	80	89
Black	68	59	72	70	83
Asians	84	84	89	72	89
Hispanics	73	68	79	76	85
Puerto Rican	68	63	76	83	84
Other Hispanic	80	78	83	78	86
Females	55	37	55	64	77
White	59	38	54	66	77
Black	56	41	60	64	80
Asians	65	63	59	61	73
Hispanics	41	31	50	55	72
Puerto Rican	34	23	45	54	74
Other Hispanic	51	45	56	56	70
Total	65%	51%	65%	70%	83%

SOURCE: U.S. Bureau of the Census, Census of Population, Public Use Microdata Sample, 1980.

and Hispanics than for whites, suggesting forms of labor-market discrimination to be discussed below.) For example, among white males the share of adults between ages of 20 and 64 with a college education is 31 percent, compared to 9 percent for blacks and 7 percent for Hispanics. In contrast, fully 37 percent of black and 55 percent of Hispanic males had not completed high school, compared to just 22 percent of whites (see Table 2.14). Similar patterns of lower educational attainment for minorities are evident among females. Moreover, more detailed analyses (not shown) by age as well as sex and ethnicity reveal that the disparities are being perpetuated among the younger age groups. For example, among white males age 16 to 24, approximately 32 percent had not finished high school, and 50 percent were in or had completed some college; in contrast, the comparable figures for black males of the same age were 58 and 25 percent, respectively, and for Hispanic males were 69 percent and 16 percent, respectively.[14]

The disparity between the educational levels of minority groups and of whites is greater in New York City than in the nation as a

TABLE 2.14

Highest Level of Education of New York City Residents
Age 20 to 64 by Sex and Ethnic Group, 1980
(percentage distribution)

	Total	Less than High School Graduate	High School Graduate	Some College	College Graduate
Males	100.0%	39.8%	23.8%	17.9%	18.6%
White	100.0	22.1	26.1	20.7	31.1
Black	100.0	36.9	32.5	21.6	9.0
Asians	100.0	25.6	17.1	19.0	38.3
Hispanics	100.0	54.5	22.9	16.0	6.6
Puerto Rican	100.0	59.7	22.7	13.6	4.0
Other Hispanic	100.0	47.6	23.2	19.2	10.0
Females	100.0	41.3	29.3	16.3	13.1
White	100.0	21.7	36.1	18.5	23.7
Black	100.0	35.4	34.5	21.9	8.2
Asians	100.0	31.7	19.6	19.0	29.7
Hispanics	100.0	57.1	24.1	13.9	4.9
Puerto Rican	100.0	60.4	24.0	12.5	3.1
Other Hispanic	100.0	52.7	24.1	15.7	7.5
Total	100.0%	40.6%	26.8%	17.0%	15.5%

SOURCE: U.S. Bureau of the Census, Census of Population, Public Use Microdata Sample, 1980.

whole (see Table 2.15). Nationally, the share of white males with a college degree is 22 percent, compared to 8 percent for blacks and Hispanics. Blacks and Hispanics in the city are not less educated than their counterparts across the country, but they are competing in New York with a white population with unusually high educational levels. Fully 31 percent of white adult males in the city completed college compared to 22 percent nationally; the respective figures for white females are 24 and 14 percent. The pronounced gap between educational levels of whites and of minority groups in New York City makes it difficult for the latter to improve their standing in the local economy.

Labor Market Discrimination. While inadequate educational preparation keeps many New Yorkers from competing successfully in the labor market, it is also true that members of minority groups encounter discrimination in the world of work regardless of their educational level. The gross effects of this discrimination are evident in the earning disparities between white males and others even after the figures are adjusted for age and education (see

TABLE 2.15

Percentage of Adults Who Have Completed Four or More Years of College by Age, Sex, and Ethnic Group, United States, Northeast, and New York City, 1980

(college graduates as a percentage of total)

	Men					Women				
	Total	White	Black	Asian	Hispanic	Total	White	Black	Asian	Hispanic
United States										
20–24	9	10	4	14	3	9	10	6	16	4
25–44	26	26	11	49	11	18	19	11	36	7
45–64	17	21	7	30	8	9	10	7	14	5
Total, 20–64	20%	22%	8%	38%	8%	14%	14%	8%	27%	6%
Northeast										
20–24	11	12	4	19	4	11	12	6	20	5
25–44	29	30	12	60	10	20	22	10	45	7
45–64	18	19	7	37	8	9	10	6	21	5
Total, 20–64	22%	23%	9%	50%	9%	15%	16%	8%	36%	6%
New York City										
20–24	14	23	4	17	3	15	24	6	20	4
25–44	29	42	11	48	8	22	34	10	38	6
45–64	17	21	8	25	6	10	12	7	15	4
Total, 20–64	19%	31%	9%	38%	7%	13%	24%	8%	30%	5%

SOURCES: Data for the United States and the Northeast from U.S. Census Bureau, Census of Population, *Detailed Characteristics* (Washington, D.C.: United States Government Printing Office, 1984). New York City data from U.S. Census Bureau, Census of Population, Public Use Microdata Sample, 1980. Nationally and for the Northeast, data for Hispanics are included as part of other racial groups as well as shown separately. In New York City, however, all catgories presented are mutually exclusive.

TABLE 2.16

Earnings of Employed Members of Selected Population Subgroups, New York City, 1980

	No High School	Some High School	High-school Graduate	Some College	College Graduate
White Males					
Age 25–44	$10,005	$13.505	$16,125	$16,003	$18,005
45–64	14,005	16,005	18,005	20,005	24,235
Other Groups as a Percentage of White Males					
Black Males Born in New York State					
Age 25–44	.90	.72	.74	.75	.83
45–64	.71	.81	.89	.90	.83
Black Males Born in Other States					
Age 25–44	1.10	.74	.74	.81	.84
45–64	.79	.77	.78	.75	.78
Puerto Rican Males					
Age 25–44	.92	.75	.74	.80	.83
45–64	.71	1.03	.95	1.20	.85
White Females					
Age 25–44	.68	.59	.62	.75	.78
45–64	.54	.50	.58	.60	.73
Black Females Born in New York State					
Age 25–44	.70	.65	.61	.68	.72
45–64	.56	.59	.64	.60	.78
Black Females Born in Other States					
Age 25–44	.70	.58	.62	.69	.78
45–64	.55	.53	.56	.60	.74
Puerto Rican Females					
Age 25–44	.88	.50	.61	.64	.64
45–64	.40	.44	.61	.65	.79

SOURCE: U.S. Bureau of the Census, Census of Population, Public Use Microdata Sample, 1980.

TABLE 2.17

Summary of New York City Population Projections, 1980–90
(in thousands)

	Total	White	Black	Hispanic	Other
Total 1980	7,092	3,686	1,702	1,429	275
Natural Increase	344	−237	234	302	45
Net Migration	−479	−578	−7	−85	191
Total 1990	6,957	2,871	1,929	1,646	511
Percentage Change	−1.9%	−22.1%	+13.3%	+15.2%	+85.8%

SOURCE: 1980 data from U.S. Census Bureau, Census of Population, Public Use Microdata Sample.

Table 2.16). In most age and education categories, black males, both those born in New York State and those born elsewhere in the United States, typically earn about three-quarters of that which white males earn. For younger Puerto Rican males the pattern is similar, but older Puerto Rican males do significantly better. White females typically earn between one-half and three-quarters as much as their male counterparts, and the relative rewards of work are even lower for most subgroups of minority women.

Pay disparities do not arise simply from employers paying some groups of workers less than others for identical work. Patterns of labor-market discrimination are often more complex and subtle. The way in which knowledge about job openings is spread, the selection criteria for promotion and hiring, and the career opportunities made available within firms are all factors that channel some groups into lower-paying jobs than others.[15]

THE OUTLOOK

The trends evident since 1970, and especially trends evident since the local economic recovery beginning in 1977, provide a basis for projecting the size and composition of the city's population in 1990. The demographic factor with the least uncertainty is natural increase. Births can be projected reasonably accurately based on current fertility rates, since little change is likely in this behavior. With respect to mortality, age-adjusted death rates improved steadily since 1970. It is reasonable to expect this trend to continue, so deaths are projected based on declines in the death rate for specific age groups paralleling those evident since 1970. These combined factors suggest that over the 1980–90 period, natural increase will add 344,000 people to the city's population (see Table 2.17). This is about 10 percent above the natural increase of the earlier decade.

More problematic are the estimated rates of migration during the 1980s. Since 1970, migration rates have varied among ethnic groups and have shifted between the period of economic contraction and the subsequent recovery. In light of these variations, a reasonable assumption for the 1980–90 period is that the limited emigration of blacks and Hispanics during the 1970s will continue, but that the emigration of whites will slow significantly from its 1970s rate due to local economic growth. Specifically, it is assumed that the emigration of whites will be halved from the previous decade to the current one. These assumptions about migration are consistent with actual developments during 1978–81, but differ from the apparent trends of the 1981–84 period. In the later period, while white emigration is estimated to remain at the projected level (i.e., one-half the 1970–80 rate), the black and Hispanic immigration may be accelerating over their previous levels. If this persists during the remainder of the decade, the total population will be approximately 200,000 greater than projected below and the minority share of that population will be somewhat larger than projected below.

The assumptions lead to a 2 percent decrease in the city's population, from 7,092,000 in 1980 to 6,957,000 in 1990 (see Table 2.18). All of the decline is among the white population, whose numbers drop more than 22 percent to 2,871,000. This is less than the 26 percent drop during the 1970s. Nevertheless, in 1990 whites may comprise only 41 percent of the population compared to 52 percent in 1980. The decline is due to the expected reduced, but still significant, emigration as well as relatively low birth rates among white women and a relatively large number of deaths linked to the age of the white population remaining in the city.

The city's black and Hispanic populations are expected to increase 13 and 15 percent, respectively, over the decade. This is a slightly higher rate than for blacks in the 1970s and a somewhat lower rate than for Hispanics in the same period (refer to Table 2.2). The "other" group is expected to grow by 86 percent, a rate well above the 49 percent growth in the 1970s.

TABLE 2.18

Projected New York City Population by Age and Ethnic Group, 1990

	Number (000s)				Percentage Change, 1980–90			
	Total	White	Black	Hispanic	Total	White	Black	Hispanic
Under 18	1,647	409	576	533	−7%	−35%	+4%	+5%
Under 5	497	99	176	182	+5	−38	+23	+24
5–17	1,150	310	400	351	−11	−34	−2	−3
18–64	4,317	1,811	1,180	1,009	−1	−21	+15	+18
65 and Over	993	651	173	104	+4	−13	+43	+55
65–74	542	340	115	70	−6	−22	+40	+52
75 and Over	451	310	59	34	+18	—	+51	+62
Total[a]	6,957	2,871	1,929	1,646	−2%	−22%	+13%	+15%
Exhibits								
16–24	845	276	263	243	−20	−40	−10	−5
20–64	4,123	1,759	1,104	959	−1	−21	+16	+20

SOURCE: See text.

a. Asians and others are included in the totals, but not shown separately.

The predicted trends will also result in significant changes in the age composition of the population. Youth, or those under age 18, will decline nearly 7 percent with all the decline concentrated in the school-age population. The projected decline in the school-age population (13 percent) is less than the 20 percent drop during the 1970s. The smaller youth population will be primarily "minority." In 1990, less than one-quarter of the population under age 18 will be white, with 35 percent black and 32 percent Hispanic.

In contrast, the city's senior citizens, those age 65 and over, are expected to increase 4 percent to nearly 1,000,000. The growth is particularly rapid among the age group over 75. The group over age 65 will remain nearly two-thirds white. However, the one-third nonwhite component of the aged population in 1990 will be well above their 1980 share of less than 22 percent.

The size of the city's prime labor force, those between ages 20 and 64, is expected to remain virtually unchanged between 1980 and 1990. This group might increase by 3 or 4 percent during the 1980s if the migration assumptions overstate the population loss. In either case, the expected trend is a marked contrast to the 8 percent decline in the population of the prime working age during the 1970s.

The so-called "youth labor force," those between ages 16 and 24, will decline 20 percent in the current decade. This is a significant acceleration of the 7 percent decline during the previous decade. This trend should improve the employment prospects of new entrants into the labor market, but the prospects are clouded by a shifting ethnic composition. In 1980, blacks and Hispanics constituted 52 percent of the city's youth labor force; by 1990, they will account for at least 60 percent.

The limited change in the size of the prime working-age population, combined with Matthew Drennan's projected growth of between approximately 250,000 and 300,000 jobs over the 1980–90 period, suggests potential for substantial improvement in the employment and income position of the city's residents (see Chapter 2). However, employment growth in the first half of the 1980s produced little benefit for local residents. A key question for the next administration is how much projected economic growth through 1990 will help New York City residents.

It is difficult to project the extent to which New Yorkers will reap the benefits of local economic growth, but a continuation of current trends would not lead to significant improvement. As noted earlier, the dominant factor in the increased incidence of poverty in New York City has been the increased number of single-parent, female-headed families, especially among blacks and Hispanics. Nearly three-quarters of the increase in poverty in New York City from 1970 to 1980 represented an increase in black and Hispanic children and adults in female-headed families. Specifically, the number of people in such families per 1000 women age 15 to 44 rose from 481 to 632 over the decade. It is not likely that this rate of increase will continue during the 1980s, but an increase at one-half that rate is conceivable. If the rate of poverty among this group also grows at one-half the rate of the 1970s, this relative improvement will still yield close to 800,000 poor members of female-headed families in 1990. Even if no other group experienced a continued increase in its poverty population, the combined total of all people in poverty in 1990 would be approximately 1.6 million or 23 percent of the projected population total.

Prospective changes in the size of the city's population below the poverty level also can be viewed as the result of an interaction between shifts in the composition of the population and the rates of poverty that characterize different subgroups. What is most significant about the population projections earlier summarized is the substantial growth indicated for precisely those groups that had the highest rates of poverty in 1980 and also experienced significant increases in this respect over the 1969–82 period. Assuming that rates of poverty for specific subgroups remain unchanged from their 1980 levels and that only the size of the various subgroups changes, 1.5 million persons would live below the poverty line in 1990 compared to the 1.3 million that did so in 1980. Some 71 percent of these poor would be black and Hispanic. The poor would represent 22 percent of the city's population, a greater proportion than in 1980 but a slightly lower share than the 1982 recession high of 24 percent.

In sum, the outlook for people and income in New York City is disturbing. The population in 1990 should be slightly smaller than a decade earlier, and the number of jobs should be larger. However, differential patterns of migration and educational achievement among ethnic groups will increase the number and share of city residents who have experienced difficulty competing for jobs in the past. If these trends persist, more and a larger share of New Yorkers will be living in poverty at the end of the next administration.

NOTES

1. For a discussion of this process, see Emanuel Tobier, "Population," in Charles Brecher and Raymond D. Horton, eds., *Setting Municipal Priorities, 1982* (New York: Russell Sage Foundation, 1981), pp. 31–37.

2. See estimates in Emanuel Tobier, "Older New York: A Socio-Economic Portrait," *New York Affairs,* Vol. 8, No. 3 (1984), p. 73.

3. The estimates are based on New York City Health Department vital statistics and an analysis of data collected as part of the triennial New York City Housing and Vacancy Survey by the U.S. Census Bureau. Vital statistics were used to estimate natural increase over the 1978–81 and 1981–84 periods in the white population and this was deducted from the Housing and Vacancy Survey figure for non-Puerto Rican whites to estimate migration for the periods.

4. See Emanuel Tobier, *The Changing Face of Poverty: Trends in New York City's Population in Poverty, 1960–90,* Community Service Society of New York, 1984, pp. 19–21 and 42–52.

5. Estimated from unpublished data provided by the U.S. Bureau of the Census, Income Statistics Branch, the Population Division.

6. Based on tables from the *1984 Housing and Vacancy Survey* made available prior to publication by the City of New York Department of Housing Preservation and Development.

7. Greg J. Duncan et al., *Years of Poverty, Years of Plenty: The Changing Economic Fortunes of American Workers and Families* (Ann Arbor, Mich.: Survey Research Center, Institute for Social Research, University of Michigan, 1984), Chapter 1, particularly pp. 18–23.

8. Data from 1980 Census of Population, Vol. 1, *Characteristics of the Population,* Chapter C, General Social and Economic Characteristics, Part 1, United States Summary, PC 80-1-C1, Table 171.

9. For one discussion of the changing assumptions behind the AFDC program, see Gilbert Steiner, *The State of Welfare* (Washington, D.C.: The Brookings Institution, 1971), Chapter 2.

10. 1980 Census of Population, Vol. 1, *Characteristics of the Population,* Chapter D, Detailed Population Characteristics, Part 1, United States Summary, PC 80-1-D1-A, Table 304, and Chapter D, Detailed Characteristics, Part 34, New York, PC 80-1-D3-1, Section 2, Table 245.

11. U.S. Bureau of the Census, *Current Population Reports,* Series P-23, No. 124, *Child Support and Alimony Advance Report: 1981* (Washington, D.C.: United States Government Printing Office, 1984), Table 1.

12. Depending upon the valuation technique employed, the poverty rate nationally is significantly reduced if account is taken of the equivalent money income value of noncash benefits programs. For blacks, it falls from 36 percent in 1982 to between 22 and 29 percent, and for Hispanics it declines from 30 percent to between 21 and 26 percent. U.S. Department of Commerce, Bureau of the Census, *Estimates of Poverty Including the Value of Non-Cash Benefits: 1979–82,* Technical Paper 51 (Washington, D.C.: United States Government Printing Office, 1984).

13. Estimates made by Anne Perzeszty, Consumer Economic Specialist, Community Council of New York. The food stamp allowance figure for a family of four is calculated on the assumption that it receives the maximum shelter allowance.

14. Bureau of the Census, Census of Population, Public Use Microdata Sample.

15. For relevant discussions, see Charles Brecher, "The Mismatch Misunderstanding," *New York Affairs,* Vol. 4, No. 1 (1977), pp. 6–12; and Thomas Bailey and Roger Waldinger, "A Skills Mismatch in New York's Labor Market," ibid., Vol. 8, No. 3 (1984), pp. 3–18.

PART TWO

Securing and Managing Resources

State Aid

CYNTHIA B. GREEN

State aid is a critical component of the City of New York's budget. Historically, the City has depended strongly on this assistance. For the future, the City anticipates that its budget will be balanced in large part by increasing amounts of State aid. This chapter analyzes the State of New York's ability to meet these expectations and identifies options available to the City for realizing its plans. The first section describes the City's dependence on State aid and identifies its future expectations. The second section focuses on four interrelated factors that influence the level of State aid to the City: the financial health of the State, its tax policies, its expenditure priorities, and its leaders' commitment to financial propriety. These variables provide the basis for the projection of future levels of State aid in the third section. The final section discusses options that would enhance future City-State fiscal relations.

NEW YORK CITY'S DEPENDENCE ON STATE AID

The City's revenues are expected to total nearly $19.2 billion in its 1985 fiscal year.[1] The three major revenue sources are locally

TABLE 3.1
State Aid to the City of New York, Fiscal Years 1975–85
(millions of dollars)

New York City Fiscal Year	Restricted State Aid	Unrestricted State Aid	Subtotal	Medicaid Adjustment	Adjusted Total
1975	$2,377	$485	$2,862	$428	$2,434
1976	2,371	510	2,881	420	2,461
1977	2,235	542	2,777	432	2,345
1978	2,303	587	2,890	334	2,556
1979	2,113	702	2,815	100	2,715
1980	2,193	683	2,876	13	2,863
1981	2,412	593	3,005	0	3,005
1982	2,700	522	3,222	0	3,222
1983	2,685	658	3,343	0	3,343
1984	2,915	693	3,608	0	3,608
1985 (estimated)	3,500	709	4,209	0	4,209

SOURCES: Restricted State aid data for fiscal years 1975–84 from the City of New York, *Annual Report of the Comptroller*, fiscal years 1975–84. Unrestricted State aid data for fiscal years 1975–84 provided by City of New York, Office of Management and Budget. For fiscal year 1985, from City of New York, *Executive Budget Fiscal Year 1986, Message of the Mayor*, May 3, 1985. Medicaid adjustments are author's calculations based on data in the annual Comptroller's reports.

generated income, aid from the State of New York, and aid from the federal government. Locally generated income, primarily taxes and fees, is the largest source; it accounts for over $12 billion or 63 percent of the total. The remaining almost $7.1 billion comes from intergovernmental transfers. The State provides most of those funds, over $4.2 billion or 22 percent of total revenues (see Table 3.1). Federal assistance is over $2.8 billion or 15 percent of the total.

The State aid that accounts for over one-fifth of the City's budget takes two forms: categorical and unrestricted. Categorical programs provide support for specific functions such as public education, higher education, social services, health, mental health, transportation, and housing. Unrestricted aid, principally the State's revenue sharing program, provides grants to be used according to locally determined priorities. In most recent years, categorical aid has exceeded unrestricted aid by a ratio of about five to one.

The manner in which the City reports its categorical State aid does not permit meaningful comparisons over time. Prior to 1978, Medicaid payments were included as restricted aid. From 1978 through 1980, the State gradually assumed direct responsibility for making most Medicaid payments. Beginning in fiscal year 1981, the payment of Medicaid claims was completely transferred to New York State. Therefore, the figures for the later years do not include these payments. In order to identify trends in State aid to New York City, adjustments must be made for the changed reporting of Medicaid. When these adjustments are made, the figures show that over the past decade, State aid to New York City increased every year except 1977. The growth generally was accelerated over the decade, with the annual increase averaging 6.5 percent since 1980.

In addition to these programs, the State assists the City through "indirect" aid. These resources are not included in the City's budget, but they nonetheless provide fiscal relief. Indirect aid is of two principal types: payments to local public benefit corporations and State assumption of obligations previously financed by the City. Payments to autonomous or semi-independent organizations such as the Metropolitan Transportation Authority and the Housing Authority aid the City by reducing the need for municipal subsidies to these organizations. Similarly, State assumption of the financing of functions such as City University senior colleges and local courts reduces municipal tax and expenditure requirements even though no direct payment is made by the State to the City government.

Reconciling State and City accounts of levels of State aid is difficult for two reasons. First, each entity has a different fiscal year for which it prepares budgets and reports expenditures or revenues. The State's fiscal year begins on April 1 and ends on March 31; the City's fiscal year runs from July 1 to June 30. Therefore, State and City financial reports do not show comparable figures. Second, the State defines as aid to the City both direct and indirect aid; in contrast, the City reports as State aid only the direct aid which flows through its budget. This generally leads to much higher reported levels of aid by the State than by the City. However, an important exception to the City's usual practice of counting only direct aid in its estimates of future increases in State aid in its financial plan documents. The City's estimates of future aid increases, labeled "gap-closing aid," may include indirect forms of State aid. For example, in the past the City has counted as gap-closing aid the monies that would be saved by State assumption of an increased share of local Medicaid funding.

TABLE 3.2
Planned Revenues, City of New York, Fiscal Years 1985–89
(millions of dollars)

	1985	1986	1987	1988	1989	Average Annual Percentage Change
Baseline Revenues	$19,188	$20,018	$21,010	$21,763	$22,863	4.5%
State Aid	4,209	4,385	4,457	4,500	4,544	1.9
Categorical	3,500	3,756	3,821	3,865	3,909	2.8
Welfare	1,190	1,280	1,341	1,384	1,426	4.6
Education	1,730	1,897	1,897	1,897	1,897	2.4
Higher Education	265	278	278	278	278	1.2
Health and Mental Health	141	144	144	144	144	0.5
Other	174	157	161	162	164	−1.4
Unrestricted	709	629	636	635	635	−2.6
Per capita	561	535	535	535	535	−1.2
Other	148	94	101	100	100	−7.5
Federal Aid	2,861	2,716	2,699	2,740	2,782	−0.7
Local Revenues[a]	12,118	12,917	13,854	14,523	15,537	6.4
Gap-closing Actions	N.A.	N.A.	870	1,065	939	5.3
City	N.A.	N.A.	595	605	615	1.7
State	N.A.	N.A.	275	525	775	69.3
Reserve for Service Enhancement, Tax Reductions and Other Contingencies	N.A.	N.A.	—	(65)	(451)	N.A.
Total Potential Revenues	$19,188	$20,018	$21,880	$22,828	$23,802	5.6%

SOURCE: City of New York, *Executive Budget Fiscal Year 1986, Message of the Mayor*, May 3, 1985, pp. 50 and 208.

NOTE: N.A. means not applicable.

a. Net of intracity revenue and disallowances against categorical grants.

NEW YORK CITY'S STATE AID EXPECTATIONS

For the near future, City officials are relying heavily on increased State aid to help them achieve a balanced budget. Part of this expected increase is evident in the City's Financial Plan for the fiscal years 1985–89 (see Table 3.2). Over this period, the City expects increases of $335 million in aid under current programs (or baseline revenue) and another $775 million in aid from gap-closing State actions. Together, these two forms of aid are expected to be increased $1100 million or 26 percent over the 1985–89 period. This compares with an actual increase in State aid over the 1981–85 period of $1204 million or almost 40 percent.

However, not included in the City's Financial Plan is indirect State aid resulting from the State takeover of certain local Medicaid costs. Effective in 1983, the State increased its share of funding for long-term care services for those eligible for Medicaid; the State's share will grow through 1986. This law provides savings to the City of $223 million in 1985, $274 million in 1986, $316 million in 1987, $342 million in 1988, and $384 million in 1989.[2] These savings appear in the City's Financial Plan as reduced expenditures rather than increased revenues. But when the savings are added to the expected direct State aid, the City's estimates of increases in State aid for 1985–89 amount to $1494 million or almost 36 percent.

THE AVAILABILITY OF STATE AID

In order to evaluate the likelihood that the City will receive aid increases as large as those anticipated in its financial plan, it is necessary to have an understanding of the factors that shape these decisions at the State level. Foremost among them is the State's own revenue-generating ability. In order to judge whether the State will be able to sustain or increase local assistance, it is necessary to assess the financial condition of the State. In addition, the share of available State resources devoted to aiding localities depends upon policy decisions that direct the allocation of the State's resources. Within its budget, there is a competitive relationship among tax reductions, expenditures for direct State operations, and local assistance. Moreover, recent interest in improving State fi-

TABLE 3.3

State of New York General Fund Operating Results and Aid to Localities, Fiscal Years 1970–79

(millions of dollars)

	Operating Results			Local Aid	
	Receipts	Disbursements	Surplus or Deficit	Amount	Percentage Change
1970	$6,207	$6,207	$0	$3,688	14.2%
1971	6,747	6,747	0	3,825	3.7
1972	7,422	7,422	0	4,291	12.2
1973	8,326	8,298	28	4,724	10.1
1974	8,635	8,631	4	5,111	8.2
1975	9,658	9,676	(18)	5,638	10.3
1976	10,204	10,651	(447)	6,319	12.1
1977	11,279	11,370	(91)	6,687	5.8
1978	11,273	11,268	5	6,634	(0.8)
1979	11,988	11,983	5	7,082	6.8

SOURCE: Data provided by State of New York, Office of the State Comptroller, Bureau of Financial Reporting.

nancial management also could require resources that might otherwise be available for local aid. An understanding of each of these factors is useful in assessing the City's outlook for fiscal aid.

THE STATE'S FINANCIAL CONDITION

The ability of the State to assist localities depends on its own level of resources and its management of these resources. The link between the State's financial condition and its ability to aid localities was particularly evident during the 1970s. In that decade, State aid to localities increased at an annual average of 8.3 percent (see Table 3.3). But there were two distinct periods during that time affected by changes in the State's fiscal conditions.

During the first half of the 1970s, the State had balanced budgets or surpluses. The year-end results ranged from a balance in fiscal years 1970 through 1972 to a $28 million surplus in fiscal year 1973, averaging an annual $6.4 million surplus over this period. Local assistance increased an average of 9.7 percent annually during the same period.

Beginning in fiscal year 1975 and continuing through fiscal year 1977, the State experienced financial difficulties that resulted in cash deficits ranging from $18 million in fiscal year 1975 to $447

million in fiscal year 1976. During the worst of these years, fiscal
year 1976, there were shortfalls in receipts from personal income
and business taxes reflective of a sluggish economy. Moral obligations for the bonds of the Urban Development Corporation and
Housing Finance Agency could not be met, requiring unplanned
State expenditures, as did the New York City fiscal crisis.[3] By fiscal
year 1978, the State's finances had improved, and it ended that
year and the next each with a surplus of $5 million. However, aid
to localities, during this period, increased only by an average of
6.8 percent annually, in contrast to the 9.7 percent average increases during the first part of the decade.

As the State's financial condition began to improve in the latter
part of the 1970s, it might have returned the annual increases in
direct local assistance to precrisis rates. However, this did not hap-
pen because competition for available resources emerged in the
form of pressures for tax reductions.

TAX POLICY

Four major factors precipitated a tax policy decision that reduced
resources available for new local assistance. First, in the second
half of the 1970s there was a strong national movement for tax and
expenditure limitations. In many states, taxpayers began to press
for ceilings or reductions in tax and expenditure levels. In 1976, a
limit on the growth of state expenditures was adopted in New Jersey. Colorado and Rhode Island adopted limits on state taxes and
expenditures in 1977. On election day of 1978, fully 13 states had
such measures on their ballots.[4]

Although the New York State electorate did not face such a ref-
erendum, this did not indicate a lack of interest in tax reductions.
In fact, there was great concern, heightened by the knowledge that
New York State was the highest taxing state in the nation. In 1978,
New York's state and local taxes accounted for 17.2 percent of per-
sonal income, a figure 34.8 percent above the national average.[5]
On a per capita basis, state and local taxes were $1308 in New York
State versus only $888 nationally.[6] Thus, the second factor contrib-
uting to the State's tax-cut decision was popular dissatisfaction with
relatively high taxes in New York State.

Third, groups representing business interests were extremely vo-
cal in their objection to the high level of State taxation. These

organizations are typically quite influential in State-level tax decisions.[7] In New York State, strong business coalitions and lobbies argued that New York State's high taxes adversely affected business location decisions. According to this view, New York State's tax structure placed its businesses at a competitive disadvantage. The State had been and continued to be in danger of losing businesses to other states. Tax reductions were seen as the key to ensuring a favorable economic climate for the state.

Finally, the State's revenue outlook had improved as high levels of inflation increased collections from the State's economically sensitive taxes, especially the personal income tax which has steeply graduated brackets. Other economically sensitive taxes are numerous consumption taxes; business taxes; taxes on estates, gifts, and parimutuel betting. Economic growth in personal income and business activity, along with high levels of inflation experienced during the late 1970s, contributed to sharply increased collections, which in turn permitted tax cuts to be considered affordable as well as desirable.

As a result of these combined forces, a series of reductions in the rates and base of the personal income tax were instituted. These tax cuts absorbed potential resources that might otherwise have been allocated to local aid. In 1978, the first year of the tax cut and the year of the State's first cash surplus since 1974, direct aid to localities actually was decreased by just under 1 percent. In fiscal year 1979, direct local assistance was increased by 6.8 percent, a figure lower than the decade's annual average of 8.3 percent (refer to Table 3.3).

It is estimated that the tax cuts reduced the State's revenues in its 1978 and 1979 fiscal years by a total of approximately $1.2 billion.[8] If the tax cuts had not been instituted and the $1.2 billion in foregone revenues had been used for direct aid to localities, then the average increases for each of these years would have been close to those seen for the first half of the decade, 10.2 and 9.7 percent, respectively. Clearly aid to localities is affected by tax reductions.

LOCAL AID VERSUS DIRECT OPERATIONS

Another source of competition for local assistance is the cost of direct operations of State agencies. In essence, the primary resource allocation decision is the division of available funds between

TABLE 3.4

Division of New York State General Fund Spending between Local Aid and Direct Operations, Fiscal Years 1983–86

(millions of dollars)

	Fiscal Year 1983 (actual)		Fiscal Year 1984 (actual)		Fiscal Year 1985 (estimated)		Fiscal Year 1986 (adopted)	
	Amount	Percentage	Amount	Percentage	Amount	Percentage	Amount	Percentage
Direct Operations[a]	$7,182	40.4%	$8,040	41.7%	$8,912	42.4%	$8,908	39.3%
Local Aid	10,574	59.6	11,229	58.3	12,123	57.6	13,773[b]	60.7
Total Disbursements	17,756	100.0%	19,269	100.0%	21,035	100.0%	22,681	100.0%

SOURCES: Fiscal years 1983 and 1984 from State of New York, *Annual Report of the Comptroller*, 1983 and 1984; fiscal year 1985 estimated and fiscal year 1986 adopted from State of New York, *Official Statement, 1985 Tax and Revenue Anticipation Notes*, April 11, 1985.

a. For all years shown, includes State Operations, General State Charges, Debt Service, Capital Construction and Transfers to Other Funds. For fiscal year 1986, the figure also includes $182 million in Resources for GAAP Balance. These funds are for reducing the deferral of education aid payments, but will not be distributed to localities until fiscal year 1987. Therefore, this money is considered Direct Operations.

b. Includes $167 million in Resources for GAAP Balance, because these funds will be distributed to localities during fiscal year 1986.

direct operations and local assistance. This division has historically
been relatively stable. However, decisions in the early years of
Governor Mario Cuomo's administration indicate the possibilities
for direct operations to draw potential resources from local aid.

The budget that newly elected Governor Cuomo inherited in
1983 allocated 40.4 percent of expenditures to direct operations
and 59.6 percent to local aid (see Table 3.4). Governor Cuomo's
new 1984 budget increased spending for both purposes, but slowed
the growth in local aid.[9] It was decreased to 58.3 percent.

This shift in State spending priorities was due to two factors.
First, the Governor inherited a deficit. In fiscal year 1983, the State
had issued $500 million in short-term notes which had to be repaid
during fiscal year 1984. Second, the 1984 budget required spending
increases of about $400 million to finance an earlier collective bar-
gaining settlement that gave State employees an 8 percent increase
in salaries. To honor these commitments, spending for direct operations had to be increased significantly. And to finance these
commitments, the Governor both curbed increases in local aid and
successfully sought passage of measures that would raise nearly $1
billion in new revenues.

The shift in spending priorities, begun in fiscal year 1984, was
continued during fiscal year 1985. During this year, the share of
the budget devoted to direct operations increased to over 42 percent. Significant resources were devoted to restoring more than
1600 jobs previously eliminated at CUNY, SUNY, and State mental
institutions. In addition, during the course of the year, spending
in two areas, corrections and mental retardation, and developmen-
tal-disability programs exceeded planned disbursements. The former was due principally to a higher inmate population than had
been anticipated in the budget, and the latter derived from federal
disallowances of requests for reimbursement for program expenses.

The adopted Budget for fiscal year 1986 reverses the trend in
spending priorities. It increases spending for local aid by 13.6 percent and reduces spending for direct operations by $4 million. This
budget returns State spending to 60.7 percent for local aid and 39.3
percent for direct operations, as it had been before Governor
Cuomo was elected. However, previous experience demonstrates
that adopted budgets may differ significantly from actual spending.
Legislative changes in the budget and unanticipated events during
the fiscal year can alter an adopted budget dramatically. As the

earlier trends suggest, increases in local aid are vulnerable to competition from pressures to increase spending on direct State operations.

IMPROVED FINANCIAL REPORTING

In recent years, the State's financial reporting practices have been improved significantly. However, these changes have exposed some undesirable State fiscal practices. This wider knowledge has, in turn, generated pressures for reforms in financial management that would require substantial budgetary resources in the short run. These pressures to use State resources to compensate for a history of fiscal mismanagement is another source of competition for increased aid to localities.

Prior to fiscal year 1982, the State of New York accounted for its operations on a cash basis. Receipts were recorded only when money was deposited in the State treasury; disbursements were recorded only when payments were made. Under such practice, State officials have the discretion to alter the amount of revenues or expenditures in a given year by adjusting the timing of disbursements. These delayed disbursements can significantly alter the amount of spending reported in a fiscal year. Financial reports will not identify all revenues that are legally owed or all expenditures for which the State is legally responsible during a fiscal year. Thus, the cash accounting system may be used to portray the State's financial position inaccurately.

To correct these problems, in 1981 the New York State legislature enacted a statute requiring new financial reporting practices beginning in fiscal year 1982. This involved a conversion from a cash basis of accounting to a system based on Generally Accepted Accounting Principles (GAAP). The new system required a modified accrual basis to measure changes in the State's position. Revenues are recorded when they are legally owed, regardless of when received. Expenditures are recorded when the State incurs a liability or makes a commitment that will require a disbursement, regardless of whether a cash payment is actually made during that fiscal year. The presentation of a budget and the completion of an audit in accordance with GAAP is now mandated. However, the budget is not required to be balanced on a GAAP basis. Instead, it must be balanced on a cash basis. The result of these new requirements is that two versions of financial documents are prepared, one on a GAAP basis and another on a cash basis.

The addition of GAAP reporting has provided the public with much more information than was previously available. The documents prepared under GAAP reveal troublesome information. New York State experienced General Fund deficits of $256 million in fiscal year 1981, $552 million in fiscal year 1982, $1076 million in fiscal year 1983, $345 million in fiscal year 1984 and approximately $125 million in fiscal year 1985.[10] Although data for previous years are not available, it is likely that deficits were present for several years prior to the preparation of GAAP audits. These annual GAAP deficits add to the imbalance between the State's financial assets and liabilities, increasing its accumulated deficit. In fiscal year 1981, it is estimated that the accumulated deficit in the General Fund was $2.3 billion. By the end of fiscal year 1985, that figure had risen to over $4.4 billion.[11]

The preparation of GAAP financial reports has made it clear that the State relies heavily on two financial management practices that, when abused, are quite dangerous. They are roll-overs and short-term borrowing. As noted above, the budget is not required to be balanced in accordance with GAAP, but cash balance is required. In order to achieve a cash balance at year end, the State has placed significant reliance on the deferral of disbursements. Put simply, the State has financed its recurring deficits largely by shifting expenses incurred in one year to the subsequent year. The deferred expenditures are then financed with short-term borrowing, and the notes are repaid with next year's revenues. The process has been repeated for several years with the net effect that the State defers paying off a cumulative deficit by annually increasing its short-term borrowing.[12]

To illustrate, New York State ended its fiscal year 1984 with over $7.3 billion in liabilities and only $2.8 billion in financial assets. In the beginning of fiscal year 1985, the State issued $4.3 billion in tax and revenue anticipation notes. Taxes are not received at even increments throughout the year, but rather are taken in much higher amounts towards the end of the year. Disbursements also are made unevenly. But unlike revenues, disbursements are made at a much faster rate at the beginning of a fiscal year. Therefore, there is always need for what has come to be known as the annual "spring borrowing." However, true seasonal borrowing needs did not total $4.3 billion that year. Only $1.6 billion of the $4.3 billion total was for seasonal borrowing needs. The remaining $2.6 billion or over 60 percent of the total borrowing was required primarily to finance the delayed payment of personal income tax refunds, aid to localities for public education, and pension contributions.[13]

Reliance on spring borrowing is costly. Interest payments are required on the notes and the underlying fiscal problems increase interest rates on the State's bonds. The interest payments required for the fiscal year 1985 short-term borrowing totaled $246 million.[14] Some $150 million of these interest payments were for financing roll-overs and deficits.

Deferring or rolling over expenditures and relying on short-term borrowing places the State in a highly vulnerable position. Should the State be denied access to these borrowed funds, the consequences would be far reaching. The State would be unable to fund school aid, tax refunds, vendor payments, pensions and various State operations. Citizens would face disruption of governmental services, and it is possible that economically harmful tax increases would be required.

The conversion to GAAP has made these imprudent financial management practices public knowledge. As the severity of the situation and its potential consequences have become clearer, there is increasing attention to reform. The State Comptroller, the New York City Citizens Budget Commission and the Governor's Council on Fiscal and Economic Priorities have called for the capping of roll-overs and a program for reducing the accumulated deficit.[15]

In response, the Governor submitted to the Legislature a budget for fiscal year 1986 that is balanced in accordance with GAAP and an amendment to the Constitution which would require the budget to be balanced under GAAP. Adoption of these measures would serve to halt the growth in the accumulated deficit and cap the size of the annual spring borrowing. However, by itself, GAAP balanced budgets will not address the need to reduce the State's large accumulated deficit. Even with a GAAP balance every year in the future, the State would remain unable to finance all of its required disbursements; a $4.4 billion cash shortfall would continue to exist. Dealing with this problem, either through a program of annual reductions or a conversion of short-term to long-term debt will require a budget allocation that reduces resources available for other purposes, including local aid.

THE OUTLOOK FOR STATE AID

The four factors that have determined the availability of State aid in the past are likely to influence the level of aid in the future. To judge whether or not the expectations for aid to the City of New York are realistic, it is necessary to consider the State's likely financial condition in coming years, the impact of State tax cuts, pressures for greater spending on direct State operations, and the impact of any efforts to improve the State's financial management.

THE STATE'S PROJECTED FINANCIAL CONDITION

Unlike the City, the State of New York does not provide the public with a multiyear financial plan. The only future-oriented document is a set of five-year financial projections that are prepared to correspond with the Executive Budget and revised only annually. However, these projections which are mandated by State law, can be misleading, and the future financial condition of the State cannot be foreseen easily.

The State's most recent projections for its General Fund show that the State will achieve surpluses under GAAP during fiscal years 1986 to 1990 (see Table 3.5). The surpluses will be quite modest in fiscal years 1986 and 1987, at $7 million and $17 million, respectively. The surplus will increase to $77 million in fiscal year 1988 and $348 million for fiscal year 1989. By fiscal year 1990, the surplus is projected at $666 million.

The State's projections must be interpreted cautiously because of the assumptions on which they rest. The revenue projections appear somewhat optimistic. The revenue estimates assume real economic growth throughout the period and inflation ranging between 4.7 and 5.9 percent. This leads to an annual average growth in taxes of 6.6 percent, which appears conservative when compared with average annual increases during the fiscal year 1982–85 period of 9.3 percent. However, these revenue projections assume a three-year reduction in the personal income tax that otherwise would have generated $395 million in fiscal year 1986, $760 million in fiscal year 1987, and $1350 million in fiscal year 1988. When the foregone revenues are included in the tax projections, it becomes clear that the governor was assuming an average growth rate between fiscal years 1986 and 1988 of 8.5 percent. Although this

TABLE 3.5

State of New York General Fund Projected Revenues and Expenditures,

Fiscal Years 1986–90

(millions of dollars)

	1986	1987	1988	1989	1990	Average Annual Percentage Change
Revenues	$24,469	$26,241	$27,585	$29,344	$31,363	6.4%
Taxes	21,419	22,955	24,340	25,974	27,905	6.8
Other Revenues	1,438	1,558	1,613	1,688	1,733	4.8
Transfers	1,612	1,728	1,632	1,682	1,725	1.8
Expenditures	$24,462	$26,224	$27,508	$28,996	$30,697	5.9%
Grants to Local						
Governments	12,991	13,897	14,615	15,616	16,750	6.6
State Operations	8,218	8,578	9,059	9,479	9,948	4.9
General State						
Charges	1,735	1,824	1,911	2,036	2,142	5.4
Debt Service	216	209	203	183	164	−6.6
Transfers	1,302	1,716	1,720	1,682	1,693	7.6
Surplus	$7	$17	$77	$348	$666	

SOURCE: State of New York, *Five Year Projections, Fiscal Years 1985–86 through 1989–90.*

figure is closer to the earlier average, it is important to note that significant tax increases were enacted during this previous period. Therefore, it is unlikely that the State revenues could continue to grow at the high rate experienced earlier.

In addition, the State legislature passed and the governor accepted tax cuts larger than those proposed in the Executive Budget. In fiscal year 1986, the State is expected to forgo $160 million more or a total of $555 million. Over the next three years the enacted tax reduction program will forgo $500 million more than was estimated in the Governor's initial four-year projections.

The expenditure projections are more troublesome. Total expenditures increase at an annual average rate of 5.9 percent; this contrasts with the 1982–85 rate of 9.6 percent annually. The small increase is based on relatively low spending for both aid to localities and direct operations. The former is projected to increase at an annual average of only 6.6 percent compared to the 1982–85 rate of 8.3 percent. Not only is this planned growth rate much lower than recent experience, but it ignores the strong likelihood of significant federal reductions of aid. The federal funds provided to the State do not appear in the General Fund, but rather in the State's Special Revenue Funds. However, in the event that federal aid, particularly for Medicaid and mass transit, is reduced, New York State very likely would be called upon to finance the shortfall from its General Fund. With respect to direct operations, the projected average annual increase of 4.9 percent annually allows for only a 2 percent pay increase for State employees and is well below the 8 percent increase over the 1982–85 period. In sum, current projections are unrealistic because they understate likely expenditures. Equally significantly, they do not take into account changed tax policies which might lower future revenues even beyond the current plans.

FUTURE TAX POLICY

As noted earlier, the State's 1978 tax reduction program was a reaction to four major factors: a national movement for tax and expenditure limitations; strong interest among New Yorkers for tax reductions in reaction to the State's high tax burden; pressure from powerful business coalitions for tax cuts; and a growing revenue base. These pressures again are being felt. As a result new tax reductions will be made that can be expected to decrease State budgetary resources in the coming years.

The tax revolt, which reached a dramatic peak with California's Proposition 13 in 1978, seemed to have ended by 1980. Of the 19 states with tax and expenditure limits in 1983, fully 17 had passed their measures by the end of 1980. However, 1984 witnessed a revival. During that year, eight states were involved in some effort to limit taxes or expenditures. Four states considered modifying their existing limits, and measures affecting state taxes were on the ballot on election days in four other states.[16]

Although interest appeared strong, only one of these states, South Carolina, passed its measure. However, in two of the seven remaining states, the proposals were defeated by very narrow margins (four percentage points or less). One measure was defeated by moderate margin of seven percentage points. In the other four states the measures were defeated by at least nine percentage points.[17]

It has been suggested that the 1984 election results do not indicate a reduced interest in state tax levels. Instead, the electorate viewed these proposed measures as excessively restrictive, potentially leaving states unable to raise needed revenue. In fact, 12 of the 13 states with gubernatorial races in 1984 elected governors who ran on a platform pledging to cut, to restructure, or at least not to raise taxes.[18] Therefore, it appears that concern over the level of state taxes is nationally still great.

And New York is still a high tax state. In 1982 (the year for which the most recent data are available), New York State was second only to Wyoming as the highest taxing state in the country. In New York, state and local taxes accounted for 15.6 percent of personal income, a figure 42 percent above the national average. On a per capita basis, state and local taxes were $1780 in New York State versus $1148 nationally.[19]

The organized-business coalitions that were effective in the 1970s are again strongly advocating tax reductions. The State's competitive disadvantage with respect to business location decisions are again cited to support tax cuts. Finally, the State's projections indicate the financial picture, and notably likely revenues, is improved. This reinforces claims for tax cuts.

In January of 1984, Governor Cuomo asked his Council on Fiscal and Economic Priorities (COFEP) to provide recommendations for reforming the State's tax structure in a manner that would promote economic development. In November of that year, COFEP called for a gradual reduction in the personal income tax.[20] Heeding this recommendation, the Governor's budget proposal for fiscal year 1986 included a three-year plan for personal income tax cuts. The proposal would phase in a reduction on the maximum tax rate on earned income, increase the personal exemption, convert the standard deduction now based on a percentage of income to a flat deduction, and widen the middle-income brackets.[21] Cumulatively, the State would forgo over $2.5 billion in revenue during this three-year period.

The leaders of the Legislature, which must approve any tax changes, have been strong proponents of tax cut. Much of the debate over the fiscal year 1986 budget centered on the size of the tax cut. The Republican leaders of the State Senate favored a larger personal income tax reduction and cuts in other taxes. The business community has registered its interest in deeper and broader tax cuts. The final decision adopted the Governor's approach to reform of the personal income tax with only minor adjustments, and also included a reduction in the minimum tax on unearned income. As a result, the adopted plan provides greater tax relief. This compromise does not necessarily end the pressure for tax reduction. The enactment in future years of higher levels of tax cuts could consume all of or possibly more than the available general fund surpluses for the years to come. Should such proposals be adopted, even greater levels of potential resources would be directed away from local assistance.

EXPENDITURE POLICY

The State's financial projections, summarized in Table 3.5, suggest that future expenditure policies will favor local aid over direct State operations. Grants to local governments are expected to increase 6.6 percent between fiscal years 1986 and 1990; in contrast, disbursements for direct operations will grow only 4.9 percent over this period.

But, as noted earlier, the projections are misleading because the assumptions regarding the costs of direct State operations are unrealistic. The figures include only a 2 percent pay increase for State employees after fiscal year 1985 despite the fact that inflation is projected to average 5.3 percent during this period. After the State budget was adopted, the largest state employee union signed a new contract providing salary increases of 5 percent in fiscal year 1986, 5.5 percent in fiscal year 1987, and 6 percent in fiscal year 1988. Therefore, additional salary expenditures of $148 million in 1986, $247 million in 1987, and $416 million in 1988 will be required.[22] Assuming that pay increases for 1989 and 1990 match the projected inflation rate, additional salary expenditures of $581 million and $773 million will be needed for these respective years. In addition, the cost of fringe benefits would increase. Moreover, there are virtually no allowances for improvements in agency programs, but there are strong pressures for many such improvements. There are growing needs in New York State, particularly in the areas of housing, mental health, training and employment, and poverty for which the Governor has consistently expressed concern. In light of the State's past record, the assumption that no spending for new initiatives will occur is questionable.

Responding to these needs and pressures could have important consequences. First, they could alter the pattern of spending between local assistance and state operations; once a reasonable adjustment is made for State employee pay increases, it is no longer the case that growth in local assistance would outpace growth in spending for State operations. Second, like tax reductions, State employee pay increases have the potential virtually to eliminate available surpluses in future years. The use of available funds for pay increases that equal or exceed the rate of inflation would significantly reduce the possibility for new initiatives to expand aid to localities. If combined with significant tax cuts, such pay increases could force aid to localities to fall below the projected levels.

FINANCIAL MANAGEMENT IMPROVEMENTS

Two types of policy decisions are necessary to rectify the State's history of poor financial management. First, the annual budget should be balanced on a GAAP basis. Second, the cumulative deficit resulting from the transgressions of earlier years should be reduced and eventually eliminated.

As mentioned previously, the Governor proposed a balanced budget following GAAP for fiscal year 1986 and thereafter. Under the Governor's proposal, balancing the budget on a GAAP basis in fiscal year 1986 would require about $300 million of additional cash disbursements. In future years, additional cash resources will be necessary to maintain a balance according to GAAP. The cost is expected to range from $297 million to $634 million annually. These sums are already incorporated in the State's financial projections.

For fiscal year 1986, the Legislature did adopt a balanced budget under GAAP. However, it required $50 million more than the Governor anticipated.[23] This change suggests that higher levels of spending than anticipated in the five-year projections will be necessary to achieve budgets balanced on a GAAP basis in future years. These additional requirements could consume resources shown as available for local assistance.

Even if the State has balanced budgets after 1985, it still must cope with an accumulated deficit that exceeded $4.4 billion at the end of fiscal year 1985.[24] Two general strategies are available to deal with this problem. The deficit could be eliminated by converting the accumulated deficit into long-term debt. The entire accumulated deficit would be funded by bond sales. Once the bonds were sold, the State could satisfy all outstanding liabilities created from the practice of resorting to rollovers. The accumulated deficit would be eliminated, and short-term borrowing for these purposes would be unnecessary. Alternatively, the deficit could be reduced gradually by committing State revenues annually to repay a portion of the accumulated deficit and rolling over a decreased amount until the deficit is fully eliminated. A combination of these two basic strategies is also conceivable.

A 15-year program of gradual reductions in short-term borrowing has been proposed by the State Comptroller.[25] Along with his Executive Budget for fiscal year 1986, the Governor submitted a proposal, consistent with that of the Comptroller's, calling for a 15-year program, beginning in fiscal year 1988, that would create a sinking fund to eliminate $1.8 billion or that portion of accumulated deficit that is attributable to deferrals of aid to education. The Governor has also suggested a restructuring of pension contributions to reduce the spring borrowing by an additional $500 million.

In any case, policies to reduce the accumulated deficit will require annual expenditures beyond those required to maintain annual GAAP balance. For example, the Governor's program would require an increase in annual expenditures of $120 million over the 15-year period. These new expenditures would compete for resources potentially available for increased local assistance.

Whether such steps will be taken remains to be seen. They require legislative action, but the Legislature is not favorably disposed to using resources for this purpose. However, the Governor and certain civic groups are likely to pressure the Legislature to adopt these fiscal reforms.

In sum, there are strong pressures to allocate available State resources to purposes other than increased aid to localities. Tax reductions, pay increases for State employees, and steps to eliminate current and cumulative deficits are likely to consume all of the surplus revenues currently projected. Municipal leaders will be required to devise particularly wise and forceful strategies to obtain the aid increases they anticipate.

STRATEGIES FOR THE CITY OF NEW YORK

The intense competition for State resources means that municipal leaders should focus on obtaining a maximum share of any increases in statewide aid to localities as well as on seeking to increase the level of such assistance. To increase their share, City leaders can use two complementary strategies. They could alter the functional mix of aid to favor categories in which the City receives a large share and alter the principle of aid distribution within categories for which the City's share is now relatively small. In contrast, there appear to be limited possibilities for expanded indirect aid.

THE LIMITED PROMISE OF INDIRECT AID

The City's recovery from its fiscal crisis was helped significantly by indirect State aid. During that period, the State assumed responsibility for funding City University senior colleges, City courts, and Supplemental Security Income payments. In addition, the State took managerial action to improve the City's financial condition, including the creation of the Municipal Assistance Corporation, the Financial Control Board, and the Special Deputy Comptroller's Office for New York City.

Based on this record, it would seem fruitful for City officials to press for further indirect aid. Sound principles of public finance point to several areas for which State financial responsibility is more appropriate than City responsibility. Such functions include special education, sheltering the homeless, and criminal justice.

However, a note of caution must be sounded. In the past, the State's willingness to provide indirect aid was related directly to New York City's poor financial condition. New efforts will be hard to justify on this ground. New York City's financial condition no longer warrants special State support. The 1984 fiscal year was the fourth consecutive period in which the City achieved a surplus according to GAAP. For fiscal year 1985, the City's adopted budget was balanced without additional taxes and even provided service enhancements. Experience during this fiscal year suggests the year-end result will be a sizable surplus. In addition, the City's future revenue-generating capacity is strong. For the next four years, the City expects local private-sector employment to grow steadily and local unemployment to decline. Growth in personal income and retail sales are expected to be greater than the rate of inflation.[26]

In contrast, other localities in the State face serious economic difficulties and may be able to make a strong case for special State aid initiatives. For example, Erie County with a population of approximately a million, is in serious trouble and may not remain solvent. The county has been suffering from severe economic problems, including the highest rate of unemployment in the State. Erie County's deficits are expected to total $90 million or 12.5 percent of expenditures in fiscal year 1985. Lackawanna, one of Erie's principal cities, lost over 75 percent of its tax base in 1984 when the Bethlehem Steel plant closed. As a consequence, Lackawanna was closed out of the credit markets. In fiscal year 1985, the State provided $1 million in transition aid and expects further assistance will be necessary.[27] Buffalo, the other major city in Erie County, may soon face financial difficulties. This City's major source of revenue is its property tax. The State Constitution limits this City's collections from the property tax to 2 percent of the average property value over the past five years. In fiscal year 1985, Buffalo was taxing at 90 percent of this constitutional capacity. State officials expect that Buffalo will require higher levels of State assistance in the near future.[28]

Additional problem areas are Niagara Falls and Yonkers. The City of Niagara Falls, faced with high costs associated with the Love Canal disaster and the construction of an unsuccessful convention center, will require $1.2 million in additional State aid in fiscal year 1986. The City of Yonkers exhausted its property tax limitation five years ago and has suffered from a stagnant tax base. Yonkers re-

TABLE 3.6
State of New York General Fund Local Assistance Appropriations,
Fiscal Year 1985
(millions of dollars)

	Statewide Amount[a]	New York City Amount[b]	New York City Share
Education	$4,937	$1,369	27.7%
Higher Education	1,166	652	73.0[c]
Social Services	3,747	2,325	62.0
Medicaid	2,136	1,440	67.4
Income Maintenance	1,611	885	54.9
Mental Hygiene[d]	554	128	23.1
Health	88	30	34.1
Housing	79	10	12.7
Environmental Conservation	46	11	23.9
Transportation	301	58	19.3
Other Categorical	874	35	4.0
Unrestricted Aid	1,068	484	45.3
Revenue Sharing	800	484	60.5
Other	268	0	0
Total Direct Aid	$12,860	$5,102	39.7%

SOURCES: Statewide amounts from New York State Legislature, *Report of the Fiscal Committees on the Executive Budget, Fiscal Year April 1, 1984 to March 31, 1985.* New York City amounts provided by New York State Division of the Budget, Fiscal Planning Unit.

a. Statewide amounts are appropriations.

b. City amounts are planned cash disbursements.

c. The New York State Division of the Budget was unable to determine New York City's share of that portion of the appropriation for Higher Education from the Higher Education Services Corporation. Therefore, the City's share is calculated on a statewide appropriation of $893 million, rather than the $1166 million shown above.

d. Mental Hygiene includes mental health, mental retardation, substance abuse, and alcoholism and alcohol.

cently instituted an income tax, the only city in the State beside New York to do so. Despite this, Yonkers incurred a deficit of $9.5 million or 4.3 percent of expenditures in fiscal year 1984. Yonkers avoided closing its schools only because of special State assistance and loans. In fiscal year 1985, the State provided Yonkers with a $9.5 million loan. In fiscal year 1986, the State will provide Yonkers with $14 million in aid and $4.8 million in State guarantees, to be repaid if the County of Westchester provides this city with additional assistance. Should such action not occur, the State will have to assume the expense.[29]

The cities of Rochester and Syracuse are currently solvent, but they may soon face serious fiscal problems. Both cities have stagnant tax bases and Rochester is already taxing close to capacity (94 percent). Suffolk County also faces potential problems. The Long Island Lighting Company has refused to pay $53 million in county, town, and school district property taxes until the dispute over its Shoreham Plant is resolved. The Suffolk County charter requires that the county make up unpaid property taxes. This has resulted in a poor bond rating for the county.[30]

The merits of a locality's claim to indirect aid depend heavily on its relative fiscal position. There are likely to be several areas in the state that have a stronger claim to special aid efforts than does New York City. Therefore, greater priority should be given to increasing aid to the City through existing local aid programs.

ALTERING THE FUNCTIONAL MIX

The categorical nature of State aid to localities plays an important role in determining how large a share of the statewide total the City of New York receives. As shown in Table 3.6, the City received $5.1 billion or 39.7 percent of all aid to localities in fiscal year 1985. However, the City's share varied from 12.7 percent for housing aid to 73.0 percent for higher education. The City receives 62 percent of the funds allocated to social services. Within this area, 67 percent of the Medicaid funds are received by New York City. The City receives less than half the local aid for five other functions, including education, mental hygiene, health, environmental conservation, and transportation. The City receives 45 percent of unrestricted aid, but in the major unrestricted aid program, general revenue sharing, it receives 60.5 percent of the appropriation.

Given these wide variations in New York City's share, it is in the City's interest to have greater increases in aid for social services, higher education, and revenue sharing. Interestingly, two of these functions have received disproportionately large increases in recent years and the outlook is favorable for continued relative growth in social service aid. As shown in Table 3.7, the overall increase in local aid was 10.3 percent between State fiscal year 1984 and 1985. However, the increase for social services was 12.9 percent including a 13.8 percent increase in Medicaid. Higher education received a slightly higher than average increase of 10.4 percent. Much of this

TABLE 3.7

State of New York General Fund Appropriations for Aid to Localities,
Years 1984 and 1985
(millions of dollars)

	Fiscal Year 1984	Fiscal Year 1985	Percentage Change
Selected Programs:			
Mental Hygiene	$469	$554	18.1%
Mental Health	166	220	32.5
Mental Retardation	204	230	12.7
Substance Abuse	80	85	6.3
Alcoholism and Alcohol	19	19	0
Environmental Conservation	40	46	15.0
Social Services	3,320	3,747	12.9
Medicaid	1,877	2,136	13.8
Income Maintenance and Other	1,443	1,611	11.6
Higher Education	1,056	1,166	10.4
SUNY	161	174	8.1
CUNY	542	579	6.8
Other	353	413	17.0
Education	4,563	4,937	8.2
Health	82	88	7.3
Transportation	287	301	4.9
Revenue Sharing	800	800	0
Housing	86	79	−8.1
Total Direct Aid	$11,659	$12,860	10.3%

SOURCES: New York State Legislature, Report of the Fiscal Committees on the Executive Budget, Fiscal Year April 1, 1984 to March 31, 1985.

increase was directed at providing higher tuition assistance to college students.

The relatively large increase for Medicaid is the result of a 1983 decision to increase the State's share of program costs and reduce the local share. This higher State share applies to long-term care services, including nursing homes, personal care, home health, and home nursing. The federal government finances 50 percent of Medicaid services and New York State and New York City traditionally shared the remaining 50 percent. In 1983, the State enacted a Long Term Care Takeover, which would phase in State assumption of a greater portion of the cost of the long-term care services. In 1984, the State share was increased from 50 percent of the nonfederal amount to 72 percent. The State's share is scheduled to increase from 76 percent in 1985 to 80 percent during 1986. In addition, beginning in 1983, eligible costs of mentally disabled persons are reimbursed by the State at 100 percent of the nonfederal share. This will result in continued disproportionately large Medicaid increases through 1986. However, the City continues to seek a greater State role in financing medical services beside long-term care and the potential exists to expand Medicaid aid further. This strategy is particularly fruitful for the City because it accounts for so large a share of statewide Medicaid expenses.

The relatively large share of revenue sharing funds allocated to the City suggests this also should be a favored target for increases. In recent years, this proved politically difficult to accomplish. The revenue sharing appropriation had been frozen in 1981, and both the Governor and the legislative leaders had resisted reversing this decision. Instead, a new program of unrestricted aid, the Supplemental State Targeted Assistance Program, was proposed by the Governor for fiscal year 1986. This program would have provided almost $52 million of unrestricted assistance to localities with demonstrated fiscal need. However, the design of the program was such that New York City was not eligible. As discussed earlier, the City's financial condition is much better than many of the State's other areas.

The Legislature did not enact the Governor's proposal. However, they did remove the longstanding freeze on revenue sharing and increased its funding by $68.5 million. New York City will receive 40 percent, or $28 million, of this additional appropriation. This policy change may continue to help the city in the future.

INCREASING THE CITY SHARE OF SELECTED PROGRAMS

While the greatest payoff in additional aid is likely to result from efforts to increase State Medicaid funding, there are significant potential gains to be made from seeking to increase the City's share of selected categorical programs. In particular, the City can obtain new funds by increasing its share of education aid, one of the largest programs, and its share of aid for mental health, a rapidly growing program under which the City has a strong case for an increased share.

Education is second to social services as the largest aid program. In fiscal year 1985, education aid accounted for over $4.9 billion or 38.4 percent of all State aid. It accounts for almost $1.4 billion or 26.8 percent of all State aid received by New York City. Because of its magnitude, even small changes in the City's share can yield large sums. Moreover, there is good reason for additional State education aid to favor New York City. As Robert Berne demonstrates in Chapter 8 of this volume, New York State provides a significantly smaller share of total education expenditures in New York City than it does in the rest of the state, despite the fact that per pupil spending is lower in the city than in the rest of the state. Berne also identifies a number of specific changes in education aid formulas that would help rectify the inequity.

Mental health aid has grown rapidly in recent years. In fiscal year 1985, it grew over 18 percent, more rapidly than any other major function. But the City receives only 23 percent of these funds, despite its apparent need for a larger share. State policies of limited admissions to its mental hospitals cause large numbers of people with psychiatric conditions to remain in the community, but the City has not received sufficient funds to provide community-based services. A recent comprehensive study of this problem found that the State's mental health policies and practices were seriously deficient.[31] Greater funding with a redirection of aid to regional or county managers was recommended in order to enhance community-based treatment. If this approach is followed, New York City is likely to benefit.

CONCLUSION

New York City's improved financial condition requires the de-

velopment of a new relationship with the State of New York. Over
the past decade, the City experienced serious fiscal problems. At
the same time, the City had been and continued to remain the
State's economic center. The City's relative need for assistance coupled with its economic promise deemed it the appropriate recipient
of substantial increments in State aid. More recently, the City's
improved financial condition and positive future outlook contrast
with deteriorating economic and financial conditions of counties and
municipalities elsewhere in the State. In the years to come, higher
levels of State resources are therefore likely to be directed at these
declining areas. The City should seriously consider the changing
context and identify strategies that will best benefit its claims to
what may prove to be scarce local aid resources.

The City typically directs much of its efforts to the various, yet
specific State aid programs. Each year after the Governor presents
the Executive Budget, the City analyzes the proposal in an effort
to determine the level of State aid the City would receive. This
amount, typically, falls short of the City's expectations. Therefore,
substantial City resources are devoted to altering this plan. The
Mayor and a number of high-ranking City officials attend public
hearings and present arguments to show why the State could increase local assistance in particular areas and to suggest how it
might be increased.

In contrast, the City pays relatively little attention to the overall
distribution of the State budget. Yet, as the chapter has demonstrated, the amount of State aid received by the City is determined
principally by the total resources the State allocates for aiding its
localities. In particular, the State's financial condition, tax policies,
expenditure priorities, and posture towards financial propriety
strongly influence the amount of local aid made available each year.

The City has important stakes in the overall distribution of the
State's budget. Therefore, the City should take a position on a
wider range of issues, rather than continuing its traditional narrow
focus on specific State aid programs. Annual decisions on taxing,
spending for State operations, and commitment to fiscal reform
influence the levels of grants to local governments. One of the
mayor's tasks should be to articulate a broader position on State
fiscal matters. The mayor, together with leaders of other local governments, should become an important influence on the State's
broad budgetary allocations.

In addition, it is important to recognize that the City has much to gain from ensuring that funds earmarked for direct local assistance are directed towards those areas that most benefit the City. The City would benefit greatly from the continued expansion of aid for social services, particularly Medicaid. In addition, the City's strong need in the areas of education and mental health constitute a claim to a greater share of the resources devoted to these purposes.

NOTES

1. Figures in this paragraph from City of New York, *Executive Budget Fiscal Year 1986, Message of the Mayor*, May 3, 1985, p. 1.

2. Data for fiscal years 1985, 1986, and 1989 from *Executive Budget*, op. cit., p. 86; for fiscal years 1987 and 1988, data provided by City of New York, Office of Management and Budget.

3. State of New York, *Annual Report of the Comptroller*, 1976.

4. Daphne A. Kenyon and Karen M. Benkor, *Fiscal Discipline Tools Developed by State Governments: Tax and Expenditure Limits and Other Mechanisms*, draft (Washington, D.C.: Advisory Commission on Intergovernmental Relations, September 1984).

5. Advisory Committee on Intergovernmental Relations, *Significant Features of Fiscal Federalism*, 1982–83 edition (Washington, D.C.: Advisory Commission on Intergovernmental Relations, 1983), Tables 29.1 and 29.2.

6. U.S. Department of Commerce, Bureau of the Census, *Governmental Finances, 1977–78* (Washington, D.C.: U.S. Government Printing Office, 1979), Table 24.

7. Richard Bingham, Brett Hawkins, and Ted Herbert, *The Politics of Raising State and Local Revenue* (New York: Praeger Publishers, 1978), Chapter 9.

8. Unpublished data provided by the Regional Division of Federal Reserve Bank. The research from which these estimates were prepared, but not the figures themselves, were published in Allen J. Proctor, "Tax Cuts and the Fiscal Management of New York State," *Federal Reserve Bank of New York Quarterly Review*, Volume 9, Number 4 (Winter 1984–85), pp. 7–18.

9. A more detailed description of Governor Cuomo's spending priorities for fiscal years 1984 and 1985 appears in Cynthia B. Green, "The State Budget: Record Spending, Fiscal Imbalance," *Citizens Budget Commission Quarterly*, Volume 4, Number 2 (Spring 1984).

10. Data for fiscal years 1981 to 1984 from State of New York, *Annual Report of the Comptroller* for 1981–84. For fiscal year 1985, the figure shown was reported in State of New York, *Official Statement, 1985 Tax and Revenue Anticipation Notes*, April 11, 1985, p. 8. The figure for fiscal year 1981 is only an estimate. For that year, a prototype of the State's financial statements in accordance with GAAP was prepared. However, since that time the Comptroller has identified errors in the original preparation of these statements. Although these problems were corrected in future years, the fiscal year 1981 figures were not restated.

11. Figure provided by New York State Division of the Budget. Also see note 24.

12. For a more complete discussion of the State of New York's financial condition and

financial management practices, see Cynthia B. Green, *Reforming New York State Finance,* Citizens Budget Commission, Volume 52, No. 1, January 1985.

13. Figures provided by State of New York, Office of State Comptroller.

14. State of New York, Office of the State Comptroller, Letter to the Underwriters of the 1984 State Tax and Revenue Anticipation Notes from Donald G. Dunn, First Deputy Comptroller, July 16, 1984.

15. State of New York, Office of the State Comptroller, "A Multi-Step Plan to Reduce the Spring Borrowing and the State's Accumulated Deficit," December 29, 1983; Cynthia B. Green, *Reforming New York State Finance,* op. cit.; and State of New York, Governor's Council on Fiscal and Economic Priorities, *Changes in New York State Taxes to Spur Economic Development,* November 16, 1984.

16. Advisory Commission on Intergovernmental Relations, "The Tax Revolt—Round II?" *Intergovernmental Perspective,* Volume 10, Number 3 (Summer 1984), pp. 14–24.

17. Data on six of the states, including California, Hawaii, Michigan, Nevada, Oregon, and South Carolina, from "November Initiative Election Results," *Initiative Quarterly* (Englewood: National Center for Initiative Review, November Update 1984), Volume 3, Issue 3A. Data for Arizona and Louisiana from *Initiative and Referendum Report* (Washington, D.C.: The Free Congress Foundation, January 1984).

18. Capitol Publications, Inc., "Voters Reject New Tax Lids," *State Budget and Tax News,* Vol. 3, No. 23 (November 8, 1984).

19. Advisory Commission on Intergovernmental Relations, *Significant Features of Fiscal Federalism,* 1982–83 edition (Washington, D.C.: Advisory Commission on Intergovernmental Relations, 1983), Tables 29.1, 29.2 and 30. Alaska is not included in this analysis because most of this state's revenue is derived from the taxation of oil production and income of oil companies. This greatly overstates the actual tax burden borne by Alaskan residents. Therefore, the data for this state are not comparable with the rest of the nation.

20. State of New York, Governor's Council on Fiscal and Economic Priorities, *Changes in New York State Taxes to Spur Economic Development,* op. cit.

21. State of New York, *Executive Budget for the Fiscal Year April 1, 1985 to March 31, 1986,* January 22, 1985.

22. The additional cost of pay increases was determined by calculating the difference between the amount of resources the State currently plans to spend for labor between fiscal years 1986 and 1990, and the amount it will cost to finance the labor contract approved for fiscal years 1986–88 and pay labor at the projected rates of inflation for fiscal years 1989–1990. The State's financial projections for fiscal year 1986 show $5567 million for State Operations, of which 66 percent or $3784 million is for labor costs. This figure was then increased annually by the 2 percent wage increase planned by the State, yielding $3863 million for fiscal year 1987, $3940 million for fiscal year 1988, $4019 million for fiscal year 1989, and $4099 million for fiscal year 1990. The pay increases for fiscal years 1986–90 are, in order: 5.0, 5.5, 6.0, 5.6, and 5.9 percent. The State's fiscal year 1986 labor figure was deflated by 2 percent to achieve a base of $3710 million. This figure was then increased by the rates shown. The total cost of tying pay increases to inflation is $3896 million in fiscal year 1986, $4110 million in fiscal year 1987, $4356 million in fiscal year 1988, $4600 million in fiscal year 1989, and $4872 million in fiscal year 1990. In fiscal year 1986, the pay increase is effective July 1, 1985. Therefore, the effective rate was 4 percent. The cost will be $3858 million, or $148 million more than in the Governor's five-year projections.

23. For the Executive Budget the cost of budget balance under GAAP is from State of New York, *Executive Budget for the Fiscal Year April 1, 1985 to March 31, 1986,* op. cit. For the adopted budget, the New York State Division of the Budget reports that in fiscal year 1986 GAAP balance will require added expenditures to make timely payment of local aid under four programs—$182 million for education, $74 million for the Division for Youth, $50 million for revenue sharing, and $43 million for Medicaid.

24. State of New York, *1984 Annual Report of the Comptroller* reports the State's accumulated deficit as $4331 million. The New York State Division of the Budget estimates that fiscal year 1985 will end with an $125 million GAAP deficit. This shortfall would increase the accumulated deficit to $4456 million by the end of fiscal year 1985.

25. State of New York, Office of the State Comptroller, "A Multi-Step Plan to Reduce the Spring Borrowing and the State Accumulated Deficit," December 1983.

26. City of New York, *Financial Plan Fiscal Years 1985–1989,* January 31, 1985.

27. Data provided by State of New York, Division of the Budget.

28. Ibid.

29. Ibid.

30. Ibid.

31. State of New York, *Report of the Governor's Select Commission on the Future of the State-Local Mental Health System,* November 1984.

4

Federal Aid

FRED C. DOOLITTLE

In 1981, Congress and the President made unprecedented changes in federal aid programs. Following the President's lead, Congress cut spending, tightened welfare eligibility, and increased the states' role in federal aid programs. These changes were made as the City of New York was working its way out of a fiscal crisis. In response to the federal aid cuts, the City used some of its own funds to replace lost federal funds. But the substitutions were selective and did not make up for all the federal actions. A new round of federal aid cuts is likely in federal fiscal year 1986. Once again, City officials must determine how to respond. This time, however, their capacity to replace federal cuts is greater because the City's finances are improved.

This chapter examines how municipal officials reacted to cuts during the first administration of President Ronald Reagan, and frames their options for responding to likely federal aid cuts in the future. The first section explains the basic structure of the federal aid system and describes the changes in the 1981–85 period. The second section analyzes the City's responses to these changes. The concluding section identifies likely future federal-aid cuts and the City's options for dealing with them.

TABLE 4.1

Federal Spending and Federal Aid to State and Local Governments,
1955–78

(billions of dollars)

Fiscal Year	Federal Spending	Federal Aid	Direct Aid to Municipalities
1955	$ 68.5	$ 3.2	$ .1
1960	92.2	7.0	.3
1965	118.4	10.9	.6
1970	195.7	24.0	1.3
1975	324.2	49.8	5.8
1978	448.4	77.9	10.2

SOURCES: Federal spending and federal aid figures from U.S. Office of Management and Budget, *Special Analyses, Budget of the United States Government, Fiscal Year, 1985,* p. H-16; direct aid to municipalities from Advisory Commission on Intergovernmental Relations, *Significant Features of Fiscal Federalism, 1981–82* (Washington, D.C.: United States Government Printing Office, 1983), p. 67.

RECENT FEDERAL AID POLICY

Although federal grants-in-aid to states and local governments have their roots in pre-Constitutional land grants, the federal aid chapter is a recent one in American history. Federal aid to state and local governments totaled $3.2 billion in 1955 (see Table 4.1). It increased nearly eightfold between 1955 and 1970, doubled again in the next five years, and nearly doubled again between 1975 and 1978. The $77.9 billion provided in 1978 was the greatest for any year. Since then, federal aid has declined in real or inflation-adjusted terms.

Before 1978, federal aid to city governments increased even faster than total aid. Direct federal aid to these governments increased from five percent of all federal aid in 1965 to 13 percent in 1978.[1] Architects of urban aid programs built up political support by distributing money to many city governments rather than solely to the most economically disadvantaged. Nevertheless, large cities—many with high proportions of low-income residents—fared well. In 1978, cities with populations over 500,000 received 41 percent of all direct federal aid to municipalities despite having only 21 percent of the city population.[2]

Congress developed many different grant programs to address specific problems, but they may be grouped into three broad cat-

TABLE 4.2

Federal Aid in Real Terms, 1978–85

(billions of 1978 dollars)

Fiscal Year	Total Federal Aid	Entitlements	Capital Grants	Operating Grants
1978	$77.9	$20.6	$18.3	$38.9
1979	76.3	21.0	18.5	36.8
1980	77.1	21.9	18.9	36.3
1981	73.1	23.9	17.0	32.1
1982	64.1	22.7	14.9	26.5
1983	64.9	22.9	14.3	27.7
1984	65.1	23.2	15.2	27.0
1985 estimated	68.9	24.3	16.6	28.0
Percentage Change				
1978–81	−6%	+16%	−7%	−18%
1981–82	−12	−5	−12	−17
1982–85	7	7	11	6

SOURCES: U.S. Office of Management and Budget, *Special Analyses, Budget of the United States Government*, various years.

NOTE: Entitlements include Medicaid, unemployment insurance administration, food stamp administration, child nutrition, supplemental security income administration, AFDC, and refugee assistance. Adjustment for inflation is based on the GNP deflator.

egories: entitlement, operating, and capital. Entitlement grants finance programs providing benefits to all persons who satisfy eligibility rules set by federal statute. These grants are provided to state governments, but in about one-third of the states (including New York) counties or other local governments administer the programs. Entitlement programs sometimes are called "open-ended" grants because spending is a function of the number of people who meet eligibility rules. Some programs are "matching-grant" programs under which other levels of government must match the federal contribution. In most states, costs that are not funded by the federal government are financed entirely with state funds, but New York State and a few others also require local governments to provide a share of the matching funds. The most important examples of entitlement grants are Medicaid, food stamps, and Aid for Families with Dependent Children (AFDC).

Operating grants typically are "closed-ended" grants that provide a specified amount of federal aid for health, social service, employment and training, and community development programs operated by state or local governments or nonprofit organizations. Many of the "Great Society" programs fall into this category. Though most operating grants must be used for specific purposes (and hence are called "categorical grants"), less restrictive "block" grants are a second category of operating grants. Most programs based on block grants were formed by consolidating related categorical programs. Block grant funds are distributed to state or local governments by formulas (rather than competition) and may be used to finance programs falling within a broad service category. An example is the Community Development Block Grant (CDBG), but health, education, and social service block grants also exist.

Capital grants help finance projects to improve the infrastructure. Historically, most capital grants were distributed on a project-by-project basis with jurisdictions competing for a limited pool of funds. Increasingly, however, capital grants have been distributed by formula. The largest such programs are for transportation, construction of wastewater treatment facilities, and housing. In 1978, operating grants accounted for about one-half of total federal aid, with the remainder split almost equally between entitlement funds and capital funds (see Table 4.2).

Real spending for federal aid was decreased in 1979, reflecting changes in national priorities. The "taxpayers' revolt" was signalled in 1978 by passage of California's Proposition 13; a year later the Soviet invasion of Afghanistan made defense spending a more important national priority. President Jimmy Carter and the Congress responded by allowing real federal aid to fall 6 percent between 1978 and 1981.

FEDERAL AID CUTS IN PRESIDENT REAGAN'S FIRST TERM

In 1981, the newly elected President, Ronald Reagan, took advantage of his big election victory to build on the trends noted above and cut real federal aid sharply. In August, 1981 Congress accepted many of President Reagan's proposals to cut federal aid spending in fiscal year 1982. Total federal aid dropped 12 percent in real terms that year. All categories were cut, but operating grants, easiest to cut quickly, experienced the largest decline (17 percent). The program for public service employment (PSE) under the Comprehensive Employment and Training Act (CETA) was eliminated because many Democrats, in addition to most Republicans, were disenchanted with it. The elimination of the PSE program accounted for almost one-half of the total reduction in operating grants in 1982. The decline in entitlement outlays in 1982 is notable because it occurred during a recession; in the past, recessions drove up spending on income security programs. The 12 percent real decline in capital outlays reflected both cancellations (called "rescissions") of appropriations from previous years and the hesitancy of state and local governments to borrow for capital projects in the face of high interest rates.

August, 1981 was the highpoint of Reagan's influence on federal aid policy during his first term in office. In real terms, spending began to rise again in 1983. Its "honeymoon" with the new president over, Congress rejected his 1983 budget proposals for further federal aid cuts and took the lead in increasing spending. New federal aid programs were introduced and old ones expanded. The Surface Transportation Assistance Act of 1982 was passed to increase federal gasoline taxes in order to increase spending for federal highway and mass transit programs; the Emergency Jobs Act of 1983 was passed to stimulate employment. Under the latter act, the CDBG program was expanded, as were social service, health, and employment and training programs—all of special importance to cities.

Nevertheless, as Table 4.2 shows, the assertion of Congressional influence beginning in 1982 did not yield large increases in federal aid during the next three years. Spending for operating grants rose only 6 percent; capital grants, because of long lead times for the projects they support, did not rise in real terms until 1984 (but rose 11 percent overall in the 1982–85 period); entitlement spending, despite the recession in 1982 and 1983, rose only 7 percent.[3]

In sum, federal grants to state and local governments were decreased in real terms beginning in 1979. During President Reagan's first year, fiscal year 1982, the decline was accelerated sharply. However, real spending for federal aid was increased in the 1982–85 period as Congress reasserted some of its traditional influence over that component of the national budget. Spending for entitlement programs in the 1978–85 period rose from 26 percent to 35 percent of the total, while operating grants fell from 50 percent to 41 percent. Capital grants retained a 24 percent share of total federal aid.

Changes in the level and mix of spending for federal grants were but one way in which federal aid programs were altered. Structural changes also were implemented in President Reagan's first term. The most significant structural changes were in welfare programs and in the role assigned to state governments. These changes affected how the City of New York and, importantly, the State of New York responded to spending cuts; they also are likely to affect future responses to any new federal aid cuts.

CHANGES IN WELFARE PROGRAMS

As governor of California, Ronald Reagan had developed a conservative welfare program and offered it, unsuccessfully, as an alternative to liberal reforms under consideration by Congress in the 1970s.[4] The AFDC program drew much of his criticism because of its fast growth and because AFDC recipients were entitled to medical care under the Medicaid program, the largest and fastest growing federal aid program. President Ronald Reagan moved quickly to change welfare programs when he took office.

The President found federal welfare programs lacking on several counts. In the mid-1960s, AFDC reforms designed to increase financial work incentives and to discourage family breakup made more families with an employed or employable adult eligible for welfare.[5] Reagan believed these changes increased welfare dependence by exposing more families to welfare. In 1981, Congress accepted his proposals to restrict AFDC eligibility for the working poor by cutting earnings disregards, limiting total income, and allowing states to impose work requirements for welfare eligibility. (Congress subsequently relaxed some of these changes in fiscal year 1985.)

President Reagan also believed federal financing formulas for welfare discouraged state efforts to control costs. Medicaid, for example, provided open-ended federal financing to states of between 50 percent and 78 percent of all eligible costs (depending on a formula that reflects, among other things, differences in per capita income). In 1981, Reagan proposed a ceiling on federal contributions to state Medicaid programs of 105 percent of spending in the previous year. Congress, instead, blocked the cap on federal Medicaid contributions and substituted a reduction of the federal matching rate. Congress permitted states that kept expenditure growth under target rates or adopted certain cost control measures to avoid

TABLE 4.3

Changes in Block Grant Appropriations, 1981–85

(millions of dollars)

Program	1981[a]	1982	1983	1984	1985
New Block Grants					
Education	$561	$503	$479	$479	$532
Community Services[b]	524	365	342	317	335
Alcohol, Drug Abuse,					
Mental Health[b]	519	428	469	462	490
Maternal and Child					
Health[b]	454	374	478	399	478
Primary Health Care[b]	324	281	360	351	360
Preventive Health	93	79	86	88	90
Modified Programs					
Community					
Development[b]	3,675	3,456	4,456	3,468	3,472
Social Services[b]	2,991	2,400	2,675	2,700	2,700
Low-income Energy					
Assistance	1,850	1,875	1,973	2,072	2,097
Total	$10,991	$9,761	$11,318	$10,336	$10,554

SOURCE: Unpublished data provided by the U.S. Office of Management and Budget.

a. Figures for 1981 are for the predecessor categorical programs.

b. These programs received funds under the Emergency Jobs Bill of 1983.

these fiscal penalties. (In 1984, Congress chose not to continue the fiscal penalties in 1985.)

Finally, Reagan believed administration of welfare programs to be lax and in need of better fraud control. Congress enacted a series of Reagan proposals requiring states to monitor recipient income and eligibility more closely.

AN EXPANDED ROLE FOR THE STATES

In January 1982, President Reagan proposed a major reshuffling of governmental responsibility for federal aid programs. Under the Reagan plan, the federal government would have assumed responsibility for Medicaid in return for state assumption of the AFDC and food stamp programs. In addition, states would have been given the option of "cashing in" categorical grants received under more than 40 programs and using the funds for unrestricted aid. In 1988, these programs would have been phased out, and federal taxes would have been lowered accordingly. States then would have had the option of raising their own taxes to support affected services.

Despite extended negotiations with Congressional representatives, governors, and mayors, the "swap-turnback" plan received a cool reception. State officials supported federal takeover of public assistance; mayors feared states would not pass on unrestricted aid realized from cashing in categorical program funds; both groups feared that new revenues turned over to state and local governments ultimately would be insufficient to support the services. In mid-1982, the administration abandoned its plan.

However, four important Reagan initiatives were approved by Congress, each of which reduced the role of city governments in administration of federal aid programs and increased the role of the states. The first was creation in 1981 of several new block grant programs and modification of preexisting programs. These block grant programs and appropriations for them are shown in Table 4.3. Previous block grants provided funds primarily to local governments; the new approach reflected President Reagan's preference for an expanded state role. The 1981 legislation imposed a common administrative structure on the programs. Federal grants were made to the states, by formula, and with greater state authority to determine the uses of funds.

The administrative changes were coupled with cuts of $1.2 billion in funding in 1982. Only the energy assistance program for low-income people received added funds (and in real terms it too was cut). In general, the block grants gave states more influence over less funding than previously had been the case.

The block grant initiatives reflected a more general effort by the Reagan administration to shift from discretionary to formula grants. President Reagan believed project grants gave large cities that were skilled at "grantsmanship" too much influence over the distribution of federal aid. The number of project grants declined about one-third between 1980 and 1984, while the number of formula grants remained almost constant. Expenditure of project grant funds declined 31 percent between 1980 and 1984, while funds distributed through formula grants, usually to state governments, increased 8 percent.[6]

A third important institutional change involved employment and training programs. As noted earlier, the CETA program, which provided grants to local governments for employment and training, was in political trouble by the time Reagan took office. In addition to eliminating the PSE component of the CETA program, the first Reagan budget cut other CETA training funds nearly 25 percent. In 1983, Congress replaced CETA with the Job Training Partnership Act (JTPA), a program of grants to states for training that envisaged a larger role for governors and representatives from the private sector and a smaller role for local governments and nonprofit organizations.

Finally, in 1981 the states were given greater authority under Medicaid to design reimbursement systems for providers, to limit "freedom of choice" for recipients, and to establish programs of their own to serve the medically indigent. These changes were supported by the National Governors' Association and other state-oriented interest groups because of rising Medicaid costs in most state budgets.

Through a combination of spending cuts and program redesign, President Reagan changed the nation's system of federal grants to state and local governments during his first term. He did not initiate the decline in spending, but he pursued that goal more aggressively and successfully than President Carter. However, he was not able to continue his successes in reducing real spending for federal grants beyond 1982. Congress put a halt to that. But Congress did approve programmatic changes in federal aid programs that not only contributed to spending cuts but shifted greater responsibility for determining the uses and administration of federal programs to state governments. Cities, including New York City, lost both money and influence.

FEDERAL AID IN NEW YORK CITY

New York City government was affected more than most city governments by the changes in federal aid policies described in the previous section. The City of New York provides a broader range of services than most municipal governments, including federally supported public assistance programs such as AFDC and Medicaid that are administered by the state or county government in most other states and require only a small (if any) match of local funds.[7] Nationwide, federal aid equaled 9 percent of local general revenues

TABLE 4.4
Federal Aid to the City of New York, Fiscal Years 1981–85
(millions of dollars)

Source	1981	1982	1983	1984	1985	Percentage Change
Local Revenues	$8,688	$9,333	$9,919	$10,756	$11,685	34.5%
State Aid	2,942	3,221	3,343	3,588	3,760	27.8
Federal Aid	2,469	2,563	2,471	2,714	2,690	9.0
Unrestricted Aid	287	283	270	272	271	−5.6
Categorical Aid	2,182	2,280	2,201	2,442	2,419	10.9
CETA/JTPA	329	158	109	90	94	−71.4
Comm. Development	267	283	302	377	331	24.0
Welfare	1,109	1,296	1,228	1,375	1,436	29.5
Education	319	338	376	393	389	21.9
Other	158	205	186	207	169	7.0
Total Revenues	$14,098	$15,117	$15,732	$17,058	$18,135	28.6%

SOURCES: Federal aid data for 1981 are from the *Executive Budget, Fiscal Year 1983, Message of the Mayor*, p. 239; federal aid data for 1982–83 are from the *Executive Budget, Fiscal Year 1984, Message of the Mayor*, p. 229; federal aid data for 1984 are from the New York State Financial Control Board, "Staff Report on the Interim Financial Plan for New York City Covering Fiscal Year 1985," June 27, 1984, p. 32; federal aid data for 1985 are from the New York City Office of Management and Budget, "Proposed Modification No. 5 to the City's Interim Financial Plan," October 22, 1984. All other 1981–84 data are from the City of New York, *Comprehensive Annual Financial Report of the Comptroller for the Fiscal Year Ended June 30, 1984*, pp. 211–14; all other 1985 data are from the *Executive Budget, Fiscal Year 1985, Message of the Mayor*, April 26, 1984, p. 26.

NOTE: Columns may not add due to rounding.

TABLE 4.5

City Agencies in Which Federal Aid is an Important Source of Funding, Fiscal Years 1981 and 1985

(millions of dollars)

Agency	Fiscal Year	Appropriation	Federal Aid	Federal Aid Percentage
City Planning	1981	$10.9	$4.9	45%
	1985	16.8	6.3	38
Board of Education	1981	2,713.3	371.2	14
	1985	3,846.0	388.8	10
Department of Social Services	1981	2,899.0	1,088.5	38
	1985	4,134.0	1,399.5	34
Human Resources Administration	1981	482.3	451.9	94
	1985	144.1	126.1	88
Department for the Aging	1981	38.6	33.4	86
	1985	41.5	29.6	71
Human Rights Commission	1981	2.4	1.7	70
	1985	3.8	2.4	62
Office of Economic Development	1981	40.5	32.9	81
	1985	28.0	20.0	72
Housing Preservation and Development Department	1981	348.1	284.9	82
	1985	348.4	251.4	72

SOURCE: City of New York, *Adopted Budget, Fiscal Year 1982* and *Fiscal Year 1985*. The federal aid allocations for the agencies are taken from the funding summaries in the expense budget. The 1981 figures are the modified appropriations for 1981 contained in the fiscal year 1982 budget.

in 1980; for the City, it accounted for 19 percent.[8] With relatively more aid, the City had relatively more to lose.

THE BUDGETARY IMPACT OF FEDERAL AID CUTS, 1981–85

Table 4.4 identifies the changing nature of federal aid to the City of New York operating budget in the 1981–85 period. The level of federal aid fluctuated in the range of $2.5 billion to $2.7 billion, but rose overall 9 percent. For the period as a whole the federal share of total revenues declined from 18 percent to 15 percent.

Federal aid is provided in unrestricted and categorical form, with the latter accounting for about 90 percent of all federal aid. Unrestricted aid, essentially general revenue sharing funds, was cut 6 percent from 1981 to 1983, but between 1983 and 1985 remained approximately $270 million annually. Categorical aid, which was increased 11 percent overall, is for four basic functions: employment and training (formerly the CETA program and later the Job Training Partnership Act or JTPA); community development (comprised largely of CDBG funds); welfare (which includes AFDC, home care, plus a few smaller programs); and education (comprised of 15 separate aid programs). The largest decline in both absolute and percentage terms was for employment and training funds, which were reduced 71 percent; the other categorical aid programs all were increased in the 1981–85 period at rates ranging from 22 percent for education to 30 percent for welfare, the largest and fastest growing source of federal aid.

Federal aid is paid into the City's general fund, but the programs' impacts are important in relatively few of the more than 100 municipal agencies. Table 4.5 presents the level of federal aid in 1981 and 1984 for the seven City agencies whose federal aid exceeded 15 percent of their revenues, plus the Board of Education. Four agencies are relatively small. They are the City Planning Commission, Department for the Aging, Human Rights Commission, and the Office of Economic Development. However, the last three each received 70 percent or more of their funds from the federal government in 1981. Of the large City agencies, the Human Resources Administration and Department of Housing Preservation and Development received federal assistance in 1981 amounting, respectively, to 94 percent and 82 percent of their total revenues. The Department of Social Services and Board of Education received 38 percent and 14 percent respectively from the federal government. By 1985, the federally funded share of each of these agencies' operations had declined.

PROGRAMMATIC EFFECTS AND CITY RESPONSES

Tracing the exact impact of a change in federal policy on a local program is difficult. For example, President Reagan persuaded Congress to tighten up welfare eligibility rules in 1981; this cut (not in AFDC benefits, but in AFDC eligibility) resulted in New Yorkers who previously had been supported by that program being taken "off the rolls"; however, federal aid for welfare in New York City continued to be increased, largely because the 1982 recession caused more people to qualify for AFDC. Spending would have risen even more without restricting eligibility, but by how much is difficult to ascertain.

The response of City or State officials to federal policy changes also is difficult to relate to specific federal decisions. They may make no response at all, in which case they may be said to "ratify" the federal cut; or they may choose to "replace" federal funding with their own funds. Replacement decisions are particularly hard to identify and characterize, however. Again, the welfare cuts illustrate the issues. The State responded to federal cuts in AFDC eligibility in a manner (described below) that forced the City to share in the added costs. The City "replaced" federal funds with its own, but it did so because of State mandate rather than local voluntarism. There were instances, however, where the City voluntarily replaced monies cut by federal policies with its own funds.

For these and other reasons discussed below it is difficult to quantify or even to draw direct causal inferences about some of the responses of local officials to cuts in federal aid. However, by analyzing State and City actions with respect to specific programs, it is possible to draw some inferences about their past responses that may serve as a guide for framing future options.

General Revenue Sharing. As Table 4.4 shows, unrestricted aid fell 6 percent between 1981 and 1985. In the 1981–82 period general revenue sharing was not the only unrestricted federal aid received by the City, though it was the dominant part; after 1982 it was the sole source. The City historically has used general revenue sharing monies to support so-called "basic" services, including police, fire, sanitation, and education, that provide services to the whole population.

In the four-year period from 1982 through 1985, the City received about $270 million annually in general revenue-sharing funds. The federal "cap" placed on that program displeased local officials, who would like to see it grow. However, the program has not been cut in nominal terms, so it raises no "ratification-replacement" issue.

Employment and Training. In contrast, funds for employment and training were cut, and sharply, in the 1981–85 period. Spending—first for the CETA program and then for its JTPA successor—

fell 71 percent, from $329 million to $94 million. The major cuts during this period arose from termination in 1982 of funds for the public service employment of the CETA program. The City continued to support approximately one-half of the persons employed under that program with its own funds; thus, funds were replaced. However, most other cities did not choose to continue such employees when federal funds were eliminated.[9]

Other federal training programs also were cut. Between 1981 and 1982, federal funding for adult training in the City was reduced from $98 million to $65 million. The City responded by cutting the number of enrollees, reducing their weekly stipends, and eliminating some supportive services. In the case of cuts for summer youth training programs, the City responded by dropping the number of available positions from 45,000 in 1981 to 35,000 in 1984. Neither the summer youth nor adult training programs received replacement financing from City funds. In other words, City officials ratified the federal decision.

Community Development and Housing. The bulk of funding for community development and housing comes from the CDBG program. The City's annual CDBG allocation peaked at $260 million in fiscal year 1981 and dropped to slightly more than $200 million in 1985. However, other federal funding for these purposes more than made up the difference, as Table 4.4 shows. The City completed an audit of its income from urban renewal property and as a result was able to collect a one-time federal payment of $30 million in 1983. The City also received a supplemental appropriation of $48 million under the 1983 Emergency Jobs Bill which was received in the City's fiscal year 1984. And finally, a HUD regulation allowed the City to redefine its community development "program year" in a way that permitted it to draw funds from two different federal fiscal year allocations at once. This provided an extra $40 million that the federal government will recoup in 1987. Thus, what the federal government was cutting with one hand, the CDBG program, it was returning to the City under other guises and in larger amounts.

Other federal grants supporting housing programs also were cut (some of which are included in the "Other" row under Categorical Aid in Table 4.4), and some of these cuts involved local replacement. Specifically, Section 8 "substantial rehabilitation" funds were ended. City officials viewed these funds as a source of money for rehabilitation of its large *in rem* housing stock preparatory for sale to tenants, community groups, or individuals. Some City funds were used to rehabilitate some *in rem* housing, but not all of these Section 8 monies were replaced. Additional federal cuts in assistance programs for low- and moderate-income renters were not replaced.

Welfare. The AFDC, Medicaid, and social service grants that fall under this category further illustrate the complexity of evaluating the City's response to policy changes higher up the intergovernmental chain, including policies of the State of New York as well as the federal government. As Table 4.4 shows, federal welfare aid rose nearly 30 percent in the 1981–85 period, keeping apace with the overall increase in local revenues. Federal policies described in the previous section were designed to reduce costs by restricting eligibility, and these effectively slowed the increase in federal welfare aid, though by how much is difficult to estimate. Subsequent State and City decisions involving public assistance, Medicaid, and social service programs further contributed to restructuring of these programs and their financing.

With respect to AFDC, federal changes in eligibility rules forced 22,000 New Yorkers to end their participation in that program, and reduced benefits for another 50,000.[10] The fiscal effect was positive for the City and State because lower federal expenditures meant lower State and City matching requirements or, put differently, freed local funds that otherwise would have been mandated for AFDC. However, the State responded by transferring some of the former AFDC recipients to its Home Relief program, including 7000 of those ineligible for AFDC in the city. This action had a direct, negative impact on local finances because the City and State finance Home Relief in equal shares. In a sense, the State replacement decision made the City a partner, albeit not a voluntary partner. The net effect on City finances, however, was positive. Instead of contributing roughly 25 percent of AFDC costs for 22,000 New Yorkers, the City contributed 50 percent of the support for Home Relief for the 7000 people transferred from AFDC to Home Relief. Thus, the federal cut and the State's response had a positive effect on local finances. Later, however, the State increased AFDC benefits (not, however, primarily because of the earlier federal cuts in eligibility). This action obliged the City to spend more on the welfare programs.

Developments in the Medicaid program illustrate further that policy decisions by the State may have more profound implications for the City than actions of the federal government. In 1982, the State passed the Human Services Overburden Law providing the City with $244 million in fiscal year 1983 to offset Medicaid expenses. In 1983, the State legislature authorized phased increases in the State's share of financing for nursing-home and home-care services. This provides substantial fiscal relief for the City. Again, though, the tradeoffs are complex. For while the State was reforming Medicaid financing to reduce the City's share of costs, it was raising AFDC and shelter benefits and thereby increasing the City's costs for these programs as well as the number of people eligible for both welfare and Medicaid.

A third component of the welfare grants shown in Table 4.4 is the social services block grant. Funding to the City under this program was decreased about $15 million in 1982, affecting the Department for the Aging and the Agency for Child Development. The effects on the City were direct, and its response was clear. City funds were used to replace the federal cuts in order to continue services at 50 daycare centers and 29 senior citizen centers.

Education. Federal funds accounted for just under 15 percent of total spending on education in 1981 (see Table 4.5). The major cut had been made in a Carter, not a Reagan, budget. After the 20 percent cut in federal aid in 1981, federal aid gradually was returned to close to its 1980 level, partly because of a $48 million allocation from the Emergency Jobs Act. Thus, there are no aggregate impacts of cuts to be identified during the 1981–85 period.

Capital Grants. Capital grants fared relatively well during the 1981–85 period. Three types of capital grants are important for the City's capital budget. Both the highway and mass transit programs received funding increases under the 1982 federal transportation legislation, as noted earlier. The largest single program, capital grants for the New York City Transit Authority, was increased from $316 million in 1982 to $361 million in 1983, before being reduced slightly to $343 million in 1984.[11] Grants for wastewater treatment facilities also were important. Changes in federal aid in recent years have had a favorable impact on the capital budget.

TABLE 4.6

Changes in Federal Aid Spending Proposed by President Reagan
for Fiscal Year 1986

Estimated Fiscal Year 1985 Outlays	**$107.0 billion**
Entitlement Grants	
Medicaid	+ .7
Food and nutrition	− .3
Other	− .4
Operating Grants	
General revenue sharing	− 3.4
Community services block grant	− .4
Community development block grant	− .4
Other	− .9
Capital Grants	
Highways	+ .6
Mass transit	− .9
Housing	− .9
Estimated Fiscal Year 1986 Outlays	**$100.7**

SOURCE: U.S. Office of Management and Budget, *Special Analyses, Budget of the United States Government, Fiscal Year 1986*, p. H-5.

FUTURE OPTIONS: RATIFICATION OR REPLACEMENT

The previous section establishes that cuts in federal aid have complex impacts on the City's budget and elicit diverse responses by City officials. In some cases, municipal officials respond to federal aid cuts by ratification; that is, they choose not to substitute local funds for federal funds. In other cases, they choose replacement; that is, they offset the federal cuts with local appropriations. Which decision they reach depends on the importance they attach to the affected program and the extent to which the federal cut involves matching funds. Some federal cuts may be ratified because they free local money that otherwise would be committed to mandated matches; some replacement decisions are not local choices at all, but result from State responses that mandate added City expenditures.

THE NATIONAL POLICY DEBATE

With the federal deficit the central domestic issue facing Congress and the President, federal aid once again is likely to be cut.

TABLE 4.7

Proposed Federal Aid Reductions to the City of New York, Fiscal Year
1986

(millions of dollars)

Program	Amount
Unrestricted Aid	$271
Categorical Aid	234
Employment and Training	12
Community Development	79
Welfare	143
Education	0
Total	$505

SOURCE: Memorandum to Mayor Edward I. Koch from Alair A. Townsend, Director of the Office of Management and Budget, "Preliminary Analysis of the President's Budget," February 4, 1985.

Congress and the President apparently agree that outlays for defense, interest on the national debt, and social security should not be cut. Together, those programs accounted for about 60 percent of the 1985 federal outlays of $949 billion. Thus, the remaining 40 percent of federal outlays ($378 billion in 1985) must suffer large cuts in order to reduce significantly a projected $215 billion deficit in 1986.[12] Federal aid, estimated at $107 billion in 1985, is a prime candidate for cuts.

The improved finances of the state and local government sector may, ironically, increase the chances of further federal cuts. Federal deficits in the $200 billion range contrast sharply with surpluses in the state and local sector. Except for the recessionary years 1975 and 1982, state and local governments as a whole have run surpluses during the past decade, although none were higher than the $13 billion surplus in 1984.[13] In recent years, the City of New York also has enjoyed surpluses.

1986 BUDGET PROPOSAL

President Reagan's 1986 budget proposes cuts that would reduce federal aid from the estimated 1985 total of $107 billion to $101 billion. Table 4.6 shows how these cuts would be allocated among entitlement, operating, and capital grants. Operating grants would be cut $5.1 billion of the overall $6.3 billion in proposed cuts, including $3.4 billion from the termination of the general revenue sharing program. Capital grants would be decreased $1.2 billion. Entitlement grant spending would be maintained because, despite proposed limits in Medicaid, its spending still would rise $700 million under the President's proposal.

These cuts, if passed, would be as large as the 1982 cuts, but their impact would differ. In 1982, the bulk of federal aid cuts came in programs aiding the poor, especially the working poor. The 1986 proposals are designed to affect general governmental services.

Senate Republicans and House Democrats view with concern the President's call for cuts in federal aid and increases in defense spending. Based on past Congressional behavior, it is possible to estimate their reaction to the 1986 budget proposals. The 1981 cuts occurred because moderate-to-liberal Republicans and Southern Democrats supported a conservative president. The stalemate in the next three years occurred because Democrats picked up 26 House seats in the 1982 election and moderate and liberal Republicans broke ranks with the President. Republicans regained 15 House seats in 1984, but the stalemate is likely to continue. Neither the President nor congressional Democrats have enough votes to make federal aid policy unilaterally. The most likely compromise would slow defense spending and cut federal aid less than the President proposed.

LOCAL IMPLICATIONS AND OPTIONS

Predictably, City officials responded to the President's proposals in a way designed to strengthen the case for moderating them. The City's Budget Director prepared a memorandum for the Mayor that estimated the City's losses at nearly $1.2 billion, but this assumed the President would convince Congress to pass all of his recommended cuts. The estimate also included cuts that would affect other local and State agencies.[14] Table 4.7 summarizes the estimated fiscal year 1986 City of New York expense budget effects.[15] The $505 million total reduction in federal aid to New York City in all likelihood will not be made given the composition of the Congress and its opposition to the President's attempt to protect defense spending from federal cuts. Nevertheless, Table 4.7 provides a basis for discussing the options City officials face in discrete programmatic areas.

Unrestricted Aid. Cuts in unrestricted aid involve the general revenue sharing program, proceeds from which currently are used to support the Board of Education. In the past, the Board has been accorded a high priority in City spending decisions. To the extent revenue sharing cuts are made, it is likely that City officials will replace them either by raising taxes or shifting funds from other programs.

Categorical Aid. In President Reagan's budget, aid to the City for employment and training would be cut $12 million, and aid for education would be maintained. The major cuts indicated involve the community development and welfare categories—$79 million and $143 million, respectively. The largest component of the cuts proposed in community development would be $52 million in CDBG funds. Most of these funds are used for housing. In the past, cuts in the CDBG program were offset by other increases by the federal government; in the future, City officials may have to make a clear choice about the importance they attach to housing.

The bulk of the threatened welfare cuts involve a $100 million cut in Medicaid expenditures. However, it is not clear how this would be affected; thus it is not clear how City officials would respond. If the cut were made by reducing benefits or eligibility, then the net effect might be to provide fiscal relief to the City. However, these savings might be lost if higher HHC subsidies were required to cover costs no longer paid for by Medicaid. If the cuts were made by freezing federal spending, as the President's proposal implies, then local expenditures would grow—assuming costs could not be controlled by City and State actions. In this event, funds would have to be shifted from other locally funded programs.

In sum, if the President's budget proposals are enacted, the City of New York will face large federal aid cuts—approximately $500 million—affecting basic services as well as programs for the poor. But the previous behavior of Congresses of similar composition to the current body suggests they will significantly moderate the President's proposals. Because of the 1981 changes in grant programs, the State is likely to play a greater role in responding to this round of federal aid cuts. Moreover, the City is in a better position than it was four years ago to replace federal aid cuts with its own funds if such replacements are in accord with municipal priorities.

NOTES

1. Federal aid to all local governments totalled $19.4 billion in 1978, 28 percent of all federal aid. In addition to direct federal aid, some federal aid to state government "passes through" to local governments. In 1980, such aid was estimated to be about $17 billion, or one-fourth of all aid to the states. See Advisory Commission on Intergovernmental Relations, *Significant Features of Fiscal Federalism, 1982–83* (Washington, D.C.: United States Government Printing Office, 1984), p. 121.

2. U.S. Bureau of the Census, *City Finances in 1978–79*, Series GF 79, No. 4 (Washington, D.C.: United States Government Printing Office, 1980), p. 10.

3. Direct federal aid to local governments fell from $22.4 billion in 1981 to $20.9 billion in 1982, and then rose to $21 billion in 1983—the last year for which data are available. See U.S. Bureau of the Census, *Governmental Finances in 1982–83*, Series GF83, No. 5 (Washington, D.C.: United States Government Printing Office, 1984), p. 51.

4. See Governor Ronald Reagan, *California's Blueprint for National Welfare Reform* (Sacramento: State of California, 1974).

5. In 1961, Congress established the AFDC-Unemployed Father program as an option for the states. In 1967, Congress required states to disregard $30, plus one-third of remaining earnings and work expenses, in calculating AFDC grants in order to encourage family heads to work their way off welfare.

6. See George Peterson, "Federalism and the States," in John L. Palmer and Isabel Sawhill, eds., *The Reagan Record* (Cambridge, Mass.: Ballinger, 1984), p. 230.

7. In fact, in New York State these are county-run programs, but the City provides consolidated administration for the five counties that comprise the city.

8. The percentage for all local governments is from the U.S. Bureau of the Census, *Governmental Finances in 1979–80* (Washington, D.C.: United States Government Printing Office, 1981), p. 17. For City percentages, see *The City of New York, Executive Budget Fiscal Year 1985, Message of the Mayor*, p. 26.

9. See Richard P. Nathan, Fred C. Doolittle, and Associates, *The Consequences of Cuts: The Effects of the Reagan Domestic Program on State and Local Governments* (Princeton, N.J.: Princeton Urban and Regional Research Center, 1983).

10. See City of New York, Office of Management and Budget, "The Impact of Federal Budget Policies on New York City—1982–85," October 1984, p. 5.

11. Data provided by New York City Transit Authority.

12. Congressional Budget Office, *The Economic and Budget Outlook: Fiscal Years 1986–90* (Washington, D.C.: Congressional Budget Office, February 1985).

13. Figures on the aggregate state and local surplus are from David J. Levin, "Receipts and Expenditures of State Governments and Local Governments," *Survey of Current Business* (May 1983) and (September 1984).

14. Memorandum to Mayor Edward I. Koch from Alair A. Townsend, Director of the Office of Management and Budget, "Preliminary Analysis of the President's Budget," February 4, 1985.

15. Excluded from Table 4.7 are certain proposed cuts in federal programs for revenues to other governmental units providing local services; the most significant of these is a $248 million proposed cut in capital grants to the New York City Transit Authority.

5

Capital Resources

JAMES M. HARTMAN

Extensive attention in recent years, both nationally and in New York City, has focused on the "infrastructure crisis." The deteriorating condition of streets, bridges, sewers, water mains, and mass-transit lines ranks high on the list of national urban issues. Estimates by the Joint Economic Committee of Congress indicate the need to invest $1100 billion in the nation's physical plant by the year 2000.[1] Much of this required spending represents "catch-up" costs for years in which state and local governments neglected the repair and maintenance of capital facilities.

The problem in New York City was aggravated during the fiscal crisis of the mid-1970s. Denied access to public long-term credit markets, the traditional source of municipal capital financing, the City halted most of its construction projects. Commitments for new construction fell to a nine-year low of $264 million in fiscal year 1977.[2] Those commitments were financed entirely with State and federal grants.

With the gradual return of its access to public credit markets, the City has revitalized its capital program. Planned commitments exceeded $2 billion in fiscal year 1985. Moreover, the City has a ten-year capital plan that proposes to invest $26.8 billion between fiscal years 1985 and 1994.

The City confronts difficult choices on where to direct its renewed capital spending. The needs are extensive, and, even with expanding access to credit, the financial limitations are serious. The first section of this chapter describes the City's annual capital budget process and its relationship to the ten-year capital development plan. Section two explains the sources of financing for that ten-year plan and assesses the uncertainty of each. The third section examines the investment priorities of the ten-year plan and considers alternative policies assuming both increased and decreased financing sources. The final section discusses the problems of implementing the City's capital budgets and plans.

THE CAPITAL BUDGETING PROCESS

The procedures for approving and executing a capital project in the City of New York are long and complicated. Once a project has been authorized in the annual capital budget, it must undergo a process of scope development, design, contract award, and, finally, actual construction. Numerous approvals are required from City agencies along the way and, on average, it takes three to five years to complete a project once the funds are appropriated. Large public work efforts, such as reconstruction of the East River bridges, often involve a series of separately budgeted projects spanning a period of many years.[3]

The lengthy process to authorize a project is initiated when a project is included in the City's annual capital budget. The development of the capital budget is begun in December, prior to the beginning of the new fiscal year, with the issuance of a report by the Comptroller that details the current status of the City's financial condition and makes a recommendation based on consideration of the debt service level during the coming four years. The process continues through community board hearings, consultations with the City Planning Commission, and hearings conducted by the Board of Estimate and City Council. By April 26 the Mayor releases the executive capital budget for the coming fiscal year. This document details the status of current capital projects and proposes the coming year's capital program. Following the release of the executive capital budget are additional recommendations and comments from the Comptroller's Office and the City Planning Commission. The Board of Estimate and City Council then conduct hearings on the executive capital budget, make any changes they desire, and adopt the budget. If changes are made, a veto provision can be imposed by the Mayor, with final adoption of the capital budget required by June 5.

The capital budget legally appropriates funds for authorized projects. Because any changes in the budget require approval by the Board and Council, appropriation levels are sufficiently higher than actual anticipated commitments in order to provide adequate leeway in implementing the budget. A commitment plan is then developed based on the approved capital budget. A commitment is incurred when the City actually obligates funds through a contract for a particular project. It, therefore, represents the most accurate measure of capital spending. The total commitment plan for a given fiscal year is approved by the Financial Control Board and comprises the overall limit on the year's obligations.

Despite the formal involvement of many parts of City government in the process of drawing up the capital budget, it is dominated by the Mayor. Capital projects originate primarily in mayoral agencies and are shaped into a single budget by the mayor's staff. In recent years, the changes made to the executive capital budget by the Board of Estimate and City Council have not involved more than 10 percent of the total appropriations.[4] These revisions usually are limited to enhancements of highly visible projects such as parks and schools or to changes in the timing and location of projects such as street reconstruction. Rarely is any serious challenge raised to the strategic choices reflected in the mayor's capital budget proposal.

The most significant development in the capital-budgeting process in recent years is the growing reliance on a ten-year plan for capital development. The importance of longer-term thinking about municipal infrastructure and facility needs became increasingly obvious as the City recovered from its fiscal crisis. In 1979 the City Comptroller estimated the City's capital requirements at $40 billion over the next decade.[5] Although some of the reported needs were disputed, the Comptroller established one point: The City could not make wise investment decisions in the context of the traditional year-to-year capital budget.

TABLE 5.1

City of New York, Actual and Planned Capital Commitments,
Fiscal Years 1977–94
(millions of dollars)

Fiscal Year	Amount	Percentage Change
Actual		
1977	$264	—
1978	302	14.4%
1979	372	23.2
1980	926	148.9
1981	837	(10.7)
1982	1,142	36.4
1983	1,442	26.3
1984	1,681	16.6
Planned		
1985	2,343	39.4
1986	1,969	16.0
1987	3,088	56.8
1988	2,117	(31.5)
1989	2,884	36.2
1990	3,735	29.5
1991	3,033	18.8
1992	2,335	(23.1)
1993	3,125	33.8
1994	2,171	(30.6)

SOURCES: Actual figures were supplied by City of New York, Office of Management and Budget; planned figures are from the City of New York, *Ten-Year Capital Plan*, April 1984. Figures exclude capital spending for the bus and subway system controlled by Metropolitan Transportation Authority.

The task of developing a ten-year plan that balanced needs with available resources fell to the Mayor's Office of Management and Budget and was supervised by the Deputy Mayor for Policy. A preliminary version of the plan was released in the spring of 1981 as part of the fiscal year 1982 Executive Budget. A more refined plan was presented in May of 1982.[6]

The Mayor's program described expenditures of $34.7 billion from fiscal year 1983 through fiscal year 1992. Of this total, $14.1 billion represented the anticipated needs of the New York City bus and subway system. Since these transit investments are controlled by the State's Metropolitan Transportation Authority, the City-managed portion of the plan was $20.6 billion.

The initial response to the ten-year plan was mixed. Civic groups applauded the long-range approach. However, within many munic-

TABLE 5.2

Funding Sources for the Ten-Year Capital Plan

(in millions of dollars)

Source	Amount	Percentage Distribution
City Sources Total	$19,620	75.1%
City General Obligation Bonds	14,010	52.4
Water and Sewer Revenue Bonds	4,235	15.8
Municipal Assistance Corporation	1,225	4.6
Other[a]	150	.6
Federal Sources	2,296	8.6
State Sources	897	3.3
Independent HHC Funding	916	3.4
Private Resource Recovery Funding	3,000	11.2
Total	$26,729	100.0%
Planned City Support for Mass Transit	(1,003)	N.A.
Adjusted City Total	$25,726	N.A.

SOURCE: Unpublished data from the City of New York, Office of Management and Budget. The City experiences a time lag between entering into a contract for a capital project and having to make payments. Thus, while the ten-year plan calls for $26.8 billion in commitments, the City must raise only $25.7 billion during that period, exclusive of its support for mass transit.

NOTES: N.A. means not applicable.

a. Largely restricted cash reserves.

ipal agencies the plan was viewed skeptically because it did not provide directions for dealing with current problems and decisions. These reservations were counteracted when the Mayor's budget staff relied upon the ten-year plan to shape the executive capital budget for fiscal years 1983 and 1984. Gradually, the agencies accepted the importance of justifying their annual capital-project proposals in terms of a long-range strategy.[7]

In April 1984, the Mayor presented a revised plan for fiscal years 1985 through 1994. This plan reflected an apparent intention to update the ten-year plan every two years. This ten-year plan has emerged as the instrument through which the City assesses its capital needs and makes strategic choices about investment priorities. The new plan proposes $26.8 billion of investment in City infrastructure and facilities exclusive of mass transit. Interestingly, the planned annual commitments are not increased steadily (see Table 5.1). The impact in certain years of massive projects, such as the third water tunnel and several waste disposal plants, cause spending to be increased and decreased during the period. In gen-

eral, however, planned spending during the ten years is between
$2 billion and $3 billion annually. This represents a tremendous
increase from the 1977 low of $264 million.

SOURCES OF CAPITAL FINANCING

To support proposed levels of capital spending, the City plans to
strengthen its access to traditional sources of financing and to seek
new methods to raise capital funds (see Table 5.2). The plan calls
for the issuance of $14 billion in general obligation debt, the tra-
ditional source of funds. To increase the available resources, the
City also initiated programs to obtain $4.2 billion in water and
sewer revenue bonds and to seek $3 billion in private funding for
its proposed network of waste disposal plants.

One basic assumption of the City strategy is that new assistance
from the State or federal government will not be available. The
State agency created to borrow for the City during the fiscal crisis,
the Municipal Assistance Corporation, saw its authority to issue
new debt expire on December 31, 1984. The $1225 million of MAC
resources in the plan represents the phased use of MAC borrowings
undertaken in earlier years. Fiscal year 1987 is planned to be the
last year in which the City relies upon MAC funds. Direct State
support, estimated at $897 million for the ten-year period, reflects
expected grants under established aid programs for highway and
bridge repair and for water pollution control.

Similarly, the City anticipates only limited federal aid in the form
of continuation of existing aid programs. The $2296 million in direct
federal aid is for the water pollution and highway repair programs.
Because work on the new sewage-treatment plants is near completion, annual federal assistance will decline over the period. The one
new federal initiative stems from a November 1983 law extending
Federal Housing Administration loan guarantees to public hospital
construction bonds.[8] This program may enable the semiautonomous
Health and Hospitals Corporation (HHC) to issue over $900 million
of its own debt. These funds are slated largely for reconstruction
of older facilities of HHC.

GENERAL-OBLIGATION DEBT

The plan to borrow $14 billion with general obligation bonds indicates the City's confidence in its prospects both for expanded market access and for operating revenues that can support the required annual debt service. Since the early 1980s, the City has expanded gradually its sale of general obligation bonds. The first such sale since the fiscal crisis of 1975 was made in fiscal year 1981 in the sum of $75 million. Then, $250 million of bonds were offered in fiscal year 1982, $450 million in fiscal year 1983, $775 million in fiscal year 1984, and $1000 million in fiscal year 1985. The City was able to increase its original targets in the last three years, and its net interest costs, as measured by the *General Obligation Bond Buyer Index*, have declined steadily in comparison to overall market trends.[9]

What explains this growing market acceptance of City debt? Three factors are important. First, impressed by a generally positive economic and budget outlook and by achievement of fiscal reforms, both major rating agencies have awarded the City their minimum investment-grade ratings. The City first received a "BBB" rating from Standard and Poor's Corporation in March 1981, and Moody's Investors Service issued the city its "Baa" rating in November 1983. Gradual upgrading of these ratings is likely. Second, City debt has proven attractive to individual investors, especially to New York State and City residents who benefit from double or triple tax exemption, respectively. Third, the overall size of the municipal bond market has grown rapidly in recent years. The annual volume of municipal bond issues increased from $18.1 billion in 1970 to $77.3 billion in 1982.[10] During that period, because of the growth, New York City bonds fell from approximately 7 percent to 1 percent of the total market.[11]

Spurred by steady progress, the City plans to continue to increase its sales of general obligation bonds. The intention is to offer $1100 million during the 1986 fiscal year, $1275 million in 1987, and $1345 million in 1988. If achieved, this plan would leave $9430 million of the ten-year plan's $14 billion total to be raised during the six fiscal years from 1989 through 1994. On average, that would mean over $1.5 billion would have to be received annually during the later period.

Certain events could undermine this ambitious plan. Any serious

TABLE 5.3

City of New York Debt Service, Fiscal Years 1976–94

(in millions of dollars)

Fiscal Year	City Long-Term	MAC	Total Debt Service	Total Revenues	Debt Service as a Percentage of Revenues
Actual					
1976	$1,460	$462	$1,922	$10,800	17.8%
1977	1,566	597	2,163	11,500	18.8
1978	1,619	373	1,993	12,224	16.3
1979	1,366	437	1,803	12,335	14.6
1980	1,364	340	1,704	13,244	12.9
1981	1,366	362	1,728	13,664	12.6
1982	1,354	392	1,746	14,748	11.8
1983	1,233	430	1,663	15,780	10.5
1984	1,172	565	1,737	17,085	10.2
Planned					
1985	1,444	335	1,779	18,067	9.9
1986	1,313	539	1,852	18,675	9.2
1987	1,433	631	2,064	19,484	10.6
1988	1,488	665	2,153	20,420	10.5
1989	1,675	840	2,515	21,849	11.5
1990	1,816	831	2,648	23,379	11.3
1991	2,011	830	2,842	25,015	11.4
1992	2,211	837	3,048	26,766	11.4
1993	2,427	657	3,084	28,640	10.8
1994	2,664	659	3,323	30,645	10.8

SOURCE: City of New York, Office of Management and Budget, April 1984 calculations. Debt service and revenues for fiscal year 1976 through 1984 are actual. Debt service and revenues for fiscal years 1985 through 1988 reflect the April, 1984 Four-Year Financial Plan assumptions. Revenues for fiscal years 1989 through 1994 are inflated at 7 percent annually. Debt service on debt issued in the 1985–94 fiscal period is calculated at a 10 percent rate of interest. Financing costs of the water and sewer program are included.

downturn in the City's economic or fiscal situation would weaken its credit standing and market access. Similarly, unforeseen changes in the credit markets that reduce investor interest in municipal bonds also could compel the City to lower its borrowing goals. One such change might result from proposed federal reforms that decrease the tax advantages for upper-income investors of municipal securities.

Barring such events, however, the City's plan seems realistic. This prognosis stems in large part from the City's projected capacity to afford the related debt service burden. Table 5.3 shows actual and anticipated debt service expenditures as a percentage of total City revenues for fiscal years 1976 through 1994. The combined City and MAC debt-service burden was at its high of 18.8 percent of total revenues in fiscal 1977. Since then it has declined steadily to 9.9 percent in fiscal year 1985. The planned program of new borrowings will not raise this percentage significantly. It is forecast to be increased to 11.5 percent in fiscal 1989, and then cut back to 10.8 percent by fiscal 1994. In sum, assuming normal growth in City revenues, the cost of financing the capital program should not burden the expense budget excessively.

WATER AND SEWER REVENUE BONDS

Debt issues backed by dedicated revenue as opposed to general obligation credit have grown increasingly popular with state and local governments in recent years. In 1970 revenue bonds represented 34.5 percent of all municipal issues; by 1982 that share had risen to 73.0 percent.[12]

Many large cities including Boston, Chicago, Philadelphia, and Detroit long have used revenue financing to support capital investment in water and sewer systems. User charges for water and sewer services provide the dedicated revenue to support this debt. However, in New York City, even though property owners pay separate water and sewer fees, City officials historically shunned a similar approach. The belief was that general obligation borrowing was preferable to earmarked revenues.

This attitude changed gradually in recent years. Restraint in property tax increases since the fiscal crisis have created more leeway to raise water and sewer fees. Moreover, the growing popularity of revenue bonds nationally encouraged City officials to explore using them to meet some portion of the City's borrowing needs. In 1981 Mayor Koch first endorsed State legislation to create a mechanism for water and sewer financing in New York City. Finally passed in July 1984, this legislation created a municipal Water Board to set and collect fees and a Water Finance Authority to undertake the borrowing. Both bodies are politically accountable to the Mayor who appoints five of the seven members of the Authority and all seven members of the Board.[13]

The City's plan called for the Water Financing Authority to offer its first bonds in the amount of $150 million in the spring of 1985. It further assumed the Authority will sell $330 million of its bonds in fiscal year 1986, $350 million in 1987, and $375 million in 1988. These amounts would leave $2995 million of the planned total to be raised in the period from fiscal years 1989 through 1994. This implies borrowing of approximately $500 million annually in that period. However, the initial goal was not achieved on time, so the total Authority borrowing over the period may have to be reduced or more of it accomplished in the later years.

In theory, the return from water and sewer revenue bonds could support all investments in the City's systems of water supply, water mains, sewers, and sewage treatment. However, the planned borrowings of $4.2 billion are below the total ten-year investments of $6.2 billion planned for these systems. If the water and sewer bonds prove easy to market, therefore, the City could increase the $4.2 billion goal. The $14 billion to be gained from the sale of general-obligation bonds then might be reduced accordingly, or it might provide additional resources for other purposes.

A constraint on the amount of water- and sewer-revenue bonds to be issued is in their impact on charges to property owners. In the past, the City has kept charges relatively low by supporting water and sewer operations with property taxes. In fiscal year 1985 the average single-family homeowner paid between $135 and $150 per year in water and sewer fees. Revenue from these charges in fiscal 1985 totalled $380 million. That amount fell $160 million below the estimated combined total of $540 million in operating costs ($250 million) and existing debt service ($290 million).[14] Thus, if the new authority assumed full responsibility for water and sewer financing, it would have to increase fees more than 50 percent before even issuing any new debt. To avoid this problem, the legislation creating the Authority permits the City to continue to cover the preexisting debt service from property taxes. This means the user charges must only cover operating costs and repayment of newly issued revenue bonds. This strategy permits existing rates to be kept low for several years. By the late 1980s, however, the combination of operating costs and repayment of revenue bonds will exert upward pressure on rates. The political decision over how much to increase those rates will determine the extent to which the effort to sell $4.2 billion in bonds could be expanded.

WASTE DISPOSAL FINANCING

The City's strategy for expanding its waste-disposal capacity assumes that private firms will construct and operate eight plants that generate marketable energy while incinerating refuse. This arrangement would relieve the City of direct responsibility for both capital financing and the complicated technical management of the plants. In return, the private operator would receive contractual commitments from Con Edison to purchase steam and from the City to pay fees to dispose of garbage at the plant.

This strategy also assumes that the private operators will finance their construction costs with tax-exempt Industrial Development Bonds (IDBs). Without the resultant tax advantages, private firms would be compelled to charge the City significantly higher fees for garbage disposal. For this reason the $3 billion of private financing for resource recovery is premised on the availability of tax-exempt IDBs.

After the City's initial plan was formulated, however, congressional action restricted the use of IDBs. [15] Concerned about the loss of revenue from expanding IDB activity, the Congress in 1984 placed an annual limit of $150 per capita on new issuances of IDBs in each of the states. This cap declines to $100 per capita in calendar year 1987.

These limits have complicated but not destroyed the City strategy. Under formulas developed by the State, the City is entitled to issue $425 million annually until calendar year 1986 and $300 million annually in subsequent years. This yields approximately $3.4 billion in the ten-year period when the City seeks $3 billion in IDB financing for waste disposal plants. Any new action by Congress to restrict the reliance on IDBs further or to change the tax-exempt status of such bonds would undermine the City's prospects for realizing its planned financing of waste disposal plants.

In sum, the City's financing plan is reasonable, but ambitious, and faces uncertainties typical of any effort to foresee developments over a ten-year period. The prospects for raising nearly $26 billion in ten years are enhanced by efforts to diversify the funding sources. The creation of a Water Finance Authority and the pursuit of private capital for waste disposal avoid the risks and limitations of exclusive reliance on general obligation bonds. However, market

TABLE 5.4

Planned Capital Commitments by Functional Area,
Fiscal Years 1985–94
(millions of dollars)

Investment Category	Amount	Percentage Distribution
Bridges	$ 1,616	6.0%
Water Supply	2,512	9.4
Water Mains	1,238	4.6
Streets	4,747	17.7
Sewers	1,762	6.6
Water Pollution Control	2,499	9.3
Waste Disposal	3,361	12.5
Hospitals	1,508	5.6
Sanitation Facilities	278	1.0
Police Facilities	264	.9
Fire Facilities	151	.5
Uniformed Service Vehicles	775	3.0
Schools	1,818	6.8
Parks	1,392	5.2
Correction	345	1.3
Economic Development	326	1.2
Housing Programs	180	.7
All Other	2,023	7.5
Total	$26,795	100.0%

SOURCE: City of New York, Office of Management and Budget, *Ten-Year Capital Plan*, April 1984.

acceptance of the proposed mix of general obligation and revenue bonds is uncertain, as is the political will of the City to impose higher user fees for water and sewer operations.

INVESTMENT PRIORITIES

The ten-year plan addresses the capital needs of a broad spectrum of municipal functions. It encompasses facilities normally defined as infrastructure, such as streets and highways, bridges, water supply and distribution, sewers, water pollution control, and waste disposal. It also deals with the capital requirements of the City's operating agencies, including police, fire, sanitation, correction, and hospitals. Finally, the plan funds projects for economic development and housing.

The capital needs for these diverse functions are extensive, and they compete for borrowed funds as they do for operating revenues. This section describes the investment choices in the current ten-year plan, and then asks two questions. First, if more funds were available, which areas should receive higher allocations? Second, by contrast, if less funds were available, which areas should be cut?

CURRENT POLICY

The current ten-year plan allocates $26.8 billion among 18 major functional areas (see Table 5.4). The amounts range from $4747 million for streets to $151 million for Fire Department facilities. However, the size of the allocations does not indicate accurately the City's priorities among competing areas. This is because the dollar needs vary tremendously among these areas. In some cases, a smaller allocation represents a more complete fulfillment of need than does a larger allocation for a functional area with greater needs. The extent to which needs are met can be considered separately for each major functional area.

Bridges. Because of its practice of regular biennial inspections, the City has relatively complete knowledge about the condition of its 852 highway, railroad, and waterway bridges. The inspection system divides bridges into four major groups based upon their structural soundness: poor, fair, good, and very good.[16] The plan funds reconstruction or repair of the 228 major bridges rated poor or fair. It also funds minor repair and maintenance to bridges now rated good or very good, thereby preventing their condition from slipping over the decade.

Water Supply. The major capital project in this category is continued construction of a new tunnel, the third in the City's system, to bring water from upstate reservoirs to the city. First begun in 1970, this project is not expected to reach completion until well into the next century. The purpose is to relieve the burden on the two existing tunnels and to improve water pressure in outlying areas of the city.

The tunnel project involves four separate stages to be completed over the course of the next 50 years and ultimately to run a distance of 60 miles. Stages One and Two will create a new transmission system for upstate supplies that will run from the Hillview Reservoir in Yonkers through the Bronx, Manhattan, Queens, and Brooklyn. The completion of Stage One and part of Stage Two will allow inspections of the existing water tunnels to take place. Stage Three will extend the tunnel to the Kensico Reservoir, the storage facility for the Catskill and Delaware watershed supplies. It will increase pressure in the distribution system. Finally, the eastern sections of the Bronx and Queens will be serviced by the completion of Stage Four. At present, work is underway on Stage One running from Yonkers to Astoria in Queens.[17]

The ten-year plan encompasses the completion of Stage One of the tunnel. It also incorporates the completion of the Brooklyn/ Queens leg and the initiation of the Manhattan leg of Stage Two. The completion of Stage One and work on Stage Two will improve water service to Queens and Staten Island and will allow the existing tunnels to be closed one at a time for structural inspection.

The other major water supply investment involves improvements in the Croton reservoir network, the oldest of the City's three upstate watersheds. The planned spending will bring the Croton dams into conformity with national safety standards and will build a treatment facility to strengthen the quality of the Croton water supply. Of the total water supply allocation of $2512 million, fully 80 percent is for the third tunnel, and the remainder is for the Croton watersheds.

Water Distribution. The City's water distribution system is composed of 6157 miles of water mains. Because over one-half of these mains were installed before 1930, and 10 percent of them before 1900, many analysts have expressed concern about the aging of the system.[18] Interestingly, however, available evidence indicates that water pipes do not deteriorate uniformly with age. Studies by the Army Corps of Engineers and other engineering consultants indicate that location and original pipe design are more important than age in causing water main breaks.[19]

Based upon these studies, the City has identified water mains that should be replaced, generally smaller pipes that cannot withstand modern surface stress or that no longer have adequate capacity for their location. The ten-year plan proposes to replace the total 735 miles of these water mains. This replacement program accounts for 68 percent of the total $1238 million allocated for water mains.

In addition, the plan provides for installation of 190 miles of entirely new water mains, mostly on Staten Island. At present, large sections of that borough lack the backup capacity that exists in the rest of the city, making residents more prone to water loss in the event of breaks. The investment in system expansion accounts for $394 million or 32 percent of the water distribution allocation.

Streets. Unlike water mains, deterioration of streets is directly related to age, that is, the period since the last reconstruction of the roadbed. Thus, the City's repair strategy for its 5852 miles of locally managed streets has relied upon the concept of average replacement cycles. Based upon accepted national standards, its long-run goals are to reconstruct primary streets, the busiest thoroughfares, every 40 years, to reconstruct secondary streets every 50 years, and to reconstruct local streets every 60 years.

The ten-year plan will not reach these desired levels of reconstruction activity until 1989. Thus, assuming that its reconstruction goals are correct, the City's streets will continue to deteriorate though 1988 and will only begin to stay even with wear and tear in 1989. In addition, the ten-year plan provides for simple street resurfacing twice within the period of major reconstruction. The total cost of this street repair program is $4747 million, of which 12 percent is for repaving, 36 percent for reconstruction of primary streets, 19 percent of reconstruction for secondary streets, and 23 percent for reconstruction of local streets.

Sewers. New York City contains nearly 6200 miles of sewers. Historically, the City has not compiled a regular or comprehensive inventory of sewer conditions. Because of this information gap, the City is now undertaking a complete inspection of the system. This work will take several years to finish.

In the meantime, some problems already are recognized. Concern in recent years has focused on the construction material of the oldest sewers. Collapses have occurred predominantly in those made of brick and cement. The troublesome, older brick sewers are located mostly in Manhattan, which has a total of 400 miles of this type, some 250 miles of which are over 100 years old. Sewers made of cement pipes, first introduced in Brooklyn, were discontinued after 1900 because of unusually rapid deterioration. However, the borough still contains 300 miles of old, cement sewers.

Based upon its current knowledge, the City has established two major priorities for sewer repair in the ten-year plan. The first is to replace sewers as they collapse. It is expected that 300 miles of sewers will have to be replaced for this reason over the decade. The second is to begin preventive replacement or repair of the troubled cement and brick sewers. The plan provides funds to replace 110 miles of cement pipe in Brooklyn and to repair 60 miles of brick sewer in Manhattan. Together the two sewer replacement programs account for 77 percent of the total allocation for sewers.

The other major investment in the sewer program is installation of new sewers. This spending is directed largely at Queens and Staten Island where development in the last 20 years has exceeded the City's installation of new sewers. An estimated 870 miles of streets lack sewers.[20] Residents in these areas experience frequent street flooding because of inadequate run-off capacity, and many rely upon septic tanks for sanitary disposal. The ten-year plan calls for about 80 miles of new sewer construction in those areas judged most needy.

Water Pollution Control. The ten-year plan provides for completion of a long-term effort, largely funded by the federal government, to provide each of the City's 14 drainage areas with a sewage-treatment plant capable of meeting the requirements of the federal Clean Water Act of 1972. The remaining links in the system are construction of the North River and Red Hook plants and upgrading of the Coney Island and Owls Head plants. All four projects are scheduled for completion by 1992. These projects account for $1329 million or 53 percent of the total allocation for water pollution control.

With this important mandate nearly met, the City has planned two new initiatives. The first is construction of facilities and vessels to dispose of sewage sludge at a site 106 miles off shore. This will replace the current site located just 12 miles from shore. The second initiative is to begin construction of facilities to prevent overflows from sanitary sewers. The problem of sanitary overflows occurs when heavy flooding causes raw sewage to flow past the holding tanks at water pollution control plants. These two efforts are allocated $124 million and $631 million respectively. The total allocation for water pollution control is $2499 million.

Waste Disposal. The City expects to exhaust nearly one-half its current landfill facilities by 1986. Confronted with the need to dispose of 22,000 tons of garbage daily, the Koch administration has proposed a twofold strategy of extending the capacity of its remaining landfill site as an interim measure and developing a network of eight resource recovery plants to serve longer-run needs.[21] The ten-year plan provides $3000 million or 89 percent of the waste disposal total for new plants and $361 million for landfill capacity expansion.

Hospitals. Seven of the 15 hospitals administered by the Health and Hospitals Corporation currently meet State standards for safety, patient space, and air and temperature quality. The ten-year plan provides for reconstruction and rehabilitation that would raise that total to 14. In addition, the plan provides funds for purchase of medical and other equipment. The $1508 million total allocation for hospitals is divided 76 percent to reconstruction and 24 percent to new equipment.

Sanitation Facilities. The facilities of the Sanitation Department had deteriorated seriously by the late 1970s. Many were dilapidated, in violation of federal occupational health and safety standards, and too small for modern sanitation equipment. The problems were most acute among leased facilities, many of which were built originally for other purposes. In 1982 the City began an effort to upgrade those facilities that it owned and to replace the leased buildings with new ones. The ten-year plan provides for rehabilitation of all City-owned facilities and construction of ten new garages to replace leased facilities. The total allocation is $278 million.

Police and Fire Facilities. The ten-year plan continues a program of upgrading and replacement of police and fire facilities that began in 1980. In the 1985–94 period the Police Department will replace ten precinct houses and reconstruct 12 others from among its 73 precincts. The Fire Department, with a total of 224 firehouses, will build ten new ones and reconstruct 60. The plan also provides for routine replacement of operating equipment. The Police Department receives $264 million for facilities and equipment, and the Fire Department receives $151 million over the ten-year period.

Uniformed Service Vehicles. In recent years the City has improved the condition of vehicles in the departments of Police, Fire, Sanitation, and Correction through establishment of regular replacement cycles. The ten-year plan maintains those standards and assures the provision of the vehicles necessary for basic service delivery. The allocation for this purpose is $775 million.

Schools. The capital needs of the City's public schools are related essentially to their age. While about 45 percent of the City's 970 school buildings were constructed after 1950, the Board of Education relies for more than one-half of its space requirements upon facilities that are 35 years old or older. Given this age profile, the Board's first priority is to maintain its basic physical structures. This encompasses replacement of roofs and windows, modernization of electrical and plumbing systems, upgrading of boilers and water heaters, and repair of foundations. Approximately $1070 million or 59 percent of the Board's capital plan is devoted to these projects.

A second major component of the plan is enhancement of vocational education facilities. Funds in this area will modernize the 16 vocational high schools and purchase new equipment for shops and labs in many such schools. This part of the capital plan accounts for $213 million or 12 percent of the Board's total.

The third major component is a limited program of new construction in districts experiencing enrollment increases. Included are ten new schools and additions to ten existing buildings. The allocation for this program is $290 million or 16 percent of the $1818 million education total.

Parks. Age, heavy use, and two decades of inadequate maintenance have caused many parks to deteriorate extensively in recent years. The leading priority in the ten-year plan is to repair about 900 neighborhood parks and playgrounds under five acres in size. The plan provides funds for improvements including new fences, play equipment, pavement, and bench repairs. This plan for repairing neighborhood parks accounts for $489 million or 35 percent of the total for parks.

The plan also includes investment in the most deteriorated recreation facilities such as playing fields, tennis courts, running tracks, swimming pools, ice skating rinks, and recreation centers. These facilities will receive $176 million or 13 percent of the total.

The City's larger parks, which encompass nearly 25,000 acres, will receive only selected improvements. The plan allows for improvements to roadways and bridges, foot paths, lights, benches, comfort stations, and for some landscaping and forestry work. The allocation for the larger parks is $446 million or 32 percent of the total $1392 million for parks.

Corrections. The first priority for the City's correction system is construction of facilities to accommodate growth in the jail population. The ten-year plan will add nearly 4000 jail spaces by 1988, bringing total inmate capacity to about 14,000. The program includes new construction on Rikers Island, completion of the White Street jail in lower Manhattan, and conversion of the Brooklyn Navy Yard Brig. This program requires $224 million or 65 percent of the corrections total.

The other major element in the plan is reconstruction of existing facilities. This includes repairs and renovations to comply with judicial orders establishing minimum standards for inmate living conditions. This program requires $102 million or 29 percent of the total.

Economic Development. The ten-year plan includes $325 million for four types of economic development projects. First, site preparation and other improvements for industrial parks are allocated $109 million or 34 percent of the economic development total. Second, improvements to physical facilities and amenities for commercial projects such as the South Street Seaport, the 42nd Street Development Area, and various outer borough office sites will receive $95 million or 29 percent. Third, street, sidewalk, and other improvements in neighborhood retail districts are allocated $47 million or 14 percent. Finally, City support for construction of the Convention Center requires $60 million or 18 percent of the total.

Housing Programs. The largest housing item in the plan, $75 million, is for completion of the church-sponsored Nehemiah and New York City Partnership programs for new home construction in Brooklyn. The plan also includes funds for property management in City Urban Renewal Areas, demolition of abandoned buildings, and site development for possible Housing Authority projects. The total capital allocation for housing is $180 million.

PRIORITIES FOR ADDITIONAL SPENDING

As the preceding descriptions indicate, the ten-year plan addresses major capital requirements in each of the City's basic service functions. In certain of those functions, the level of planned investment appears to be reasonably adequate. However, because of the financing limitations, the plan clearly does not meet all the identified needs. For many functions, additional intelligent investments could be made.

The functional areas in the ten-year plan can be divided into three major categories based upon their potential for additional investment. The first category includes those functions in which higher capital spending is unnecessary. The second category involves those functions in which marginal increases are desirable. The third category includes those functions in which identifiable needs justify additional investments. These classifications are as follows.

Adequate Investments. The ten-year plan meets nearly all recognized capital needs in six major functions. First, the plan provides for repairs of all major bridges where problems have been identified. Second, the plan includes all investments needed to upgrade the Fresh Kills landfill and to develop the eight resource-recovery plants needed to create a viable waste disposal system for the public. Third, the plan includes adequate funding to maintain desired replacement cycles for vehicles in the Police, Fire, Sanitation, and Correction departments. Fourth, in water supply, the plan will correct the structural and water quality problems in the Croton reservoir network and proceed at the most rapid pace feasible on the third water tunnel. Fifth, the program for water mains would replace all the pipes that are likely to fail. Finally, the strategy for streets is to define and to achieve an optimal level of reconstruction activity. Theoretically, more funds might allow that goal to be reached before the 1989 target date. As the next section of this chapter indicates, however, the City probably could not implement the streets program any faster, even if more funds were provided.

Marginal Increases Desirable. The ten-year plan addresses major capital needs for six services, but some additional spending could produce obvious benefits. Perhaps the clearest examples are hospitals and correction facilities. The plan includes spending to bring 14 of the City's municipal hospitals into compliance with State health facility codes. The program in corrections is designed to meet court mandates on minimal jail conditions. Despite these scheduled improvements, however, the City could make further investments that would enhance the quality of patient care and inmate life. Even at the conclusion of the ten-year plan, City hospitals and jails undoubtedly will lack many services and amenities present in similar facilities in other cities.

A similar argument can be made for the improvement of Police, Fire, and Sanitation facilities. The current City program will gradually replace older facilities and upgrade other units. However, funding constraints dictated the pace and the extent of these improvements. All three agencies could operate more efficiently with additional new construction and more extensive refurbishment of remaining facilities.

A final area where marginal spending increases would be beneficial is water pollution control. The ten-year plan contains approximately $500 million to begin construction of facilities to prevent overflows from sanitary sewers during rainy periods. However, the adequacy of that amount is questionable. The City is attempting to arrive at a policy on the extent to which it wishes to limit sewage overflows. If the objective is to reduce the frequency of sanitary overflows to reasonable levels, then increased funding will be required.

Large Increases Possible. For five functions capital spending that exceeds the allocations in the ten-year plan by large amounts is required to address all identified needs. These are schools, parks, sewers, housing, and economic development.

In schools, as discussed previously, the ten-year plan is focused on keeping the physical structure of existing buildings sound. While elimination of leaky roofs and windows will be an improvement, it represents a minimal goal. With the exception of vocational education, the ten-year plan contains almost no improvements designed to enhance the educational program. New construction is limited mostly to relief of overcrowding in selected neighborhoods.

According to the Board of Education, approximately 150 schools, mostly built in the 1930s and 1940s, lack gymnasiums, auditoriums, cafeterias, and other such common facilities. Similarly, over 100 buildings 30 years or older never have been modernized. Most of these facilities lack media centers, laboratories, and space for other kinds of contemporary learning programs. One 1982 estimate by Board officials placed the cost of such educational additions and modernizations at from $3 billion to $4 billion.[22]

Education is the major area in the ten-year plan where no replacement of any significant portion of the capital plant is contemplated. The City's intention is to rely on the same school buildings. Conceivably, proper maintenance can extend the useful life of these school buildings, and many older buildings may constitute perfectly adequate facilities. However, some older buildings probably should be replaced with new schools. To replace just the 60 buildings dating to before 1900 would cost at least $1.2 billon.[23]

The ten-year plan provides only for selected improvements in the City's 227 large parks, which encompass nearly 25,000 acres. The needs for improvement of parkland exceed the planned investments of $446 million. Master plans for Central, Prospect, and Flushing Meadows parks indicate that hundreds of millions of dollars could be spent in just those three locations. Thorough rehabilitation of man-made infrastructure and green spaces in the 227 large parks might require several billion dollars.

As indicated previously, the City has approximately 700 miles of trouble-prone brick and cement sewers. The ten-year plan allocates $340 million to begin the replacement or repair of 170 miles. The decisions on where and how to expand this prevention effort await more thorough inspection of the system, which is underway. This inspection is likely to indicate the desirability of replacing much of the 700 miles of brick and cement sewers. Full replacement would suggest quadrupling the allocation or adding well over $1 billion.

In addition, higher spending could be directed at installing new sewers. The ten-year plan provides for 80 miles of new sewer construction at a cost of $300 million. However, the City Planning Commission has identified 870 miles of developed but presently unsewered streets in Queens and Staten Island. If the funds were available, the City could expand sewer construction several times over.

In housing programs, which traditionally have been supported with federal funds, the City's planned investment of $180 million represents a minimal allocation. Given the reduction in federal housing programs, and the enormous need for new middle- and low-income housing, the City's capital expenditure for housing could be increased substantially. The political pressures to address this need were reflected in Mayor Koch's January 1985 proposal for a $4.4 billion program to create or rehabilitate 100,000 housing units over a five-year period through a combination of grants and low-interest loans largely outside the regular capital budget and plan. Most of the financing for the Mayor's plan would come from an increase in federally guaranteed bonding by the independent Housing Development Corporation and from the Port Authority.[24] In principle, however, the City's own capital spending for housing purposes also could be increased.

A comparable situation exists with economic-development programs. The ten-year allocation of $325 is relatively modest in comparison to potential investment. During the formulation of the ten-year plan, the Mayor's economic development staff reportedly identified between $3 billion and $4 billion of projects they judged worthwhile. While much of this request probably constituted a "wish list," it suggests that substantially increased City-sponsored investment could be made.

AREAS FOR POTENTIAL INVESTMENT REDUCTION

Another basic issue involves areas in the City's ten-year capital plan that most easily could withstand a reduction in planned investment. Such reductions could be necessitated by the City's inability to achieve its financing objectives or by changed priorities that sought to reduce debt service burdens and increase service expenditures beyond planned levels.

Again, the functional areas of the ten-year plan can be divided into three categories. The first is those functions that should be reduced first in any situation of financing difficulty. The second category is those functions where some reductions could be justified. The third category is those functions in which reductions should be avoided. The rationale for this grouping follows.

Most Potential for Reduction. Construction on the third water tunnel was suspended during the fiscal crisis of the mid-1970s. Should the City experience a shortage of capital dollars, suspension or construction slowdown would be sensible. The value of the tunnel project is essentially to prevent disruptions in service. Assuming that the two existing tunnels can be kept in service, further delay on the third tunnel would pose no immediate problems.

A second major candidate for any cutback should be street repair. The City could choose not to reach its optimal goals for reconstruction. Stretching out repairs would generate large capital savings.

The result, a postponement of the anticipated improvement in street conditions, would not produce any major catastrophe—though it would be unpleasant and potentially expensive for motorists.

The situation in parks is similar to that concerning streets. To forego scheduled park improvements, especially the ambitious program for neighborhood facilities, would not disrupt a basic City function.

Finally, the new police precincts, fire houses, and sanitation garages funded in the ten-year plan could also be delayed without major service disruptions. Construction of new facilities for these services was suspended during the fiscal crisis and could be postponed again. If necessary, these agencies could make do with a less ambitious program of repairs to existing facilities.

Potential for Some Reduction. A second group of functions could withstand reduced investments without causing short-run service disruptions. Preventive replacement of the most troubled components of the network of sewers and water mains is crucial to the city's long-term viability; in the short-term, however, the City could suffice, as it has in recent years, with emergency repairs. Similarly, structural repair of school buildings is important, but the current goal of fixing all roofs and windows within five years could be extended. The City should keep its basic fleets of police, fire, sanitation, and correction vehicles in good working order, but current replacement cycles could be lengthened. In the case of economic development and housing programs, the City commitment is minimal in comparison to potential needs, but both areas could be cut back without threatening basic municipal functions.

Least Desirable for Reduction. The ten-year plan contains five areas in which the City should not spend less than is now planned because of their critical importance, external mandates, or funding sources. Critical function is most evident in waste disposal. Inability to dispose of garbage poses a fundamental health and sanitation problem, leaving the City with little choice but to construct a needed waste disposal capacity. Should the financing scheme or technology of planned resource-recovery plants prove unfeasible, alternatives must be found even at higher cost.

The situation is comparable, albeit somewhat less critical, for bridges. Bridge failures or closures would disrupt traffic, and mass transit, and the economy. Heavy State and federal funding for bridge repairs protects this area, assuming those sources do not diminish.

In the case of hospitals, correction facilities, and water pollution control, State and federal mandates argue for planned capital spending levels. The City is under pressure from the State to bring its hospital facilities into compliance with safety and patient environment codes. In corrections, the City is under federal court mandate to improve the conditions of inmate life. (And given the City's November 1983 experience with premature inmate releases, a mayor would be well advised to resist cuts in the program of jail space expansion.) Federal mandates and funding for completion and upgrading of the network of sewage treatment plans make reductions for water-pollution control undesirable.

IMPLEMENTATION OF THE CAPITAL PLAN

The final phase of the capital budget process is project execution. The City encountered serious difficulty in undertaking this task when it reactivated the capital program in the late 1970s. When funds became available, the City often was unable to get work started. Although most capital projects are handled by private contractors and construction firms, City agencies must be able to outline the scope of the work and award the contracts. The City's performance in this process has improved in recent years. Nonetheless, implementation of the ten-year plan still represents an ambitious goal in several major areas.

RECENT GAINS IN IMPLEMENTATION

The City incurs a capital commitment when it contracts for a particular project. As discussed previously, the City develops an overall commitment plan each year based upon its approved capital budget. At the conclusion of each fiscal year, the City compares actual dollar commitments with the year's plan. These comparisons are shown in Table 5.5 for fiscal years 1981 through 1984.

In fiscal year 1981 the City experienced considerable difficulty in reaching its goals. The City committed a total of $837 million,

TABLE 5.5

City of New York Planned and Actual Capital Commitments, Fiscal Years 1981–84
(millions of dollars)

	Fiscal 1981			Fiscal 1982			Fiscal 1983			Fiscal 1984		
	Plan	Actual	Percentage Achieved	Plan	Actual	Percentage Achieved	Plan	Actual	Percentage Achieved	Plan	Actual	Percentage Achieved
Streets and Bridges	$131	$88	66.9%	$211	$180	85.4%	$186	$150	80.5%	$244	$281	114.9%
Water Supply	155	111	71.9	115	85	74.0	100	134	133.9	95	89	94.1
Water Mains	34	21	62.2	46	67	145.2	32	37	118.2	57	55	95.9
Sewers	170	120	70.8	100	110	109.5	69	62	90.8	60	68	112.5
Water Pollution Control	382	95	24.8	306	75	24.5	374	373	99.8	429	418	97.3
Education	97	96	99.2	140	117	83.4	115	117	102.3	128	150	117.0
Correction	32	29	90.1	29	17	56.1	28	24	86.3	77	89	115.2
Sanitation	73	43	59.3	104	94	90.7	102	123	121.0	152	133	87.8
Police	22	14	61.7	25	21	83.1	20	18	87.9	20	15	75.6
Fire	13	7	55.1	18	20	111.9	19	18	95.8	22	20	90.6
Housing	23	9	38.6	30	24	77.6	22	19	86.9	54	60	112.6
Hospitals	53	37	69.3	78	84	107.1	60	67	112.5	62	89	142.0
Parks	61	55	90.8	84	80	94.6	68	78	115.1	75	66	87.4
Economic Development	47	40	84.1	66	32	48.7	47	58	122.4	66	39	59.5
Other	128	72	56.2	189	136	72.0	189	162	85.7	220	109	49.5
Total	$1,422	$837	58.9%	$1,543	$1,142	74.1%	$1,431	$1,442	100.8%	$1,762	$1,681	95.4%

SOURCES: Plan figures for 1981 are based on Office of Management and Budget, "Capital Commitment and Cash Flow Plan For New York," October 6, 1980. Fiscal year 1981 actual figures and all subsequent figures are based on Office of Management and Budget, "Quarterly Capital Plan" for October of fiscal year 1982 through fiscal year 1985. (October figures represent the commitment plan as modified by the City Council.) The plan for fiscal year 1984 has been interpolated from authorization goals based on the total plan target of $1850 million.

TABLE 5.6
City of New York Capital Commitments, Actual and Planned, Fiscal Years 1981–94
(millions of dollars)

	Fiscal 1981–1984 Actual	Fiscal 1985–1988 Plan	Percentage Change	Fiscal 1985–1994 Ten-year Plan	Four-year Plan As Percentage of Ten-year Plan
Bridges[a]	[$700]	$746	[158.7%]	$1,616	46.2%
Streets[a]		1,065		4,747	22.4
Sewers	360	399	10.8	1,762	22.6
Water Pollution Control	961	996	3.6	2,499	39.9
Water Supply	419	395	(5.7)	2,512	15.7
Water Mains	180	401	122.8	1,238	32.4
Education	480	818	70.4	1,818	45.0
Correction	159	301	89.3	354	84.9
Sanitation	393	1,949	395.9	4,213	46.3
Police	68	103	51.5	285	36.2
Fire	65	113	73.8	315	35.9
Housing	112	69	(38.4)	180	38.2
Hospitals	277	576	107.9	1,508	38.2
Parks	279	435	55.9	1,392	31.2
Economic Development	169	307	81.7	521	58.9
Other	478	841	75.9	1,833	45.9
Total	$5,102	$9,515	86.5%	$26,795	35.5%

SOURCE: Actual commitments for fiscal years 1981–84 are from Table 5.5. Planned commitments for fiscal years 1985–94 are from the City of New York, *Ten-Year Capital Plan, Fiscal Years 1985–94*, April 1984.

a. Separate data for actual commitments of streets and bridges were not reported for the 1981–84 period.

which represented only 59 percent of its planned $1422 million. No City agency achieved its objective for the year.

Performance began to improve in fiscal year 1982. The City planned total commitments of $1543 million, and achieved 74 percent of that goal or $1142 million. Interestingly, while some agencies still encountered difficulties, others exceeded their goals. The City strengthened its capacity to monitor the situation and made midyear adjustments to accommodate variations in the performance of the agencies.

In fiscal year 1983 the City exceeded its overall commitment target of $1431 million. In part, this accomplishment resulted from reduced goals, since the 1983 objective was lower than the planned goal for the previous year. Significantly, many of the agencies that had fallen behind in 1982 caught up with their project work by exceeding their 1983 targets.

In fiscal year 1984 the City raised its goal to $1762 million, and achieved $1681 million in commitments, or 95 percent of the plan. Most of the major agencies reached or exceeded their targets. Clearly, the City made significant strides in implementation during the 1981–84 period. The 1984 total of $1681 million in commitments was double the 1981 total of $837 million.

IMPLEMENTATION OUTLOOK

Implementation of the ten-year plan will require further management gains, some major, in City agencies. Table 5.6 shows the level of planned commitments for the four-year period from fiscal year 1985 through 1988 and the actual level in the preceding four-year period. The table also indicates the relationship of the planned commitments in the fiscal year 1985–88 period to the goals for the total ten-year plan.

Overall, the City plans to commit $9515 million in the 1985–88 period, an 86 percent increase from the $5102 million committed in the preceding four years. If this goal is met, the City will have achieved only 35 percent of its ten-year goal, indicating that commitment levels need to grow steadily in the last six years of the plan.

Plans for individual agencies vary considerably from the citywide pattern. Commitments for corrections, education, bridges, and sanitation are concentrated in the early years or "front-loaded." In corrections, for example, intention to complete the program of jail expansion by 1988 requires that 85 percent of the ten-year allocation for corrections be committed in the first four years. In education, where the goal is to do most roof and window repairs early, the ten-year plan will be 45 percent committed by 1988. Because of the massive work being carried out on the four major East River bridges, this plan should be 46 percent committed by 1988. The objectives in these three areas seem achievable. In sanitation, however, where the City hopes to obligate funds for four resource recovery plants by 1988, the outlook is less promising. Initiation of plant construction still faces large political and technical hurdles.

In many agencies, the four-year objective resembles the citywide goal of committing between 30 and 40 percent of the ten-year allocation by 1988. Included in this group are water pollution control, water mains, police, fire, housing, hospitals, and parks. No major obstacles appear to prevent reaching these agency goals, although commitments for water mains and hospitals will be increased more than average by 1988—122 percent for water mains and 108 percent for hospitals. This goal will challenge the management skills of officials in these two agencies.

Three areas—water supply, streets, and sewers—are "backloaded" in terms of meeting the ten-year goals. Only 16 percent of the ten-year funds are to be committed to enhance water supply facilities by 1988 because major construction on Stage Two of the third water tunnel is not scheduled to begin until 1989. The intervening years are required to complete survey and design work preceding construction.

The four-year goal for streets and sewers accounts for only 22 percent of the ten-year plan. Street repair may present the most difficult implementation problems in the entire ten-year plan. Development of strategies for handling traffic disruption and improvement of construction management in the Department of Transportation are necessary before the City can reach planned commitment levels for street reconstruction. Because sewer replacement usually accompanies the opening of roadbeds, the preventive program of sewer repair also must wait until the later years of the ten-year plan.[25]

CONCLUSION

The expansion of investment in the City of New York's physical plant is well underway. The City's ten-year capital plan addresses a wide range of infrastructure and facility needs. Consequently, many of the City's capital assets will be improved demonstrably. However, not all of the City's needs are included in the ten-year plan, and some areas will receive only modest or limited investment.

Two major hurdles could thwart the City's program. The first is inability to raise the funds required to support planned investment. To date, however, the City has met its goals of selling general-obligation bonds in increasing yearly amounts, and has moved to diversify its financing sources by seeking private capital for waste-disposal facilities and establishing an independent system of water and sewer revenue bonding. The second potential obstacle is inability to initiate and complete construction on time. Again, the City's record on capital execution has improved in recent years. Its chances for implementing the ten-year plan seem reasonably good.

NOTES

1. National Infrastructure Advisory Committee to the Joint Economic Committee of the U.S. Congress, *Hard Choices: A Report on America's Increasing Infrastructure Needs and Our Ability to Pay for Them,* February 1984.

2. See David A. Grossman, *The Future of New York City's Capital Plant* (Washington, D.C.: The Urban Institute, 1979). The previous low capital commitment level was $210 million in fiscal year 1968; the previous high was $1112 million in fiscal year 1973.

3. For a depiction of the stages over many years in the completion of a capital project, see The League of Woman Voters of the City of New York, "A Visual Aid Toward Understanding the Procedures Which Turn Capital Budgets Into Infrastructure," League of Women Voters, April 1983.

4. Estimate arrived at from a discussion with staff of the City Office of Management and Budget.

5. City of New York, Office of the Comptroller, *Rebuilding During the 1980s,* May 1979.

6. City of New York, *Executive Budget, Fiscal Year 1983, Message of the Mayor,* May 1982.

7. This change in attitude is the author's interpretation, based upon interviews with agency officials.

8. See Merrill Lynch Capital Markets, Health Care Finance Department, "FHA Mortgage Insurance for Publicly Owned Hospitals," March 1984, prepared for the National Association of Public Hospitals.

9. *The Bond Buyer Index* is an indicator of municipal bond interest rates that is compiled weekly based on averages of dealer quotes for 20 municipal bond issues. For discussion, see Office of the Special Deputy Comptroller, "The City's FY 1985–1994 Capital and Financing Program," Report No. 41–85, November 1984.

10. U.S. General Accounting Office, *Trends and Changes In the Municipal Bond Market As They Relate To Financing State and Local Public Infrastructure*, September 12, 1983.

11. Office of the Special Deputy Comptroller, op. cit.

12. U.S. General Accounting Office, op. cit.

13. Provision in the State Constitution requires separate entities for the rate-setting and borrowing functions. The Water Board also is empowered to operate the water and sewer system, but the City's intention is to retain that responsibility in the New York City Department of Environmental Protection.

14. Data on the current revenues and costs of the water and sewer system were provided by the staff of the Department of Environmental Protection.

15. The legislation is the Deficit Reduction Act of 1984 passed in June of that year.

16. For discussion of bridge condition ratings, see New York City Department of Transportation, *Annual Condition Report, Bridges and Tunnels*, 1983.

17. For discussion of the third water tunnel project, see the Citizens Union Research Foundation, *Issues and Options in Regional Water Supply*, 1979.

18. For a discussion of water-main replacement based upon age, see the City Comptroller, "Water Distribution," *Rebuilding During the 1980s*, op. cit.

19. U.S. Department of the Army, District Corps of Engineers, *New York City Water Supply, Infrastructure Study, Volume 1, Manhattan*, May 1980.

20. New York City Planning Commission, *Capital Needs and Priorities for the City of New York*, Spring 1982.

21. For a more detailed discussion of these plans, see Chapter 13 by John Kaiser in this volume.

22. Board of Education, Division of School Buildings, internal memorandum on ten-year assessment of capital needs.

23. Estimate based upon an average construction cost of at least $20 million for a new school building.

24. City of New York, *The State of the City, Housing Initiatives*, January 30, 1985.

25. For a discussion of the related problems of capital implementation in streets and sewers, see City Planning Commission, *Capital Needs and Priorities for the City of New York*, April 1984.

6

Human Resources

RAYMOND D. HORTON

In the next four years, the City of New York will spend about $90 billion mainly to pay employees to deliver services. In allocating these resources to provide services to residents and visitors, the City's leaders will make four important and related decisions. First, they will split spending between municipal employees and others— those who loan the City capital, with interest; those who deliver services but are not employees; those who provide space, supplies, and materials; and finally those who must rely on government for basic needs, the poor. Second, the sums available for compensating employees will be allocated based on a trade-off between paying fewer employees more or paying more employees less. Third, the work force will be allocated among competing agencies. Fourth, the sums allocated for compensating the work force will be allocated among competing groups of employees.

These decisions will be reached in different phases of a quad-rennial political cycle, in different settings, by different people. To borrow the concept of a well-known economist, they will be separated in time and space.[1] These decisions will affect and will be affected by the productivity of the work force. In the next four years, managers will attempt to increase productivity by better utilizing the City's human resources. These decisions, too, will be separated in time and space, spread across many operating agencies and separated from the more centralized decisions establishing staffing and compensation policies. Thus, in the next four years, important decisions concerning the management of human resources will be reached under circumstances that make it difficult for municipal officials to consider them strategically and to recognize their interdependence.

The premise of this chapter is that a more comprehensive view of human resource management would aid the City in providing citizens with improved services. The first three sections examine, respectively, staffing, wage, and productivity policies. In each case earlier patterns of decision-making are examined and opportunities to develop a more comprehensive framework for policy are reviewed. The final section identifies options for better managing the City's human resources.

STAFFING POLICIES

The optimal staffing level for the City as a whole or for a given agency is difficult to determine. In theory, managers are able to rely on the principle of declining marginal utility. In practice, they find it difficult to determine the level at which the addition of a single employee would produce less benefit than the cost of employing that worker. To some extent, this reflects the inherent difficulty in government of determining the basis of benefit, but structural characteristics that separate staffing decisions from other allocation decisions contribute to the difficulty.

PAST STAFFING POLICIES

While their decisions reflect considerations other than principles of marginal utility, municipal officials still establish and implement policies that define the size and mix of the work force. Numerous factors shape these decisions, including the availability of revenues, intergovernmental mandates, and elected officials' interpretations of the voters' priorities. In so complex a system, municipal staffing policies may evidence discontinuity and contradiction. By examining past staffing policies, it is possible to develop some understand-

TABLE 6.1

City of New York Expenditures and Employment, Fiscal Years 1970–85

(millions of dollars)

	Current Dollar Expenditures		Constant (1970) Dollar Expenditures		Employees	
	Amount	Percentage Change	Amount	Percentage Change	Number	Percentage Change
1970	$6,154	—	$6,154	—	275,211	—
1971	6,832	11.0%	6,408	4.1%	271,853	−1.2%
1972	7,701	12.7	6,876	7.3	274,766	1.1
1973	8,118	5.4	6,927	0.7	278,088	1.2
1974	8,878	9.4	6,925	0.0	293,025	5.4
1975	10,690	20.4	7,587	9.6	285,856	−2.4
1976	10,799	1.0	7,195	−5.2	245,549	−14.1
1977	12,288	13.8	7,680	6.7	232,355	−5.4
1978	12,578	2.4	7,568	−1.5	239,805	3.2
1979	12,591	1.0	7,085	−6.4	236,586	−1.3
1980	13,454	6.9	6,844	−3.4	228,784	−3.3
1981	13,971	3.8	6,435	−6.0	232,330	1.6
1982	15,076	7.9	6,432	−0.1	236,813	1.9
1983	15,699	4.1	6,351	−1.3	236,057	−0.3
1984	17,013	8.4	6,584	3.7	242,926	2.9
1985	18,219	7.1	6,811	3.4	251,720	3.6
1970–75	+4,806	78.1%	+1,433	23.3%	+10,645	3.9%
1975–80	+2,764	22.8	−743	−9.8	−57,072	−20.0
1980–85	+4,765	35.4	−33	0.0	+22,936	+10.0

SOURCES: Employment data for 1970–84 are year-end figures supplied by the New York State Financial Control Board and the New York City Office of Management amd Budget. Expenditure data for 1970–84 are adjusted operating budget totals from annual additions of the *Comprehensive Annual Report of the Comptroller.* Adjustments were made to take into account the reporting practices that removed State and federal Medicaid expenditures from the City operating budget over a period beginning in fiscal year 1978. Constant dollar adjustments reflect the Consumer Price Index for all Urban Consumers (CPI-U) for the New York-Northeastern New Jersey area. For fiscal year 1985, expenditures are from the adopted budget; fiscal year 1985 employment figures are for December 1984 as reported by the New York City Office of Management and Budget.

ing of why they changed. This, in turn, helps understand how they may change in the future.

Size of the Work Force. The size of the work force is widely perceived as being determined by the availability of revenues. When revenues are growing, it is assumed that employment will rise; when resources decline, it is expected that employment will fall. Indeed, when the City's revenues decreased in the mid-1970s, employment did fall; and as the City moved from fiscal crisis to recovery, employment increased. But revenue and employment trends do not necessarily move in parallel or even similar directions because municipal spending priorities may change. The value accorded staff may rise or fall independently of the supply of resources, since expenditures for staff compete with other purposes of public expenditure, including compensating the work force.

Table 6.1 shows changes in municipal staffing during the 1970–85 period and changes in real (or inflation-adjusted) total expenditures.[2] The correlation between employment and expenditures is not close. In the 1970–75 period, real spending rose a wholesome 23 percent, but employment rose only 4 percent. In the next five years, when employment declined 20 percent, real spending fell only 10 percent. In periods of both financial growth and financial decline in the 1970s, other purposes of public expenditure were valued more highly than maintaining or expanding the size of the work force. In the 1980–85 period, employment rose 10 percent, but spending was stable; in this later period, employment was valued more highly than in the 1970s.

The figures in Table 6.1 also highlight another determinant of municipal staffing policy. In fiscal year 1974, the number of employees rose 5 percent, but real spending was kept stable. In fiscal year 1978, in the midst of the New York City fiscal crisis, real spending declined 1 percent, but employment rose more than 3 percent. In fiscal year 1982, another year when real spending was kept stable, employment rose 2 percent. A mayoral election was held during each of these fiscal years; in the years immediately following, employment declined. Staffing levels in fiscal years 1986 and 1987 will provide further evidence to test the proposition that the size of the work force is affected by elected officials' quadrennial imperative to use clearly temporary staff additions to improve their odds of being reelected.

TABLE 6.2

Employment by Agency, City of New York, Fiscal Years 1970, 1975, 1980, and 1985

Agency	Percentage Distribution				Percentage Change		
	1970	1975	1980	1985	1970–75	1975–80	1980–85
Total Employment	100.0%	100.0%	100.0%	100.0%	3.9%	−20.0%	+10.0%
Major Tax Levy Agencies	53.8	47.4	52.8	52.5	−7.9	−10.9	9.4
Education	30.1	25.0	30.9	30.4	−13.6	−1.2	8.2
Police	12.6	12.5	11.7	12.1	2.8	−24.9	13.9
Fire	5.6	4.9	5.4	5.4	−8.5	−11.6	9.3
Sanitation	5.6	5.0	4.8	4.6	−7.0	−23.3	6.7
Hospitals and Welfare	24.3	26.9	26.7	27.0	15.1	−20.4	10.0
HHC	14.6	16.4	17.1	17.3	16.8	−16.3	11.3
HRA	9.7	10.5	9.6	10.0	12.4	−26.8	10.3
City University	5.5	7.0	2.1	1.5	31.5	−76.1	−22.1
Other Large Agencies	11.9	11.2	12.1	12.9	−2.1	−13.3	17.0
Corrections	1.3	1.5	2.1	3.0	19.2	7.8	58.6
Environmental Protection	1.8	1.7	1.9	1.8	−3.4	−10.1	7.3
Housing Preservation	1.9	1.5	1.5	1.3	−19.6	−18.1	4.1
Transportation	2.0	1.9	2.4	2.4	1.4	−0.4	8.4
General Services	1.5	1.2	1.2	1.2	−14.1	−23.1	12.4
Parks	2.1	1.6	1.7	1.7	−18.4	−14.2	9.2
Health	1.7	1.7	1.4	1.5	8.3	−37.6	20.3
All Others	4.1	7.5	6.2	6.1	89.5	−33.6	8.6

SOURCE: See Table 6.1.

NOTE: Columns may not add due to rounding.

Functional Distribution of the Work Force. The distribution of employment among competing municipal agencies also reflects a variety of factors. Intergovernmental policies may mandate certain staffing decisions; but at other times higher levels of government provide unrestricted aid that increases local discretion. The independent or semiautonomous legal status of some local agencies may enable them to resist the control of municipal officials better than other agencies. But these structural variables are not always dispositive. The mix of staffing, like staffing levels, may change because municipal leaders alter their priorities. They may allocate workers based on changes in the demand for a service or in the productivity with which a service is delivered, or they may choose not to recognize such considerations, preferring to "muddle through" and allocate workers on an "equal shares" basis.

The trends in municipal employment, summarized in Table 6.2, indicate that City officials do alter service priorities. Municipal employment is concentrated in a relatively few agencies. In 1970, seven agencies accounted for about 80 percent of all municipal employees. Four of these agencies—the Board of Education and the departments of Police, Fire, and Sanitation—are "tax-levy" agencies, financed largely by local revenues. The three other large agencies in 1970, the Health and Hospitals Corporation (HHC), Human Resources Administration (HRA), and the Board of Higher Education (CUNY), received substantial shares of their funds in the form of intergovernmental aid.

The four major tax-levy agencies provided 54 percent of the total employment in 1970 compared to 30 percent for the three "intergovernmental" agencies. By 1975, the comparable figures were 47 percent and 34 percent. The HHC, HRA, and CUNY added 14,860 employees between 1970 and 1975; the remainder of the municipal bureaucracy shrank. This appreciation of employment in the hospitals, welfare, and higher-education agencies reflected a relatively rapid growth in intergovernmental aid during this period. However, local priorities were not static. Municipal officials revised their employment priorities within the tax-levy agencies between 1970 and 1975. The Board of Education staff was decreased from 30 percent to 25 percent of total employment.

The mix of municipal employment changed again after the fiscal crisis of 1975. Agencies with declining employment shares during the period included two of the large tax-levy agencies (Police and

Sanitation) and HRA. Employment at CUNY dropped dramatically because in 1976 the State began to assume responsibility for operating senior colleges, shifting many workers from municipal to State payrolls. The only agency that grew in absolute terms was the Department of Corrections, the growth of which reflected increased demand for jail space and federal judicial mandates to expand staffing to constitutionally acceptable standards.

In contrast to the previous periods, the mix of municipal employment remained relatively stable after work force expansion began again in 1980. In both 1980 and 1985, the four major tax-levy agencies accounted for 53 percent of the staff; the combined employment share in HHC and HRA stayed at 27 percent. Corrections employment was increased 59 percent due to continued federal court orders to improve jail conditions, but, in general, City officials opted to increase employment after 1980 in a way that was much closer to an across-the-board approach than was evident in earlier periods of expansion and contraction.

FUTURE EMPLOYMENT POLICIES

The recovery from the fiscal crisis and recent growth in spending provide municipal officials a more stable environment than existed in the 1970s within which to plan and implement staffing policies. Since there is wide agreement that municipal government should provide improved services, particularly as its financial resources grow, the City's goal is not in question.

The Size of the Work Force. The Executive Budget for fiscal year 1986 projects year-end employment of about 267,000, a target that would increase staffing nearly 6 percent over 1985. This would represent the largest percentage increase in employment in the post-1970 period. However, 1986 employment still would represent only 91 percent of the 1974 employment peak of 293,000. The City's longer-term staffing policies cannot be identified because the four-year financial planning process does not include staffing projections over a number of years. Presumably, given projected increases in available resources, staff expansion will continue.

Whether the City should continue to increase employment is a different issue than whether it will. A larger work force will not necessarily produce more and better services because it may be less productive. At some point, the costs of obtaining incremental service improvements by expanding the work force will outweigh the benefits. How soon that occurs will depend in part on municipal policies on wages and productivity.

The Mix of Employment. The expansion of the work force since 1980 has been allocated on a basis that is closer to "equal shares" among agencies than was the case in earlier periods of change. Except for corrections, no major municipal agency experienced a change in its share of total employment of more than one-half of one percentage point. (Refer to Table 6.2.) The 1986 Executive Budget continues this pattern, although police employment also is projected to grow at a somewhat faster rate than employment in most of the other major agencies. In this sense, there is a priority for criminal-justice agencies—police and corrections—in the most recent years.

Across-the-board expansion of the work force has all the virtues of incremental decision-making: simplicity for planners, conflict avoidance among competing agency managers, the appearance of fairness to different service constituencies. But it has all the vices, too. The demand for some services is growing, for others declining. Some services are being delivered more productively, others less. Raising employment on an across-the-board basis is a blunt policy.

WAGE POLICIES

Determining how much to pay municipal employees is a second major issue related to human resource management. Municipal wage decisions involve issues that are similar in kind to those City officials must consider in formulating employment policy. These decisions determine whether or not the real pay of employees is to increase or fall; and unless the salaries of all employees are to rise in (percentage) tandem, decisions must be reached about how to differentiate among categories of employees.

Because the City's financial resources are finite, municipal wage and staffing policies are interdependent. Increases in municipal wages reduce the funds available to finance staff increases, and vice versa. The interdependence of wage and staffing policies suggests that municipal officials should consider them in concert, and attempt to strike a purposeful balance in allocating funds between the numbers of workers and their pay. If more staff is desired, for example, it is essential not to use all available funds for higher wages; if pay is too low to attract a qualified work force, it is important not to use all available funds to add more staff. However, striking the appropriate balance is difficult because the process by which staffing decisions are reached differs from the process by which wage decisions are reached—in time, space, and managerial control. Staffing policies generally are decided when the City's budget is formulated and are within the control of municipal officials; wage policies, in contrast, may not be established when the City's budget is formulated (indeed, usually are not), and are determined in collective bargaining between officials and municipal-union leaders. City officials may be in a stronger bargaining position when revenues are in short supply, but even then determining wages is a bilateral rather than a unilateral process.

PAST PAY POLICIES

Before examining past municipal wage policies, it is useful to review the structural characteristics of collective bargaining. These arrangements help shape policies establishing how the City's funds for wages are allocated among employee groups.[3]

When collective bargaining for municipal employees was introduced in the early 1960s, it ended an "administered" wage-setting system whereby the Board of Estimate, usually acting on recommendations of the Department of Personnel, established pay rates unilaterally. Municipal workers and their leaders were not without influence in the Board of Estimate, but their role and influence was increased after the introduction of collective bargaining.

Collective bargaining required that union officials be granted the right of exclusive recognition for bargaining units that numbered hundreds initially. Aside from the time involved in bargaining with so many units and translating agreements into legal contracts, bargaining was complicated by competition among union representatives who sought to outdo one another at the collective bargaining table. In response to these demands, negotiators adopted certain simplifications. To cut their work, negotiators adopted the practice of entering into multiyear contracts, usually for two years; this

TABLE 6.3

Pay Relationships among Selected New York City Municipal Employee Groups, Fiscal Years 1970–84

	Police Officer 1st Grade		Sanitationman 1st Grade		Lower Paid Civilian		Higher Paid Civilian	
	Basic Salary	Added Cash	Basic Salary	Added Cash	Basic Salary	Added Cash	Basic Salary	Added Cash
1970	$10,425	—	$ 9,383	—	$ 6,667	—	$13,334	—
1971	10,950	—	9,855	—	7,200	—	14,400	—
1972	12,800	—	11,520	—	7,704	-	15,408	—
1973	13,550	—	12,195	—	8,243	—	16,487	—
1974	15,000	—	13,500	—	8,737	—	17,474	—
1975	16,470	—	14,823	—	9,436	—	18,872	—
1976	17,458	$ 220	15,712	$ 220	10,000	$ 220	20,000	$ 220
1977	17,458	641	15,712	641	10,000	590	20,000	590
1978	17,458	1,113	15,712	1,113	10,000	1,062	20,000	1,062
1979	17,458	1,191	15,712	1,191	10,000	1,140	20,000	1,140
1980	18,597	750	16,782	750	10,841	750	21,241	750
1981	21,082	750	19,024	750	12,177	750	23,858	750
1982	22,769	750	20,546	3,045	13,151	750	25,767	750
1983	25,401	—	23,000	2,550	13,901	—	26,517	—
1984	27,433	—	24,840	2,550	16,064	—	30,643	—
Percentage Increase								
1970–75	58.0%		58.0%		41.5%		41.5%	
1975–79	6.0		6.0		6.0		6.0	
1979–84	57.1		58.1		60.6		53.2	
1970–84	163.1		164.7		140.9		129.8	

SOURCES: Salary and added cash data provided by the New York City Office of Municipal Labor Relations, except that added cash data for sanitationman in 1982, 1983, and 1984 were provided by Program Planners Inc.

NOTES: Basic salary rates are for July 1 of each fiscal year; civilian salary data for 1970–74 period are based on the most common civilian settlement for those years; the 1976 wage increase was deferred, in whole or in part depending on the employee's salary, but is credited to 1976 because the deferred amounts were repaid in accord with a negotiated settlement; in 1980 and 1983, employees had $441 and $750, respectively, added to their base pay for purposes of computing that year's percentage salary increase; added cash for sanitationmen in 1982, 1983, and 1984 includes bonuses paid according to a gainsharing agreement of $2295, $2550 and $2550, respectively.

helped separate determination of wage policy from staffing policy, as well as from the larger budgetary process.

A second set of customs were based on rules designed to regulate conflict over the allocation of wages. This issue posed few problems with respect to uniformed personnel (police, fire, sanitation, and correctional personnel, plus Housing Authority and Transit Authority police). Parity rules long had existed for uniformed personnel; they were simply continued under collective bargaining. The basic salaries of all uniformed employees were linked in fixed ratios that applied vertically within a single uniformed agency (from entry level through various superior officer positions) and horizontally across the uniformed agencies. This meant that once a settlement was reached for a single uniformed bargaining unit (usually the entry-level positions in either the Police Department or Fire Department), its terms would be extended throughout the uniformed work force. Thus, uniformed workers' salaries rose in lock-step fashion, preserving the salary ratios. (Pay for sanitation workers equaled about 90 percent of the pay for other uniformed personnel.)

No precise parity rules existed for other groups, however. In the early years of collective bargaining, conflict over pay relationships among civilian bargaining units complicated negotiations. Gradually, the practice of "pattern bargaining" emerged whereby civilian units generally (though not always) received the same percentage salary increase. However, the civilian pay increases typically were lower than the uniformed settlements.

In sum, by 1970 the general rules for distributing salary increases to the unionized work force were as follows. Employees are divided into two broad groups on the basis of whether or not they wear uniforms to work; those who wear uniforms are treated better. This "uniformed preference" rule caused the salaries of uniformed workers increasingly to exceed those of lower-paid civilian workers and to approach (and perhaps pass) those of higher-paid civilian employees.

Wage Allocation Policies. Table 6.3 shows the uniformed-preference rule in operation between 1970 and 1975. Salaries of uniformed personnel, including sanitation workers, rose 58 percent. Salaries for typical lower-paid and higher-paid civilian workers rose 42 percent.

In the 1975–79 period, however, an "equal shares" rule was substituted for the uniformed preference rule in municipal wage policy. All unionized employees were treated alike in the sense that identical salary increases preserved the pay relationships that obtained in 1975. Salaries were increased 6 percent across the board in 1976 and then were frozen through the next three fiscal years.[4]

Another principle to establish pay rates was followed during the 1975–79 period, but it was implemented outside of the basic salary structure. Beginning in 1976 (and continuing through 1982), employees received "added cash" in the form of various cost-of-living adjustments and bonuses that were nearly uniform, regardless of uniformed status or salaries.[5] Thus, payment of added cash rather than basic wages resulted in a "progressivity rule" that increased earnings of lower-paid workers relative to higher-paid workers.

In the 1979–84 period, another allocation rule was established through collective bargaining. The basic salaries of lower-paid workers were increased faster than those of higher-paid workers. In essence, the progressivity rule previously adopted to provide added cash was extended to basic salary relationships. This rule obtained despite the fact that uniformed employees' contracts conveyed a higher percentage increase than did civilian employees' contracts in two of the five years. This was made possible through flat payments ($441 in 1980 and $750 in 1983) added to the basic salaries of all employees. Lower-paid civilians enjoyed 61 percent salary increases between 1979 and 1984, followed by sanitation workers (58 percent), police officers (57 percent), and higher-paid civilians (53 percent). This new practice also broke preexisting par-

TABLE 6.4

Percentage Change in Real Salaries of Selected Uniformed and Civilian Employees of the City of New York, Selected Periods, 1970–84

Employee Groups	1970–75	1975–80	1980–84
Police Officer 1st Grade	13.5%	−18.5%	9.2%
Sanitationman	13.5	−18.3	9.6
Lower-Paid Civilian	1.7	−17.1	9.7
Higher-Paid Civilian	1.7	−18.7	6.8

SOURCE: Basic salary data are from Table 6.3 adjusted for price changes by the U.S. Department of Commerce, Bureau of Labor Statistics, Consumer Price Index for All Urban Consumers (CPI-U) in the New York-Northeastern New Jersey area.

ity rules among uniformed workers. Sanitation salaries moved closer to other entry-level uniformed salaries, and entry-level uniformed workers in the other services gained relative to their superior officers.

Note also that sanitation personnel received more "added cash" in 1982 than other employees and continued to receive additional payments of $2550 in 1983 and in 1984. These sums represent bonus payments made under a "gainsharing" plan (discussed more fully below) whereby sanitation workers received bonuses for each shift they worked on two-man as opposed to three-man sanitation trucks. When these bonuses are added to their base pay, the earnings of sanitation workers nearly equal the basic salary of other entry-level uniformed personnel.

To summarize, the rules for distributing salary increases to municipal workers have changed repeatedly since 1970. Initially, uniformed workers were favored over civilians; then all unionized workers were given similar percentage increases. More recently, wage discrimination was based on relative income; later, an additional basis for distinguishing among employees was productivity.

Real Wage Policies. Changes also occurred in the extent to which municipal wage policy protected the salaries of City employees from inflation. In the first half of the 1970s, all City employees received real wage gains (see Table 6.4). However, the salaries of uniformed workers were increased eight times faster than those of civilians in real terms. The preference for uniformed employees reflected more than a judgment that they were more "valuable" or more "deserving" than civilians. Partly, these divergent wage trends reflected the general chaos in municipal labor relations in the early 1970s. The extraordinary increase in uniformed salaries was caused in part by the City agreeing to pay them a large, one-time salary increase in order to reestablish a set of parity relationships broken by an earlier negotiating debacle (for the City) that created two inconsistent sets of parity rules. A potential series of increases in uniformed salaries arising from the inconsistency was foreclosed by the one-time bonus.[6]

After the fiscal crisis, the policy of raising real pay changed abruptly. Wages fell sharply from 1975 to 1980, when they began to rise again. In the 1980–84 period, all employees received real wage increases; however, lower-paid civilian salaries, reflecting the progressivity rule, rose the most (9.7 percent), followed by sanitation workers (9.6 percent), police officers (9.2 percent), and higher-paid civilians (6.8 percent). It is worth adding that collectively bargained wage policies "spill over" to salaries for managerial employees. The City's practice is to apply civilian settlements to managerial salaries. In this context, the progressivity rule reduces the differences in salaries between managers and their subordinates.

Confusion after 1984. The events surrounding negotiations for a contract beginning in fiscal year 1985 indicate the City may be entering a collective bargaining era with confusion approaching that of the early 1970s. When negotiations for a new contract began in 1984, the City offered successive salary increases of 2 percent for 1985 and 1986. The City's offer was raised to 3 percent after fiscal year 1985 began. These offers signaled the City's intent to return to an "equal shares" method of allocating wage increases and to discontinue the practice of increasing real wages (since inflation rates between 4 and 5 percent were projected for 1985 and 1986). These proposed changes in policy, coupled with a decline in the cohesion of the coalitions of uniformed and civilian workers, caused wage negotiations to be stalemated through the first six months of fiscal year 1985. The City eventually petitioned for arbitrated settlements. This was another policy change; the City (and unions) had eschewed arbitration for a decade.

Shortly after the arbitration was requested, the City announced a three-year settlement with the leadership of the firefighters' union that would have continued to raise real salaries. The proposed contract granted pay increases of approximately 6 percent annually over the three-year period. The City then assumed in its preliminary budget for fiscal year 1986 that uniformed salaries would increase 6 percent and civilian salaries 4.5 percent. Leaders of the civilian unions then proclaimed they would not settle for less than uniformed personnel and thereby revert to the "second class" status they had not experienced for a decade. Leaders of the other uniformed unions urged the rank-and-file firefighters to reject the proposed settlement, claiming that they could negotiate a better settlement under a united front of all uniformed workers. The fire-fighters voted against the proposed contract in February 1985. At this point, the City again petitioned for arbitration. Mayor Edward I. Koch stated that the City no longer could afford the 6 percent increase he already had agreed to with one union and already had budgeted for in the January 1985 financial plan. Thus, City officials neared the end of fiscal year 1985 and initiated planning for fiscal year 1986 with no clear definition of municipal wage policy for the past and future, no firm date of when it would be determined, and not certain whether it would be decided by negotiation or arbitration.

FUTURE WAGE POLICY

Given the events described above, there is no basis (at this writing) for deciphering what present wage policy is or predicting what it is likely to be. But future options may be identified on the basis of past policies. One option is to treat all employees alike, that is, to allocate salary increases on an "equal shares" basis. A second option is to discriminate among workers on some basis. One such basis used in the past was the clothes employees wear to work. This approach favored uniformed employees. A second basis of discrimination had been based on an employee's relative income. This approach favored low-paid workers. A third basis for differential treatment, which has been applied to sanitation workers, was related to productivity.

Municipal wage policies that treat all employees as an undifferentiated mass are convenient, but inefficient. Wage rules based on clothing are more discriminating, but no less inefficient; the same may be said of wage rules that favor lower-paid workers (and that, over time, would cause the pay of messengers to near that of managers). Paying employees on the basis of productivity is a more rational basis for wage discrimination. Pay rules based on productivity would stimulate and reward arrangements similar to the gain-sharing plan by paying bonuses outside of the regular salary structure. Another variation of the rule based on productivity pay would raise basic salaries for those in positions whose salaries are too low to attract enough qualified applicants.

In addition, future wage policies will be made to decide whether to reduce, maintain, or increase workers' real pay. Since 1980, the City has increased the real wages of low-paid civilians and uniformed employees more than 2 percent a year. The rationale for this policy was that real wages should be restored to the levels they had been at before the fiscal crisis.

The case for not continuing to increase the real pay of municipal workers, except where justified by productivity considerations, rests in part on its implications for future productivity gains. An examination of municipal productivity policies is in order before returning to consideration of future wage and staffing options.

PRODUCTIVITY POLICIES

Productivity gains are desirable because they permit service enhancements without staff expansion. This frees funds for other purposes, including higher pay. It is paradoxical that something as desirable as productivity improvement is so difficult to achieve. Since 1970, the City's productivity programs have focused almost exclusively on improvements in the utilization or management of municipal employees. Improvement of the quality of the work force, another way to increase productivity, has received little consideration by the City.

HUMAN RESOURCE MANAGEMENT

The premise underlying efforts to utilize staff resources more efficiently is that people do not work up to their potential. The means of improving management of an organization's human resources are well known. They include the introduction of technology, the rationalization of goals and the methods of accomplishing them, and increasing motivation—all things, according to the traditional view, that "managers" should do to narrow the gap between the actual and potential performance of workers.

Problems abound with this approach to human resource management. One problem arises if managers are not up to the task. Frequently, the inability of managers to narrow the gap between their own actual and optimal performance is a major reason why workers do not realize their potential. Also, workers have a stake in how they are utilized, substantial insight into how they could be utilized better, and substantial discretion to do as they please in any event.[7] The City's "street-level" bureaucrats do not produce widgets on an assembly line; they deliver a wide range of services through day-to-day contact with residents under conditions that make supervision difficult. These realities—one involving the quality of the City's managers, the other labor's role in human resource management—have shaped the City's productivity programs since 1970 and will continue to do so in the future.

Past Policies. The task of analyzing the City's efforts to manage its human resources more effectively during a complex period covering four different administrations is eased by Mary McCormick's work.[8] She developed a typology of the City's productivity programs, described their history in the 1970s, and evaluated their accomplishments. This study provides a basis for evaluating municipal productivity efforts since 1980 and for assessing the City's future options.

McCormick distinguished between productivity programs that rely on "management initiatives" and those that require "labor-management" interaction. An early example of the latter, during the second administration of Mayor John V. Lindsay, was the City's attempt to justify increases in real wages by "buying out" inefficient work rules in collective bargaining. That program proved to be a better vehicle for increasing real wages than improving productivity.[9]

A second major labor-management program, the Productivity-COLA program initiated in 1976, sought to devise a justification for paying cost-of-living adjustments when wages were frozen during the fiscal crisis. This program worked in the sense that it provided a rationale for such payments in the 1976–78 period; like the earlier program, however, it did not yield productivity gains.[10] After 1978, the pretense of the Productivity-COLA program was dropped; added cash payments were made through 1982 without the need to argue that productivity gains were involved. Subsequent wage negotiations have agreed to salary increases without linking them to productivity "buy-outs" or "give-backs."

Management-initiated productivity programs were less focused than the labor-management programs in the 1970s. One line of programs recognized that the quality of the City's managers inhibited their potential to utilize staff more productively and sought "structural" changes to help develop better managers. The last example of such an approach was introduced in 1979 when Mayor Edward I. Koch unsuccessfully attempted to persuade the State legislature to modify civil service rules he believed limited the number of managers over whom he could assert effective control. In 1977, a group appointed by Mayor Abraham D. Beame, the Mayor's Management Advisory Board, had recommended that the City develop a greater sense of "identification" among its managers by changing their recruitment, pay, selection, and evaluation.[11] These two efforts followed a recommendation of the State Charter Revision Commission, made in 1974 and approved by referendum in 1975, to create a Management Service (discussed below). Attempts to improve the quality of the City's managers by structural solutions ranging from charter reform to civil-service reform have borne little fruit.

The second type of management-initiated productivity program in the 1970s was designed to upgrade the quality of managerial performance rather than the quality of managers per se. These initiatives were begun in the second Lindsay administration with an attempt to develop productivity measures for selected services. After the fiscal crisis, these efforts were expanded and received institutional embodiment in 1977 with creation of an Office of Operations responsible for developing a management information and reporting system. The Office of Operations was assigned responsibility for preparing the *Mayor's Management Report*, another charter mandate resulting from the previously noted State Charter Revision Commission. If a managerial class did not emerge from efforts at structural reform in the 1970s, at least the City's managers ended the decade with more systematic information upon which to act (no small achievement in a government that could not identify how much money it was spending or how many people it was employing when the fiscal crisis began).

In reviewing the City's productivity record in both management-initiated and labor-management programs, McCormick concluded

TABLE 6.5
Productivity and Management Improvements in the City of New York, Fiscal Years 1983–86
(millions of dollars)

	1983		1984		1985		1986	
	Amount	Percentage	Amount	Percentage	Amount	Percentage	Amount	Percentage
Adjusted Expenditures[a]	$13,882	100.0%	$14,530	100.0%	$15,979	100.0%	$17,797	100.0%
PEG Plans	854	6.2	1,068	7.4	463	2.9	407	2.3
State or Federal Actions	297	2.1	120	0.8	220	1.4	200	1.1
City Actions	557	4.0	948	6.5	243	1.5	207	1.2
PMI Plans	158	1.1	214	1.5	63	0.4	105	0.6
PMI Achievement	139	1.0	94	0.6	63	0.4	N.A.	N.A.
Cumulative PMI Achievement[b]	139	1.0	272	1.9	309	1.9	N.A.	N.A.

SOURCES: Adjusted expenditures and PMI achievements for 1983 and 1984 from New York State Financial Control Board, *The New York City Productivity Program*, annual reviews, 1983 and 1984; adjusted expenditures for 1985 and 1986, and 1985 PMI achievement and cumulative achievement figures, provided by Financial Control Board staff; PEG program plans and PMI plans from City of New York, *Financial Plans*, fiscal years 1982–86 through 1985–89; cumulative PMI achievement figures for 1983 and 1984 from City of New York, *Financial Plan, Fiscal Years 1985–89*, addendum.

a. Adjusted expenditures exclude debt service and general reserves.

b. PMI achievements do not cumulate precisely because their carryover savings change over time.

that they accomplished little in the way of direct productivity gains. They did, however, provide a foundation for the development of productivity programs in the 1980s.

Since 1980, the City has pursued productivity improvement in straightforward fashion informed by past failures. With one failed exception, the City has not attempted to achieve productivity gains in general wage bargaining.[12] Nor has it attempted to create a larger, more responsive managerial class by civil service reform. The City's major productivity program has involved the annual Program to Eliminate the Gap (PEG).

Each January, the City releases its preliminary budget for the next fiscal year, the centerpiece of the four-year financial planning process that emerged in response to the fiscal crisis. Pursuant to the methodologies employed by the City to forecast revenues and expenditures, the City's preliminary budget identifies a "gap" accompanied by a Program to Eliminate the Gap (or PEG program). It identifies intergovernmental aid that would contribute to closing the gap, but "City Actions" typically is the larger of the two PEG components. City actions are divided into three categories: Productivity and Management Improvements (PMIs), other expenditure actions, and other revenue actions. The PMI category provides a useful basis for evaluating productivity initiatives because it involves only actions that permit services to be maintained at lower cost or improved for the same cost. The two other categories involve actions that contribute to closing the gap by cutting services or raising revenues. Thus, they are not regarded as productivity gains.

Table 6.5 traces changes in the City's PEG programs in the 1983–86 period (earlier data are not comparable), and shows the contribution of PMI plans and achievements to closing the gap.[13] Improvements in the City's finances are evident in the declining shares of expenditure represented by the PEG program and by City actions in particular. Productivity and management initiatives, both planned and achieved, also have declined. Most significant for this analysis is the relative insignificance of the PMI programs. In 1983, 1984, and 1985, they accounted, respectively, for 1 percent, 0.6 percent, and 0.4 percent of adjusted municipal expenditures (excluding nonoperational allocations for debt service and the general reserve).

The City's candid explanation for the declining importance of the PMI program is that "new agency PMIs are becoming harder to come by."[14] About $60 million of the $105 million PMI total planned for fiscal year 1986 would come from improved tax enforcement efforts of the Finance Department, and $5 million would be realized from other revenue enhancements. Only $40 million would result from savings due to improvements in productivity in the operating agencies. In an organization that will spend $18 billion to deliver services and will employ more than a quarter-million persons, how is it possible not to plan productivity savings greater than one-fifth of one percent of operating expenditures and averaging only approximately $150 per employee?

The answer is that in recent years the City's managers have exhausted their "easy marks," those productivity gains they could implement on their own initiative, and have been unwilling to take on harder—but perhaps more important—initiatives requiring basic changes in the work patterns of unionized civil servants. The major exception is the previously mentioned gainsharing program, under which important productivity gains were realized in refuse collection.

Future Options. The City's record of achieving productivity improvements by utilizing the work force better is modest, at best, and its plans for 1986 continue that pattern. Review of past policies suggests that labor-management initiatives involving delivery of major municipal services—education, police, fire, sanitation, social services, health and hospitals—are desirable. But consider how the City's human resource management affects its productivity record and potential. Managers have little incentive to undertake the hard job of attempting to utilize the work force differently because workforce expansion promises the opportunity to enhance services without doing so; civil servants have little incentive to work differently because municipal wage policy promises them rising real-wage gains without doing so. Continuation of the City's productivity program in the context of the annual PEG program promises small gains, particularly if past staffing and wage policies are continued.

An alternative approach is to fashion staffing and wage policies that encourage productivity gains achieved by labor-management initiatives. Before considering the relationships among staffing, wages, and manpower utilization further, one often-forgotten dimension of productivity policy warrants brief discussion.

HUMAN RESOURCE DEVELOPMENT

The assumption underlying attempts to improve the quality of the City's human resources is straightforward. Otherwise similar organizations will exhibit productivity differences based on the quality of their workers. Thus, an organization that is able to upgrade its human resources can expect to benefit from increased productivity.

The means by which the City can accomplish this goal are the same means available to other organizations. The City can attract qualified applicants for its positions; it can select the right people to hire or promote, to demote or dismiss; it can train the work force to perform better.

The potential benefit from successful implementation of these strategies appears substantial. The City of New York is able to draw applicants from a metropolitan labor force of unmatched size, diversity, and quality. Based on current rates of attrition and a work force of constant size, the City will have the opportunity in the next four years to hire more than 80,000 new employees, to promote tens of thousands of people from among this group and its able current employees, and to train more than a quarter of a million human beings in ways that could make them both richer and more productive. Not to focus on this general approach to improving the work force and, by extension, the services it produces seems at odds with many desirable things. Why have municipal policy makers resisted the approach?

Past Policies. An answer to that question is suggested by turning the clock back to 1954. In that year, the City's Charter was amended to create a Department of Personnel following recommendations of successive commissions.[15] The Department was to be separated from the City's Civil Service Commission, headed by a director appointed by the mayor (who would be chairman of the three-member Civil Service Commission and an advisor of standing in the mayor's cabinet). It was assigned a broad range of responsibilities for personnel administration. The administrative theory underlying its creation was that the civil service system had grown so cumbersome in pursuit of protecting civil servants from arbitrary managerial behavior, the original purpose of the merit system of personnel administration, that it did not meet the growing need of the municipal government for a more "responsive" civil service. The political reality, however, was quite different. What quickly became clear was that a centralized personnel system had no client within government, including the mayors for whom it was created.

Most explanations for the demise of the Personnel Department begin with the attitudes and actions of budget officials in the 1950s and 1960s.[16] They viewed the centralized civil service administration, particularly the scheduling and conduct of examinations and making appointments therefrom, as interfering with their ability to regulate expenditures. Budget directors were joined in attack by heads of operating agencies. Frustrated with the Personnel Department's pace in producing candidates for jobs (which was partly the budget bureau's responsibility), and with civil service rules that forced them to select the top scorer on examinations, agency heads appointed employees on a provisional basis. But budget directors and commissioners are agents of mayors who permitted the former to block appointments from civil service lists and the latter to appoint workers outside of the civil service system.

In his last term, Mayor Robert F. Wagner, Jr. supported the introduction of collective bargaining, thereby eliminating the Personnel Department's role in pay administration and reducing its role as protector of civil servants in grievance administration and other functions. Mayor John V. Lindsay, who succeeded Wagner, permitted large numbers of provisional appointments. By the late 1960s, the experiment with centralized personnel administration was a failure, primarily because the City's chief executives failed to support the Personnel Department.

In the early 1970s, another generation of municipal reformers addressed the problem, this time through the State Charter Revision Commission. Its 1974 recommendations, approved by referendum in 1975, rested on two basic findings. First, the mayor lacked an effective managerial service; second, the civil service system was not responsive to the needs of the City's operating agencies. Findings similar to those of the earlier charter reformers produced a different recommendation: Shift the responsibility for personnel administration to the operating agencies.[17]

The fiscal crisis intervened, preventing the transition from a centralized to a decentralized personnel system. For the next several years, municipal priorities focused on other issues, including cutting employment and real wages. The impact of these and other policies on the quality of the work force was seldom questioned, least of all by the Personnel Department. In the late 1970s, Mayor Koch tried to convince the State legislature that the number and authority of municipal managers were inadequate, and that relief from restrictive civil service laws would improve the situation; the City's municipal unions prevented his proposal from reaching the floor of either the Assembly or the Senate. Since then, municipal officials have tried to beat the system rather than change it.[18]

Future Options. Based on the past record, there are a number of approaches that could be taken to improve the quality of the municipal work force. One option is to rebuild the Personnel Department. It now is unable to capitalize on available recruitment, selection, and training opportunities. An alternative is to learn from the failure of centralized personnel administration and follow the spirit of the City Charter by devolving the primary responsibility for personnel administration to the operating agencies.

Another option is to revamp the City's civil service exams, for both entry-level positions and promotions, to ensure that they test applicants for relevant skills in a nondiscriminatory fashion. Testing is one of the most nettlesome problems in personnel administration; however, if the civil service system is to be continued, the integrity of its central function should be beyond reproach. This is not the case in the City of New York, as attested by a string of law suits challenging (often successfully) the legitimacy of many of its civil service tests.

A third option involves the City's managers. In 1980, 2 percent of the employees of mayoral agencies were managers not represented by unions for collective bargaining; in 1984, the comparable figure also was two percent.[19] The management of the City probably would be improved by reducing the ratio of unionized civil servants to managers below 50-to-one. The leadership of the Metropolitan Transportation Authority and New York City Transit Authority successfully won reforms in the civil service and union systems in 1985 that increased the number of managerial employees over whom they could exercise control. Mayor Koch supported this initiative. The next administration might profit from pursuing the same policy for the City.

A final option to improve the quality of the work force is to raise managerial pay more rapidly than was done in recent years. Managerial salaries do not lend themselves to the same kind of analysis as civil service salaries because the Managerial Pay Plan has multiple grades or levels to which managers can be promoted. In recent years, salaries under the Managerial Pay Plan have been raised in proportion to the civilian pattern. As noted previously, this effectively has reduced the difference between the pay of managers and of their subordinates.

CONCLUSION

Discontinuity and contradiction are recurring characteristics of the human resource management policies of the City of New York. Employment rose and then fell sharply in the 1970s; so, too, did the real wages of municipal employees. Abrupt changes in the City's financial condition contributed to swings in policies affecting human resources, but so did structural features of municipal management. Total municipal employment grew prior to the fiscal crisis because staff increases in three agencies supported primarily with intergovernmental funds more than offset employment declines in the remainder of the municipal work force; in the same period, the real wages of uniformed workers rose eight times faster than those of civilian workers, an outcome that reflected municipal officials' difficulties in adjusting to the nascent institution of collective bargaining.

In the 1980s, the City's human resource management policies have exhibited less discontinuity: Staffing has increased steadily; real wages have increased steadily; productivity gains as reflected in the annual PMIs have declined steadily. The City's poor productivity record is due, at least in part, to staffing and wage policies that reduce managerial and worker incentives to improve productivity. Future discontinuity is likely. The next administration will

TABLE 6.6
Residents per Municipal Employee, Selected Years 1970–86

	1970	1974	1980	1985	1986
Residents per Employee	29	26	31	28	26
Adjusted Residents per Employee[a]	30	28	32	28	27

SOURCES: For 1970, 1974, 1980, and 1985, employment data used to compute the ratios are the same as those in Table 6.1; 1986 employment figures from City of New York, *Executive Budget, Fiscal Year 1986, Message of the Mayor,* May 3, 1985; population data used in the 1970, 1974, and 1980 computations are from U.S. Department of Commerce, Bureau of the Census, *Current Population Reports,* with the 1975 reported population used for the 1974 calculation; 1985 and 1986 ratios computed on the basis of the 1984 population estimate provided by the staff of the National Planning Association.

a. This ratio is derived by subtracting the number of employees of the Board of Higher Education from the total number of municipal employees.

find it increasingly difficult to continue building a larger and better-paid, but less productive, work force. Alternative policies to resolve the key issues of staffing, wages, and productivity could improve and expand services in a less costly fashion.

STAFFING POLICIES

Municipal wage and productivity policies require City managers and employees to initiate change jointly, but elected officials retain primary influence over the size and mix of the work force. Hence, staffing policies are an appropriate place to begin outlining a revised human resource management strategy.

The Size of the Work Force. In the 1980–85 period, the City's policy of work force expansion increased municipal employment an average of 2 percent a year, from 229,000 to 252,000. Implicitly if not explicitly, the City's staffing policies were driven by the desire to restore services to their status before the fiscal crisis. Lacking data on the level and quality of municipal services during that period, City officials used the size of the work force as an indicator of how well restoration of municipal services was proceeding. Given the apparent need to improve services, work force expansion was appropriate. The City plans to accelerate this policy to increase staff to 267,000 in 1986, compared to 275,000 in 1970 and 293,000 at the 1974 high point. The new administration might continue this policy of work-force expansion beyond 1986. Should it, or is it time, to begin enhancing services in other ways?

The rationale for continuing to increase staff in order to restore services to some unknown level and quality is weak. The number of employees delivering municipal services is only one determinant of their level and quality; another is the number of persons to whom services are delivered. While municipal employment is lower in 1986 than in 1974, the population to be served is also smaller. Table 6.6 shows the number of residents per employee for selected years between 1970 and 1986. The first set of ratios are for total population and total municipal employment; the second set of ratios use employment figures that are adjusted for the State's takeover of the CUNY senior colleges during the second half of the 1970s. The 1986 ratio is as low as it was in 1974, when the City had one employee for every 26 residents and is substantially lower than it was in 1970. When staffing for CUNY senior colleges is removed from the equation, the 1986 resident-to-employee ratio (27) is lower than in 1974 (28).

A second variable affecting the relationship between employment and services is the quality of management. It is likely, though dif-

TABLE 6.7

Municipal Employment for Common Functions Per 10,000 Population in New York City Compared to the Average for all Other Cities Over 1,000,000 Population, 1983

Functions	New York City	Other Cities[a]
Police	43.8	41.3
Fire	19.0	15.5
Sanitation	16.3	8.1
Parks & Recreation	6.4	7.0
Financial Administration & Control	15.8	12.6
Highways	9.7	6.4
Total	111.0	90.9

SOURCE: Computed from data in U.S. Department of Commerce, Bureau of the Census, *City Employment in 1983* (GE83-No. 2), Table 4, pp. 6, 11, 15, 19, 21, 23.

a. Includes Chicago, Los Angeles, Philadelphia, Houston, and Detroit.

ficult to document, that services are managed better today than in 1974.[20] From this perspective, the City may not be understaffed relative to the era before the fiscal crisis.

Of course, there is no special reason why the goal of municipal officials should be to restore services to levels and qualities that obtained more than a decade ago. The goal of municipal officials should be to enhance services from the present base. New York is America's preeminent city; its services should be second to none. There are no data that compare service quality in all the cities, but data describing employment relative to population size show how staffing inputs vary among cities. Table 6.7 compares New York City municipal employment per 10,000 population for common functions to the average of the five other United States cities with populations of over 1,000,000. In 1983, the most recent year for which data are available, New York's municipal employment-to-population ratio was lower than the big-city average only in parks and recreation. Overall, New York City's staffing level for common functions was 22 percent higher than the average. Thus, the need to increase the number of municipal employees cannot be well justified either on the basis of restoring earlier service levels or of competing with other areas. Nevertheless, the goal of enhancing services is important. The means, not the end, are the issue.

The Mix of the Work Force. The functional distribution of the municipal work force should be based on three factors: the priority assigned to the service by elected officials, the productivity of the workers, and the level of demand for the service. Other things being equal, the services that officials view as most important should be assigned additional available manpower. But other things—notably productivity in the agencies and citizens' demand for services—are rarely equal. In services like refuse collection, where productivity gains can be accomplished more easily (and more measurably), employment could be reduced; in agencies like the Board of Education, where the relationship between employment and services is more direct, staff could be expanded. Similarly, functions such as social services for children are experiencing a marked increase in demand due to the sad and serious social forces described in Emanuel Tobier's chapter of this volume. In contrast, demand for firefighting services, as evidenced by the incidence of serious fires, is declining. The allocation of manpower should reflect these diverse demand trends.

In recent years, the City's allocation of staff has changed relatively little, except for the mandated increase in the Department of Corrections. Presumably, the incremental allocations reflected the belief that all services were diminished proportionally by the fiscal crisis, and should be restored by proportionate staff additions. The support for both perceptions is shaky. Earlier research indicates that services of some agencies improved while their work force was being reduced; in others, services declined by less than the magnitude implied by their employment reduction.[21]

In sum, establishing service priorities and then staffing agencies in accord with those priorities and with changes in demand and productivity, will achieve more, and more, appropriate services. Controlling employment growth in this fashion is likely to yield two important byproducts. First, it would raise the incentives for agency heads to seek increased productivity, particularly if the policy were accompanied by instructions from the leader of the next administration that better services were expected. Increasing staff without considering these factors provides managers an easy way to enhance services without having to manage better. Second, controlling expansion of the work force in the next four years would save considerable sums of money that could be used for other purposes, including new productivity programs.

PRODUCTIVITY POLICIES

Two means of increasing productivity were surveyed earlier, improving the quality of the work force and improving its utilization or management. Added expenditures and new incentives are required for both.

Upgrading the Quality of the Work Force. Upgrading the quality of the work force involves a set of actions that fall under the heading of personnel administration. The failure of centralized personnel administration in the last three decades suggests that the primary responsibility for most personnel functions should devolve to the operating agencies. If agency heads are to be assigned greater responsibility for improving the management of the work force, it is sensible to assign them greater influence in the recruitment, selection, and training functions by which the quality of the work force could be upgraded.

One immediate option for improving the quality of the work force is to increase salaries for those civil service and managerial positions where wages are too low to attract an adequate number of talented applicants. This requires changing current wage policies that discourage salary increases that "break the pattern." This policy would require modest additional expenditures. A second personnel initiative, revising civil service tests to ensure high standards and discrimination among applicants only on the basis of quality, also requires added expenditures. But such revisions are necessary to protect the integrity of the civil service system. Investing more in training municipal employees, both civil servants and managers, also would yield desirable returns.

Improving the Management of the Work Force. A major challenge facing the next administration is to improve the previous record of productivity gains. In recent years, savings resulting from improvements in productivity have not exceeded more than 1 percent of operating expenditures, and the trend is down. With the exception of the sanitation gainsharing program, no major steps have been taken to improve utilization of the work force. One reason for this record, as emphasized earlier, is the absence of incentives for managers and workers to change established methods of delivering services inherent in current municipal staffing and wage policy.

Extending gainsharing to other major agencies would increase productivity by improving work-force utilization. However, agencies vary in the extent to which their operations lend themselves to gainsharing agreements modeled after that achieved for sanitation. Labor-intensive activities where services can be measured (to ensure that quality is not sacrificed for quantity and that productivity gains continue with payment of productivity bonuses) are the most likely candidates for extension of gainsharing. Examples include reduced manning of radio patrol cars, fire equipment, and refuse collection trucks; extension of street-sweeping routes and expansion of teacher "contact" hours with students are other possibilities. Additional "mini-gainsharing" experiments could be fashioned with smaller groups of employees providing services to other agencies rather than directly to the public. Office workers and other support personnel need not be excluded from productivity bonuses simply because their contribution to enhanced productivity is indirect.

The potential gains from extension of gainsharing agreements should not be overestimated; nor should the difficulty of negotiating and administering them be underestimated. They do provide a vehicle, however, for increasing productivity that should be pursued by the next administration.

WAGE POLICIES

The City's search for standards in municipal wage policy has not yielded much progress. During the second half of the 1970s, real wages fell sharply; since 1980, they have been rising steadily. In the first half of the 1970s, the real wages of uniformed employees rose at a faster pace than those of other workers. Thereafter, wage policy froze relative pay patterns throughout the work force; more recently, the salaries of higher-paid workers, including managers, have fallen relative to lower-paid workers.

From a managerial perspective, wage policies that treat all employees alike or that reward workers on the basis of their clothing or income are no more sensible than discriminating on the basis of race or sex. But developing more selective bases for allocating wage increases complicates collective bargaining and threatens to intensify interunion conflict. Thus, wage allocation rules have tended to sacrifice productivity for convenience and stability.

However, municipal wage policy should reflect a greater concern for productivity in the future. The bonuses paid to sanitation workers have not caused a rebellion among police officers and firefighters; the extension of gainsharing to them would provide a basis for their earning more money. Another modification of wage-allocation rules sensitive to productivity concerns, raising disproportionately salaries for those titles where present salaries are inadequate to attract a large and talented pool of applicants, also is warranted.

A more difficult issue is the extent to which municipal-wage policy should continue to increase the real pay of municipal workers. Wage policy since 1980 nearly has restored real salaries to the levels before the fiscal crisis. Continuing increases in real pay of municipal workers cannot be justified indefinitely on the grounds of sacrifices during the 1975–80 period. Nor can real pay increases be justified on the basis of pay trends in the local private sector, where average real wages grew only 0.5 percent in the 1980–84 period.[22] In addition, City officials would find it easier to achieve gainsharing agreements if productivity bonuses represented the primary means for municipal employees to increase their living standards.

The City's human resource management policies have changed in the past and will change again. Underlying contradictions in human-resource management policies are a source of their discontinuity. Contradiction in policies prior to the fiscal crisis led to altered policies in the remainder of the 1970s; contradiction in policies during the first half of the 1980s is likely to engender new policies in the future.

Municipal officials lack the authority to determine unilaterally the City's human resource management policies. While they are able to exercise considerable discretion over decisions determining the size and distribution of the work force, the processes by which wage and productivity policies are fashioned ensure that civil servants are involved in their formulation. Ultimately, then, the options recommended in this chapter must be persuasive to the City's quarter-million civil servants and their representatives, as well as elected and appointed leaders. If they jointly are able to fashion a strategy in the next four years that moves toward a consistent set of human resource management policies, then the City of New York will have taken a large step towards ensuring its ability to meet other, new challenges.

NOTES

1. Karl Marx believed the separation in time and space (location) between production, where surplus value was expropriated, and distribution, where profit would result from surplus value, provided capitalists could sell their goods at prices above costs, was the central problem facing business policy makers. Municipal policy makers attempting to formulate

consistent human resource management policies face an even greater problem than Marx's capitalists because the former share policy-making power with today's labor.

2. The employment figures in Tables 6.1 and 6.2 reflect the City's current reporting system, except that the tables include the Health and Hospitals Corporation. While the Corporation is a semi-independent agency, it was included because it provides an important municipal service, receives City funds, and is controlled by a Board of Directors over whom the mayor exercises substantial authority. Transit Authority and Housing Authority police are excluded from the tables because, while they are paid for by the City, they are not City employees.

3. The discussion of the structural issues involved in the new collective bargaining system is drawn from Raymond D. Horton, *Municipal Labor Relations in New York City: Lessons from the Lindsay-Wagner Years* (New York: Praeger Publishers, 1973), particularly Chapters 1–4.

4. The 6 percent salary increase was deferred after the outset of the fiscal crisis, in whole or in part depending on the salary of the unit involved. In this sense it could be argued that the operative pay rule then was not one of equal shares but, rather, progressivity in that low-paid workers received the full percentage increase as scheduled, and workers earning over $15,000 received nothing. However, the deferred salaries were repaid eventually, consistent with understandings reached at the time the deferral was negotiated. For this reason, the 1976 settlement is considered to initiate the equal-shares wage rule, and the 1976 salaries shown in Table 6.3 are treated as paid.

5. For more detail on the nature of these items, see Mary McCormick, "Labor Relations," in Charles Brecher and Raymond D. Horton, eds., *Setting Municipal Priorities, 1982* (New York: Russell Sage Foundation, 1981), pp. 207–08.

6. For somewhat competing versions of how this situation developed, see Horton, op. cit., pp. 87–90 and Charles Morris, *The Cost of Good Intentions* (New York: W. W. Norton & Co., 1980), pp. 120–24. Both versions, however, support the use of the word "debacle" to describe what occurred.

7. For elaboration of this point, see Michael Lipsky, *Street-Level Bureaucracy: Dilemmas of the Individual in Public Service* (New York: Russell Sage Foundation, 1980).

8. Mary McCormick, "Productivity Programs and Issues," in Raymond D. Horton and Charles Brecher, eds., *Setting Municipal Priorities, 1980* (Montclair, N.J.: Allanheld, Osmun & Co., 1979), pp. 171–193.

9. Ibid., pp. 180–82.

10. Ibid., pp. 182–84.

11. Mayor's Management Advisory Board, *Personnel* (March 1977).

12. In 1982, the City thought it had achieved agreement with municipal unions that $50 million of productivity savings would be made as part of the agreement raising salaries in 1983 and 1984; the union leaders had a different interpretation, and their view prevailed.

13. Financial Control Board, *The New York City Productivity Program*, annual reviews.

14. City of New York, *Financial Plan, Fiscal Years 1985–89*, addendum.

15. They were the the the Mayor's Committee on Management Survey and the Josephs Commission on the Government of New York City, which reported in 1952 and 1954, respectively.

16. For example, see David Stanley, *Professional Personnel for the City of New York* (Washington, D.C.: The Brookings Institution, 1963), pp. 71–76.

17. The fullest analysis of the issues is found in a staff report prepared for the State Charter Revision Commission for New York City, "Personnel Reforms for New York City" (January 1975).

18. This conclusion might be contested by some, but it was the conclusion affirmed by all persons interviewed on the subject both within and outside of the Department of Personnel. The current leadership of the Department is rated for qualities other than its professionalism in personnel administration or commitment to the civil-service system. More

objective data supporting this conclusion is the fact that, by 1984, the number of provisional appointees exceeded 23,000 of the roughly 200,000 municipal employees falling under civil-service rules.

19. The 1980 figure is from McCormick, "Labor Relations," op. cit., p. 216; the 1984 figure was computed on the basis of information provided by the Department of Personnel.

20. For discussion, see Charles Brecher and Raymond D. Horton, "Introduction," in Charles Brecher and Raymond D. Horton, eds., *Setting Municipal Priorities: American Cities and the New York Experience* (New York: New York University Press, 1984), pp. 1–11.

21. See Raymond D. Horton and John Palmer Smith, "Expenditures and Services," in Charles Brecher and Raymond D. Horton, eds., *Setting Municipal Priorities, 1983* (New York: New York University Press, 1982), pp. 77–119.

22. Citizens Budget Commission, "Toward a Responsible Municipal Wage Policy," Volume 51, Number 2 (July 1984), p. 30.

PART THREE

Delivering Services

7

Services to Children

DAVID TOBIS

Times are hard for many children in New York City. Despite a significant decline in the size of the population under age 18, the number and share of children living in poverty have increased dramatically. In 1980, nearly one of every three children in the city was being raised by a family in poverty; the share has increased since. At the same time, government has been doing less for poor children. Excluding medical care and education, the City of New York spends nearly $2 billion of federal, state, and local funds annually on income maintenance and other services for children and their families, but this sum is used to provide services reduced from those available before the fiscal crisis of 1975. Since that time the standard of living provided to children in needy families has been lowered, and the supply of supportive services available to them has been restricted. Moreover, these services are typically provided only after a crisis, when it may be too late to repair the damage.

It will require large sums of money and restructuring to build adequate services to help children reach their full potential. This chapter suggests a framework for making such an effort. The first section summarizes the trends that are changing the characteristics of the city's children and increasing their problems. The second section reviews current efforts to aid poor children and identifies the shortcomings arising both from reduced spending and the poor design of current programs. The final section presents a blueprint for establishing a more humane and more effective system of services to cultivate the city's greatest long-term asset, its children.

CHILDREN AND POVERTY

The facts regarding the size of the New York City population under age 18 are clear. As documented in Chapter 2 of this volume, the number of children declined 21 percent in the 1970s and is projected to fall another 7 percent by 1990. At the end of this decade there are likely to be about 1.6 million children in the city compared to 2.2 million in 1970.[1]

Most of the city's children are black and Hispanic, and this has become increasingly the case during the 1980s. At the time of the 1980 census, about 49 percent of the population under age 18 were non-Hispanic whites, 25 percent were non-Hispanic blacks, and 22 percent were Hispanics. By 1990, the combined number of blacks and Hispanics is likely to rise to two-thirds and the number of whites to fall to one-quarter.[2]

The falling number of children masks a substantial increase in the population requiring the aid of public programs. A large and growing number of children are being raised in families with incomes below the federal poverty threshold and in single-parent, female-headed families. In 1980, the latest year for which detailed data are available, less than six of every ten children lived in two-parent families (see Table 7.1). Of this group only 16 percent, or 164,000 children, lived in families with incomes below the poverty level. About 546,000 children lived in single-parent, predominantly female-headed, families. Among this group over two-thirds were living in poverty. Restated, these figures reveal that about 552,000, or 31 percent, of the city's children lived in poverty in 1980, and 67 percent of this group were members of female-headed families.

TABLE 7.1
Selected Characteristics of Children in New York City, 1980

	All Children		Poor Children		Percentage Poor
	Number	Percentage	Number	Percentage	
In Married-Couple Families	1,023,481	58.0%	163,805	29.7%	16.0%
In Other Families	713,963	40.4	383,867	69.6	53.8
Female-headed	546,313	30.9	369,527	67.0	67.6
Other	167,650	9.5	14,340	2.6	8.6
Not in Families	28,023	1.6	3,861	0.7	13.8
Total	1,765,467	100.0%	551,533	100.0%	31.2%

SOURCES: Figures from U.S. Department of Commerce, Bureau of the Census, *1980 Census of Population, General Population Characteristics, New York*, PC80-1-B34, Table 28, pp. 34–139; and *General Social and Economic Characteristics, New York*, PC80-1-C34, Table 125, pp. 34-366; and Public Use Microdata Sample.

By 1982, over 40 percent of the city's children were living in poverty, a situation which is likely to increase during the next four years.[3] These are the children toward which services are primarily aimed.

Poverty is the main factor consistently associated with problems that are damaging to children and highly costly to society. Among these are abuse and neglect, teenage pregnancy and parenthood, and homelessness.

Abuse and neglect involve situations in which the physical or mental health of a child is harmed or threatened by his or her parents or others responsible for the child's welfare. These situations include physical and sexual abuse, and exposure to a range of unwholesome circumstances. Typically, such neglect involves malnutrition, improper shelter, or lack of supervision. Poverty is one of the factors most often and most strongly correlated with abuse and neglect. As one expert has stated:

Every national survey of officially reported child neglect and/or abuse incidents has indicated that the preponderance of the reports involves families from the lowest socio-economic levels. . . . Poverty is not merely "associated" with child abuse and neglect; there is good reason to believe that the problems of poverty are causative agents in the abusive and negligent behaviors, and the resultant harm of children.[4]

The harm caused by abuse and neglect is enormous. Maltreated children show abnormally high levels of emotional disturbance, below-normal physical and emotional development, and below-average or failing academic performance.[5] One study, including New York City children, reported that one-half of the families with abused or neglected children had at least one child later taken to court as delinquent or ungovernable.[6] Another study compared family histories of children who had committed extremely violent offenses with those of children who committed less violent offenses and found that more violent behavior was strongly associated with having been abused.[7]

In New York City the reported incidence of child abuse and neglect has outpaced growth in the poverty population, perhaps because growing attention to the problem has raised the likelihood that it will be reported officially. Between 1978 and 1984, the number of reported cases more than doubled from approximately 15,000 cases involving 28,200 children to 32,827 cases involving 54,452 children.[8] When City officials reviewed reports of child abuse and neglect in 1984, they found 41 percent were substantiated and required some form of intervention.[9] This share applied to the 54,452 children reportedly abused or neglected yields a total of 22,325 children abused or neglected. The actual number no doubt is many times greater due to the discrepancy between the frequency with which offenses are committed and reported.

Another troublesome problem related to rearing of children in poverty is teenage parenthood. Pregnancies among teenagers occur in all income groups, but the rate is higher among low-income groups, and so is the likelihood that poor teenagers will give birth rather than have an abortion. In 1983, fully 32,398 teenagers in New York City, or over 12 percent of the females between the ages of 15 and 19, became pregnant.[10] Of those becoming pregnant, 13,749 or 43 percent gave birth. Almost two-thirds (64 percent) of those giving birth were enrolled in Medicaid, suggesting they came from low-income families.[11] The share of pregnant teenagers giving birth was higher in low-income neighborhoods than in more affluent communities. For example, in Flushing 26 percent of the pregnant teenagers gave birth; in poorer Williamsburg-Greenpoint the rate was 56 percent.[12] A rough extrapolation is that between 15 and 20 percent of all poor, females aged 15 to 19 become pregnant each year, and that between 7 and 10 percent become parents.

The consequences of teenage parenthood often are severe for both parent and child. For the mother, teenage parenthood interrupts the normal transition to adulthood and contributes to an array of problems. It is estimated that between 60 and 80 percent of teenage mothers do not finish high school.[13] An estimated two-thirds of the teenage mothers require public assistance at some time during the first five years of their child's life.[14] Loneliness, depression, and frustration often produce bitterness and anger for the teenage mother; and these, in turn, contribute to domestic violence, child abuse, and suicide. Teenage mothers kill themselves ten times more frequently than the national average.[15]

The growth and development of children of teenage mothers often are adversely affected. In 1981, fully 11 percent of such children in New York State had low birth weights, compared to 7 percent of the children born to women between 20 and 34 years old. Low birth weight is linked with infant death, epilepsy, cerebral palsy, mental retardation, deafness, and blindness.[16]

Finally, a significant number of poor children and their families

TABLE 7.2
Expenditures for Selected Public Services for Children, 1984

	Amount (millions)	Number of Children Served
Income Maintenance Services	$1,354.2	520,898
AFDC	1,299.6	498,263
Home Relief	54.6	22,635
Day Care Services	173.8	52,652[a]
Group Day Care	121.1	34,157
Family Day Care	16.7	6,910
Head Start Programs	36.0	11,585
Family Support Services	52.0	N.A.[b]
Preventive Services	26.7	37,900
Protective Services	25.3	54,452
Family Substitute Services	365.5	N.A.[b]
Foster Care	335.2	16,963
Completed Adoptions	30.3	1,607
Total	$1,981.5	N.A.

SOURCES: Income maintenance expenditures are from New York State, Department of Social Services, "Social Statistics"; children served from City of New York, Human Resource Administration, Office of Policy and Economic Research, "Cases and Persons Receiving Assistance During Month of December 1984." Day care expenditures for total and Head Start program are from City of New York, Human Resources Administration, "Consolidated Services Plan, Federal Fiscal Years 1982–84," September 1984, p. 9. Estimates for group day care and family day care are from City of New York, Agency for Child Development, "Submission for the Consolidated Service Plan for City Fiscal Years 1985–87," July 1984, p. 5. Family support services expenditures are from "Consolidated Service Plan," op. cit., p. 9; children served under protective services are from City of New York, Office of Operations, *The Mayor's Management Report*, September 17, 1984, p. 486. Family substitute expenditures are from "Consolidated Services Plan," op. cit., p. 9; foster care children served are from Child Welfare Information Service Report STAT 100P, June 1984, Table A; children served by completed adoption provided by City of New York, Human Resources Administration, Special Services for Children, Office of Management Analysis.

NOTES: N.A. means not available.

a. Average number served during the year.

b. Subcategories for family-support services and family substitutes are not mutually exclusive and therefore cannot be summed.

are homeless. Approximately 7000 children in 3000 families slept in municipal shelters or hotels because they had no home in 1984.[17] These figures exclude many more families who have no regular home and live with friends or relatives or resort to other forms of shelter, like subways.

Homelessness is a major disruption to life. Families housed at municipal shelters and in hotels stay an average of more than six months before they find other housing.[18] Often, children are exposed to potential harmful circumstances in the shelters and hotels. Homelessness can also cause children to be separated from their families. A recent study found that the families of 20 percent of the children in foster care are homeless, and that 11 percent of this group had been living in the streets or subways, another 19 percent in a hotel or shelter, and that most had been living temporarily with friends or relatives.[19]

PUBLIC PROGRAMS

More fortunate residents of the city and the nation have not abandoned New York's more than one-half million poor children. Large and expensive public programs have been established to serve them and others. Two of the most significant efforts, the public schools and medical services funded by Medicaid and provided by the New York City Health and Hospitals Corporation, are analyzed in other chapters of this volume.[20] The remaining governmental efforts are of four types: income maintenance, day care, supportive services to families, and family substitutes.

Together, these four types of programs were allocated nearly $2 billion in the City of New York's fiscal year 1984 budget (see Table 7.2). The program receiving the largest amount was income maintenance, accounting for nearly $1.4 billion or 68 percent of the total. Nearly 265,000 families containing about 521,000 children received monthly allowances as part of the two income maintenance programs for families: Aid to Families with Dependent Children (AFDC) and Home Relief (HR). Day-care programs received approximately $174 million or 9 percent of the total. These funds provided nearly 53,000 children with either full-day or after-school day care. Family-support services consisting of investigations of child abuse and neglect and counseling by caseworkers received the smallest portion of the funds, $52 million or less than 1 percent. Finally, family substitutes consisting of foster care and adoption services were allocated over $365 million, 18 percent of the total, to serve 17,000 children in foster care and 1600 adopted children. These programs do not reduce to minimally acceptable levels the problems experienced by poor children. Each type of program is seriously deficient.

INCOME MAINTENANCE

Public assistance programs are intended to provide families with a minimally adequate standard of living during periods when their own resources do not make that standard possible. By ensuring adequate food and shelter, cash allowances are designed to help families remain together and provide sufficient material and emotional nourishment for their children. In practice, however, these goals are not reached. Benefits are too low, and not all those in need are served.

In a relatively affluent country such as the United States, the specification of a minimum adequate living standard becomes a normative decision based on relative rather than absolute standards of need. There is no broad consensus on such a standard, but the federal government has pursued two approaches to establishing and measuring minimum standards. One approach is the federal-poverty threshold. Established in 1963, this figure represents the estimated consumption needs of families, assuming they purchase food for a minimally adequate diet and have other expenses that bear the same relationship to food expenditures, as was the case among families in 1963. While an admittedly crude approach to the issue, the federal poverty threshold has become a widely used minimum standard. In 1984, the federal poverty threshold was $10,200 for a family of four.[21]

A second approach is based on a Lower Level Living Standard budget established by the Bureau of Labor Statistics (BLS) that was discontinued in 1981. The figure was based on the actual cost of a "package" of goods and services in a particular area considered to represent a low living standard. This standard can be modified to make it relevant to welfare families by removing expenditures for medical care (which are paid by Medicaid), adjusting for the presence of only one adult, and other modifications. An update of the most recent figures based on overall consumer price changes yields a 1984 modified standard of $14,168 for a family of four.

A comparison of the package of benefits (that is, cash grants, shelter allowance, and food stamps) available to a family of four fully dependent on AFDC with the two federal standards of minimum adequacy reveals a significant shortfall that has worsened over the past decade (see Table 7.3). In 1976, the benefits actually exceeded the poverty threshold by about 13 percent, but were 76

TABLE 7.3

Comparison of New York Income Maintenance Benefits for a Family of Four with the Federal Poverty Level and BLS Lower Budget Standard, 1975–84

Year	Maximum Benefits	Poverty Level	Maximum Benefits as Percent of Poverty Level	BLS Lower Budget[a]	Maximum Benefits as Percent of BLS Lower Budget
1975	$5,667	$ 5,500	103.0%	$ 8,239	68.8%
1976	6,564	5,815	112.9	8,661	75.8
1977	6,564	6,191	106.0	8,872	74.0
1978	6,612	6,662	99.2	9,628	68.7
1979	6,756	7,412	91.1	10,336	65.4
1980	6,876	8,414	81.7	11,503	59.8
1981	7,392	9,287	79.6	12,551	58.9
1982	7,968	9,862	80.8	13,061	61.0
1983	8,208	10,178	80.6	13,521	60.7
1984	8,688	10,200	85.2	14,168	61.3

SOURCES: City of New York, Human Resources Administration, Policy and Program Development, "Policy Brief No. 1: The Public Assistance Standard of Need in New York City," January 1985, Table 2, p. 6. The figures for maximum benefits were incorrectly presented in the report and were recalculated.

a. The Bureau of Labor Statistics lower budget, minus the medical expense component, multiplied by .88, the factor used to convert the amount for a two-parent family of four to that for a single-parent family of four. Since 1981, when BLS discontinued updating the family budgets, increases in the overall Consumer Price Index were applied for each year.

TABLE 7.4

Poverty and Public Assistance Status of New York City Population under Age 65, 1975–82

Year	Estimated Number of People (Under Age 65) Below Poverty Level	Number of People Receiving Public Assistance	Percentage Receiving Public Assistance
1975	1,009,000	991,033	98.2%
1976	1,147,185	995,425	86.8
1977	1,225,900	961,927	78.5
1978	1,198,100	905,822	75.6
1979	1,232,100	875,566	71.1
1980	1,271,300	868,803	68.2
1981	1,370,900	861,346	62.8
1982	1,528,600	851,737	55.7
1983	N.A.	889,004	N.A.
1984	N.A.	918,653	N.A.
Percentage Change 1975–84[a]	+51.5%	−7.3%	—

SOURCES: Poverty population estimates based on unpublished tabulations by the New York City Human Resources Administration from the annual Current Population Survey sample data; public assistance figures from New York City Department of Social Services, *Monthly Statistical Report*.

NOTES: N.A. means not available.

a. Percentage increase for number below poverty level for 1975–82.

percent of the BLS standard. Between 1976 and 1980, inflation increased the standards by 45 and 33 percent, respectively. However, AFDC grants were not raised. Increases in benefits from food stamps were sufficient to increase the total value of benefits by only 5 percent. As a result, the benefits package fell to only 82 percent of the poverty threshold and 60 percent of the BLS standard in 1980. Between 1980 and 1984, the AFDC grants were increased. As a result, the combined benefits package rose 26 percent in nominal dollars and narrowed the standards' gaps slightly.

Because maximum benefits correspond to the income eligibility level for public assistance, the deterioration in the constant dollar value of benefits also has meant that fewer poor families are eligible for assistance. As shown in Table 7.4, between 1975 and 1982 (the latest year for which population data are available), public assistance recipients fell from 98 to 56 percent of the New York City population under age 65 with incomes below the federal poverty threshold. In other words, only slightly more than one-half of the non-aged poor are receiving income maintenance benefits. If the same proportion of the non-aged poor had been reached by public assistance in 1982 as in 1975, then an added 649,000 people would have brought the rolls to more than 1.5 million.

In addition to reduced benefits, administrative practices of the New York City Human Resources Administration (HRA) limit the share of poor people reached by public assistance programs. Since 1975, HRA has altered eligibility procedures to increase the number of times clients must report to welfare centers, and individuals failing to report often have their assistance terminated despite continued eligibility under the income criteria. Some client advocates report that approximately 60 percent of all terminated welfare cases are closed for such reasons.[22] A review of HRA case closings by the State found that 25 percent were closed erroneously and that another 30 percent of the closings were reopened because there was no change in the family's income status.[23] An estimated 15,000 to 30,000 New Yorkers have their welfare cases closed erroneously each month, more than one-half of whom are children.[24]

Finally, it should be noted that changes in federal AFDC regulations effective in 1982 disqualified some recipients. These changes in eligibility rules are estimated to have cut 4000 families from welfare rolls, and prevented as many as 5000 more families from becoming eligible.[25]

DAY CARE

The major source of publicly funded day care in New York City is HRA programs that in fiscal year 1984 served 52,526 children. The vast majority (74 percent) of these children were preschoolers between the ages of three and five who received full day care (8 A.M. to 6 P.M.), or Head Start for half the day. A small share (6 percent) were infants below the age of three, and 20 percent were school-age children who received care after school hours.[26]

Most of the funds supporting day care are provided under two federal programs: the Social Services Block Grant and Head Start. In recent years, block grant funding for day care has fallen, but funding for Head Start has risen. The City has tried to maintain the scale of its day care programs by lowering the unit costs of day care and by supplementing federal funds with local revenues. In fiscal year 1985, the Agency for Child Development (ACD), the

HRA unit that administers day care programs, was allocated $48.4 million in local revenues, compared to $39.5 million three years earlier.[27] Due to these efforts, the number of day care opportunities funded by HRA has increased slightly. However, stretching available funds has resulted in reduced quality.

Eligibility criteria for public day care vary between programs funded under the two federal programs. For the Head Start program, 90 percent of the children served must come from families with incomes below the federal poverty level; the other 10 percent must be handicapped. For programs funded under the Social Services Block Grant, families must meet both social criteria (parents must be working, looking for work, enrolled in an education or training program, or be ill or incapacitated) and income criteria that vary with family size and distinguish between those who receive free services and those who must pay on a sliding scale. For example, in 1984 a family of four with an income below the federal poverty threshold could obtain free care, and families with incomes up to $29,935 paid weekly fees ranging from $2 to $70 per child.[28]

There are no recent, detailed data on the characteristics of families using public day care, but a 1980 survey found that 84 percent were headed by females, and that in 62 percent of the cases the parent or parents were employed.[29] More than one-third (38 percent) of families using day care have incomes above the federal poverty threshold. However, their incomes are relatively low (a median of $13,600 annually), and they paid average weekly fees of $16 in 1984.[30]

To provide these sevices, HRA contracted with 385 private, nonprofit organizations in 1985. The average enrollment at these centers was 99, with sizes ranging from 33 to 195.[31]

In addition to HRA, the Board of Education also is an important source of public day care. In the 1984–85 school year, the Board provided full-day kindergarten to more than 5000 five-year olds. The Board also provided a limited (i.e., three hours a day) prekindergarten program for about 3500 four-year olds. Most of this latter group (approximately 2000) were from families who met the eligibility criteria for day care services under the Social Services Block Grant.[32]

Finally, there are approximately 500 private day care centers, often known as nursery schools, that serve approximately 32,000 preschool age children.[33] These facilities are licensed by the City's

Department of Health. In many cases, the care at these facilities is indirectly subsidized through federal income-tax credits available to working parents. Local tax credits are unknown but nationally, the federal day care subsidy through tax credits exceeded $2 billion in 1983—more than the $1.6 billion spent on day care through Head Start and the Social Savings Block.[34]

The network of public day care programs in New York City is large in both an absolute sense and in comparison to the efforts of local government in most other cities. Nonetheless, there are too few public day care programs to meet demand. Day care programs also are characterized by less-than-desirable standards of quality and, perhaps most importantly, by a financing system that segregates children by income and race.

Unmet Need. There are significant conceptual problems in defining need for day care. It is relatively easy to use available data to identify the groups of New York City children who meet eligibility criteria, which HRA's Agency for Child Development has done.[35] The figures indicate that 72,000 children under three years old and another 72,000 aged three to five were eligible for public day care in 1985. In addition, another 208,000 children between the ages of six and 12 were eligible for after-school day care. However, not all of these children need day care. Particularly for younger children, parents may not want to enroll them in day care; in other cases, more likely involving older children, parents may make other arrangements with family members or friends they believe preferable to group programs.

In order to deal with some of these issues, the HRA employs another approach to estimating the need for day care.[36] For those under age six, it defines as "in need" currently enrolled children and children not able to be placed in group day care. The latter category in 1985 included approximately 16,000 children (see Table 7.5). For those between ages six and 12, the HRA equates unmet need with so-called "latch-key" children who return home after school without any adult present, estimated at 47,000. In both cases, the definition of need is relatively stringent. Parents of younger children may not have made a serious effort to obtain public day care. Families with older children may make unsatisfactory arrangements for children while they are not home. Therefore, the HRA estimates may be viewed as conservative.

TABLE 7.5

Estimated Need for Day Care in New York City, 1985

	Eligible for Public Day Care	Currently Enrolled	Eligible but Not Enrolled	Seeking or Needing Care but Not Enrolled
Children under 3	72,000	3,000	69,000	16,000[a]
Children 3 to 5 Years	72,000	69,000[b]	3,000	
Children 6 to 12 Years	208,000	10,000	198,000	47,000
Total	352,000	82,000	270,000	63,000

SOURCES: City of New York, Human Resources Administration, Agency for Child Development, "The ACD Submission for the Consolidated Services Plan for City Fiscal Years 1985–87," July 1984, pp. 9–12.

a. The figure includes the under three and three to five age groups.

b. Includes an estimated 2000 children in the Board of Education preschool program who are eligible for full day care and includes all five-year olds eligible for day care on the assumption they are enrolled in Board of Eucation kindergarten programs.

Nevertheless, there remains significant unmet need (see Table 7.5), particularly for after-school care. The approximately 10,000 children age six to 12 receiving such care in 1985 contrast sharply with the 198,000 who are eligible but not enrolled and the 47,000 estimated to need care. For children age three to five, the current enrollment of 69,000 falls only 3000 short of the number eligible; but among the youngest group, the 3000 children currently served falls far below the eligible group. Even by the more conservative measure, a total of 63,000 children require but do not receive day care.

Low Quality. The efforts to sustain programs in the face of a fiscal crisis and federal aid reductions have led the City to lower standards for public day care programs. When the City's day care facilities were expanded in the early 1970s, all centers included a family counselor who identified problems and worked with a child's parents to correct them. Following the 1975 fiscal crisis, family counselors were eliminated in day care centers.

Staff levels for day care also were reduced. Originally, three full-time equivalent instructors were provided for each group of up to 15 children to cover the ten hours of daily care. This ensured that at least two people were available throughout the day, and three were available during midday hours when most children were in attendance. In 1976, this was reduced to 2.5 full-time staff members per group, causing some groups to have but one adult available at the start or end of the day.

Finally, salary levels for aides who comprise many of the staff are low. Salaries in fiscal year 1985 were under $6000 annually for the typical half-time position. This has restricted the pool of interested applicants to a relatively small group, some of whom have questionable qualifications.

Segregating the Poor. Perhaps the most serious long-run problem facing current programs is financing arrangements that produce one system for poor children and another for more affluent children. The HRA-funded agencies are limited to serving those in low-income families. In contrast, wealthier families use private day care and nursery schools that few poor children attend.

The City of New York purchases some private day care through Limited Purchase of Service (LPOS) agreements and places publicly subsidized children in them. This encourages socioeconomic integration in these programs, but the LPOS programs tend to be in marginal neighborhoods, thus limiting the mix of families using the program. The LPOS program accounts for 6 percent of all children provided City-funded day care; expanded, it could play an important role in reducing segregation of the city's children by race and class.

Other cities with large public programs encourage a broader spectrum of social classes to participate in both public and private day care. Hennepin County in Minnesota, a metropolitan area of a million people containing Minneapolis, developed a voucher system allowing families to use day-care services of their choice. This helps to make day care accessible to low-income parents and to create racially and economically integrated programs.

FAMILY SUPPORT SERVICES

People can benefit from a wide range of services at various points in their lives, ranging from tutoring to more specialized supportive services to help them confront developmental problems. Sometimes people need intensive help because they experience a catastrophe that disrupts their families. Such crises may require services from many agencies, including homemakers, parent training, and temporary foster care.

In New York City, prior to reforms initiated in early 1985, family-support services were made available through two units of HRA. The Department of General Social Services (GSS) nominally made services available to all families receiving public assistance, but it relied on clients to initiate them through requests. The GSS focused its energies on providing home care to adults rather than family cases. It made a total of only 74 referrals to day care in fiscal year 1984.[37] The Special Services for Children agency of HRA focused on services to families in which there either was a report of neglect or abuse or where a family was identified as being at high risk of having a child placed in foster care.

In 1985, a reorganization plan was developed by a mayoral commission to merge a part of the Department of General Social Services with Special Services for Children and other parts of HRA into a single unit serving families and children. However, reorganization will not deal with the basic problems. Most families who could benefit from supportive services do not receive them, and most that do receive them too late to be effective. Poor families may have a range of problems that require supportive services to resolve. Properly addressed, a child's development will not be harmed; neglected, however, a child and a family can be destroyed.

Therefore, children's services require an early warning mechanism to identify and meet needs in timely fashion. This is not provided by the City's social service system. Early warning mechanisms available in the past were decreased during the fiscal crisis period and were never restored. As noted earlier, family care workers at day care centers were eliminated; public-school guidance workers, also in a position to spot troubles early, were cut significantly.

The problem goes beyond the fact that there are inadequate numbers of trained personnel who can perform the early warning function. A related problem is fragmentation in the delivery of services. Several thousand separate organizations contract with a number of City agencies to provide day care, recreation, family counseling, homemakers, drug and alcohol treatment, family planning, and other services. Additional programs run by the State and the federal government increase fragmentation. As a result, people from several services may be working with the same child, unaware of each other's involvement. Also, clients may be referred from agency to agency without receiving the assistance they need. These problems have been well documented, most recently by the Mayor's Commission on Human Services Reorganization. Its review of services for children and families concluded

Programs remain uncoordinated, resources are not rallied. Most significantly, the present division of agencies virtually guarantees that no comprehensive approach will be undertaken to deliver the many services New York has to offer to the children within it. [38]

Because of the lack of coordination and the loss of key personnel, family support services depend on self-initiation or belated crisis intervention by Special Services to Children (SSC). Well-intended services like counseling typically are inappropriate or inadequate for the families' immediate needs—frequently money or direct services. For example, 93 percent of the families served by SSC in December 1983, received counseling; only 13 percent received emergency cash or food, 8 percent were referred for day care, and

2 percent were assigned a homemaker.[39] The failure to provide homemakers to those eligible for them is striking. In January 1984, only 388 families received a homemaker out of approximately 50,000 families who were eligible.[40]

More distressing is the failure to provide services after a pattern of abuse or neglect has been discovered. In 1984, the State Department of Social Services reviewed a sample of cases in which investigations of abuse and neglect had been made by the SSC office in Brooklyn. It reported, "Forty percent of the families needing services were not offered or provided with either direct services or referred for services."[41] A follow-up study in the field offices of SSC in the five boroughs found that

The review of the 200 sample cases indicated a need for service in 162 (81 percent) of the records. These services included day care, homemaker/chore, foster care, alcohol/drug counseling, parenting training, and other. In 65 (40 percent) of these cases, the families identified as needing the services were not offered or provided them. The case documentation also showed that 97 (60 percent) of the families were offered services, and that only one family (in Brooklyn) refused the service upon being offered it.[42]

The consequences of this public neglect are devastating. The Mayor's Task Force on Child Abuse examined all abuse-related deaths of children in New York City during the first six months of 1980, and it found: "One fourth of the children who died in case families (i.e., cases involving abuse) were involved with an active child-protective service case at the time of their deaths. All of these cases had been open for a long time before the deaths."[43] In 1984, the HRA Inspector General investigated 22 abuse and neglect cases alleged to have been mishandled in SSC field offices. The report concluded that "SSC was seriously negligent in not adequately protecting the lives of 51 children living in high risk situations."[44] Nine children died, and the Inspector General found SSC performance seriously inadequate for eight of the dead children.

Conducting investigations of reported cases of abuse and neglect is a difficult job. Workers may find a child in imminent physical danger; families often are overwhelmed with problems that workers lack the resources to solve and take out their anger, at being investigated, on personnel; investigations require interviews with members of the family, neighbors, witnesses, physicians, and other

TABLE 7.6
Discharge Objectives for Children in Foster Care, 1984

Objective	Number	Percentage
Discharge to parents	6,509	34.1%
Discharge to relatives	648	3.4
Discharge to own responsibility	5,326	27.9
Adoption	4,289	22.4
Adult custodial care required	729	3.8
Unknown	57	0.3
Not Reported	1,552	8.1
Total	19,110	100.0%

SOURCE: Child Welfare Information Services, Inc., Report I.D., STAT 100P, Table H.

NOTE: Figures include children in active care as well as on suspended payment and trial discharge. A total of 16,960 children were in active care.

relevant parties. In light of these difficulties, the New York State Department of Social Services recommends that workers be assigned no more than four new cases a month in addition to continuing 20 cases from previous months.[45] At times, however, City workers have more than twice the number of new cases recommended by the State. Newly assigned cases in the city were increased from an average of 5.3 per worker in 1980 to 8.3 per worker in August 1984.[46]

In response to public pressure resulting from reports that cases had been mishandled, 150 new workers were added in 1984, bringing the regular staff available for investigations to 560 and reducing the average number of new cases to seven. Another 150 workers are needed to reduce caseloads to the level recommended by the State Department of Social Services.[47]

TABLE 7.7
Trends in Foster Care in New York City, 1981–84

Year	Expenditures (in millions)	Children in Active Care	Admissions	Discharges	Adoptions
1981	$281.4	19,907	N.A.	N.A.	1,134
1982	292.2	19,127	N.A.	N.A.	1,137
1983	308.0	17,793	9,820	10,971	1,347
1984	335.2	16,963	10,651	10,419	1,607

SOURCES: Expenditure data from City of New York, Human Resources Administration, "Consolidated Services Plan, Federal Fiscal Years 1982–84," September 1984, p. 9; data on children in active care from Child Welfare Information Service, STAT 100P.

FAMILY SUBSTITUTES

When efforts to assist children in their homes fail, it may become necessary to place them in foster care. In many cases, this should be temporary placement until crises are overcome. Then, the child can be released to his or her natural family. In other cases, the family may no longer exist or be incapable of assuming responsibility. In such instances adoption should be planned.

As shown in Table 7.6, placement is intended to be temporary only for a minority of children in foster care. Less than 38 percent of the children in care were intended to be returned to parents or relatives. City and State standards require that this be achieved in less than two years. Adoption is the objective for another 22 percent. Current standards call for adoption to be achieved within 27 months of the time it is established as the objective and within 45 months from the time a child is placed in foster care.

For a large group of children, over 30 percent, foster care is the setting in which they will reach maturity. About 4 percent will be transferred to a custodial institution due to physical or mental disability. The remaining 28 percent will be released to their own responsibility. Most of these children are teenagers who lived with their families until recently or who were not placed or returned home by an agency in previous years. These children are supervised by foster care agencies until they reach age 18.

The dominant trend in foster care has been a decline in the number of children in care. As Table 7.7 shows, the number of such children declined steadily in the 1981–84 period, some 15 percent. This is generally viewed as a positive trend. Historically, the City's foster care agencies were criticized for the excessive length of time children remained in foster care.[48] The primary reason for the declines was more rapid discharges rather than reduced admissions.

In addition to the extent of foster care activities, two important concerns are the quality and cost of these services. In each case, some progress has been made in addressing the issues, but serious problems remain.

Standards of Care. Most foster care is provided and supervised by some 60 voluntary agencies under contract with the City. Prior to 1979, no formal standards were imposed by the City to ensure that these agencies provided adequate service, nor was their performance monitored. In that year, HRA, after prodding from the Board of Estimate, established a Program Assessment System (PAS) under which contract agencies are systematically evaluated annually. Agencies performing poorly are subject to losing their contracts or other sanctions.

Since then, performance has improved, but the standard of care remains well below desirable norms. Evidence of improvement includes the increase in adoptions, particularly in 1983 and 1984; also, the average time to achieve adoption fell from seven to six years, along with a decline in the average length of stay in foster care from five to four years in 1984.[49] These gains resulted in part from the City's willingness to impose sanctions on poorly performing agencies. Since 1979, HRA has closed four programs, reduced the number of placements in another by approximately 100 children, and temporarily suspended placements at six agencies for periods ranging from one to nine months.[50] Nonetheless, these efforts still leave children in care longer than necessary and the quality of foster care services below established professional standards. As noted earlier, adoption is supposed to take 45 months, not the current six years; return to a family is supposed to take 24 months, not the current four years. Moreover, in recent years there has been a growing number of confirmed reports of abuse or neglect among children in foster care—from 173 in 1981 to 266 in 1983.[51]

One area of notable failure among foster care agencies is their inability to prepare adequately and provide follow-up services to the more than one in four children who are discharged to their own responsibility. In 1984, fewer than two-thirds of the agencies satisfactorily met the modest standards for providing services after discharge which, among other things, required only one face-to-face contact with the child in three months.[52] Indicative of the poor services for youth who become independent is the finding that 27 percent of the homeless men aged 18 to 23 in the municipal shelters previously were in foster care.[53]

High Cost. Despite the significant decline in the foster care population, expenditures for providing foster care have been rising. As shown in Table 7.7, between 1981 and 1984 expenditures grew 19 percent, from $281.4 million to $335.2 million. Average costs per child rose from $14,135 to $19,760 or 40 percent.

A major factor behind the costs for foster care is the system by which the City pays foster care agencies. They are paid a daily rate per child, thereby creating an incentive to retain children. The rate is based on the agencies' actual costs, but the City lacks standards for assessing their reasonableness. Agencies are classified into four categories for purposes of setting payment rates. These categories— basic, intensive, intensive/extraordinary, and extraordinary—describe the level of care necessary for the children they serve. Over the years, increasing numbers of programs have been classified to care for the more difficult children and thus receive more money. Of 48 programs in 1981 classified as basic, intensive, or intensive/ extraordinary, 20 had their classifications and thus their receipt of funds increased by 1984.[54] This resulted partly because older, more difficult children were provided with care, but more importantly, agencies became more sophisticated in classifying the children's disabilities in order to maximize their revenues. Costs are also high because the declining population has not been matched by a contraction in the agencies' administrative costs. As a result, the City finances excess costs.

FUTURE POLICY DIRECTIONS

Current governmental policies do not address adequately the sad and serious problems of many children in the city. Children in poor families suffer the daily desperations that derive from inadequate family incomes. The economic and emotional stresses are cumulative and manifest themselves in short-term crisis situations, including a growing incidence of abuse and neglect, growing numbers of families who literally do not have a place in which to live, and teenagers who become parents. All of these crises become expensive social burdens; more importantly, they are personal disasters which destroy individuals' lives.

Major departures from established policies are necessary to improve the futures of the City's children, especially of its poor children. These efforts will require substantial new public expenditures. Much of the funding can be derived from State and federal sources, but greater local commitment will be necessary. In addition, municipal leaders need to restructure services in each major program area. The basic requirement, of course, is that the new administration be committed to doing more for children.

IMPROVE BASIC LIVING STANDARDS

Four years ago, Reynold Levy and Margaret Bald recommended in *Setting Municipal Priorities, 1982* that the next administration work with the State to pursue a multiyear program that would restore public assistance benefits to a level equal to the modified BLS lower-level budget.[55] Municipal leaders did not assign a high priority to this goal. Since 1981, benefit levels have reached no more than 62 percent of the BLS standard. The continued escalation of social problems among poor families since then suggests the need is even greater to consider again a multiyear program of improved basic benefits.

Substantial additional expenditures will be required to achieve this objective. In 1984, the gap between the modified BLS standard and current benefits for those families receiving assistance is estimated to be about $1 billion. But the new standards would make additional families eligible for supplements to their current incomes. The additional cost of this expanded eligibility is difficult to estimate precisely. The figures in Table 7.4 suggest nearly 700,000 people have incomes between current benefit standards and the poverty level. If this gap averages as little as $500 annually, the added expenditure would be approximately $350 million. Thus, more than $1.3 billion may be required to provide the city's children with minimally adequate living standards. The costs would be shared by the federal (50 percent), State (25 percent), and City (25 percent) governments. The State would have to bear the costs of providing equivalent benefits statewide, as well as in New York City. By pursuing a State program of improvements in basic living standards, the City would leverage significant intergovernmental revenues to aid children.

In addition, the City's HRA could do more on its own to ensure that those currently eligible receive the benefits to which they are entitled. Changed administrative practices would avoid short-term closings of otherwise eligible cases that result from restrictive federal, State, and local policies. More equitable handling of applications would reduce the number inappropriately rejected.

EXPAND AND INTEGRATE DAY CARE

The City of New York is not equipped financially to provide universal day care, but it should be made available for the large number of poor and near-poor children currently eligible for public day care who are now unattended after school hours, and for the smaller group of preschoolers whose parents seek but cannot find an available place to provide them with care. As described earlier, meeting those needs would require at least an additional capacity to serve 16,000 children with full day care services and 46,000 with afterschool care. At respective annual costs of $68 million and $144 million, these new services together would require additional expenditures of $212 million.[56]

The expansion of services for the indigent should be accompanied by better integrating the two day care systems—that of contract agencies serving the poor and "private" schools serving the middle class with the aid of tax subsidies. The precise mechanism for achieving this goal should be developed through experimentation with alternative methods, such as vouchers and conversion of tax subsidies to direct provider subsidies linked to requirements for more economically integrated enrollments. Detailed analysis is necessary to develop plans for achieving greater social and economic integration, but the basic objective of eliminating segregation among preschool age children is clear.

CREATE A SYSTEM OF SUPPORTIVE SERVICES TO FAMILIES

Current expenditures of approximately $52 million annually for family support services underwrite activities that reach too few families too late and often fail to provide enough, or even any, material assistance. To improve this situation will require restructuring services to establish a network of family service centers able to help families in a variety of ways. Such centers exist in some European countries and have been proposed in the United States.[57] They require staffing with professionals who are capable of identifying problems early and who are given the authority and resources to provide assistance the families require.

To function effectively, professionals must interact with families at risk in two settings. First, families seeking or receiving public assistance and evidencing specific problems, including reports of abuse or neglect or teenagers who have become pregnant or parents, should have access to a family service program offering a broad range of services. Linking the services to income-maintenance benefits will help ensure that poor, high-risk families are not left unaided. Second, problems among younger children can be detected by deploying family counselors at day care centers to screen systematically the children in care. As problems arise, these workers would authorize appropriate supportive services.

Establishing this dual network of caseworkers would not be highly expensive. Adding counselors to the staff of existing day care centers would require approximately $24 million, and including them in the recommended day care expansion would add another $37 million.[58] The added costs of identifying troubled families on public assistance cannot be estimated because plans are underway to redeploy existing workers; most of the added cost could be covered with the funds presently allocated to casework services in units of HRA.

IMPROVE THE QUALITY AND EFFICIENCY OF FOSTER CARE

The present foster care system provides an expensive service that often fails to meet its objectives. Many children who should be returned to their families remain in care too long; children who should be prepared for independent living often are not.

The recently established accountability system should be expanded and used more vigorously to encourage accountability among foster care agencies. Special Services for Children should expand the use of administrative and financial sanctions for agencies that continue to perform unsatisfactorily in reunifying children and families. Bad programs should be closed, and good programs should be expanded. Finally, the reimbursement system should be restructured, replacing per diem reimbursement with a system that would tie payment to the delivery of specific services of specified quality.

NOTES

1. See Emanuel Tobier, chapter 2 in this volume.
2. See Robert Berne, chapter 8 in this volume.

3. See Emanuel Tobier, *The Changing Face of Poverty: Trends in New York City's Population in Poverty, 1960–1990* (New York City: Community Service Society, 1984), pp. 47–51 and 105–107.

4. Leroy Pelton, "Child Abuse and Neglect—The Myth of Classlessness," *American Journal of Orthopsychiatry*, Vol. 48, No. 4 (October 1978), pp. 608–617.

5. See A. H. Green et al., "The Psychiatric Sequellae of Child Abuse and Neglect," paper presented at the Annual Meetings of the American Psychiatric Association, 1974; also see B. Johnson and H. Morse, "Injured Children and their Parents," *Children*, Vol. 15, No. 4 (July–August 1968), pp. 147–152, and E. Elmer and G. Gregg, "Developmental Characteristics of Abused Children," *Pediatrics*, Vol. 40, No. 4 (1967), pp. 596–602.

6. Jose Alfaro, "Report on the Relationship Between Child Abuse and Neglect and Later Socially Deviant Behavior," in R. Hunner and Y. Walker, eds., *Exploring the Relationship Between Child Abuse and Delinquency* (Montclair, N.J.: Allanheld, Osmun, and Co., 1981), p. 191.

7. Dorothy Otnow Lewis et al., "Violent Juvenile Delinquents: Psychiatric, Neurological, Psychological and Abuse Factors," *Journal of the American Academy of Child Psychiatry*, Vol. 18 (1979), pp. 307–319.

8. City of New York, Office of Operations, *The Mayor's Management Report*, September 17, 1984, p. 486; and City of New York, Human Resources Administration, Office of the Inspector General, "A Review of Twenty-two Cases of Child Neglect and Abuse as Case Managed by the Brooklyn Field Office," April, 1984, p. 7.

9. City of New York, Office of Operations, *The Mayor's Management Report*, op. cit., p. 486.

10. Ronald Soloway, "Pregnancy, Births and Abortions Among New York City Teenagers, 1980–1983," Center for Public Advocacy Research, Inc., New York City, 1984, p. 1; also see "Special Report: Adolescent Pregnancy," New York State Council on Children and Families, Albany, June 1984, p. 3.

11. City of New York, Department of Health, Bureau of Health Statistics and Analysis, "Summary of Vital Statistics, 1983," p. 13.

12. Soloway, "Pregnancy, Births and Abortions," op. cit., p. 7.

13. New York State Temporary Commission to Revise the Social Services Law, "Teenage Motherhood and Public Dependency," Albany, New York, March 1983, p. 17.

14. New York State Council on Children and Families, op. cit., p. 4.

15. New York State Temporary Commission, op. cit., p. 18.

16. J. Menken, "The Health and Social Consequences of Teenage Childbearing," and J. Trussell, "Economic Consequences of Teenage Childbearing," in F. Furstenberg, Jr., J. Lincoln, and J. Menken, eds., *Teenage Sexuality, Pregnancy and Childbearing* (Philadelphia: University of Philadelphia Press, 1981), as reported in New York State Council on Children and Families, op. cit., p. 4.

17. Citizens' Committee for Children, "7000 Homeless Children: The Crisis Continues," New York City, October, 1984.

18. Citizens' Committee for Children, op. cit., p. 8.

19. Office of the City Council President, "Children and the Housing Crisis: From No Home to Foster Home," October 1984, p. 5; also see, for discussion of the related problem of runaway youth, David Shaffer and Carol Caton, "Runaway and Homeless Youth in New York City," New York State Psychiatric Institute, Division of Child Psychiatry and Columbia University College of Physicians and Surgeons, January 1984, p. 24.

20. See Berne, op cit., and Chapter 9 in this volume.

Human Resources Administration, Policy Brief No. 1, op. cit., p. 5.

21. City of New York, Human Resources Administration, Office of Policy and Economic Research, "The Public Standard of Need," March, 1985.

22. Timothy Casey, "The Maladministration of Public Assistance in New York," Downtown Welfare Advocate Center, New York City, 1984, p. 3.

23. New York State Department of Social Services, "Administrative Closings of New York City Public Assistance Cases," April, 1984, p. 2 and p. 6.

24. Casey, op. cit., p. 3.

25. City of New York, Human Resources Administration Policy and Program Development Project Bulletin, "Effects of Budget Cutbacks on Employed AFDC Recipients," April, 1984, p. 1.

26. City of New York, Human Resources Administration, Agency for Child Development, "The ACD Submission for the Consolidated Services Plan for CFY 1985–1987," July 16, 1984, p. 5.

27. Human Resources Administration, "Consolidated Services Plan, Federal Fiscal Years 1982–1984," p. 19; and draft "Consolidated Services Plan, Federal Fiscal Years 1982–1984," p. 17.

28. Agency for Child Development, Memorandum from Deputy Administrator Doby Flowers, "Advance Notification of Revised Daycare Fee Schedule," May 10, 1984, Appendix E.

29. City of New York, Human Resources Administration, Office of Policy and Program Development, "Socio-Demographic Characteristics of Clients and Applicants in New York City's Daycare Programs," April 1981, pp. ii, 26.

30. City of New York, Human Resources Administration, Agency for Child Development, Memorandum from Louis Wilker, December 18, 1984.

31. Figures based on data provided by Agency for Child Development, Office of Planning and Research, based on a sample of 71 fully-funded public daycare programs.

32. The ACD Submission, op. cit., p. 11; Community Council of Greater New York, "Trends and Forecasts: Child Day Care in New York City," January 1984, p. 6; New York City Board of Education, Chancellor's Draft "State Aid Proposal, 1985–86," 1984, p. 6.

33. Community Council, op. cit., p. 6.

34. The federal funding for day care nationally in 1983 included $540 million from the Social Services Block Grant and $1,075 million for Head Start. The tax credits were $1.91 billion for credits to individuals and $100 million in employer tax deductions.

35. Agency for Child Development, "ACD Submission," op. cit., pp. 9–11.

36. Ibid., p. 12.

37. Mayor's Commission on Human Services Reorganization, "Outline for Action: New Directions for HRA," January 1985, p. 31.

38. Ibid., p. iv.

39. Letter from Gail Kong, Deputy Administrator, Special Services for Children, to David Tobis, June 6, 1984.

40. David Tobis and Bernard Horowitz, "Homemaker Services in New York City," Welfare Research Inc., New York City, 1984, p. 45 and pp. 54–57.

41. New York State Department of Social Services, "Review of the Child Protective Services Program, Brooklyn Field Office, Special Services for Children," November 14, 1983, p. i.

42. New York State Department of Social Services, "Review of New York City Child Protective Services Program, Special Services for Children," December 10, 1984, p. 21.

43. Mayor's Task Force on Child Abuse and Neglect, "Report on the Preliminary Study of Child Fatalities in New York City," 1983, p. 53.

44. Human Resources Administration, Office of the Inspector General, A Review of Twenty-two Cases of Child Neglect and Abuse as Case Managed by the Brooklyn Field Office," OIG/OLAP 84-03, April 1984, p. 163 and p. 177.

45. Letter to colleagues from Norris Phillips, Deputy Commissioner, State Department of Social Services, May 26, 1982, p. 12.

46. City of New York, Office of Operations, *The Mayor's Management Report,* September 17, 1984, p. 466; and "Foster Care Monitoring Committee," op. cit., p. 18.

47. Foster Care Monitoring Committee, "Foster Care 1984," The Committee, 1984, pp. 20–21.

48. See Office of the City Council President, "Compendium of Research on Foster Care in New York City," May 1979. The report summarizes 24 studies during the previous ten years that document the problems in the City's foster care system, including excessive length of time in care. See also, the Mayor's Task Force on Foster Care, "Redirecting Foster Care," June 1980.

49. Special Services for Children, Program Assessment System, "Systemwide Performance in Discharge and Adoption, in Foster Care 1984," as reported in Foster Care Monitoring Committee, Appendix B, p. 2 and p. 123.

50. Foster Care Monitoring Committee, op. cit., Appendix C, p. 124.

51. City of New York, Human Resources Administration, "FY83 Management Plan," p. 198, and "FY84 Management Plan," p. 125.

52. Foster Care Monitoring Committee, op. cit., p. 40.

53. City of New York, Human Resources Administration, "Homeless Youth in New York City Municipal Shelter System, Demographic Profile I," 1984, p. 13.

54. Foster Care Monitoring Committee, op. cit., p. 112.

55. Reynold Levy and Margaret Bald, "Income Maintenance," in Charles Brecher and Raymond D. Horton, eds., *Setting Municipal Priorities, 1982* (New York: Russell Sage Foundation, 1981), pp. 373–393.

56. Preschool day care costs an average of $82 per child per week. For 16,000 additional children the yearly cost would be $68 million. After-school care costs an average of $60 per child per week. For 46,000 new slots, the yearly cost would be $144 million. A portion of this cost would be paid by the families that use the program. Currently 38 percent of user families pay an average of $15.60 per child per week. If the same rate of payment occurred in the expanded program, fees would total $19 million.

57. Alfred Kahn and Sheila Kamerman, *Not for the Poor Alone* (Philadelphia, Pa.: Temple University Press, 1975); also see Kenneth Keniston, *All Our Children* (New York: Harcourt Brace Jovanovich, 1977).

58. The salary for counsellors is $23,000 plus 30 percent for fringe benefits and administration costs, or roughly $30,000. One counsellor is needed per 50 children for a total of 800 counsellors. Since the recommended expansion would add 62,000 slots, an additional 1240 counsellors would be required at a total cost of $37 million.

8

Education

ROBERT BERNE

Few people need to be convinced of the importance of education as a municipal function. Education shapes the values of individuals and their preferences as citizens, but its impact goes beyond politics. While education often is not included in discussions of economic-development policy, its effects on a city's economy are far reaching. The cost and quality of primary and secondary education are key factors in determining where people live and where firms locate, and they influence the ability of residents to obtain jobs and contribute to the economic base.

This chapter examines four subjects closely related to the future of education in New York City and hence to the economic future of the city and its residents. The first section describes recent changes in the school age population, public school enrollment, and the implications of these trends for future demands on the public schools. The second section considers the financing of public schools in New York City including both the level of expenditures and the sources of revenues. Policy options for improving financing arrangements are identified and assessed. The third section presents evidence relating to the performance of the public schools with respect to attendance, reading achievement, and high school

TABLE 8.1

New York City Total and Youth Population by Race and Ethnic Group,
1970, 1980, and 1990

Population Group	Population (in thousands)			Percentage Change	
	1970	1980	1990	1970–80	1980–90
Total Population					
White	4,997	3,686	2,871	− 26.2%	− 22.1%
Black	1,514	1,702	1,929	11.0	11.8
Hispanic	1,201	1,429	1,646	19.0	15.2
Other	185	275	511	48.7	85.8
Total	7,895	7,092	6,957	− 10.2	− 1.9
Population Under Age 5					
White	290	159	99	− 45.2	− 37.7
Black	156	143	176	− 8.3	23.1
Hispanic	152	147	182	− 3.3	23.8
Other	18	23	40	27.8	73.9
Total	616	472	497	− 23.4	5.3
Population Age 5 through 17					
White	814	471	310	− 42.1	− 34.2
Black	414	410	400	− 1.0	− 2.4
Hispanic	349	362	351	3.7	− 3.0
Other	40	53	89	32.5	67.9
Total	1,616	1,292	1,150	− 20.1	− 11.0

SOURCES: Figures for 1970 and 1980 from decennial Census; figures for 1990 based on projections developed by Emanuel Tobier. The projection assumptions are described more fully in Chapter 2 of this volume.

dropouts. The final section is concerned with the private schools, which educate one of every four children in New York City. The characteristics of these schools and the implications of expanded public support for private schools are analyzed.

STUDENTS, FAMILIES, AND SCHOOL DISTRICTS

The performance of the school system is affected strongly by the nature of the students they service, the support available from the students' families, and the way in which the schools are organized. In New York City, the number of students and the nature of their families have changed dramatically in the past decade. However, the boundaries of school districts have remained nearly constant, with potentially adverse consequences for the ability of some dis-

TABLE 8.2

New York City Public School Enrollment by Race and Ethnic Group,
1970–71 to 1983–84

	Total Enrollment	Percentage Distribution			
		White Non-Hispanic	Black Non-Hispanic	Hispanic	Other
1970–71	1,141,075	37.8%	34.4%	26.2%	1.6%
1971–72	1,137,741	36.4	35.1	26.9	1.7
1972–73	1,122,788	35.2	36.1	26.9	1.8
1973–74	1,102,391	34.3	36.6	27.1	2.0
1974–75	1,096,302	33.2	36.6	28.0	2.2
1975–76	1,096,460	32.1	37.4	28.2	2.3
1976–77	1,074,945	30.5	37.9	29.0	2.6
1977–78	1,033,813	29.6	38.1	29.4	3.0
1978–79	996,555	28.7	38.5	29.5	3.3
1979–80	960,242	27.8	38.6	29.8	3.8
1980–81	941,159	26.9	38.6	30.5	4.1
1981–82	920,911	25.9	38.6	31.1	4.4
1982–83	914,782	24.8	38.5	31.8	4.9
1983–84	921,131	23.7	38.5	32.5	5.4

SOURCES: Data from 1970–71 to 1981–82 are from City of New York, Board of Education, *School Profiles, 1981–82*, Fall 1983, Table IV, p. 8. Data from 1982–83 and 1983–84 are from New York State, Information Center on Education. Excluded from totals are prekindergarten and postgraduate enrollment.

tricts to provide effective services. The changing size and nature of the student population and possible reorganization of the school districts warrant consideration.

CITYWIDE DEMOGRAPHIC CHANGES

The city's youth population, and particularly the school age population, declined significantly during the 1970s. While the total population declined 10 percent, the population under five fell 23 percent, and the population between five and 17 decreased 20 percent (see Table 8.1). The sharp decline was due to emigration as well as declining birth rates.

The decline in the youth population is likely to abate, perhaps end, during the 1980s. Improved local economic conditions and other factors have stemmed the rate of emigration, and birth rates have remained relatively stable in the late 1970s and early 1980s. Under assumptions described more fully in Chapter 1 of this volume, the school age population is projected to decline by 11 percent between 1980 and 1990. However, almost all of the decline is expected to occur during the first half of the decade; stable school enrollments are possible in the last half of the 1980s. In addition, the population under age five is projected to increase approximately 5 percent over the decade.

Past and projected declines in the school age population are associated with marked changes in their racial and ethnic composition. The non-Hispanic white population (hereafter, "whites") in this group declined over 42 percent in the 1970s and are expected to fall again by over one-third in the 1980s. In contrast, the nonHispanic black population (hereafter, "blacks") and the Hispanic population in the five to 17 age group have been and are projected to remain relatively stable over the same period. While one-half the school age population were whites in 1970, only slightly more than one-quarter are projected to be whites in 1990. In that year whites under age 18 will be smaller in number than either blacks or Hispanics of the same age.

The changing size and mix of the youth population influence trends in public school enrollment (see Table 8.2). From 1971–72 through 1982–83, total enrollment declined 20 percent, or over 220,000 pupils. However, in 1983–84 enrollment increased for the first time in over a decade. Modest enrollment increases are expected for the remainder of the 1980s due primarily to the demographic changes described above.

Primary and secondary enrollments did not change uniformly. Enrollment in the primary grades declined from 1971–72 through 1982–83 and then rose in the following year. Some of the increase was due to the introduction of all-day kindergartens, but increases were also evident in several grades. Secondary school enrollment generally increased from 1971–72 through 1976–77, but then declined through 1983–84. Thus, stable enrollments anticipated in the later half of the 1980s consist of more elementary school students and fewer high school students.

Changes in the racial and ethnic mix of the youth population also can be seen in public school enrollments. From 1970–71 through 1983–84, white enrollment declined 50 percent, or over 213,000. Black and Hispanic enrollments increased slightly from the early to the mid-1970s, declined until 1982–83, and then increased again in 1983–84. The growth in the "other" category, which is comprised primarily of Asians, was substantial over the entire period. By

1983–84, black, Hispanic, white and other children comprised 38.5, 32.5, 23.7, and 5.4 percent of the total public school enrollment, respectively.

In addition to the size and ethnic mix of the student population, the characteristics of these youths' parents also are critical to demands placed on the city's schools. Two important family characteristics that shape a child's education are income and parental education. In New York City, the trends in these characteristics have been mixed.

Median family income in New York City rose from $9682 in 1970 to $16,818 in 1980, a 73 percent increase.[1] During the same period, however, the Consumer Price Index in the area increased 99 percent.[2] Thus, real median family income actually declined 13 percent, from $9682 to $8438.

At the same time there has been an alarming increase in the number of children and families with low incomes. In 1970 about 12 percent of families had incomes below the federal poverty threshold; this figure increased to over 17 percent in 1980. Despite the total population decline, the number of families in poverty increased from 236,500 in 1970 to 304,000 in 1980. The incidence of poverty was particularly high in female-headed families with children under 18. In 1970 there were 216,000 such families, of which 98,700 or 46 percent were below the poverty level; in 1980 there were 307,500 such families, 169,400, or 55 percent, of which were living in poverty.

The trends in poverty of children are similar. While 480,000, or 21 percent of the city's 2.2 million children, were living in poverty in 1970, the number increased to 551,500, or 32 percent of the city's 1.7 million children, by 1980. Among children under six, the problem is even worse. In 1970, about 23 percent of the 741,600 preschool children were in poverty; by 1980, this increased to 35 percent of the 545,200 preschool children.

Given the economic trends described above, the complex and difficult educational problems associated with poverty also intensified over the past decade. Increased learning-related problems, increased behavioral problems involving attendance and discipline, and increased emotional problems stemming from a stressful family life are related to the growing number of children in poor families. The substantial increase in children in poverty will have effects on the public school system lasting into the next decade.

TABLE 8.3

Median Income, Demographic Characteristics, and School Enrollment for Community School Districts, New York City, 1980

District Number	Median Family Income	Population	Percentage of Population Under Age 18	Public Elementary School Enrollment[a]	Percentage of Population			
					White non-Hispanic	Black non-Hispanic	Hispanic	Other
Low-income Group								
32	$7,536	91,147	39.6%	16,280	15.7%	26.1%	56.4%	1.7%
9	7,933	174,245	37.3	29,443	4.8	52.7	40.3	2.3
7	8,510	94,335	35.3	14,822	5.3	38.9	54.9	1.0
4	8,582	91,534	33.0	12,768	6.5	37.6	54.5	1.3
23	8,667	73,022	40.4	13,482	2.2	81.0	15.5	1.3
16	9,454	73,032	35.7	11,603	1.0	88.9	9.6	0.6
12	10,126	107,975	33.9	16,043	11.3	34.2	53.6	1.0
5	10,153	123,547	24.0	12,660	4.1	83.0	11.7	1.2
1	10,352	109,785	24.4	11,656	36.3	11.5	44.3	7.8
14	10,437	166,243	34.1	19,045	42.5	14.4	41.3	1.8
Mean	$9,175	110,487	33.8%	15,780	13.0%	46.8%	38.2%	2.0%
Middle-income Group								
13	11,573	158,097	28.1	18,704	20.0	64.3	13.8	1.8
19	11,679	157,893	37.6	25,860	19.1	44.3	34.6	2.0
6	12,113	236,078	25.2	21,504	23.3	24.2	49.9	2.6

17	12,129	227,070	31.7	28,717	7.9	78.9	10.4	2.8
10	13,517	298,764	27.7	32,483	47.6	17.6	31.7	3.2
15	14,207	230,926	27.3	22,590	54.5	9.0	33.0	3.4
8	14,825	195,055	30.1	22,659	36.7	23.0	39.3	1.0
21	16,956	264,943	21.8	20,788	83.1	7.1	7.4	2.4
30	17,158	322,029	21.6	22,847	62.4	9.5	21.5	6.7
20	17,362	321,265	22.8	19,647	86.8	1.2	8.9	3.2
24	18,356	341,140	22.7	24,461	63.1	6.2	22.7	8.0
11	18,366	298,599	21.8	21,265	54.5	29.2	14.7	1.5
Mean	$14,853	254,322	26.5%	23,460	46.6%	26.2%	24.0%	3.2%
High-income Group								
18	18,751	149,495	27.0	15,113	47.1	44.9	6.4	1.6
3	19,339	258,478	14.9	12,773	57.4	22.2	17.4	3.1
27	19,347	296,249	26.1	27,795	67.0	21.9	9.3	1.7
22	20,000	321,885	23.0	24,000	73.7	17.3	6.4	2.7
28	21,052	255,211	21.5	20,762	55.2	26.7	13.1	5.1
29	21,982	243,241	28.2	26,126	30.1	57.0	9.8	3.0
25	22,552	262,146	21.1	18,460	76.6	5.4	9.7	8.3
31	23,842	352,121	29.1	37,417	85.4	6.9	5.5	2.2
2	26,473	604,781	11.0	16,072	76.8	4.3	9.8	9.1
26	26,678	171,310	19.6	10,129	89.8	2.1	3.9	4.3
Mean	$22,002	291,492	22.2%	20,865	65.9%	20.9%	9.1%	4.1%

SOURCE: U.S. Bureau of the Census, School District tapes.

a. These are children residing in the physical boundaries of the district who attend public school but not necessarily the schools in the district.

The trend in the education level of adults in the city is more positive. In 1970 over one-third of the population above age 25 had less than a ninth grade education; this dropped to 23 percent in 1980. Moreover, in 1970 approximately 47 percent of the population over 25 were high school graduates, and 11 percent had graduated from college; in 1980 these figures increased to 60 percent and 17 percent, respectively. Thus, while the decline in real family income makes the educational task more difficult, the improved education levels of the adult population should have an opposite and partly offsetting effect.

In sum, demographic and economic changes present a series of challenges for the public schools. Although enrollment declined over the past decade, the period of contraction is ending. This will increase the pressures on the already-constrained resources of the system. In addition, changes in the ethnic and racial mix of the students, along with the higher incidence of poverty, mean that changes in the educational process will be needed simply to maintain existing levels of effectiveness.

IMPLICATIONS FOR COMMUNITY SCHOOL DISTRICTS

The economic and demographic changes in the city's youth population have not been felt evenly among the 32 community school districts. In fact, as will be shown, the demographic changes have exacerbated inequalities in the demands placed on local school districts and in their ability to meet these challenges efficiently.

To facilitate comparisons among the 32 districts, districts are organized into three groups based on average family income in Tables 8.3 and 8.4. Citywide, median family income in 1980 was $16,818. The ten districts in the low-income group have median family incomes ranging from $7536 to $10,437; the 12 districts in the middle-income group range from $11,573 to $18,366; the ten districts in the high-income group range from $18,751 to $26,678.

The groups of districts differ from each other in size, ethnic composition, and the capacity of families to aid in the educational process. The low-income districts have fewer residents and public

TABLE 8.4
Poverty Status and Education of Adult Residents for Community School Districts, New York City, 1980

District Number	Percentage of Total Families in Poverty	Female-headed Families with Children Under 18 in Poverty as a Percentage of Total Families	Percentage of Children Under 18 in Poverty	Percentage of Over-25 Population	
				Without High School Graduation	With College Graduation
Low-income Group					
32	45.5%	31.5%	61.7%	68.2%	2.9%
9	43.7	31.5	58.1	56.1	4.5
7	41.2	25.4	54.8	62.5	3.4
4	39.3	24.5	52.1	63.2	5.0
23	41.4	29.2	54.5	58.1	3.5
16	36.4	23.9	50.6	54.0	4.0
12	34.0	22.1	50.3	59.3	4.5
5	31.7	19.0	48.0	53.2	8.6
1	31.5	16.8	50.3	50.4	17.5
14	32.7	16.3	51.6	63.3	4.6
Mean	37.7%	24.0%	53.2%	58.8%	5.9%
Middle-income Group					
13	29.4	19.7	45.9	40.5	19.9
19	30.6	20.3	44.3	52.8	5.2
6	24.7	14.6	40.5	52.0	11.3
17	25.6	16.0	38.2	39.0	9.6
10	24.9	16.8	44.8	44.2	14.8
15	21.5	11.8	36.2	48.7	15.9
8	21.1	12.7	34.2	51.9	5.9
21	13.0	5.2	24.6	44.8	11.7
30	11.6	4.5	22.1	43.9	12.0
20	12.5	4.5	23.6	44.7	11.2
24	10.3	4.0	17.8	45.5	11.0
11	9.8	4.7	17.1	42.9	10.0
Mean	19.6%	11.2%	32.4%	45.9%	11.5%
High-income Group					
18	12.5	6.9	20.3	36.4	11.1
3	15.3	8.3	30.5	24.3	42.4
27	12.0	6.0	22.5	42.3	9.8
22	10.2	4.4	18.6	32.7	16.2
28	10.1	4.7	21.8	30.1	22.4
29	8.3	4.1	13.9	32.5	13.4
25	5.7	1.7	10.3	29.9	19.9
31	7.0	3.3	10.8	31.4	14.7
2	7.8	2.7	17.4	19.3	45.5
26	3.1	0.8	5.9	24.2	24.6
Mean	9.2%	4.3%	17.2%	30.3%	22.0%

SOURCE: U.S. Bureau of the Census, School District tapes.

TABLE 8.5

*Changes in Median Family Income, Population, and Public Primary
School Enrollment in Community School District Groups,
1970 to 1980*

	Groups of Community School Districts		
Variable	Low Income	Middle Income	High Income
Average Percentage Change in Median Family Income	45.2%	57.0%	83.0%
Average Percentage Change in Public Primary Enrollment	−41.7	−6.1	−16.3
Average Percentage Change in Population	−31.7	−8.1	−3.0

SOURCES: Data for both years from census data computed for each community school district. Measures for 1980 calculated from data on tape provided by U.S. Bureau of the Census; measures for 1970 calculated from data in New York City Planning Commission, *Community School District Profiles*, July 1974.

school students. The middle-income districts are larger and have more students. The high-income districts have the largest populations, but have a smaller share of this population of school age. This and a greater propensity to use private schools make the public school enrollment of high-income districts smaller than it is in middle-income districts.

The low-income districts have a racial and ethnic mix of residents which differs significantly from the middle- and high-income districts. Only about 13 percent of the low-income district populations were whites compared to nearly 47 percent of the middle-income district residents and nearly two-thirds of the high-income district residents. In contrast, fully 85 percent of the residents in low-income districts are blacks or Hispanics compared to about one-half those in the middle-income districts and 30 percent in the higher-income districts.

Families in the low-income districts are more likely to be in poverty and to have lower levels of educational attainment. Nearly 38 percent of the families in the low-income districts are in poverty, and fully 53 percent of the districts' children are in these poor families. In contrast, the respective figures for the middle-income districts are 20 percent and 32 percent, and for the high-income districts 9 percent and 17 percent. Similarly, nearly one-quarter of the families in low-income districts are both in poverty and headed

TABLE 8.6

Measures of Inequality for Median Family Income, Population, and Public Primary School Enrollment among Community School Districts, New York City, 1970 and 1980

Variable	Year	Coefficient of Variation	Minimum Value	Maximum Value
Median Family Income	1980	.3692	$7,536	$22,002
Median Family Income	1970	.2733	5,765	14,319
Public Primary Enrollment	1980	.3042	10,129	37,417
Public Primary Enrollment	1970	.2158	16,468	38,582
Population	1980	.5034	91,147	604,781
Population	1970	.3865	112,565	583,221

SOURCE: See Table 8.5.

by females, while the equivalent figure for the high-income districts was only 4 percent.

The low-income districts are also limited by the relatively low educational attainment of their adult residents. Nearly 59 percent of the adults in low-income districts did not have a high school diploma compared to 46 percent in the middle-income districts and 30 percent in the high-income districts. Similarly only about 6 percent of the adults in low-income districts have college degrees; this figure doubles for adults in the middle-income districts and doubles again for adults in the high-income districts.

The differences in the educational environments of the community-school districts widened over the past decade. Table 8.5 shows the average percentage change for median family income, population, and public primary school enrollment between 1970 and 1980 for each group of districts. The low-income districts had the smallest increase in income and the largest declines in population and enrollment. In other words, the low-income districts became relatively poorer and smaller.

Another more sophisticated indicator of increasing disparity in the educational environments of school districts is the coefficient of variation for the factors examined. The coefficient of variation (defined as the standard deviation divided by the mean) measures the dispersion around the mean. A coefficient of variation of .25, for example, means that approximately two-thirds of the observations will fall between 125 percent and 75 percent of the mean. Perfect equality is indicated by a coefficient of variation of zero; as inequality increases, the coefficient of variation increases.

The coefficients of variation and minimum and maximum values for median family income, primary school enrollment and population among all school districts in 1970 and 1980 are displayed in Table 8.6. Inequality increased substantially for all three measures from 1970 to 1980. In addition, the magnitudes of the coefficients of variation for all three variables by 1980 are rather large, indicating a high degree of inequality.

The large and growing disparities among school districts suggest a need to reconsider their boundaries. The State law that created the community school boards in 1969 stated that the "common educational needs of the communities" should be taken into account along with the number of pupils necessary for efficient management, geographic size, and heterogeneity of pupils.[3] Moreover, the law permits the district boundaries to be changed every other year, although there has been only one minor change since the law was passed. Thus, the educational needs of communities should be a major consideration in the design and redesign of school districts.

There is a strong desire for neighborhood schools. With only 32 districts in New York City, each district necessarily includes many neighborhoods. Thus, neighborhoods can be combined into districts in alternative ways. Since children are likely to choose among different schools within their district, the decisions on district boundaries can affect social separation along economic, racial and ethnic, and educational dimensions. Maintaining existing boundaries has intensified economic and ethnic segregation; changing district lines could serve educational objectives by providing less segregated environments. The possibilities for effective redistricting are enhanced because every low-income district shares a border with at least one middle- or high-income district.

While the trends documented here argue strongly for a redefinition of district boundaries, other factors should be considered before change is implemented. Initially, there are likely to be transitional problems. After the transition, pupils would probably have to travel farther to school to take full advantage of new district boundaries. The full costs of this additional movement may offset other improvements.

In addition, the management efficiencies that can be realized from realignment should be carefully assessed. While more uniform district size and the elimination of extremely large and small districts should ease administration, other potential problems and inefficiencies should not be ignored. The disadvantages of disrupting the political and administrative structures of the districts should be assessed. Finally, the potential change in the attractiveness of the public school system for various groups should be considered. It is sometimes argued that parents want a homogeneous educational environment of their children.[4] If so, realigned districts may increase the utilization of private schools to the detriment of public schools.

The foregoing are important caveats, but they do not necessarily argue against change. The current boundaries divide children in harmful ways by creating school districts of haves and have nots. While budgetary allocations across districts partly compensate for the disparities, money alone cannot adequately offset the social and economic divisions. Although the final decision on district boundaries will be a complex and difficult one, the burden of proof should be on the side of those who argue that increasing educational segregation should not be changed.

FINANCING THE PUBLIC SCHOOLS

Operating New York City's large and complex public school system requires substantial resources. However, evidence presented below indicates that the city's public schools receive relatively fewer resources than other schools in New York State. An analysis of the sources of funds for public schools in New York City and in the rest of the state reveals that the lower expenditures result primarily from lower levels of State aid rather than lower levels of local tax support. Consequently, policy options for enhancing the public schools' revenues should focus on reforms in the State's programs to aid education.

EXPENDITURES FOR PUBLIC EDUCATION

Public school financing is structured at the state level. State laws create local school districts and determine both the available local revenues and their level of State aid. Accordingly, it is instructive to examine the financing of New York City's public schools in comparison to that of public schools in the rest of the state. The city is

TABLE 8.7

*Approved Operating Expenses per Pupil and Price-adjusted Approved
Operating Expenses, New York City
and Rest of New York State, 1966–83*

Year	Per Pupil AOE in New York City	Per Pupil AOE in the Rest of the State	Ratio of per Pupil AOE in New York City to the Rest of the State	Price Adjusted per Pupil AOE in New York City	Ratio of Price Adjusted per Pupil AOE in New York City to the Rest of the State
1966	$736	$690	1.07	$663	.96
1967	792	766	1.03	714	.93
1968	775	839	.92	699	.83
1969	925	947	.98	834	.88
1970	983	1,015	.97	886	.87
1971	1,182	1,137	1.04	1,066	.94
1972	1,154	1,217	.95	1,040	.86
1973	1,299	1,308	.99	1,171	.90
1974	1,625	1,415	1.15	1,465	1.04
1975	1,879	1,585	1.19	1,694	1.07
1976	1,754	1,711	1.03	1,581	.92
1977	1,880	1,842	1.02	1,695	.92
1978	2,100	1,988	1.06	1,893	.95
1979	1,962	2,158	.91	1,769	.82
1980	2,145	2,496	.86	1,934	.78
1981	2,539	2,781	.91	2,289	.82
1982	2,882	3,158	.91	2,598	.82
1983	3,360	3,503	.96	3,029	.87

SOURCE: State Education Department, Information Center on Education, *Annual Education Summary, 1965–66* through *1982–83*. For an explanation of the price index, see the text.

a significant part of the state public school system, representing 34 percent of all public school pupils.[5]

The most appropriate measure of public school expenditures is "approved operating expenses" (AOE). As defined by the State, AOE are the day-to-day operating expenses of the schools funded from state and local sources. Excluded are expenses for building construction, transportation of pupils, payments made to purchase services from a Bureau of Cooperative Educational Services (BOCES), tuition payments to other districts, and expenses for programs that do not conform to law or regulation. Also excluded are all expenses funded by federal aid, proceeds from borrowing, and State aid for a few experimental programs and for textbooks.[6]

TABLE 8.8

Ratios of Approved Operating Expenses per Weighted Pupil, with and without Price Adjustments, in New York City to the Rest of the State, 1966–83

Year	Without Price Adjustment	With Price Adjustment
1966	.93	.84
1967	.90	.81
1968	.80	.72
1969	.85	.77
1970	.84	.76
1971	.90	.81
1972	.82	.74
1973	.86	.78
1974	1.00	.90
1975	1.03	.93
1976	.89	.80
1977	.89	.80
1978	.92	.83
1979	.79	.71
1980	.75	.67
1981	.79	.72
1982	.79	.71
1983	.83	.75

SOURCE: AOE and pupil data from State Education Department, Information Center on Education, *Annual Educational Summary, 1965–66* through *1982–83*. For an explanation of the price index, see the text.

To facilitate comparisons AOE are expressed on a per pupil basis using all enrolled students as the base.[7]

In recent years, New York City's AOE per pupil have been significantly lower than in the rest of the State (see Table 8.7). The 1983 figure for New York City of $3360 per pupil was less than 96 percent of the average for the rest of the state. In the four preceding years the New York City figure was between 86 percent and 91 percent of the average in the rest of the state.

However, these figures understate the disparity between spending in New York City and the rest of the state. Two types of adjustments to the figures provide more meaningful comparisons. First, because prices are higher in New York City for the items (principally teachers) required by schools, expenditures should be adjusted with an appropriate price index. Second, the City's public schools have greater proportions of handicapped, foreign language, and disadvantaged children. The measure of AOE per pupil can also be adjusted to reflect the presence of greater numbers of children with special education needs.

Fortunately, a price index for teacher inputs has been calculated for all districts in New York State.[8] This index reveals that prices in New York City were 10.9 percent higher than average prices in the rest of the state in 1978. Assuming that the price differences for teachers represent differences for prices in all educational inputs and that the price differences measured in 1978 hold for all years, it is possible to calculate price adjusted AOE per pupil for New York City. These figures, shown in Table 8.7, indicate that public school spending in New York City was only 86 percent of the average in the rest of the state in 1983 and that expenditures in the city have been below average in all but two of the last 18 years. During the five most recent years spending in the city never exceeded 86 percent of the average in the rest of the state.

To adjust for the presence of large numbers of pupils requiring extra resources a set of weights developed by the New York State Task Force on Equity and Excellence in Education can be employed.[9] The weights are defined as the extra cost of educating a pupil in a particular category. The weights for each type of pupil are:

Handicapped pupils in special classes 2.00
Handicapped pupils in resource rooms 1.00
Speech-impaired pupils 0.15
Pupils With Special Education Need (PSEN) 0.35
Bilingual pupils 0.40

Using these weights, the number of weighted pupils in New York City and the rest of the State are calculated and used to determine AOE per weighted pupil (see Table 8.8).

The weighted figures reveal that expenditures on New York City were only 83 percent of the average in 1983. Moreover, when the price adjustments and the pupil category are both used in the calculations, the city's expenditures fall to only 75 percent of the average in the rest of the state. Using both price adjustments and pupil weights, spending in the city has not exceeded 92 percent of the average in the rest of the state during the past 18 years and has been 75 percent or less of that level in the past five years. Because education is a cumulative process, a pupil who entered kindergarten in 1971 and graduated from high school 12 years later

TABLE 8.9
Sources of Public School Revenues, New York City and the Rest of the State, 1966–83
(percentage distribution)

Year	New York City				Rest of the State			
	Total	Local	State	Federal	Total	Local	State	Federal
1966	100.0%	65.7%	30.7%	3.6%	100.0%	46.8%	50.5%	2.7%
1967	100.0	61.2	30.9	7.9	100.0	45.5	50.9	3.6
1968	100.0	63.2	33.1	3.6	100.0	46.1	51.0	2.9
1969	100.0	56.2	39.4	4.4	100.0	45.6	51.7	2.7
1970	100.0	54.3	38.3	7.5	100.0	48.3	49.1	2.6
1971	100.0	55.6	32.7	11.6	100.0	47.8	49.7	2.5
1972	100.0	57.8	32.2	10.0	100.0	49.3	47.3	3.4
1973	100.0	59.7	31.7	8.6	100.0	51.2	45.8	3.0
1974	100.0	65.7	28.3	6.1	100.0	52.4	44.5	3.1
1975	100.0	61.9	26.4	8.7	100.0	51.7	45.3	3.0
1976	100.0	60.8	31.3	8.0	100.0	52.6	44.8	2.6
1977	100.0	60.4	31.9	7.8	100.0	54.3	43.2	2.6
1978	100.0	61.5	29.9	8.7	100.0	55.3	41.6	3.1
1979	100.0	57.2	33.0	9.7	100.0	54.9	41.5	3.6
1980	100.0	55.8	32.4	11.8	100.0	55.0	41.6	3.4
1981	100.0	55.8	35.0	9.2	100.0	55.3	41.5	3.2
1982	100.0	58.3	34.5	7.2	100.0	56.2	41.2	2.6
1983	100.0	56.8	37.0	6.2	100.0	56.1	41.7	2.2

SOURCE: State Education Department, Information Center on Education, *Annual Education Summary, 1965–66 through 1982–83.*

TABLE 8.10

State Aid and Price-adjusted State Aid per Pupil, New York City and Rest of the State, 1966–83

Year	Per Pupil State Aid			Per Pupil Price-Adjusted State Aid in New York City	Ratio of Per Pupil Price Adjusted State Aid in New York City to the Rest of the State
	New York City Amount	Rest of the State Amount	Ratio of New York City to the Rest of the State		
1966	$291	$453	.64	$262	.58
1967	325	508	.64	293	.58
1968	375	549	.68	338	.62
1969	492	630	.78	444	.70
1970	505	642	.79	455	.71
1971	536	733	.73	483	.66
1972	527	752	.70	475	.63
1973	565	770	.73	509	.66
1974	604	814	.74	545	.67
1975	725	926	.78	654	.71
1976	734	991	.74	662	.67
1977	780	1,014	.77	703	.69
1978	823	1,063	.77	742	.70
1979	945	1,180	.80	852	.72
1980	1,055	1,311	.80	951	.73
1981	1,217	1,482	.82	1,097	.74
1982	1,375	1,645	.84	1,240	.75
1983	1,542	1,829	.84	1,390	.76

SOURCES: For price adjustment, see text; other data from State Education Department, Information Center on Education, *Annual Education Summary, 1965–66 through 1982–83.*

TABLE 8.11

Per Pupil Local School Revenues, New York City and the Rest of the State, 1966–83

Year	New York City	Rest of the State	Ratio of New York City to Rest of the State
1966	$621	$420	1.48
1967	643	454	1.42
1968	716	497	1.44
1969	703	556	1.26
1970	716	632	1.13
1971	911	706	1.29
1972	946	783	1.21
1973	1,066	860	1.24
1974	1,405	960	1.46
1975	1,528	1,056	1.45
1976	1,427	1,164	1.23
1977	1,477	1,275	1.16
1978	1,696	1,413	1.20
1979	1,637	1,562	1.05
1980	1,816	1,736	1.05
1981	1,939	1,976	.98
1982	2,323	2,242	1.04
1983	2,364	2,458	.96

SOURCE: State Education Department, Information Center on Education, *Annual Education Summary, 1965–66* through *1982–83.*

experienced a significant shortfall compared to the average student in the rest of the state. Expressed more dramatically, expenditure gaps averaging 15 percent over 12 years could be viewed as the equivalent of denying a child nearly two years of schooling.

PUBLIC SCHOOL REVENUES

School districts raise local revenues primarily through the property tax, and they receive revenues from the State and federal governments. In New York City, local sources provided 57 percent of total revenues in the most recent year (see Table 8.9). This proportion has been between 55 and 58 percent in each of the last five years. The State share in New York City was 37 percent in 1983, but it has varied in recent years including a low figure of 25 percent in 1974. The federal share peaked at nearly 12 percent in 1971 and 1980. The most recent trend is downward, with the 1983 figure at 6.2 percent.

TABLE 8.12

Local Education Revenue Effort, New York City and the Rest of the State, 1966–83

	Local Education Revenues as a Percentage of Full Value of Property		
Year	New York City	Rest of the State	Ratio of New York City to Rest of the State
1966	1.52%	1.62%	.94
1967	1.56	1.75	.90
1968	1.74	1.91	.91
1969	1.66	2.09	.80
1970	1.62	2.30	.70
1971	1.95	2.36	.83
1972	1.87	2.41	.78
1973	1.92	2.40	.80
1974	2.27	2.39	.95
1975	2.35	2.25	1.04
1976	2.13	2.25	.95
1977	2.13	2.22	.96
1978	2.26	2.21	1.02
1979	2.09	2.18	.96
1980	2.19	2.17	1.01
1981	2.18	2.24	.98
1982	2.44	2.30	1.06
1983	2.44	2.40	1.02

SOURCES: Revenue data from State Education Department, Information Center on Education, *Annual Education Summary, 1965–66* through *1982–83*; property value data from State of New York, Office of the State Comptroller, *Financial Data for School Districts,* various years.

In the rest of the state the revenue pattern is somewhat different. The federal share is substantially larger in New York City (6.2 percent) than in the rest of the state (2.2 percent). The recent local shares are nearly equal, but the State provides a larger share of revenues in the rest of the state. In those districts the State provided nearly 42 percent of all revenues in 1983 compared to 37 percent in New York City.

To analyze the importance of State aid further, it is instructive to examine aid per pupil (see Table 8.10). For most of the past 18 years, state aid per pupil has been increased more rapidly in New York City than in the rest of the state, but in 1983 the figure still remained at 84 percent of the average outside of New York City. When the previously described price adjustments are taken into account, State aid per pupil in the city falls to only 76 percent of the average in the rest of the state. Finally, when the pupil weights described earlier are also used in the calculations, State aid per pupil in the city drops to just 66 percent of the average in the rest of the state (figures not shown). Thus, the distribution of State aid appears to be an important source of lower expenditures in New York City.

The role of State aid in creating expenditure inequities is also suggested by analysis of local revenue efforts. As noted earlier, the local share of revenues is approximately equal in New York City and the rest of the state. Further analysis, using a measure of local revenues per pupil, points to a similar conclusion (see Table 8.11). In all but two of the past 18 years, local revenues per pupil, unadjusted for price differences, have been higher in New York City than the average in the rest of the state. However, the gap has been narrowing over time, and in the most recent year the New York City figure was below the average in the rest of the state.

Does this suggest that New York City's contribution is unjustifiably low and contributes to the per pupil expenditure shortfall? If the City is responsible for the funding requirements generated by the character of its student population and by higher prices, then the City should be contributing more. But it is widely agreed that the City should not be responsible for funding these unavoidable obligations. Intergovernmental finance for education is based on the concept that the State and federal levels should be responsible for educating handicapped, bilingual, and learning-disadvantaged pupils.

It is more appropriate to examine the local contribution in terms of the revenue effort exerted by the local government. In school finance, revenue effort is often measured by the fraction of the property tax base that is contributed to education through local revenues. This measure shows that in 1983 $2.44 was contributed to education for every $100 of local property value; the comparable figure in the rest of the state was $2.40 (see Table 8.12). In most recent years New York City's tax effort for education has been close to or greater than the comparable effort of districts in the rest of the state.

Another way to assess New York City's local contribution to education is to examine the proportion of the municipal budget devoted to education. Since 1976 a subdivision of the State Education Laws, commonly known as the Stavisky-Goodman law, has required that the proportion of the total City expense budget devoted to primary and secondary education must be at least equal to the average proportion over the previous three years. It is important to note that the requirement is specified in terms of the total budget, not solely local resources. Thus, as the State and federal aid systems become more or less generous toward New York City, the local resources needed to maintain the prescribed proportion decrease or increase accordingly.

Data gathered to examine the effect of this law show that the proportion of the City's total expenses devoted to education rose from about 21 percent in 1977 to about 24 percent in 1980 and remained between 24 and 25 percent for the next four years.[10] However, during this period certain expenditures such as Medicaid were removed from the City's expense budget thereby reducing the base for the Stavisky-Goodman computation and inflating the proportion of the budget devoted to education. Calculations of the proportion of the expense budget devoted to education that adjust for the change in Medicaid financing show that the general increase in the proportion of the budget continued in recent years.[11] In fact, estimates of the amount that the City has funded education over the amount mandated by the Stavisky-Goodman law range from $650 million to $1 billion for 1978 through 1984.[12]

In sum, the City of New York is making a greater-than-average local revenue effort to support education and is devoting an increased share of its budget to education, but expenditures for public schools still fall below those of the rest of the state. While even greater local efforts may be justified, a more desirable approach is to reform the financing system, especially State aid.

OPTIONS FOR SCHOOL FINANCE REFORM

Every state has its own school finance system based on local districts that raise resources and a state aid program to distribute revenues to the local districts. Public financing, and particularly state financing, of education is intended, in part, to promote equity. But equity has multiple definitions, each characterized by different value judgments.

Three principles are available to analyze the equity of a state's school finance system. *Horizontal equity* calls for equality of inputs, usually expenditures, for equally situated pupils. *Equal opportunity* seeks to eliminate any systematic relationship between inputs

TABLE 8.13

*Full Value of Property per Pupil, New York City and the
Rest of the State, 1966–83*

Year	New York City	Rest of the State	Ratio of New York City to Rest of the State
1966	$40,784	$25,841	1.58
1967	41,140	25,971	1.58
1968	41,258	26,030	1.59
1969	42,259	26,620	1.59
1970	44,240	27,452	1.61
1971	46,712	29,958	1.56
1972	50,513	32,427	1.56
1973	55,578	35,851	1.55
1974	61,811	40,099	1.54
1975	65,094	46,890	1.39
1976	66,965	51,787	1.29
1977	69,410	57,380	1.21
1978	74,903	63,854	1.17
1979	78,232	71,574	1.09
1980	82,818	80,103	1.03
1981	88,880	88,344	1.01
1982	95,159	97,276	.98
1983	96,865	102,237	.95

SOURCE: State of New York, Office of the State Comptroller, *Financial Data for School Districts*, various years.

and a school district's wealth or racial composition. *Vertical equity* seeks inequality of inputs for pupils judged to be deserving of unequal resources; handicapped pupils and others are expected to receive greater-than-average expenditures.[13]

When judging the equity, or fairness, of a state's school finance system, it is inappropriate to examine the relationship of only one district to the rest of that state. The policy objective should be to design a school finance system that is equitable from that state's perspective. Once this is accomplished, any problems faced by an individual district can be reduced to an acceptable level. If the system in New York State is reasonably equitable but problems remain for New York City, the recommended changes should be different than if the entire State has problems, only one of which is New York City. The available evidence strongly suggests that the latter case is true; New York State's school finance system is not equitable, and New York City's problems are part of this larger problem. Several studies completed in the late 1970s showed that New York State is less equitable than most other states when judged in terms of horizontal equity and equal opportunity with respect to wealth.[14] Moreover, an analysis of the horizontal equity, equal opportunity, and vertical equity of New York State school finance system over the 14-year period from 1965 to 1978 found that for many definitions and measures of equity, New York State was more inequitable during the 1970s than during the late 1960s and early 1970s.[15] Thus, studies show that New York City's problems are not just a squeaky wheel in an otherwise well-running machine.

Some readers may question how the State's system can be inequitable when the State's Court of Appeals ruled in 1982 that the State's school finance system was constitutional. The decision explains that while New York State's school finance system meets constitutional standards, it is still inequitable; remedies for this inequity should be found through the legislative process, not the courts. The Court stated:

It is not whether there are great and disabling and handicapping disparities in educational opportunities across our State, centered particularly in our metropolitan areas; many recognize and decry this state of affairs. The ultimate issue before us is a disciplined perception of the proper role of the courts in the resolution of our State's educational problems, and to that end, more specifically, judicial discernment of the reach of the mandates of our State Constitution in this regard. . . . [T]he urgings of those who would alleviate the existing disparities of educational opportunity are properly to be addressed to the Legislature for its consideration and weighing in the discharge of its obligation to provide for the maintenance and support of our State's educational system.[16]

What options are available to the State Legislature to remedy the inequities? The answer is to provide more State aid to districts with a lower ability to pay. This could be accomplished through a variety of aid formulas, most of which use the relationship of the district's ability to pay to some statewide average to allocate more aid to the low ability to pay districts. The formulas can vary according to the degree of equalization; some formulas may provide only a little more aid for districts with a low ability to pay, while a more equalizing formula might provide substantial differences between those districts and districts with a high ability to pay. Moreover, the formulas can vary in their definition of ability to pay, the inclusion of flat grants, "save harmless" features, the definition and weighting of pupils, and other features.

TABLE 8.14

Attendance Rates, New York City and the Rest of the State,
1965–66 to 1983–84

| | Ratio of Attendance to Enrollment | | |
| | New York City | | Rest of the State |
Year	Data from State Sources	Data from City Sources	Data from State Sources
1965–66	.858	N.A.	.931
1966–67	.855	N.A.	.934
1967–68	.855	N.A.	.934
1968–69	.853	N.A.	.929
1969–70	.820	N.A.	.937
1970–71	.825	.837	.938
1971–72	.814	.834	.940
1972–73	.812	.834	.931
1973–74	.818	.823	.937
1974–75	.809	.837	.934
1975–76	.817	.824	.926
1976–77	.800	.827	.921
1977–78	.802	.834	.919
1978–79	.809	.842	.921
1979–80	.829	.843	.922
1980–81	.826	.842	.933
1981–82	.828	.843	.925
1982–83	N.A.	.851	N.A.
1983–84	N.A.	.846	N.A.

SOURCES: State data from State Department of Education, Information Center on Education, *Annual Educational Summary, 1981–82*; City data from New York City Board of Education, *School Profiles, 1981–82*, and New York City, *The Mayor's Management Report*, for 1982–83 and 1983–84 data.
NOTE: N.A. means not available.

The traditional measure of ability to pay used in school finance formulas is full (equalized) property value per pupil. Since the New York State aid system has, to varying degrees, allocated aid inversely in relation to ability to pay, it is instructive to compare full value per pupil in New York City and in the rest of the state (see Table 8.13). Until recently, New York City's full value of property per pupil exceeded the level in the rest of the State. Thus, one explanation for the lower levels of state aid for New York City compared to the rest of the State is the City's higher ability to pay as measured by full value of property per pupil.

However, during the most recent two years the decline in per

TABLE 8.15

Reading Achievement Test Scores in Grades Two through Nine,
New York City, 1977–78 through 1983–84

	Percentage of Students Reading at Various Levels				
Year	At or Above Grade Level	1.0 Grade Below Grade Level	1.1 Grades Below Grade Level	2.0 Grades Below Grade Level	2.1 Grades Below Grade Level
1977–78	43.0%	N.A.	N.A.	N.A.	N.A.
1978–79[a]	40.3	N.A.	N.A.	N.A.	N.A.
1979–80	46.7	28.2%	N.A.	11.3%	N.A.
1980–81	50.8	26.8	N.A.	10.9	N.A.
1981–82	51.0	26.6	24.6%	10.2	9.9%
1982–83	55.5	N.A.	21.6	N.A.	8.4
1983–84	52.9	N.A.	22.5	N.A.	8.6

SOURCES: Data for 1977–78 through 1981–82 from New York City Board of Education, *School Profiles*, 1981–82; data for 1981–82 through 1983–84 from New York City, *The Mayor's Management Report*, September 1983 and September 1984; data on percentages of pupils 1.0 and 2.0 grade levels and below calculated from New York City Board of Education, *School Profiles*, 1979–80. 1980–81, and 1981–82 editions; data on percentages of pupils 1.1 and 2.1 grade levels and below from Board of Education, City of New York, News Bureau releases dated May 26, 1983 and May 2, 1984.

NOTES: N.A. means not available.

a. Due to different testing conditions, the 1978–79 test results may not be fully comparable with the results from other years.

pupil full value in New York City relative to the rest of the State has reversed the relationship that held for the previous 16 years. Yet, New York City continued to receive lower amounts of State aid per pupil.

One reason why State aid for New York City lags behind aid for the rest of the State is that the measure of the ability to pay in the State aid formula now combines income per pupil with full value of property per pupil. Since on an income per *pupil* basis (but not on an income per capita basis) New York City is better off than the rest of the state, the change in the measure of the ability to pay in the formula from property value only to property value and income lowers aid in New York City relative to the rest of the state.[17]

Other changes could be made in the State aid system to increase simultaneously the overall equity of the State's school finance system and increase the relative advantage for New York City. Many of these changes have been considered and recommended by various groups, including the New York State Task Force on Equity and Excellence in Education.[18] Examples of these changes include the elimination of flat grants that provide a minimum amount of aid to any district, regardless of its wealth; the elimination of save-harmless provisions that guarantee aid will not decrease in a district, despite a formula that calls for reduced aid; the utilization of enrollment in conjunction with or instead of attendance as the basic pupil count; more realistic weightings of pupils that are costly to educate, including handicapped, bilingual, and learning disadvantaged; and the inclusion of price adjustments that recognize that prices vary within New York State.[19] These latter two options, adjustments for prices and pupil needs, are on the firmest ground in terms of educational and financial arguments, and practices such as save harmless provisions and flat grants are difficult to justify from an equity perspective.

Each of these changes, if implemented, would partially remedy the discrepancies in State aid for New York City compared to the rest of the State and taken together they have the potential to close the gap considerably. The important point is that these changes could be structured in a way that improves the equity of the entire State system, and as a byproduct, State aid for New York City would increase. Unfortunately, despite the availability of changes that would improve the State's system as a whole, the Legislature has not taken the required steps.

PUBLIC SCHOOL PERFORMANCE

One reason for the concern over financing is the belief that school performance may suffer if finances are inadequate. Increased financial support provides the potential to improve educational performance if the dollars are used effectively. Due to the multiple and complex goals of urban public schools, more than a section of a chapter is required to assess completely the schools' performance. Nevertheless, it is useful to examine three key performance measures: attendance rates, reading scores, and dropout rates.

ATTENDANCE

Recent studies conclude, not surprisingly, that children who spend more time on a task are likely to perform it better. A necessary, but not sufficient, condition for spending time on an educational task is being in school. In other words, attendance is critical for education.

For at least nearly two decades attendance has been significantly lower in New York City public schools than in districts in the rest of the State (see Table 8.14). Moreover, while attendance in the rest of the State has remained relatively steady over the period, attendance levels in New York City at the beginning of the 1980s were lower than they were in the mid-1960s. As a result, the discrepancy between the city and the rest of the state has grown to nearly 10 percentage points. In the most recent year for which comparable data are available, school year 1981–82, attendance in New York City schools was 82.8 percent of enrollment compared to 92.5 percent in the rest of the state. Data available only for New York City show that in the two years since 1981–82 attendance increased slightly from historical levels, but that attendance is not uniform in the entire school system. For example, in 1983–84, the attendance rate was 88.2 percent in the elementary schools, 84.5 in the intermediate and junior high schools, and 78.8 percent in the high schools.[20]

New York City has a serious problem due to low attendance, but this problem is not the sole fault of the school system. Attendance rates are profoundly influenced by factors beyond the school's control. The low attendance rates in New York City's schools are both indicative of the problems facing the schools and a reflection of the schools' performance.

It should also be noted that the low attendance rates in New York City have detrimental fiscal effects because State aid is based on attendance as opposed to enrollment. Although the City cannot fully control attendance rates, the aid formula penalizes the City for its low attendance.

READING ACHIEVEMENT LEVELS

Reading is important, in and of itself, but also is a key input to further learning. Accordingly, standardized reading test scores are used as an important indicator of school performance. New York City has used the same reading test, the California Achievement Test (CAT), since 1977–78. The CAT is normed to a national sample from the 1976–77 school year. This means that comparisons of New

TABLE 8.16

Twelfth Graders as a Proportion of Tenth Graders Two Years Earlier by Racial and Ethnic Groups, New York City Public Schools, Selected Years

Year	White	Black	Hispanic
1983–84	.61	.39	.38
1981–82	.62	.42	.39
1973–74	.72	.51	.43

SOURCES: New York State Information Center on Education and Emanuel Tobier, "The Changing Face of Poverty: Trends in New York City's Population and Poverty: 1960–1990," revised draft report, Community Service Society of New York, October 1984, Table 24, p. 92.

York City results for a given year are made to a national sample in 1976–77.

Between 1977–78 and 1983–84 the percentage of New York City students taking the CAT and scoring above grade level has increased from 43.0 to 52.9 (see Table 8.15). Progress is also evident in terms of a reduced share of students who read very poorly. The percentage of students reading one and two grades below their norm has declined noticeably in recent years. Despite unfavorable demographic trends and attendance problems, the reading level of students has improved.

Two additional points about these reading scores deserve attention. First, since the scores are reported in terms of 1976–77 national norms, the percentage of pupils reading at or above grade level are *not* being compared to current national norms. Since reading performance has improved nationally since 1976, the norm for the test is a relative low point. Comparisons of testing norms provided by McGraw-Hill indicate, for example, that a reading score of 50 percent of pupils at or above grade level using the 1977 norm converts to 40 to 44 percent at or above grade level using the 1981 norm.[21] Therefore, the actual percentage of pupils reading at or above grade level in New York City compared to *current* national norms is probably lower than the reported figures and may be under 50 percent. Since New York City is planning to use a new test in the next several years, a more precise estimate of this difference will soon be available.

Second, the test scores are reported for only those who take the test. The percentage of pupils enrolled in grades two through six who took the CAT in 1979–80, 1980–81, and 1981–82 were 86, 90, and 91 percent, respectively.[22] Although these figures compare favorably with those of elementary school attendance, about 10 percent of the pupils do not take the test. The effect of these absentees on the reading scores depends on who is absent. If, as is likely, reading ability is positively correlated with attendance, then there is an upward bias in the reported scores. If school officials encourage certain students to stay home on the day of the test or otherwise manipulate the group of students who take the test, then this also would introduce an upward bias in the scores. Without additional research, however, the effects of absenteeism on the reading scores remain undocumented.

Although there are important qualifications to the data, recent test scores indicate reading achievement has improved in the New York City public schools. Since, however, national norms also have improved, it is uncertain whether the City has gained relative to current national averages. Nonetheless, there is no doubt that reading achievement has improved relative to New York City's own performance in 1977–78.

DROPOUTS

It is an important sign of failure if a youngster drops out of school without achieving a twelfth grade education. However, the New York City Board of Education began only recently to measure the magnitude of its dropout problem. Consider the following from *The Dropout Report* of 1979.

This report is the first attempt in recent years by the staff of the central administration to identify the scope of the dropout problem our schools are experiencing. . . . This report . . . confirms that about 45 percent of the entering 9th graders never complete a high school education. There is no question that our responsibilities to these young people have been grievously unfulfilled.[23]

Since this initial attempt to measure the dropout rate, some of the data problems encountered in 1979 were solved, and this led to varying definitions of dropouts in subsequent years. There has been no attempt by the Board to adjust the more recent data so that it is comparable with the earlier figures. The resulting changes in definitions make comparisons of the dropout rate over time poten-

TABLE 8.17

Private School Enrollment, New York City, Selected Years, 1971–72 to 1983–84

Year	Private School Enrollment			Private Enrollment as a Percentage of Total Enrollment		
	K–6	7–12	Total	K–6	7–12	Total
1971–72	230,538	164,160	394,688	26.7%	24.4%	25.7%
1975–76	192,175	141,738	333,913	25.2	21.3	23.3
1979–80	180,375	129,470	309,845	27.7	20.9	24.4
1980–81	180,854	128,933	309,787	28.2	21.2	24.8
1981–82	179,608	128,472	308,080	28.3	21.7	25.1
1982–83	177,457	127,660	305,117	28.2	21.7	25.0
1983–84	176,278	129,130	305,408	27.5	22.1	24.9

SOURCE: New York State, Information Center on Education.

TABLE 8.18

Enrollment in New York City Private Schools by Racial and Ethnic Status, Selected Years, 1971–72 to 1983–84

(percentage distribution)

Year	Total	Black	Hispanic	White	Other
1971–72	100.0%	8.4%	11.9%	78.9%	0.8%
1975–76	100.0	11.1	13.7	73.8	1.4
1979–80	100.0	14.8	15.8	66.7	2.8
1980–81	100.0	15.8	16.0	65.3	3.0
1981–82	100.0	16.8	16.3	63.5	3.3
1982–83	100.0	17.3	16.5	62.5	3.6
1983–84	100.0	17.9	16.6	61.6	3.9

SOURCE: New York State, Information Center on Education.

tially misleading. Between 1977–78 and 1981–82 the definitions are reasonably comparable, and the dropout rate in this period remained between 44 and 47 percent in these years. In 1982–83 the definition of both the numerator and denominator of the dropout rate were changed significantly, and some double counting was eliminated. This reduced the rate to under 42 percent, but the figure cannot be compared meaningfully to the earlier years' rates. [24]

Although the dropout rates are not published by race and ethnicity, alternative measures can be relied upon to document the alarming differences. [25] One such measure is to compare the number of twelfth graders to tenth graders two years earlier. This comparison does not take into account factors such as migration, changes in the hold-back rate, and return to school after twelfth grade. As a result, it does not provide dropout rates comparable to those reported earlier. Nevertheless, this ratio identifies substantial differences in dropout rates among racial and ethnic groups. This alternative measure indicates that in 1983–84 about 61 percent of whites completed high school; in contrast, only 39 percent of blacks and 38 percent of Hispanics did so (see Table 8.16). Moreover, the rates for all groups have fallen significantly over the past ten years.

Regardless of whether there have been increases or decreases in the dropout rate in most recent years, the most striking fact is that there is a high dropout rate. With approximately four out of ten New York City youth failing to graduate from high school, the public schools are helping to create a group of young adults whose chances for economic advancement are severely limited.

PUBLIC FUNDS AND PRIVATE SCHOOLS

Public schools are often discussed as *the* educational system in New York City. In fact, however, a large number of children in the city attend private schools the financing, especially public financing, of which is a critical educational issue. Some basic information about private elementary and secondary schools in New York City provides an instructive background for a consideration of the merits of increased public support for private schools.

CHARACTERISTICS OF PRIVATE EDUCATION

In 1983–84, the most recent year for which data are available, over 305,000, or nearly one of every four, school age children attended private school (see Table 8.17). The number of private school children has fallen significantly over the past decade, but the decline is not markedly greater than that of public schools. As a result, the share of New York City children attending private school has not changed significantly since the start of the 1970s.

The private schools have a larger share of total enrollment in the primary grades than in the secondary grades. A significant enrollment shift occurs after the eighth grade because many private schools do not continue through high school.

Religiously oriented schools dominate private enrollment in New York City. In 1982–83, for example, 66 percent of the private school pupils attended the Roman Catholic Archdiocese's schools. Children in schools administered by Jewish organizations comprised nearly 16 percent of the private school enrollment, and other religious schools accounted for another 7 percent. Thus, religious schools enrolled 89 percent of the private school students in New York City. The remaining 11 percent attend nondenominational schools.[26]

The racial and ethnic composition of private schools differs noticeably from that of the public schools (see Table 8.18 and refer to Table 8.2). The private schools enroll a smaller percent of minority pupils than the public schools. In 1983–84, black and Hispanic students comprised 17.9 and 16.6 percent of private school enrollment compared to 38.5 and 32.5 percent, respectively, of public school enrollment. However, minority enrollment in the private sector has increased both as a share of the total and absolutely since 1971–72.

Private schools enroll children from families that are wealthier than those sending their children to public school (see Table 8.19). In 1980 about 40 percent of children in public schools had family incomes under $10,000; in contrast, only 18 percent of children in private schools had family incomes that low. Only 20 percent of children in public schools had family income over $25,000; the corresponding figure for private school children is 41 percent. Church-related schools did not have as many pupils drawn from the upper-income classes as the other private schools.

In sum, private schools in New York City have remained relatively stable in their enrollment share. Religiously affiliated schools account for the vast majority of private school pupils. Although private schools have a higher percent of white pupils than the public schools, minority enrollment in the private schools is increasing. Private schools also draw their students from families with significantly higher family incomes than do the public schools.

ISSUES RELATING TO PUBLIC FUNDING

The issue of public support for private education is likely to be seriously debated in the city and state, as well as nationally, within the next four years. The issue will arise, or more accurately rise again, because a recent U.S. Supreme Court decision broadens opportunities for states to support private schools. The fact that the State sought in earlier years to help fund private schools suggests that new initiatives will be launched in response to the changed judicial posture.

Public support for specific aspects of private education is already an established practice in the United States. In many states, including New York, public funds are used for transportation and textbooks for private school students, and state aid for learning disadvantaged and handicapped pupils is available to private schools. Over a decade ago, New York State enacted statutes to provide aid to parents for private school tuition, but this was struck down by the U.S. Supreme Court.[27] However, in 1983 the U.S. Supreme Court ruled that Minnesota's plan to provide tax deductions for education expenses, including private school tuition, is constitutional.

TABLE 8.19

Family Income of Children Aged Five through 18 by Attendance in Public and Private Schools, New York City Residents, 1980

(percentage distribution)

Income Class		Public Schools	Private Schools		
			Church-related	Other Private	Total
Less than	$ 5,000	19.3%	7.8%	8.8%	8.0%
$ 5,000	–$ 7,499	12.0	5.3	5.1	5.2
$ 7,500	–$ 9,999	8.8	5.0	4.4	4.9
$10,000	–$14,999	16.1	13.7	10.1	13.0
$15,000	–$19,999	13.0	14.8	10.4	13.9
$20,000	–$24,999	10.5	14.5	11.1	13.8
$25,000	–$34,999	12.2	22.0	15.1	20.5
$35,000	–$49,999	5.9	11.2	13.1	11.6
$50,000	–$74,999	1.8	4.3	10.0	5.5
Greater than $75,000		0.5	1.6	11.9	3.8
Total		100.0%	100.0%	100.0%	100.0%

SOURCE: U.S. Bureau of the Census, Census of Population, Public Use Microdata Sample.

The U.S. Supreme Court's new ruling signals that certain state-level programs of support for private schools are constitutional.[28] Minnesota's statutes allow an income tax deduction for tuition, textbooks, and transportation up to a maximum of $500 for children in elementary school and $700 for children in secondary school. While the deduction is available to all parents, the vast majority of such expenses are incurred for private rather than public education. This is the first time tuition deductions have been deemed constitutional, even though 95 percent of children who attend private schools in Minnesota are enrolled in religiously affiliated institutions. This landmark decision suggests that the U.S. Supreme Court will not block state-level plans similar to Minnesota's. Consequently, in New York State legislative consideration of public support for private schools is likely in the near future. In order to guide City and State officials in their consideration of such programs, it is useful to consider the impacts of such actions on schooling in New York City.

Impacts on Private School Enrollment and Tuition. A critical argument in favor of public support for private schools is that such programs will increase educational choice. The programs are expected to make private schools more affordable for a larger number of families. By increasing the options for many families, the programs improve the match between students and schools. This, in turn, should enrich educational outcomes.

Whether such outcomes are achieved will depend on how many and which types of students change their schools as a result of the available subsidy. Many citizens want schools, especially public schools, to serve an important socialization mission. If public support for private schools encourages more separation along economic, racial, and religious lines than currently exists, then the benefits from increased choice may not offset the costs to society from increased separation. To explore these tradeoffs it is necessary to understand the impacts on enrollment and tuition of a potential State program of tax deductions for private school tuition.

There are three likely immediate effects of State tax deductions to support private schools. The parents previously sending their children to private schools will receive a new subsidy; some parents who previously enrolled children in public schools will put them in private schools; and the tuition charged by private schools will increase because the new demand is unlikely to be met fully by private school expansion. It is difficult to estimate the magnitude of each of these impacts, but they deserve further consideration.

Since, as noted earlier, private schools in New York City enroll a disproportionate share of wealthier families, a significant portion of public support for private schools would go to families in relatively high income brackets. This pattern would be accentuated with a tax deduction program as opposed to a tax credit program, because the value of the tax deduction increases as marginal tax rates increase, while the value of a credit is constant across income groups. Blacks and Hispanics also would receive relatively small shares of the public support for private schools because of their underrepresentation in private schools. If public support for private schools is provided, discrimination as a cause of this underrepresentation should be scrutinized carefully.

Public support for private schools would also lead to changes in enrollments in private and public schools and in the tuition that private schools charge. Enrollment shifts from public to private schools would occur because the net price to parents of private schools would be reduced. At the same time, as more openings in private schools are created, the tuition of existing schools would be increased because new private schools would bid up the costs of teachers, managerial talent, space, and other inputs. If few new private school openings are created, enrollment in private schools will not increase as much, and tuition will increase even more.

It is difficult to estimate how much of the public support would go towards increased tuition and how much would benefit parents of children in private schools; however, it is likely that all of the support will not end up in net price reductions and that some of the support will be absorbed by increased tuition. An attempt to estimate these effects using national data found that with a tax credit of 50 percent of tuition up to $500, private-school enrollment in primary and secondary schools would increase by 10 and 18 percent, respectively, and tuition in private primary and secondary schools would increase by 50 and 10 percent, respectively.[29] Only if the public support is intended to improve the financial condition of private schools as well as provide support for parents should such outcomes be welcomed.

Impact on Public Schools. Public support of private schools has the potential either to improve or worsen the public schools. On the positive side, the increased choice for parents may increase the competitive spirit and responsiveness of the public schools and force improvements and innovations that would not otherwise occur. But this increase in responsiveness is not guaranteed. Those who stand to lose their jobs if students shift from public schools to private schools are the most recently hired staff, and they may not have a significant influence on the responses made by the public schools.

On the negative side, public support for private schools could result in the departure from the public schools of many educationally desirable children, leaving behind the less desirable. The research cited above estimated that private school enrollment will increase between 10 and 18 percent, but found that children from low-income families would be less likely to be shifted to private schools in response to a price change. Or, as a different observer notes, if tuition tax credits were enacted,

I suspect that the quality of public schools would probably decline. The gainers would be those families who would be financially enabled to shift from public to private school; the losers would be those students who remain behind, particularly in schools where the tax credit leads to the loss of a significant percentage of brighter students.[30]

A related issue is how a program of public support for private schools would affect the budget of New York City. Of course, the answer depends on the form of the initial support combined with any alterations in federal and State aid programs. At a very simple level, if only the federal government were to enact income tax deductions and nothing else changed, then the City's budget would benefit because the City would have fewer children to educate without reduced resources. But if State and City income tax deductions are used, the eventual impact on the City's budget is uncertain because other aspects of State and federal aid are likely to change simultaneously.

Finally, it should be added that tax support for private schools could alter residential patterns. At present, some people who have school-age children but who do not want to send them to New York City's public schools move to a suburb where their children attend public school. For these people, it is now preferable to live in the suburbs and pay suburban property taxes, instead of living in the city, paying City taxes, and utilizing private schools. The enactment of a tax credit or deduction that lowers the cost of private school may provide the incentive for some of those who would move to the suburbs to remain in the city.[31] Thus, lowering the net cost of private schools may improve the city's social and economic base, assuming that it is desirable to keep those who would otherwise leave in the city.

In sum, the merits of a program of public support for private schools should be assessed with multiple criteria, for using any one will result in much uncertainty regarding the likely impact. As specific proposals are formulated, they should be assessed in terms of their affects on tuition, enrollment patterns, and residential decisions as well as on questions of religious convictions. At present there is no clear cut judgment on the merits of these proposals, but as programs are designed, the foregoing framework should provide a basis for public officials to weigh the issues and inform their constituents about their positions.

SUMMARY

The analysis of four issues related to educational policy provides both discouraging findings and some evidence of progress. Socioeconomic trends affecting the educational environment are generally negative. Within the city, real family incomes have fallen and the incidence of poverty is increasing. These changes make education more difficult. Moreover, public school enrollments may begin to increase after a long period of decline. This will increase the demands on existing resources.

Perhaps even more serious is the uneven impact of socioeconomic changes in different community school districts. Among three sets of school districts identified, the differences between the most and least well off are both striking and widening. Social, educational, and management concerns call into question the current community school district boundaries and, at a minimum, the boundary issue deserves careful study.

The findings with respect to public school financing are also discouraging. Expenditures for public education in New York City are lower than in the rest of the State. When adjustments for price differences and special-student populations are taken into account, per pupil expenditures in the City lag behind the rest of the State by one-third.

With federal aid diminishing, the desirable increases in education expenditures must be derived from State and local sources. While the City can provide some additional resources, it is already making a greater tax effort to support education than the average district in the rest of the state. The most appropriate source of new funds is the State. Approaches to making the State-aid program work more equitably, for the state as a whole as well as for New York City, are available and warrant action by the legislature.

The findings with regard to public school performance are mixed. The good news is that reading achievement has improved relative to the city's performance several years ago. However, the degree to which this also represents progress relative to the national average awaits a new testing procedure. The bad news relates to attendance and dropout rates. These indicators reveal that a significant portion of the pupil population is not being reached effectively by the public schools and that a substantial group of undereducated adults continues to leave the public schools.

Finally, a major uncertainty for education in New York City is the future role of the private sector. Several factors suggest that a new program of public support for private schools will appear on the legislative agenda before the end of the decade: A recent U.S. Supreme Court case finds certain State tax deductions for private school tuition constitutional, and there is support for such moves in the federal executive and legislative branches. This legal environment, combined with the fact that one in four New York City youth attends private school, makes State action a likely prospect.

It is too early to assess accurately the impact of expanded public support for private schools, but the consequences would undoubtedly be significant. Those already sending their children to private school would receive some subsidy but would also face higher tuitions. Others will shift their children from public to private schools, while still other families might remain in or relocate to New York City because they have expanded options. The new options might also improve school performance. But the magnitude of these effects is largely unknown and cannot be estimated until specific proposals are designed. As the issue emerges, elected officials should weigh the likely impacts. While part of the population may choose a position on ideological grounds, a careful assessment of some of the effects of public support for private schools raised in this chapter should help others make up their minds.

NOTES

1. Unless otherwise noted, all data in this section are from documents and tapes from the U.S. Department of Commerce, U.S. Bureau of the Census.

2. U.S. Department of Labor, *Handbook of Labor Statistics* (Washington, D.C.: United States Government Printing Office, December 1983), Table 114, p. 328.

3. See New York State Education Law, Article 52, Section 2590, and Marilyn Gittell, "School Governance," in C. Brecher and R. D. Horton, ed., *Setting Municipal Priorities, 1981* (Montclair, N.J.: Allanheld, Osmun, 1980).

4. See Nathan Glazer, "The Future under Tuition Tax Credits," in T. James and H. M. Levin, eds., *Public Dollars for Private Schools* (Philadelphia: Temple University Press, 1983).

5. State Comptroller, State of New York, *Financial Data for School Districts for Fiscal Year Ended June 30, 1983*.

6. For a precise definition of AOE, see New York State Education Department form SA 122 and the Annual Financial Report, ST-3. Approved operating expenses are actual expenditures.

7. Enrollment is used rather than attendance because schools must make available services to all enrolled pupils.

8. Wayne Wendling, "Cost of Education Indices," discussion paper prepared for the New York State Special Task Force on Equity and Excellence in Education; Education Commission of the States, Denver, Col., October 23, 1979.

9. New York State Education Department, "Providing State Aid for the Education of Children with Handicapping Conditions Based on a Study of Program Costs," a report required by Chapter 789 of the Laws of 1978, Pt. 2, November 1979; J. M. Gaughan and R. J. Glasheen, "Study on Special Pupil Needs, Interim Report," New York Special Task Force on Equity and Excellence in Education, November 1979.

10. See Percy Aguila, "Analysis of the Stavisky-Goodman Law," New York University, Graduate School of Public Administration, unpublished paper, 1984.

11. Adjusted expenditure data from C. Brecher and R. D. Horton, "Expenditures," in C. Brecher and R. D. Horton, eds., *Setting Municipal Priorities, 1984* (New York: New York University Press, 1983).

12. P. Aguila, op. cit., p. 10.

13. For a more complete presentation of equity concepts in school finance, see R. Berne and L. Stiefel, *The Measurement of Equity in School Finance: Conceptual, Methodological and Empirical Dimensions* (Baltimore, Md.: The Johns Hopkins University Press, 1984).

14. See, for example, National Center for Education Statistics, "School Finance Equity: A Profile of the States, 1976–77," Draft Review Copy, December 1979; and R. Berne, A. Odden, and L. Stiefel, *Equity in School Finance* (Denver, Col.: Education Commission of the States, October 1979).

15. These empirical results are presented in R. Berne and L. Stiefel, *The Measurement*

of Equity in School Finance, op. cit. Note that some measures of equity that place a heavier weight on the lower end of the distribution do not show this consistent trend.

16. *Board of Education, Levittown v. Nyquist,* Ct. App. 453 NYS 2d 643 in West Publishing Co., *New York Supplement,* Series 2, Vol. 453, NYS 2d (St. Paul, Minn.: West Publishing Co., 1983): see p. 21, note 9 in the majority opinion.

17. In 1982–83, adjusted income per pupil (as defined by the State's formula) was $43,800 in the entire New York State and $48,815 in New York City. In contrast, 1980 median household income was $16,662 in New York State and $13,854 in New York City. See State Education Department, "Averages Conceal Trends in a Heterogeneous State: An Analysis of Selected Characteristics of New York State School Districts," *Draft Report,* September 1984.

18. See *The Report and Recommendations of the New York State Task Force on Equity and Excellence in Education,* February 1982. For other discussions of the issues, see City of New York, Office of the Comptroller, "Analysis of Inequities, The State Education Operating Aid Formula," May 26, 1981; and Joan Scheuer, "Robin Hood's Unhappy Adventures in New York State," paper presented at the American Education Finance Association, Orlando, Fla., March 1984.

19. For an analysis of the effects of flat grants and save-harmless provisions in New York State, see New York State, Division of the Budget, Education Unit, "Analysis of $977 Million—New York State Operating Save Harmless and Special Aids, and of $565 Million—all 1982–83 Aids Not Fully Equalized," September 14, 1982.

20. City of New York, Office of Operations, *The Mayor's Management Report,* September 17, 1984, p. 426.

21. Data provided by John Stuart, Senior Marketing Manager, McGraw-Hill.

22. Calculated from New York City Board of Education, *School Profiles,* 1979–80, 1980–81, 1981–82.

23. New York City, Board of Education, "The Dropout Report," October 15, 1979, p. 1.

24. Dropout rates for 1977–78, 1978–79, 1979–80 and 1981–82 from New York City Board of Education, *School Profiles,* 1981–82; dropout rates for 1982–83 from New York City Board of Education, "Dropouts from New York City Public Schools, 1982–83," Educational Management Information Unit, Office of Student Information Services, Spring 1984.

25. See Emanuel Tobier, "The Changing Face of Poverty: Trends in New York City's Population in Poverty, 1960–90," revised draft report, Community Service Society of New York, October 1984, pp. 91–3.

26. These data are from the New York State Education Department, Information Center on Education.

27. *Committee for Public Education v. Nyquist,* 413 US 756, 93 S. Ct. 2955, June 25, 1973.

28. *Mueller v. Allen,* No. 82-195, 103 S. Ct. 3062, June 29, 1983.

29. Donald E. Frey, "The Cost of a Tuition Tax Credit Reconsidered in the Light of New Evidence," *Journal of Education Finance,* Vol. 7, No. 4 (Spring 1982).

30. David W. Breneman, "Where Would Tuition Tax Credits Take Us? Should We Agree to Go?" in T. James and H. M. Levin, eds., *Public Dollars for Private Schools,* op. cit., p. 112.

31. Nathan Glazer, op. cit., p. 97.

9

Health

UNITED HOSPITAL FUND STAFF*

The City of New York spends approximately $1.5 billion of local tax funds to subsidize municipal hospitals, purchase medical care for the indigent, finance health insurance for municipal employees, and provide other health services. In recent years, municipal officials have focused on operating some of these programs more efficiently and on securing greater State aid for the purchase of care for the indigent under Medicaid. Their efforts have been fruitful. There is much good news to report about the management of the municipal hospital system and changes in Medicaid financing.

The effectiveness of the City's health care policy is less clear. The impact of municipal programs is influenced by their relationship to the larger health care system, which includes voluntary hospitals, medical schools, private physicians, and insurance companies, and which is heavily regulated by the State and federal governments. But municipal leaders have not yet developed strategies for dealing with these important institutions. Efficient man-

*This chapter was written by Dina Keller Moss, under the direction of Bruce C. Vladeck, with contributions from Melvin Krasner, Emily Goodwin, Willine Carr. Significant additional contributions were made by Nancy Bella, Toni Heisler, MaryAnn Holohean, Diana Stager, Natan Szapiro, and Mary Windels.

277

agement, while important, is no substitute for effective strategy. In the next four years, the primary challenge in municipal health policy will be to expand the influence of the City government over the entire health care system, so that its critical stake in the entire system will be better promoted.

This chapter considers three major aspects of the City's role in providing health care: Medicaid, the Health and Hospitals Corporation, and the Department of Health. In each case, recent progress is reviewed and ways in which the City's role can be expanded are identified. These sections are preceded by an examination of the changing environment in which municipal health policy is made.

THE HEALTH POLICY ENVIRONMENT

The formulation of municipal health policy is shaped by three important forces. First, the health status of the population determines the problems confronting health care providers and funders. Second, the economic magnitude of the health care industry in the city adds the element of economic development to policy making. Finally, the intergovernmental division of authority over health care finance and policy limits the options available to local leaders. In important respects, the environment of health policy has been improving, thereby providing municipal leaders some new leeway in the initiatives available to them.

HEALTH STATUS

Available measures provide only a limited picture of the health status of New Yorkers, but the evidence points to a variety of improvements. These include lower (age-adjusted) death rates, a reduced incidence of several communicable diseases, and reduced infant mortality (see Table 9.1). Between 1970 and 1980, age-adjusted death rates fell 15 percent, with major causes of death other than homicide declining. Between 1970 and 1982, the infant mortality rate dropped by over one-third. During this period, the incidence of tuberculosis, syphilis, and hepatitis also declined, although the improvement was not steady and the incidence of some communicable diseases, such as gonorrhea, increased.

TABLE 9.1
Health Status Indicators for the United States and New York City

| | New York City | | | United States | |
	1970	1980	1982	Actual 1980	As Percentage of New York City, 1980
Age-Adjusted Deaths per 100,00 Population					
Total	771.1	655.8	N.A.	585.8	89.3%
Selected Causes					
Heart disease	306.6	294.0	N.A.	202.0	68.7
Cancer	161.2	154.3	N.A.	132.8	86.1
Accidents	22.7	17.5	N.A.	42.3	241.7
Flu and Pneumonia	29.0	20.7	N.A.	12.9	62.3
Diabetes	15.9	11.8	N.A.	10.1	85.6
Homicide	14.0	23.0	N.A.	10.8	47.0
Infant Deaths per 1000 Live Births	21.6	16.1	14.3	12.6	78.3
Cases of Selected Diseases per 100,000 Population					
Tuberculosis	26.3	16.8	17.6	12.3	73.2
Syphilis	47.9	33.7	36.7	14.6	43.3
Gonorrhea	465.9	617.9	662.7	443.3	71.7
Hepatitis	56.9	15.3	27.9	26.5	173.2
Measles	14.6	17.1	0.7	6.0	35.1

SOURCES: New York City Department of Health, *Summary of Vital Statistics, 1982*, Tables 8 and 22; U.S. Department of Health and Human Services, Public Health Service, *Health: United States, 1983*, Table 15; and *Morbidity and Mortality Weekly Report*, "Annual Summary 1982," December 1983, Vol. 31, No. 54.

NOTE: N.A. means not available.

Despite these significant improvements, the health status of New Yorkers is, on average, poorer than that of other Americans. National death rates were significantly lower for all major causes except accidents and the national infant death rate was 12.6 per thousand births compared to 14.3 in the city. Related to the higher infant mortality is the fact that 19 percent of births in New York City were characterized by late or no prenatal care, compared to 5 percent nationwide.[1] New Yorkers also have higher rates of communicable diseases than the rest of the nation. Moreover, some communicable diseases such as tuberculosis and hepatitis, which had been decreasing throughout the city, are now beginning to increase.

Certain groups within New York City bear a disproportionate risk of disease or death. The poor generally have more serious health problems and less access to health services than others. New York City's poverty population was 20 percent of the total compared to a national average of 12.4 percent.[2] The city's minority groups also bear disproportionate risks. White males in New York City can expect to live 3.7 years longer than nonwhite males; for white females, the advantage is 2.9 years.[3] The infant mortality rate for whites is 11.4 per thousand live births; the rates for blacks and Puerto Ricans are 18.1 and 13.3, respectively.[4]

Other large segments of the population with potentially serious health problems are those among whom Acquired Immune Deficiency Syndrome (AIDS) is most likely to occur. Two such groups are homosexuals and Haitians, of whom New York City has disproportionate shares. As of 1984, fully one-third of the nation's AIDS cases were diagnosed in New York City. The city's residents accounted for over one-third of the nation's deaths due to AIDS.[5] The emergence of AIDS as a major public health problem since 1979 illustrates the extent to which the heterogeneity of the city's population creates a parallel heterogeneity in health problems to which the City must respond.

HEALTH CARE AS AN INDUSTRY

Municipal health care policy must be shaped by economic-development considerations, as well as the changing health status of New Yorkers. Local health care providers draw substantial expenditures from residents of other parts of the region and nation, which

TABLE 9.2

General Care Hospitals in New York City, 1973 and 1983

Hospital Ownership	General Care Hospitals		General Care Beds		
	1973	1983	1973	1983	Percentage Change
Voluntary	66	54	24,694	23,586	−4.5%
Municipal	16	11	8,172	5,770	−29.4
Proprietary	33	14	4,567	2,375	−48.0
State	1	1	310	320	+3.2
Total	116	80	37,743	32,051	−15.1%

SOURCE: United Hospital Fund, *Health and Health Care in New York City: Local, State and National Perspectives*, 1985 edition.

become income for New Yorkers who work in the health care system. Health care is a significant export industry in New York City; and given the earlier noted relationship between health and poverty, expansion of the health services industry might even be viewed as an indirect means of improving the health status of New Yorkers.

In 1983, the most recent year for which estimates were prepared, health care expenditures in New York City totaled $15.7 billion.[6] Of the total, approximately 44 percent was for hospital care, 19 percent for physician care, 8 percent for nursing home care, and the remainder for all other types of health services, supplies, and research. A large proportion of these expenditures, especially for

TABLE 9.3

Expenses per Hospital Admission, New York City and the United States, 1978–83

	New York City		United States	
	Adjusted Expense per Admission	Percentage Change	Adjusted Expense per Admission	Percentage Change
1978	$2,690	—	$1,474	—
1979	2,843	5.7%	1,642	11.3%
1980	3,167	11.4	1,851	12.8
1981	3,558	12.4	2,171	17.3
1982	3,800	6.8	2,501	15.2
1983	4,212	10.8	2,789	11.5

SOURCE: American Hospital Association, *Hospital Statistics*, annual editions.

NOTE: Adjusted expenses per admission are total expenses less outpatient expenses divided by total admissions.

hospitals and physicians, are made by nonresidents. Approximately one of every ten inpatients treated in New York City hospitals lives outside the city, and for hospitals in Manhattan the figure approaches one in five.[7]

These figures have remained relatively constant over the past 25 years despite suburbanization. The city's major medical centers apparently have lost less of their market to suburban health facilities than other industries have lost to suburban shopping malls, office parks, and industrial zones. While increasingly sophisticated medical facilities are available in the suburbs and the proportion of suburban residents treated in New York City hospitals has declined, Manhattan has retained its role as *the* center for health care in the region. In addition, hospitals in the Bronx and Queens continue to attract large numbers of nonresidents, principally from adjacent Westchester and Nassau counties.

Health care provides numerous job opportunities for New Yorkers. According to the 1980 census, the industry employed 266,906 New York City residents, or 9.1 percent of the employed population. In 1982, health care accounted for close to 20 percent of all private sector employment in the Bronx and Richmond, and 14 percent of employment in Brooklyn. Moreover, the hospital industry is probably the largest source of entry level, unskilled jobs in the city. Employment opportunities have grown steadily in recent years despite the large decline in population and other jobs during the 1970s. While total resident employment fell almost 9 percent during that decade, the number of New Yorkers employed in health care increased over 78,000—a striking 41 percent.[8]

INTERGOVERNMENTAL CONSTRAINTS

The ability of municipal officials to set local health care policy is constrained by the shift in sovereignty from City Hall to the State capitol that has occurred over time, particularly since the 1970s. Concern with escalating costs led State officials to assume expanded regulatory authority over the health care industry, leaving City officials a peripheral role in cost-containment strategies.

State health policy has had two related components. First, the State controlled planning and capital expenditures to reduce the size of what was generally conceded to be an industry that had more inpatient care capacity than was necessary and thus was excessively expensive. Second, after the 1975 fiscal crisis, the State aggressively used its regulatory authority over Medicaid and Blue Cross (and, subsequently, private insurers') payments to hospitals to restrain their price increases.

Both policies were relatively successful, but they had dramatic consequences for New York City hospitals. Largely as a result of State policy, the city lost almost one-third of its institutions and 15 percent of its hospital beds between 1973 and 1983 (see Table 9.2). Municipal hospitals contracted disproportionately during this period. City officials closed five municipal hospitals resulting in a 29 percent reduction in the number of beds. In contrast, the number of beds in voluntary hospitals was reduced less than 5 percent, although 12 voluntary hospitals closed.

The State's rate regulation policies effectively slowed hospital price increases. As shown in Table 9.3, New York City hospital costs per admission rose by 56.6 percent between 1978 and 1983, compared to almost 90 percent nationally. In 1978, the city's costs per admission were 82 percent higher than the national average; by 1983, they were only 50 percent higher.

Rate regulation resulted in many obsolete and qualitatively dubious institutions being closed, but other needed institutions were seriously threatened by State policies. The Jewish Hospital and Medical Center of Brooklyn became the paradigmatic example. Heroic efforts, including the infusion of more than $25 million in City, State, and federal funds, and unprecedented labor-management cooperation were required in the 1978–82 period to keep a needed institution—and also the largest employer in Bedford-Stuyvesant—alive until it could be merged with another hospital. Between 1975 and 1982 a large majority of voluntary hospitals incurred operating losses. The annual net deficit of voluntary hospitals amounted to nearly $86 million in 1979; the cumulative deficit incurred by all voluntary hospitals over the 1975–83 period exceeded $475 million (see Table 9.4).

Largely in response to the fiscal plight of voluntary hospitals the State, with federal acquiescence, implemented a three-year experimental system of hospital payments in 1983 called the New York Prospective Hospital Reimbursement Methodology (NYPHRM). It applies uniformly to all payers, including Medicare. The federal government waived its usual principles of reimbursement under Medicare in order to participate. The NYPHRM provides funds to

TABLE 9.4
Bottom Line Results of New York City Voluntary Hospitals, 1975–83

| Year | Number of Hospitals | | Amount (in millions of dollars) | | | |
	With Deficit	With Surplus	Annual Surplus	Annual Deficit	Annual Net Deficit	Cumulative Deficit
1975	33	24	$13.1	$47.9	$34.8	$34.8
1976	32	25	18.2	36.3	18.1	52.9
1977	42	15	9.3	75.0	65.7	118.6
1978	40	17	17.7	82.7	65.0	183.6
1979	40	17	10.5	96.4	85.9	269.5
1980	37	18	13.1	66.9	53.8	323.3
1981	38	17	24.8	79.0	54.2	377.5
1982	37	14	26.2	111.1	84.9	462.4
1983	21	24	39.5	51.9	12.4	474.8

SOURCES: Hospital Association of New York State, *Fourth Annual Voluntary Hospital Fiscal Pressures Survey, 1975; Ninth Annual Voluntary Hospital Fiscal Pressures Survey, 1981*; and unpublished data.

NOTE: Bottom line results are determined by subtracting total costs from total revenues, including all non-operating revenues.

pay hospitals for serving patients without insurance or the means to pay for their care, as well as to aid hospitals in financial distress. These funds are generated by surcharges (set at 2.3 percent in 1983, 3.85 percent in 1984, and roughly 4 percent in 1985) on insurance and other payments to hospitals. In 1983, such special funds paid $86.8 million to New York City voluntary and proprietary hospitals, and another $24.5 million to municipal hospitals. In 1984, the amounts were $147.9 million and $36.4 million, respectively.[9]

NYPHRM appears to be achieving some of its intended results. As shown in Table 9.4, a reduced number of hospitals incurred deficits in 1983, and the net deficit incurred by voluntary hospitals fell from $84.9 million to $12.4 million. Moreover, by providing partial compensation for previously uncompensated care, NYPHRM helps maintain access to hospital care for many poor and near-poor New Yorkers. The new system also benefits the municipal treasury. While NYPHRM increases the City's Medicaid expenditures, the bad debt and charity payments provide funds to offset HHC costs otherwise paid by local tax funds. The net effect is a fiscal gain for the City, estimated to be at least $10 million annually.

In recognition of the importance of NYPHRM and of the need for a thorough evaluation of both NYPHRM and alternative systems, the State may seek a one year extension of the federal waiver. Whether or not there is an extension, the City's most important health policy agenda item in 1986 will be the renegotiation of hospital payment formulas, an issue discussed in the next section.

In sum, the environment in which municipal health policy is formulated has become more favorable in recent years. The health status of New Yorkers has improved in many ways; and the health care industry has become an increasingly important sector of the local economy and has begun to be recognized as such. Furthermore, the State has adopted a hospital payment system more favorable to the City. The City faces a series of choices in designing health care policy, however, which have emerged from its three major operational concerns: Medicaid, the Health and Hospitals Corporation, and the Department of Health.

MEDICAID

Under federal law, the State of New York, like all states, main-

TABLE 9.5

Projected Medicaid Expenditures, New York City,
Fiscal Years, 1984–88
(millions of dollars)

	1984	1985	1986	1987	1988
Total	$3,609.7	$4,354.0	$4,833.0	$5,362.8	$5,980.1
City	919.0	1,017.0	1,079.0	1,181.0	1,319.0
State	1,122.1	1,417.5	1,596.5	1,783.6	1,980.6
Federal	1,568.7	1,919.5	2,158.0	2,398.2	2,680.6

SOURCES: City of New York, *Message of the Mayor, Executive Budget, Fiscal Year 1985,*
April 26, 1984; and unpublished data supplied by the Office of Management and Budget.
NOTE: Data do not include expenses for New York City Department of Health.

tains administrative authority over the Medicaid program and must
implement the program uniformly throughout the state. It must
determine eligibility criteria, payment rates for providers, and the
scope of services covered under Medicaid. Localities certify the
eligibility of applicants within State guidelines.

Twelve states, including New York, require local governments to
share the cost of the Medicaid program.[10] In New York State, localities must pay one-half of the nonfederal share of Medicaid costs,

TABLE 9.6

Medicaid Expenditures by Eligibility Category, New York City, 1983

	Percentage of Total Medicaid Expenditures	Average Annual Expenditures per Recipient	Monthly Average Number of Eligibles
Total	100.0%	$3,058	1,231,452
Aid to Dependent Children	21.8	949	741,046
Aged and Disabled	16.7	2,578	204,058
Medical Assistance Only	15.5	4,594	75,124
Chronic Care Population	31.8	25,205	40,687
Home Relief Adults	13.1	3,053	138,937
Other Children	1.1	1,120	31,600

SOURCE: New York City Human Resources Administration, Office of Policy and Economic
Research, *Medicaid Data Report, 1983 Year-End Summary and July–December 1983* (June
1984).
NOTE: The chronic care population includes all recipients institutionalized in skilled nursing or health-related facilities, even if the recipient was originally eligible under the SSI or
medical assistance-only program. Only expenses that could be allocated to a category of
assistance were used to calculate the percentage of expenses; unallocated expenses include
retroactive rate adjustments and Citycaid expenditures.

or 25 percent of federally qualified expenditures. No other state requires as large a local share. Moreover, since New York State extends coverage and benefits beyond those mandated and reimbursed by the federal government, a locality's share of the total Medicaid expenditures may exceed 25 percent.

Approximately $3.6 billion was spent on Medicaid in New York City in fiscal year 1984. Between fiscal years 1984 and 1988, Medicaid expenditures are projected to increase at an average annual rate of 13.5 percent to almost $6 billion (see Table 9.5), including over $1.3 billion in local tax receipts.

Given these costs and constraints, municipal leaders' strategic decisions regarding Medicaid usually involve bargaining with State officials designed to reduce local Medicaid costs, and to improve the quality of care to those who are eligible. Recently, the City has enjoyed considerable success in pursuing those objectives, but much remains to be achieved.

EXPENDITURE PATTERNS AND FINANCING CHANGES

One option for reducing the City's Medicaid costs is to serve fewer people by reducing eligibility standards. Another is to reduce the share of expenditures that must be financed by the City. The first option is undesirable. Prevailing on the State to increase its share of Medicaid funding should remain the major policy goal of municipal officials.

While Medicaid spending in New York City averaged $3058 per person in 1983, there were significant variations in spending among categories of beneficiaries (see Table 9.6). Five major groups are eligible for Medicaid: those receiving Aid to Families with Dependent Children (AFDC); the aged and disabled receiving Supplementary Security Income (SSI); persons who are "medically needy" because of high medical expenses relative to their incomes but who do not qualify for public assistance payments; a chronic care population consisting of elderly and disabled people living in nursing homes; and persons receiving Home Relief, a welfare program principally for adults who do not qualify for AFDC. In 1983, these groups comprised 1.2 million New York City residents.

The most expensive group of Medicaid beneficiaries is the chronic care population. These disabled, and generally elderly, individuals require nursing home care as well as additional care from physicians, episodic hospitalization, and continuing medication. At an average cost in excess of $25,000 annually, the 3 percent of all Medicaid beneficiaries in the chronic care population account for nearly 32 percent of all Medicaid expenditures. (Reforms in the financing and administration of long-term care services are treated in Chapter 10.)

Those in the medically needy category also incur above-average expenditures. The high expenses arise because their eligibility is a function of the size of their medical bills relative to their income. Medicaid functions for these groups as a catastrophic medical insurance program for formerly working-class or near-poor families. Other than taking measures to contain costs, which affect the entire industry, there is little the City can do to lower costs for this group.

For the two largest groups of Medicaid beneficiaries, SSI and AFDC enrollees, per person expenditures are well below average. The figure for SSI beneficiaries is $2578. Medicaid costs are relatively low for SSI recipients, who are all disabled or elderly, because they usually qualify for Medicare, which covers their acute care costs. For this group Medicaid functions largely as a supplemental insurance program to cover copayments and services excluded under Medicare.

The more than 740,000 people eligible for AFDC required Medicaid expenditures that averaged only $949 per person in 1983, below the estimated national average per capita expenses for persons under age 65 of $1,121.[11] The low spending for beneficiaries of AFDC strongly suggests they are not receiving all necessary services. The State Department of Social Services has found that 20 percent of children eligible for Medicaid receive *no* medical care during the course of a year; moreover, most of the remaining children see a physician *only* when they are sick.[12] Those receiving AFDC, mostly children, need more medical service, not less.

Because of the limited possibilities for savings in costs per enrollee, the most appropriate municipal strategy is to reduce local spending by seeking an increased State share of Medicaid funding. To a limited extent, this goal has already been achieved. As is evident in Table 9.5, the City share of funding dropped from just over 25 percent in 1985 to a projected 22 percent in 1988. This change is a result of the City's success in increasing the State's share of Medicaid costs. The first step in this process was enactment of the Human Services Overburden Aid (HSOA) program for calendar year 1983. Under HSOA, the State assumed all Medicaid costs for the mentally disabled, 35 percent of the local share of that portion of the Medicaid program which receives no federal funding, and 17 percent of the remaining local share of the Medicaid program.

HSOA was replaced in 1984 with the Long-Term Care Medicaid Takeover Act (LTCMTA). Under this law, the State assumes an increasingly larger share of Medicaid costs for most categories of chronic care. In 1984, 1985, and 1986, the State has assumed or will assume 72, 76, and 80 percent, respectively, of the nonfederal share of local Medicaid costs for nursing homes and home care. Subsequently, the State will continue to assume 80 percent of the nonfederal share of these costs. Beginning in 1984, the State also assumed all of the local Medicaid costs for the mentally disabled. Under LTCMTA, the City estimates it will save more than $1.3 billion between 1984 and 1988.[13]

Despite these reforms, the State continues to impose a heavy financial responsibility on the City for Medicaid. After LTCMTA is fully implemented, the City still will be forced to pay one-fifth of the nonfederal share of chronic care costs and one-half of the non-federal share of the costs of other services. Furthermore, the State takeover of costs for the mentally disabled is incomplete because its definition of the mentally disabled excludes a large number of individuals never admitted to State facilities as a result of the State's restrictive admissions policies. In 1985, the City's costs for caring for those individuals exceeded $40 million.[14]

Thus, with regard to lowering local expenditures for Medicaid, the City's agenda is clear. Increased State funding should remain the first priority. Delays in implementation of the LTCMTA should be avoided and extension of the program to other services should be pursued for the period after 1988.

EXPANDING ELIGIBILITY

Pressing for more State assumption of local Medicaid costs should not, however, be the only policy the City pursues. Medicaid eligibility should also be expanded. Limiting Medicaid eligibility is often the most politically convenient strategy for containing Medicaid expenditures. In periods of inflation, a state can cut Medicaid eligibility simply by failing to adjust income criteria for the effects of price increases and economic growth. This policy was pursued in New York State during the mid-1970s. The constant dollar (1967) maximum income level for Medicaid eligibility for a family of four declined 46 percent, from $4202 to $2277, between 1970 and 1983.[15] During this period, the number of Medicaid beneficiaries in New York City declined 18 percent, largely because of a 58 percent decline in the number of those who were eligible only for medical assistance. In 1982, only about 11 percent of the Medicaid population was not receiving cash assistance, compared with 22 percent in 1970.[16]

The limitation in Medicaid eligibility has created serious inequities. While the standards for medically needy one- and two-person households are linked to annually indexed federal SSI benefits, standards for larger families are not automatically adjusted for inflation. In 1973, the income-eligibility standards for two-person and seven-person families were 113 percent and 90 percent of the poverty level, respectively. By 1983, income eligibility for a two-person household was still 102 percent of the poverty level; the standard for a family of seven had fallen to 48 percent of that standard (see Table 9.7). This "silent" policy change is particularly troubling since most of those left uncovered are children.

That low eligibility standards coupled with inequities related to family size exclude many needy individuals from Medicaid is illustrated by several indicators. At the time of the 1980 census, the number of Medicaid enrollees was only 85 percent of the number of persons below the poverty level in New York City. Moreover, the ratio of Medicaid enrollees to the poor and near-poor population (defined as those with incomes below 125 percent of the poverty level) was only 66 percent.[17]

Another indicator is the existence of a large, poor, uninsured population consisting of approximately 400,000 persons in the state with incomes below the poverty level and without health insurance. Another 390,000 near-poor New Yorkers are without coverage.[18] The lack of insurance is a barrier to medical care. While not all of these individuals have serious health problems, many do not obtain preventive health care as a result of their uninsured status.[19] This failure inevitably results in more serious and more costly health problems subsequently.

Medicaid eligibility restrictions also create financial problems for the hospitals that serve the poor and uninsured. The number of

TABLE 9.7

Medicaid Income Eligibility Standards by Family Size, New York State, 1973 and 1983

| | 1973 | | 1983 | |
Family Size	Maximum Annual Income	Maximum Income as Percentage of Federal Poverty Level	Maximum Annual Income	Maximum Income as Percentage of Federal Poverty Level
1	$2,500	104.0%	$4,500	88.9%
2	3,400	113.0	6,600	102.0
3	4,000	115.0	6,700	84.4
4	5,000	109.0	6,800	66.8
5	5,700	103.0	6,900	57.2
6	6,400	101.0	7,000	51.4
7	7,200	89.8	7,400	47.7

SOURCES: United States Census Bureau and New York State Department of Social Services, "Memorandum in Support of Legislation to Amend the New York State Social Services Law."

uninsured patients discharged from New York City voluntary hospitals in 1980 was nearly 55,000, or about 7 percent of all those discharged from voluntary hospitals. The number of uninsured patients discharged from the municipal hospitals was nearly 31,000, some 13 percent of their total.[20]

Expanding Medicaid eligibility and eliminating the inequities for larger families would not only improve the health of the poor and near poor, and improve the financial status of hospitals, but it would make sense fiscally for the City of New York. Approximately 75 percent of the cost of care for those eligible for Medicaid is paid by the State and federal governments; when a poor, uninsured patient uses municipal hospitals, the City must finance the costs entirely from local tax dollars. The net effect of increasing Medicaid eligibility would be to shift costs to higher levels of government, better equipped to finance them.

NEW DELIVERY SYSTEMS

Financing reforms and expanded eligibility will not address all of the health-care problems of those receiving Medicaid because Medicaid services are often not satisfactory. Given the shortage of private physicians in many of the city's poorer neighborhoods and the reluctance of physicians generally to accept low Medicaid fees, enrollees typically are dependent on hospital clinics, emergency rooms, and shared health facilities (which used to be more pungently described as "Medicaid mills"). The care rendered in such facilities tends to be highly episodic. As a result, Medicaid recipients receive more diagnostic tests and more inpatient care than if they were under the continuing care of doctors who knew them.

One approach to dealing with this issue is prepaid capitated practice arrangements, the most effective form of which is the health maintenance organization (HMO). Under appropriate circumstances, HMOs can deliver continuous, high-quality care while reducing tests and inpatient utilization. As a result, development of HMOs to serve Medicaid recipients has become popular in many parts of the country, supported by the federal government and private foundations.

A decade of small-scale experimentation with HMOs for the Medicaid population in New York State culminated in the passage of the Medicaid Reform Act of 1984. It authorized the development of up to ten plans, including three that had already been in the developmental stage. One of those three is Health Care Plus, sponsored by Lutheran Medical Center in Brooklyn.

While there is much to be said for the performance of well-managed prepaid delivery systems, a decade of experience with governmental attempts to foster their development for the nonpoor suggests that they are not a panacea.[21] Capitation is not merely a financing device. It requires organizational innovation and managerial sophistication of a level often difficult to achieve. Moreover, the start-up capital requirements can be considerable. As a result, a significant number of the new plans may be failures.

There are also particular problems with prepaid plans started for the Medicaid population. The plans can create financial incentives to underprovide services. Further, experience with HMOs for the nonpoor population indicates that enrollments of 20,000 to 30,000 individuals per plan over a three- to four-year period is an optimistic target. To enroll even one-half of those eligible for AFDC in such plans would require the creation of between 12 and 18 HMOs, assuming that only some of the initial efforts would be unsuccessful. Achieving enrollments of this scale will be difficult because there are few incentives for those eligible for Medicaid to enroll in HMOs. Benefits already are extensive under the Medicaid program, so the range of HMO services is not necessarily greater; moreover, the enrollee sacrifices freedom of choice among providers.

The relative success of Lutheran Medical Center's Health Care Plus program is enlightening. In addition to all Medicaid-covered services, Health Care Plus offers its approximately 300 enrollees reduced waiting times, a "pharmacy express" service, and a case manager to coordinate their care from different physicians. The hospital also guarantees all enrollees eligibility for ambulatory care for six months even if their Medicaid eligibility terminates. However, the hospital's strong ties to its local community and the lack of alternative providers also explain the program's success. It is not clear that similar programs would be as successful in areas of the city where there are alternative sources of care.

The results of the program at Lutheran Medical Center suggest that promotion of capitated plans is desirable, but that it would be a mistake for the City or the State to rely too much on HMOs. At least for the next four years, other efforts to improve the quality of services to the Medicaid population will be required. While a variety of initiatives involving voluntary hospitals and community health care centers are desirable and possible, a particularly important effort involves reorganization of the ambulatory care services of the Health and Hospitals Corporation. The Corporation is the single largest provider of services to the Medicaid population.

HEALTH AND HOSPITALS CORPORATION

The City of New York has been in the hospital business since 1736 when it opened its first almshouse, Bellevue Hospital. Since then, the City has provided for the health care of its residents by operating its own hospital facilities and subsidizing voluntary institutions. In the 1950s and 1960s, the expanded potential for medical care to improve dramatically the lives of patients highlighted the deficiencies of the municipal facilities and led to the formation of several investigative groups and blue ribbon panels. The most influential of these was the Commission on the Delivery of Personal Health Services, also known as the Piel Commission. In its 1967 report, the Piel Commission recommended the formation of a semi-autonomous public-benefit corporation to operate New York's municipal hospitals.[22] In 1970, the Health and Hospitals Corporation (HHC) was formed to improve the management of the City's diverse municipal hospitals.

The challenges facing the HHC in the remainder of this decade arise from the roles it is asked to perform. They are shaped by the progress made since 1970, and particularly in the past five years, in improving the operations of its hospitals. To help identify plausible options for the future, it is useful to review the scope of the Corporation's activities and the past efforts which provide a basis for new initiatives.

CURRENT ROLE

Municipal hospitals serve multiple, often overlapping, roles. They are providers of last resort to a population unable to obtain services elsewhere; they provide services otherwise unavailable to the community at large; they are sole providers of care in some neighborhoods. In sum, the municipal hospitals play a unique role arising both from the special population they serve and their ability to fill gaps left by the private health care delivery system.

The broad responsibilities of the HHC create an atypical set of challenges in patient care and hospital management, going beyond the obvious fact that a substantial proportion of the municipal hospitals' patients are uninsured and cannot pay out of pocket, to the more subtle challenges of caring for a predominantly poor population. The special characteristics of municipal hospitals are reflected in the high proportion of admissions that come through their emergency rooms, the high volume of ambulatory, psychiatric, and rehabilitation services they provide, and HHC's responsibility over emergency medical services.

Emergency Room Admissions. While HHC facilities account for less than 20 percent of all hospital admissions in New York City, they provide almost 40 percent of all emergency room visits throughout the city. (See Table 9.8.) More than two-thirds of the patients admitted to municipal hospitals enter through the emergency room, compared to less than one-third at voluntary and propriety facilities.[23] This difference arises largely from lower rates of elective surgery in HHC facilities which, in turn, reflects both the inadequacy or unavailability of care from private physicians in poor communities and patterns of care that delay intervention until illness is relatively advanced.

The high proportion of emergency cases means that municipal hospitals cannot accurately anticipate demand and must, therefore, maintain excess capacity to accommodate emergency needs. The need to maintain slack resources to meet unpredictable surges in admissions means that occupancy rates will be—indeed, should be—lower at municipal hospitals than at voluntary and proprietary hospitals. Beyond that, the HHC must devote relatively more resources to patient care because so many of its patients are in advanced stages of illness when admitted. Though it has been difficult to demonstrate with objective evidence, those on the staffs of municipal hospitals assert that their patients, by virtue of their poverty, are likely to have special problems complicating treatment and delaying discharge.

Although the municipal hospitals' emergency rooms are used primarily by the disadvantaged, the community at large also is served by their extensive network of emergency services and their

TABLE 9.8

Role of Municipal Hospitals in the New York City Hospital System, 1983

| | Total | Hospitals | | | |
		Municipal	Voluntary	Proprietary	State
Inpatient Services					
General Care Discharges					
Number	1,128,362	219,021	812,756	85,245	11,340
Percent	100.0%	19.4%	72.0%	7.6%	1.0%
Admissions from Emergency Room					
Number	438,123	169,226	245,624	23,273	—
Percent	100.0%	38.6%	56.1%	5.3%	—
Mental Health Discharges					
Number	3,179	1,401	1,498	246	34
Percent	100.0%	44.1%	47.1%	7.7%	1.1%
Physical Rehabilitation Discharges					
Number	1,075	646	411	—	18
Percent	100.0%	60.1%	38.2%	—	1.7%
Outpatient Services					
Emergency Room Visits					
Number	3,318,065	1,318,095	1,857,086	142,884	—
Percent	100.0%	39.7%	56.0%	4.3%	—
Outpatient Department Visits					
Number	6,604,961	3,024,167	3,514,129	—	66,665
Percent	100.0%	45.8%	53.2%	—	1.0%

SOURCE: United Hospital Fund, *Health Facilities in Southern New York*, 1985 edition.

capacity for handling large-scale disasters. The trauma services at Bellevue, the kidney treatment services at Kings County, and the respiratory care at Goldwater hospitals, for example, serve the special medical needs of the community at large. In a fundamental sense, HHC facilities provide an emergency capacity for individual or collective disasters.

Ambulatory Care. The municipal hospitals also provide a relatively high volume of ambulatory care. Almost one-half of all outpatient visits (excluding emergency rooms) in New York City are provided at HHC facilities.

While the role of municipal hospitals as the family doctor for poor communities is well recognized, the financial burden this places on hospitals only recently has begun to be fully understood. Ambulatory care is a financial drain because Medicaid, which is the major source of funds for hospital-based ambulatory care, pays hospitals at rates per visit that often are below cost. Moreover, establishing the eligibility of outpatients for Medicaid is difficult because of the relatively brief contact with the patient. Finally, and most importantly, a large proportion of uninsured, poor patients who are not covered by Medicaid seek outpatient care at municipal hospitals because they have no means to pay either private physicians or voluntary hospitals.

Mental Health and Physical Rehabilitation. The Corporation also plays a major role in providing mental health and physical rehabilitation services for inpatients. Municipal facilities account for some 44 percent of discharges from mental health units at acute-care hospitals and 60 percent of discharges from physical medicine and rehabilitation units. Patients in these units often lack health insurance and present obvious management and discharge planning challenges.

The dominant issue relating to mental health services in the city has been the State's lack of commitment to serving patients for whom it has been historically responsible. The average daily number of patients cared for at State psychiatric hospitals in the city decreased 53 percent, from 10,634 to 5020, between 1970 and 1983.[24] Thousands of mentally ill individuals were released without adequate provision for community-based care. Although the State has assumed responsibility for some of these patients by fully financing their Medicaid coverage, this addresses only a small part of the problem because appropriate services are not available, and many former State clients have not received Medicaid coverage. Local hospitals are left to cope with the State's rejects, a burden that falls heavily on municipal hospitals.

Unfortunately, municipal hospitals have not been particularly effective in caring for the mentally ill. A recent report from the City Hospital Visiting Committee of the United Hospital Fund describes continued poor direction and inadequate staffing in both mental health and rehabilitation services.[25]

Ambulance Services. The HHC does not provide all of the ambulance service in the city, but it is responsible for overseeing the citywide Emergency Medical Service (EMS) that coordinates responses by ambulances assigned to municipal hospitals as well as ambulances assigned to voluntary hospitals and other organizations. New York City's EMS responded to approximately 8600 calls per 100,000 residents in 1983, an 8.5 percent increase over 1980. In comparison, Los Angeles reported approximately 5300 EMS responses per 100,000 residents in fiscal year 1983.[26] (However, more than 50 percent of the calls in Los Angeles turned out to be unnecessary or unfounded compared to about 35 percent in New York City. The higher volume of responses in New York City is attributable to several factors, including the general lack of private transportation in New York, its greater proportion of older people, and the easy access of New York's unified 911 emergency telephone system which Los Angeles still lacks.) The HHC handles this difficult task relatively well. The EMS response time (the time between receiving the call and the arrival of the ambulance) has decreased dramatically in recent years, despite increases in call loads. The response time for life-threatening situations fell from 18.8 minutes in 1980 to 11.7 minutes in 1983, and to 9.4 minutes in 1984.[27]

This improved performance by the EMS reflects the impact of new medical leadership at the vice-presidential level of HHC and the attendant commitment to increased staff and equipment. Most directly responsible for more rapid responses is a new medical communications system introduced in 1977 and upgraded significantly in 1981 and 1983. Additional staff, including 228 new personnel hired in 1984, are expected to reduce average response time further.

Neighborhood Roles. While the high proportion of emergency room admissions and the large volume of ambulatory and inpatient mental health care are characteristic of the entire municipal hospital system, the roles played by individual hospitals are far from identical. Some City hospitals are the sole providers of care in their communities and draw the bulk of their patients from the immediate neighborhood, while others draw patients from a far wider geographic area.

The relation of a hospital to its local community can be gauged by examining the share of all inpatient and outpatient services used by the neighboring residents that the specific hospital provides. This measure of the hospital's "market share" has been calculated using two definitions of the local area; in one case, the area is the *three* zip codes from which the hospital draws the largest number of patients; in the other it is the *five* principal zip codes served by the hospital (see Table 9.9).

Municipal hospitals generally are the major source of care for residents of their surrounding communities. Citywide, municipal hospitals account for about one-fifth of all inpatient discharges. The market share of individual municipal hospitals in their respective service areas generally is higher, with most municipal hospitals discharging between 25 and 30 percent of all local inpatients. Harlem Hospital and Kings County Hospital Center serve neighborhoods that are particularly dependent on them. The principal exception is North Central Bronx Hospital, which serves a section of the Bronx with several other hospitals including Montefiore Medical Center, a major voluntary institution located across the street.

For emergency room and outpatient department visits, the municipal hospitals' importance to their surrounding communities is even greater. Municipal hospitals provide about one-third of all emergency-room visits in New York City, but at least six municipal hospitals account for more than 40 percent of all emergency room visits by residents of their service areas. City Hospital Center at Elmhurst, Metropolitan Hospital Center, and North Central Bronx Hospital provide an unusually low proportion of local residents' emergency room care due to the availability of alternative sources of emergency care. Coney Island Hospital, however, is the only major medical facility in southern Brooklyn, and thus provides an unusually large share of all emergency room care to its community.

For outpatient department visits, the market shares of municipal

TABLE 9.9

Percentage of All Hospital Care in Local Service Area Provided by Each Municipal Hospital

	Local Service Area Defined by Three Zip Codes			Local Service Area Defined by Five Zip Codes		
	Inpatient Discharges	ER Visits	OPD Visits	Inpatient Discharges	ER Visits	OPD Visits
Woodhull Hospital	—	45%	38%	—	41%	33%
Coney Island Hospital	29%	54	81	22%	41	76
Metropolitan Hospital Center	30	37	35	22	23	32
Harlem Hospital Center	42	47	37	36	42	38
Lincoln Hospital	28	39	61	28	36	49
North Central Bronx Hospital	13	30	24	12	25	20
Kings County Hospital Center	35	61	33	32	49	24
City Hospital Center at Elmhurst	26	28	67	24	27	65
Bronx Municipal Hospital Center	24	48	48	22	43	50
Queens Hospital Center	29	42	51	24	37	48
Bellevue Hospital	30	45	56	27	42	24

SOURCE: United Hospital Fund Patient Origin Information System.

NOTE: Data on inpatient discharges are for 1980; data on emergency room and outpatient department visits are for second quarter, 1983. Woodhull Hospital was not in operation during 1980.

hospitals vary widely depending, again, on the availability of alternative providers. Coney Island Hospital and City Hospital Center at Elmhurst, located in areas with no nearby alternative sources of hospital-based outpatient services, account for a large majority of outpatient visits by residents of the surrounding community. In contrast, the unusually low market share for Kings County Hospital Center reflects the nearby presence of several voluntary hospitals with extensive outpatient services.

In sum, the specific role played by a municipal hospital within its community varies among facilities. Sole community providers will have a distinctly different character and different responsibilities from those of hospitals that serve a smaller, more skewed proportion of the market. Identifying and organizing to serve these widely different roles is a major challenge facing the Corporation.

RECENT IMPROVEMENTS

It has taken almost 15 years for the Health and Hospitals Corporation to produce tangible results. In its early years, the Corporation was plagued by the same problems that the municipal hospitals faced when under jurisdiction of the Department of Hospitals: the lack of good, stable leadership; inadequate budgets; deteriorating physical plants and equipment; poorly qualified, unmotivated staff. For many years, the Corporation not only failed to solve these problems, but added to them.

Throughout most of the 1970s, the Corporation's central office endured frequent turnover of top-level management and senior staff, as did many of its hospitals. The early 1970s also were characterized by political tension revolving around community control and minority representation. The fiscal crisis had a profound impact on HHC for the rest of the decade. Then too, municipal hospitals found themselves affected dramatically by the changing regulations and reimbursements, described earlier, that constrained the level of funds available to them.

However, notable progress in defining a rational role for HHC facilities and significant gains in managing the daily operations of the municipal hospitals have been achieved, particularly since 1980. These gains include improved occupancy rates, decreased dependence on tax levy funds for operating support, and development of a ten-year capital plan.

TABLE 9.10

New York City Health and Hospitals Corporation Operating Budget and Tax Levy Subsidy, Fiscal Years 1978–85

(millions of dollars)

Fiscal Year	Total Budget	Tax Levy Subsidy[a]	Subsidy as a Percentage of Total
1978	$1,075.5	$280.5	26.1%
1979	1,095.5	266.5	24.3
1980	1,035.3	114.2	11.0
1981	1,068.7	149.2	14.0
1982	1,337.5	208.1	15.6
1983	1,468.2	241.9	16.5
1984	1,638.4	232.4	14.2
1985	1,719.5	268.8	15.6
Percentage Change 1978–85	59.9%	−4.2%	−40.2%

SOURCE: The City of New York, Expense Budget as adopted, fiscal years 1978 through 1985.

a. Excludes appropriations for mental health, Medicaid, and capital funds.

Higher Occupancy Rates. In 1973, the occupancy rate for general-care services at municipal hospitals was less than 76 percent; by 1983, it had increased to 83 percent.[28] Although this figure remains significantly below the occupancy rate at voluntary hospitals in the city, the high volume of emergency room admissions at municipal hospitals suggests that their occupancy rates should be lower than those at voluntary hospitals.

The improved occupancy rates result largely from reductions in beds. Between 1973 and 1983, the HHC cut its general care capacity from approximately 8200 to fewer than 5800 beds.[29] This required a significant reconfiguration of the system's physical plant. Facilities for providing inpatient services at four hospitals were closed; bed capacity at eight others was reduced; and two new inpatient facilities were opened.

Noteworthy, too, is the fact that higher occupancy rates occurred during a period when average lengths of stay were falling. In 1973, the average stay for general care services at municipal hospitals was 10.9 days; by 1983, this had declined to 8.1 days. The average length of stay also decreased at voluntary hospitals during this period, but the decrease was significantly smaller, from 10.3 to 9.4 days.[30]

Greater Financial Independence. In recent years, and most no-

TABLE 9.11

Capital Plan for the New York City Health and Hospitals Corporation
Fiscal Years 1985–94
(millions of dollars)

	Amount	Percent
Sources of Fund		
City Funds	$ 585.0	38.8%
FHA-insured Hospital Revenue Bonds	712.7	47.3
HHC Alternative Financing	203.1	13.5
State and Federal Funds	7.1	0.5
Total	$1,507.9	100.0%
Uses of Funds		
Major Reconstruction of Hospitals (Elmhurst, Coney Island, Bronx Municipal, Kings County, Queens)	$957.7	63.5%
Major Equipment	198.9	13.2
Routine Reconstruction	187.2	12.4
Information Systems	66.1	4.4
EMS Equipment	59.1	3.9
Telecommunications	29.3	1.9
Energy Projects	9.7	0.6
Total	$1,507.9	100.0%

SOURCE: City of New York, *Executive Budget, Fiscal Year 1985, Message of the Mayor,*
April 26, 1984; p. 220.

NOTE: Columns may not add due to rounding.

tably since 1978, the HHC has reduced its dependence on subsidies
from the City for its operating expenses. While the HHC budget
grew nearly 60 percent from 1978 to 1985, from less than $1.1 to
more than $1.7 billion, the subsidy required from City tax funds
fell 4 percent, from $281 to $269 million (see Table 9.10). As a share
of total expenses, the subsidy from local taxes fell from 26 to under
16 percent.

This greater financial independence resulted from a number of
efforts to improve revenues from third parties. A major investment
in financial management and legal services paid off in higher Medicaid rates and in significant retroactive payments from the settlement of reimbursement appeals. The decline in average length of
stay and the increase in occupancy rates had significant implications
for reimbursement because reimbursement formulas take into account occupancy and length of stay. The Corporation also improved
its collections efforts by installing automated billing systems at the
City hospitals. This accelerated the processing of previously back-

logged claims and enabled more timely and accurate handling of current billing activities. Finally, the Corporation has been increasingly successful in securing Medicaid enrollment for eligible patients, largely by permitting patients to apply for Medicaid at individual hospitals rather than requiring them to apply at central offices in mid-Manhattan. As a result, approval rates for applications have increased, while the length of time for approval has decreased.[31]

Establishing a Capital Plan. As part of a ten-year planning process for the entire city, the Corporation produced a ten-year capital plan in 1983 for the municipal hospital system. Before then, the capital needs of the municipal hospitals were reviewed only on an ad hoc basis.

The ten-year plan was revised in 1984, again as part of a citywide capital planning process. This plan allocates over $1.5 billion to HHC. (See Table 9.11.) Nearly two-thirds of the money will be used to reconstruct five municipal hospitals, Elmhurst, Coney Island, Bronx Municipal, Kings County and Queens. Other large expenditures are for major equipment (13 percent) and routine reconstruction of other facilities (12 percent).

The planned sources of these funds indicate both the serious commitment of municipal funds to the HHC and its growing financing capacity. Nearly 39 percent of the funds, or $585 million, will be provided by the City. However, the HHC plans to issue federally insured revenue bonds to raise another $713 million, and is seeking additional independent financing for another $203 million.

LOOKING AHEAD

The progress made by HHC leaders in recent years still leaves much to be done. Nursing services are inadequate; mental health services need improvement; response times for the EMS could be decreased; geriatric care must be improved. Each of these efforts deserves more consideration by municipal and HHC leaders, but for the long-run future of HHC it is important to focus on broader strategies that would help promote its mission. Two issues in particular need resolution: affiliation relationships with teaching institutions, and the restoration of a leadership role by City officials in citywide health planning.

Relationship with Affiliates. The ability of HHC to fulfill its various missions is profoundly influenced by its program of "affiliation" with medical schools and voluntary teaching hospitals. This program was begun in 1961 in an effort to bring qualified professional staff into the municipal hospitals. Through expansion of this program, as well as through other agreements to affiliate with private hospitals, the city's medical schools have become a major instrument for the delivery of health care services to the city's population. Hospitals affiliated with medical centers account for 75 percent of all New York City hospital discharges, 80 percent of all emergency room visits, and 92 percent of all outpatient visits.[32] The medical schools play a particularly crucial role in the delivery of professional and medical services at municipal hospitals. Six of the seven medical schools with teaching programs in the city are affiliated with municipal hospitals. In exchange for the professional services they provide at municipal hospitals, the HHC-affiliated institutions were paid nearly $263 million in fiscal year 1984. This sum represented nearly 15 percent of HHC total operating expenses.[33]

The unresolved issue that has permeated the affiliation is the clash between individual patient care and community service goals of the municipal hospitals, on the one hand, and the academic mission and independent tradition of the medical schools and voluntary hospital affiliates, on the other. Because of the dependence of the Corporation on the affiliates for staff and services, affiliation contracts historically represented agreements between unequal partners. While affiliation has improved the quality of care at municipal hospitals, the academic centers have not been often as zealous in maintaining quality standards at municipal facilities as they have been at their "home" institutions. The affiliates have resisted attempts by municipal officials to impose standards and have often been able to determine what kinds of services and staffing would be provided at the municipal facilities.

Since 1982, the HHC has sought to ensure that activities of its affiliates better reflect the primacy of the Corporation's basic purpose of providing health services over competing interests of the voluntary medical centers. In addition, the Corporation has begun to specify, in the affiliation agreements, HHC expectations for staffing levels and services. Furthermore, HHC hospital administrators have assumed responsibility for many hospital functions previously delegated to affiliates, including admissions, medical records, discharge planning, and utilization review. Discussions also are underway at several hospitals to create key medical positions that report directly to the hospital administrator rather than to the affiliate. Nevertheless, the types and levels of services provided to the municipal hospitals by the affiliates continue to be inadequate in many instances.

Current trends in the number of physicians available, however, may provide a new opportunity for HHC to recruit and manage a medical staff for its hospitals independently. As the number of qualified physicians increases, municipal hospitals can become less dependent on affiliates to provide medical services—at least in theory. By hiring their own doctors—or planning to—HHC should be able both to insist on higher standards of patient care in the municipal hospitals and exert significant influence on medical education policies in the city.

The objective to be realized from building up its own staff or using the opportunity to recruit its own physicians as a negotiating strategy with the affiliates is to reduce the level of resources that have supported medical education at the expense of the kinds of patient care most needed by HHC patients. Highly specialized care and sophisticated equipment should be available at municipal hospitals only to the extent they are necessary to serve HHC patients, not because they help meet the affiliates' educational and research agendas.

HHC emphasis on primary care should prove beneficial to medical education in the long run. Expensive, impersonal, discontinuous care, however technologically sophisticated, is under attack by leading medical educators; HHC's business, focused on primary care, is a valuable ingredient in physician education that municipal hospitals can help provide. The municipal hospitals thus represent to the affiliates an opportunity to influence positively the direction of medical education by providing training that emphasizes primary and long-term care.

Leadership in Citywide Planning. The coordination of services from many sources on a broad geographic basis or "regionalization" long has been a goal of health planners throughout the city. The strongest push for regionalization has come from the Corporation, which has sought to avoid the costly duplication of equipment and programs while ensuring availability of a full range of services to all residents of an area. Yet, the Corporation's historical weakness in its relationships with voluntary hospitals, plus its own internal management problems, limited its effectiveness as an advocate for system-wide change. Now, because of its improved internal management and planning capabilities, its expanded capacity to raise capital, and its increasing equality in relations with affiliates, the Corporation is in a position to exert more influence over the larger health care system in New York City.

It is important, however, to recognize that much of the legal authority for health planning rests with State officials. The State's capacity to control capital investment by means of the Certificate of Need requirement and its control over operating income through regulation of third-party payment rates make it the most powerful source of public control over the health care industry. But the case for an expanded role for municipal officials also is strong. The City, like the State, finances a share of all hospitals' operating expenses through its share of the Medicaid program. Also, City officials have an important stake in decisions about both public and private facilities because of the vital role of health-care services in the local economy.

There are numerous opportunities for municipal officials to take a lead in planning. In western and southeastern Queens, northern and central Brooklyn, and much of the Bronx, health planners face formidable problems in terms both of modernizing facilities and providing expensive new technologies. Similarly, the Corporation's planning for long-term and psychiatric care should be better integrated with the planning carried out by private institutions.

Leadership from municipal officials in health planning is desirable and feasible. In addition to increased managerial capacity at HHC, the City has political resources through its generalized negotiations with Albany and legal authority through its land-use review process to participate more effectively and aggressively in health planning than it has in the past. The future of health care in the city will be shaped in the next few years by this planning process whether or not the City adopts such a role. It would be a pity for it to miss the opportunity.

THE DEPARTMENT OF HEALTH

The general mission of the Department of Health (DOH) has

remained essentially unaltered for over 100 years. Since creation of the Metropolitan Board of Health in 1866, a municipal agency has been legally responsible for regulating "all matters affecting the health in the city" and for "performing those functions and operatins performed by the City that affect the health of [its] people."[34] However, changes in its environment have altered the role of the Department in protecting public health. A review of these changes provides an essential background for suggesting an appropriate future role for the DOH.

THE CHANGING ENVIRONMENT

For nearly a century after its birth, the New York City Department of Health was a model public agency. It took the initiative—in fact, led the way nationally—in areas such as school health, vital statistics, laboratory research and bacteriology, maternal and child health, and public-health research. The DOH took a particular interest in maternal and child health, and over time became increasingly involved in the direct delivery of personal health services. By the 1960s, the Department's district health centers that had been targets of opposition from private medical practitioners earlier in the century, who feared the competition, were providing pediatric, geriatric, and general medical care.

Over the past two decades the roles and responsibilities of the Health Department have changed or, more precisely, have contracted. Four important factors have greatly altered the DOH mission.

First, the nature of public health problems changed. Contemporary public health problems, unlike the communicable diseases that dominated public health practice in the Department's glory days, increasingly have been replaced by chronic, degenerative, and social disorders. The cures for these "new" ills lay in large part outside the scientific foundation upon which the Department had built its earlier reputation for excellence.

Second, following the effective control of many communicable diseases, there was a gradual diffusion of many of the Department's former responsibilities to other agencies or departments, such as sanitation and environmental protection. In addition, the State Department of Health gradually assumed many of the City's regulatory and standard-setting functions.

Third, in the 1960s there were major changes in the delivery and financing of care for the poor—the major clientele of the Department's services historically. These changes enabled poor people to choose from an increasingly wide range of options for health services. Federal support of free-standing health centers led to the development of neighborhood-based comprehensive care clinics, strong competitors providing a full range of preventive and treatment services at reduced or no cost to patients in new or renovated physical structures. Another source of competition was the reorganized Health and Hospitals Corporation which offered improved services at municipal hospitals for the poor. Finally, access to both public and private health care was improved with the enactment of Medicaid, which substituted purchasing power for direct service and increased the ability of the poor to choose among available delivery systems. The result was that the Department no longer was the primary protector of public health but simply one of several agencies with parallel, if not overlapping, responsibilities.

The fourth factor that changed the Department's role was mayoral choice. As an agency under direct mayoral control, in contrast to Medicaid or HHC, the DOH has been particularly vulnerable to budgetary cutbacks. Reorganizations and other accounting changes make comparisons to budgets drawn up before the fiscal crisis potentially misleading. Since 1979, a period when figures are more reliable, the DOH budget has remained nearly stable despite inflation and the City's fiscal recovery.

The DOH child health programs provide a dramatic illustration of the impact of these forces. Prior to the fiscal crisis, annual City budgets provided continually expanding support for the conversion of many of the DOH's 78 Child Health Stations to comprehensive clinics for both well and sick children. During the fiscal crisis, however, more than a quarter of the Child Health Stations were closed. Currently, the City's health stations deliver a narrow range of services, centering on immunizations and monitoring healthy babies. Major reductions in virtually all other DOH services also occurred.

LOOKING AHEAD

Having lost some of its historical roles to competition and fiscal stringency, the Department of Health must now define a role appropriate to today's and tomorrow's public health needs. The improved financial outlook of the City no doubt will be accompanied by public pressures from a range of interest groups to replace or expand programs that were cut during the fiscal crisis. However, the Department should rebuild itself by purposefully setting an agenda for the next four years. This will permit the DOH to make a stronger claim for resources and to manage its resources more effectively.

The current Commissioner of Health, David Sencer, has suggested that the ideal urban health department should "(1) treat the community, not the individual, as the patient; (2) have the primary responsibility in its community for assuring primary prevention with the capability of providing such services if others are not so doing; (3) divorce itself from all curative programs except those that are themselves a means of primary prevention (such as ambulatory treatment of tuberculosis); (4) live on local financial resources or funds earmarked for its operation and avoid becoming a conduit for other resources (such as home health care services) that do not relate to its primary mission; and (5) possess the technical expertise that is a prerequisite for leadership."[35]

Sencer's suggestions provide a useful basis for distinguishing the DOH mission from other City health programs. What remains distinctive about the DOH is its community orientation. Protecting *public* health implies a different range of activities than does protecting the health of each individual within a population. The Department should maintain a community-based perspective in defining its objectives.

Surveillance, data collection, epidemiological studies, the setting and monitoring of health and sanitary standards, and the maintenance of public health laboratory services are all logical activities for the DOH since they represent "public goods" of various sorts. In these areas, the Department has both the opportunity and the tools to make significant contributions. Its data-gathering and standard-setting functions place the Department in a unique position to identify unmet health needs and changing patterns of diseases or treatment. The Department's data-collection efforts rest on a solid foundation; the DOH is the only local health department that maintains its own vital and health statistics capability. This capacity should be enlarged to include stronger research and analytic capabilities.

In setting and monitoring health care standards, the Department should expand its focus and monitor access to and quality of care. In today's highly cost-conscious environment, it is important that the effects of cost-cutting experiments be independently evaluated. Both these epidemiological and standard-setting activities should be tied to renewed and stronger public information, health education, and advocacy activities in the Department. The Department is uniquely situated to act as an advocate on a range of public health issues. It should seek to educate the public about risks to their health and available sources of screening and treatment.

There are, unfortunately, strong political disincentives to playing such a role. Elected officials rarely publicize problems which they do not have the resources or ability to solve; they invite too much opportunity for blame, too little for praise. Yet, as protectors of public health with sole access to the information upon which successful advocacy can be based, the Department should be encouraged by the next administration to perform this function. At a minimum, the Department should enhance its capacity to make available a broad range of data necessary for identifying unmet community health needs. Continuing assessment of community health needs is of vital importance to planning for the city's entire health care system.

Direct delivery of primary prevention services, another area of departmental involvement recommended by Sencer, merits close scrutiny. A case can be made for a departmental role in the delivery of services that are preventive rather than forms of disease treatment, since they are aimed at the health of whole populations rather than individuals. For example, preventive activities such as lead-poisoning screenings or maternal and child health services that are tied to epidemiological findings regarding the high risks of certain populations for certain kinds of disease fit within the mission of a community-based department.

Immunization—the most basic preventive service—generally is provided through physicians in private practice. To the extent that it is not, groups at risk of infectious disease pose a risk to themselves and to the general public health. The DOH thus has a role to play in maintaining surveillance of immunization levels and in acting directly where private providers have not. The Department should immunize anyone who requests it and be particularly energetic in finding other potential cases among high-risk groups.

A case also can be made for a departmental role in school health programs. The economies of scale, the citywide scope of such activities, and potential cost savings from disease prevention justify departmental responsibility for these programs. The DOH strength in this area will depend not solely on whether screenings are carried out and problems are identified, but whether appropriate follow-up and treatment is received. It is in this area that efforts by the DOH have fallen short in the past, and in which demonstration projects should thus be encouraged.

It is more difficult to make the case for departmental delivery of prenatal and family-planning services for which there is mounting public pressure. These services are currently provided by all the municipal hospitals and many voluntary hospitals. Establishing a duplicate set of services under DOH auspices not only would be inefficient itself but may also reduce the efficiency with which care is delivered at other institutions by reducing their patient load. Instead, the Department should expand its outreach activities and develop mechanisms to require that HHC fill gaps in services that DOH identifies.

Ironically, many of the Health Department's successes helped put it out of business—or at least out of the businesses for which it was best known. Yet much remains to be done. The remaining tasks, highlighted above, may not be as exciting or glamorous as those related to the great public health struggles of the past, but some agency has to address them. No City or private agency is as well equipped to do so as the Department of Health.

CONCLUSION

The City has made important progress in meeting the health needs of its population. It has done so by more efficiently managing those resources and institutions over which it has direct control. More progress is needed, but a different emphasis is needed as well. The City should no longer concern itself solely with managerial improvements, nor with the allocation of City resources alone. Municipal officials have an opportunity to be leaders in system-wide health planning, an opportunity they should realize.

Recognizing the City's stake in its health care system and its new ability to shape this system is a crucial first step towards using their leverage effectively. There are, however, additional steps that should be taken. First, the City should forge stronger relationships with voluntary institutions. The public and private sectors need to join forces to defend common, citywide interests in the intergovernmental arena. New York City's health care system will lose to competing upstate interests if municipal and voluntary sector leaders do not speak with a single voice.

In addition, to represent and promote citywide interests, municipal leaders will be required to articulate what those needs and interests are. The Department of Health can play a critical role here. The expanded surveillance, monitoring, and data gathering efforts advocated earlier should be placed in the service of broad health planning. Those responsible for setting the City's agenda in intergovernmental and other negotiations should be able to look to the Department for assessments of unmet needs.

Finally, a capacity should be developed at the mayoral level not only to supervise executive agencies but also to undertake strategic planning. Conflicts will inevitably arise between the City's long-run interest in its health care system, broadly defined, and other more immediate demands of managing narrowly defined City health activities. Balancing these competing interests requires well-defined priorities and the ability and authority to make politically difficult choices. Capital budgeting is one crucial example; further development of emergency medical services is a second; reorganization of ambulatory care facilities to serve poor patients better a third.

The next administration should not be satisfied with merely doing things right. It should, instead, ask whether it is doing the right things. The shift to consideration of such strategic questions is a mark of how far the City has come and how far it has to go.

NOTES

1. See New York City Department of Health, *Summary of Vital Statistics, 1983*, and U.S. Department of Health and Human Services, Public Health Services, *Health: United States, 1983*.

2. U.S. Department of Commerce, Bureau of the Census, 1980 Census of Population, *General Social and Economic Characteristics: United States Summary*, PC80-1-C1; and *General Social and Economic Characteristics: New York*, PC80-1-C34.

3. New York City Department of Health, op. cit.

4. Ibid.

5. Unpublished data from New York City Department of Health, AIDS Surveillance Office and from the federal Centers for Disease Control.

6. United Hospital Fund, "Health Expenditures in New York City, 1983," UHF Paper Series #1, February 1985.

7. United Hospital Fund, *Inpatient Hospital Use in New York City, 1980,* Vol. 1 Summary Report.

8. U.S. Department of Commerce, Bureau of the Census, *1970 Census of Population and Housing: Characteristics of the Population,* New York and the United States; and *1980 Census of Population,* New York and the United States, op cit.

9. New York State Department of Health, Office of Health Systems Management, unpublished data.

10. U.S. Department of Health and Human Services, *The Medicare and Medicaid Data Book, 1983* (Health Care Financing Administration), HCFA Publication No. 03156, December 1983.

11. Authors' estimate based on methodology cited in David Rogers, Robert Blenden, and Thomas Moloney, "Who Needs Medicaid," *New England Journal of Medicine,* Vol. 307, No. 1 (January 1982), pp. 13–18. The methodology described was projected forward to 1983, based on 1978 national health care expenditures and the national rate of inflation for health care expenditures.

12. State Communities Aid Association, *Albany Bulletin* #18, The Association, May 3, 1984.

13. City of New York, *Message of the Mayor, Executive Budget,* April 26, 1984, p. 75.

14. Ibid., p. 76.

15. New York State Department of Social Services, *Statistical Supplement to the Annual Report,* 1968 and 1983 editions.

16. New York State Department of Social Services, op. cit., 1970 and 1982 editions.

17. New York State Department of Social Services, op. cit., 1980; and New York State Department of Commerce, Data Center, *Summary of 1980 Census of the Population.*

18. Council on Health Care Financing, Subcommittee on Health Insurance, Draft Final Report, 1983; p. 19.

19. Louis Harris and Associates, Inc., *Health Care in New York City* (New York: Commonwealth Fund, October 1982).

20. United Hospital Fund, *Inpatient Hospital Use in New York City, 1980,* op. cit.

21. Lawrence D. Brown, *Politics and Health Care Organization: HMOs as Federal Policy* (Washington, D.C.: The Brookings Institution, 1983).

22. *Comprehensive Community Health Services for New York City,* Report of Commission on the Delivery of Personal Health Services, Gerard Piel, Chairman, 1966.

23. United Hospital Fund, *Health Facilities in Southern New York,* 1985 edition.

24. Figures from New York State Office of Mental Health, Bureau of Statistical Analysis.

25. United Hospital Fund, *The State of New York City Municipal Hospital System,* Report of the City Hospital Visiting Committee, 1983.

26. City of New York, *The Mayor's Management Report,* September 17, 1983, p. 361, and unpublished data from New York City Emergency Medical Services; also Los Angeles City Fire Department, *Annual Report,* 1982–83 edition.

27. *The Mayor's Management Report,* September 17, 1983, p. 361, and unpublished data from New York City Emergency Medical Services.

28. United Hospital Fund, *Profiles and Trends: Hospital Inpatient and Ambulatory Care in Southern New York,* 1984 edition.

29. Ibid.

30. Ibid.

31. Based on informal reports by the staff of the Health and Hospitals Corporation, Office of Finance.

32. I. J. Lewis, H. Lukashok, and C. G. Sheps, "The Academic Medical Center in New York City," United Hospital Fund, New York, no date, p. 24.

33. Unpublished data from Health and Hospitals Corporation, Office of Finance.

34. *New York City Charter*, Chapter 22, Section 556.

35. David Sencer, "Major Urban Health Departments: The Ideal and the Real," *Health Affairs*, Volume 2, Number 4 (Winter 1983), pp. 88–95.

10

Services to the Elderly

CHARLES BRECHER AND
JAMES KNICKMAN

From the early 1960s through the mid-1970s, American society substantially improved its social welfare programs for the elderly. As a result, the most recent decade was one of substantial improvement, both absolute and relative, in the living conditions of the elderly. Compared to the rest of the population, a smaller percentage of the elderly live in poverty and are without health insurance. Little more than 20 years ago the situation was exactly the opposite.

But this progress has not solved social welfare problems for the elderly and has created counter-pressures. The unsolved problems derive from the still significant proportion of elderly who remain in poverty, and from the relatively large and increasing proportion of elderly who need long-term care services they cannot afford. These problems are mainly due to the rapidly escalating costs of public programs for the elderly which are financed largely by taxing

TABLE 10.1

Number of Persons Age 65 and Over, New York City and United States, 1970–90

	New York City	United States
Number of Persons Age 65 and Over		
1970—Actual	947,878	20,065,502
1980—Actual	951,732	25,549,427
1990—Projected	993,000	31,799,000
Aged Persons as a Percentage of Total Population		
1970—Actual	12.0%	9.9%
1980—Actual	13.5	11.3
1990—Projected	14.3	12.7
Percentage Change in Number of Aged Persons		
1970–80—Actual	+0.4%	+27.3%
1980–90—Projected	+4.3	+24.5

SOURCES: The 1970 and 1980 figures are from U.S. Department of Commerce, Bureau of the Census, *1980 Census of Population, General Population Characteristics*, PC80-1-B34, Table 26, and PC80-1-B1, Table 44. The 1990 national projections are from U.S. Bureau of the Census, *Current Population Reports*, Series P-25, No. 922. The 1990 New York City projections are by Emanuel Tobier; see Chapter 2.

the working-age population. Another issue associated with the federal government's expanded commitment to the elderly is the lack of comprehensive local planning for services, particularly long-term care. The frail elderly confront a fragmented system to deliver social services that often fails to produce appropriate services or directs them to agencies that provide services that are more intensive and expensive than they require.

These issues and problems are best addressed at the federal level, but the effects of a large and growing federal deficit combined with the nation's more conservative political mood suggest national solutions will not be coming promptly. In the remainder of the 1980s, state and local governments are the most likely source of leadership for efforts to improve public programs serving the elderly.

This chapter identifies a set of opportunities for municipal leaders, in concert with State officials, to enhance the functioning of public programs for the elderly in New York City without significant increases in public expenditures. It begins with a description of the elderly population, with emphasis on their living arrangements and disabilities. The second section describes three categories of public

TABLE 10.2

Housing Status of Households with Head Age 65 and Over by Household Type, New York City, 1980

| | Number | | | Percentage |
	Total	Owner Occupied	Renter Occupied	Owner Occupied
Married couple	232,671	87,039	145,632	37.4%
Single Individual	317,288	54,476	262,812	17.2
Male	68,999	10,940	58,059	15.9
Female	248,289	43,536	204,753	17.5
Other Elderly Head	84,495	28,044	56,451	33.2
Male	19,823	6,647	13,176	33.5
Female	64,672	21,397	43,275	33.1
Total	634,454	169,559	464,895	26.7%

SOURCE: U.S. Department of Commerce, Bureau of the Census, *1980 Census of Housing*, Vol. 2, Metropolitan Housing Characteristics, New York, N.Y.–N.J., HC80-2-260, Tables D-3, D-4 and D-11.

programs serving the elderly: income maintenance, acute medical care, and long-term care. It highlights the problems that exist despite the substantial commitment of public funds. The final section specifies a set of options local leaders can pursue to alleviate some of these problems within the context of a federal system.

THE ELDERLY POPULATION

The elderly population of New York City is large and growing. At the time of the 1980 census, the city's population included approximately 950,000 persons over age 65: this group represented more than one of every eight New Yorkers (see Table 10.1). The number of aged is estimated to increase to 993,000 in 1990 despite a projected decline in the city's total population. By the end of the current decade approximately one of every seven New York City residents will be elderly—a higher proportion than is expected for the nation as a whole.

The elderly predominantly live in three types of households (see Table 10.2). Most numerous are the nearly 233,000 married couples who represent almost one-half the city's elderly population. Another group of approximately 317,000 elderly live alone; they represent about one-third of the elderly population. Among those living alone, a large majority (78 percent) are female. The third major group, involving approximately 85,000 elderly households, are older household heads who live with someone other than a spouse. Often, these are other family members. Two additional groups not included in Table 10.2 are the nearly 38,000 elderly who are institutionalized, usually in nursing homes, and those elderly who live in households headed by someone under age 65.

A large majority (73 percent) of elderly households rent their housing. Homeowners comprise a significant share (37 percent) of elderly married couples, but represent only 16 percent of single males and less than 18 percent of single females. The share of homeowners among elderly households including two or more people other than a married couple, is approximately one-third.

The more than one-quarter of elderly households that own a home tend to be in relatively good financial condition (see Table 10.3). Their homes had an average value in 1980 of over $48,000, and only 23 percent had a mortgage. For more than one-half the owners, housing costs consumed less than one-quarter of their income; less than one-third of the owners devoted more than 35 percent of their income to housing. However, elderly homeowners other than married couples, and especially females living without their husbands, fared less well. Nearly 15 percent had incomes below the poverty level, and over 47 percent devoted more than 25 percent of their income to housing costs.

Compared to elderly homeowners, older renters have lower incomes and spend more of their incomes on housing. The group in most difficult circumstances is elderly females living without husbands. More than one-quarter (27 percent) had incomes below the poverty level; over 54 percent spent more than 35 percent of their income on rent. Married couples who rented were in somewhat better circumstances. Their median income was nearly $12,200, and 55 percent spent less than one-quarter of their income on rent.

For the planning of services for the elderly, three characteristics of the population are of greatest importance: (1) whether the person is part of a household whose income is sufficient to meet most of his or her needs; (2) whether the person has a chronic condition that limits the ability to function independently; (3) whether the person's living arrangements include another household member who may be available to provide assistance when an elderly person is limited in his activities. Each of these characteristics can be

TABLE 10.3

Selected Characteristics of Housing Arrangements of Households with Head Age 65 or Over, New York City, 1980

		All Households		
	Total	Married Couple	Male, No Wife	Female, No Husband
Owner Occupied—Number	169,559	87,039	17,587	64,933
Median Value	$48,100	$50,700	$44,900	$45,600
Median Income	$12,824	$16,677	$11,106	$ 8,125
Percentage with Income below Poverty Level	9.1%	4.9%	9.3%	14.7%
Percentage with Mortgage	22.8%	27.8%	19.2%	16.0%
Monthly Costs as Percentage of Income[a]	100.0%	100.0%	100.0%	100.0%
Under 25%	50.6	61.9	48.6	35.9
25–34%	17.4	17.8	18.0	16.8
35% or more	32.0	20.3	33.4	47.3
Renter Occupied—Number	464,895	145,632	71,235	248,028
Median Monthly Rent	$203	$240	$187	$186
Median Income	$7,400	$12,156	$6,396	$4,896
Percentage with Income below Poverty Level	19.8%	8.4%	19.6%	26.6%
Rent as Percentage of Income	100.0%	100.0%	100.0%	100.0%
Under 25%	38.1	55.3	37.6	28.1
25–34%	17.7	18.0	17.4	17.6
35% or more	44.2	26.7	45.0	54.3

SOURCE: U.S. Department of Commerce, Bureau of the Census, *1980 Census of Housing*, Vol. 2, Metropolitan Housing Characteristics, New York, N.Y.-N.J., HC80-2-260, Tables D-1 to D-4, and D-10.

a. Includes mortgage costs for mortgaged units.

TABLE 10.4

Elderly Persons with Selected Types of Functional Disability,
New York City, 1980

	Number	Percentage of Total
No Major Functional Disability	791,849	83.5%
Some Functional Disability	156,991	16.5
Institutionalized	37,560	4.0
Disabled in Community		
(net subtotal)	119,431	12.6
Require Home Management Assistance	107,315	11.3
Require Assistance with		
Physical Activities	75,176	7.9
Remain in Bed Most or All Day	20,441	2.2
Total Elderly Population	948,840	100.0%

SOURCE: Estimates derived from Health Interview Survey and 1980 Census of Population; see Note 1. Total number of elderly differs slightly from that shown in Table 10.1 because the figure in Table 10.1 is from the full census count, while this figure is from the 5 percent Public Use Microdata Sample.

estimated using selected data sources to provide a profile of the city's elderly population in terms of their degree of dependence on public programs.

For this analysis, the elderly can be divided into three income groups reflecting the adequacy of resources available to help them obtain needed services: the poor, the near poor, and others. The poor are those elderly in households with annual incomes below the federal poverty line. In 1983, the poverty threshold was $4775 for a single person over age 65 and $6023 for an aged couple. People with incomes below this level have no discretionary income for purchase of services to assist in household management or activities of daily living. The near poor are those in households with incomes between 100 percent and 200 percent of the federal poverty line. This group has some, but probably still inadequate, income for purchasing needed assistance. The third group is those with incomes more than twice the federal poverty threshold; they are able to purchase most of the assistance they might require.

Estimates of the number of people with various types of disabilities can be derived using three categories of disability assessed in recent Health Interview Surveys conducted by the federal government.[1] The first category of disability is an inability to perform one or more home management activities including shopping, preparing meals, handling money, or doing other routine chores. These people require assistance of other persons to manage their households. The second, and usually more serious, category of disability is an inability to perform specific physical activities of daily living—eating, walking, going outside, bathing, dressing, using the toilet, getting in and out of bed or a chair. These people require assistance of another person to perform one or more of these activities. The third, and generally most severe, category of disability is the necessity to remain in bed all or most of the day due to a chronic health problem. Generally, the categories of disability overlap. People remaining in bed usually require assistance in performing physical activities; people with limited physical activities often require assistance to manage their households.

Table 10.4 presents estimates of the number of elderly New Yorkers wih each type of disability. While 84 percent of the elderly have no major functional limitation, approximately one of every six is disabled. This group of approximately 157,000 people is divided between over 37,500 who are institutionalized, predominantly in nursing homes, and nearly 119,500 who live in the community. Of those in the community, 90 percent require assistance to manage their homes, and 63 percent require assistance with the physical activities of daily living. A smaller number remain in bed most or all day.

Table 10.5 presents estimates of the elderly population in different groups defined in terms of income, disability status, and living arrangements. A useful way to summarize the figures is to divide the elderly into four groups: those with no major problem, those whose only problem is their low income, those whose only problem is their physical disability and those with both income and health problems.

The largest group, including 46 percent of the elderly, are those with no major health or income problems. The majority of this group live with someone else, although a substantial number live alone.

The remaining elderly, more than one-half million people, have one or more major problems. For over 356,000 elderly or 36 percent of the total, the problem is low income. This segment of the elderly population has no disability but is poor or nearly so. This group is almost evenly divided between those living with someone and those living alone.

For about 6 percent of the elderly, the only problem is their

TABLE 10.5
New York City Elderly Population by Income, Disability Status, and Living Arrangements, 1980

	Some Disability		No Disability		Total	
	Number	Percentage	Number	Percentage	Number	Percentage
Total	157,225	16.6%	791,615	83.4%	948,840	100.0%
Institutionalized	37,560	4.0	—	—	37,560	4.0
Living in Community	119,665	12.6	791,615	83.4	911,280	96.0
Living Alone	38,473	4.0	269,607	28.4	308,080	32.4
Poor	13,057	1.4	62,923	6.6	75,980	8.0
Near Poor	21,146	2.2	111,954	11.8	133,100	14.0
Higher Income	4,270	0.4	94,730	10.0	99,000	10.4
Living with Someone	81,192	8.6	522,008	55.0	603,200	63.6
Poor	6,226	0.7	51,554	5.4	57,780	6.1
Near Poor	22,345	2.4	129,875	13.7	152,220	16.1
Higher Income	52,621	5.6	340,579	35.9	393,200	41.5

SOURCES: Estimates derived from Health Interview Survey and 1980 Census of Population. See Note 1.

physical disability. These nearly 53,000 individuals have relatively high incomes and live with another person who may be available to help with activities of daily living.

The remaining 105,000 elderly have multiple problems, including a physical disability. Fully 37,560 are institutionalized; among the remainder who live in the community, almost all are disabled and relatively poor. Almost one-half live with another person, but fully 34,000 suffer the multiple hardships of physical disability, low incomes, and living alone.

In sum, the planning of services for the elderly should take into account their diverse nature. Most are not poor or even nearly poor; the overwhelming majority have no physical disability. But nearly one-half have relatively low incomes, and additional elderly people with higher incomes must cope with physical disabilities. Particularly vulnerable are the nearly 63,000 elderly who must cope with both limited incomes and physical disabilities.

PUBLIC PROGRAMS

The federal, state, and local governments have established a significant but complex network of programs to help meet the needs of the elderly. These activities can be assessed in terms of three types of programs: income maintenance, acute medical care, and long-term care. The income maintenance programs are intended to help meet basic needs of food and shelter through cash payments, vouchers such as food stamps, and direct housing subsidies. The acute medical care programs finance health care for the elderly. The long-term care programs pay for a variety of services which help the elderly cope with limitations in their activities due to chronic conditions.

INCOME MAINTENANCE

The largest and most important income maintenance program for the elderly provides cash payments from the federal Old Age, Survivors and Disability Insurance (OASDI) trust funds, a program commonly referred to as Social Security. Persons over 65 are eligible to receive benefits if they have a work history that includes employment for at least ten years in an industry or position that is covered by the program. The amount of benefits is related to earnings while employed, and benefits are increased periodically to reflect the impact of inflation. Beneficiaries between the ages of 65 and 72 who continue to work have their benefits reduced during their continued employment by an amount equal to one-half of their earnings above $6960 annually.

Approximately 90 percent of New York City residents over age 65 receive Social Security benefits. Their monthly benefit payments at the end of 1983 totaled $386.7 million for an annual equivalent of over $4.6 billion in Social Security expenditures for the elderly in New York City.[2] These figures also suggest average annual payments of nearly $5600 per beneficiary. However, the average obscures the existence of a wide range of payment, with minimum monthly benefits as low as $5 and as high as $704 in 1984.

Two important points should be made about the role of Social Security in the income of the elderly. First, for a significant portion of the elderly, Social Security makes the difference between a life of poverty and a more adequate standard of living. Estimates from the 1980 census indicate that more than one-fifth of the city's elderly enjoyed income above the poverty level because of their Social Security benefits.[3] This group includes nearly 98,000 elderly whose incomes were increased to more than twice the poverty threshold by Social Security.

Another important aspect of Social Security is that a large portion of the beneficiaries have relatively high incomes even without their benefits and that this group receives a major share of the benefits. In 1980, nearly 357,000 elderly in New York City had incomes more than twice the poverty threshold excluding their Social Security payments. This relatively high-income group received over 39 percent of all Social Security payments in the city.

While Social Security helps a large and diverse group of New Yorkers, it also leaves a significant number in poverty. Either because their work histories fail to qualify them for benefits or because they receive relatively low benefits, many elderly New Yorkers are not brought out of poverty by Social Security. For this group, an important source of aid is the Supplemental Security Income (SSI) program. In New York State, benefits under the SSI program consist of payments up to a federal standard plus a supplement funded by New York State. Deductions are made from benefits for other sources of income, but OASDI benefits are treated more favorably than other sources of income. The federal share of the SSI benefit is increased annually to reflect the effects of inflation; the State supplement is adjusted periodically by the State legislature, and these adjustments have generally served to "pass-on" to beneficiaries the federal increases. In 1984, SSI benefits provided a single, elderly individual with a minimum annual income of $4499 and an elderly couple with $6576. Relatively few elderly in New York City live at the minimum annual income level. At the end of 1983, only 72,027 persons aged 65 and over received SSI benefits in New York City.[4] This group represents about 8 percent of the city's total elderly population. Annual payments to this group were $203 million in 1982.[5]

The low-income elderly in New York City also may be eligible for benefits under the federal food stamp program. Food stamps are available to persons meeting income and other criteria that vary with family size and living arrangements. The amount of benefits diminishes as household income increases. Benefit levels are adjusted periodically to reflect changes in food costs. In the last quarter of 1983, an average of 454,896 households in New York City including 1,090,670 people received about $596 million in food stamps.[6] This represents an average benefit per person of $48 monthly. It is not known precisely how many food stamp beneficiaries are 65 or over, or what the value of their benefits is. However, a reasonable estimate based on a 1981 survey is that nearly 76,000 families with a head age 65 or over receive food stamp benefits in New York City, and the value of these benefits is nearly $57 million annually.[7]

Social Security, SSI, and Food Stamps are the major income maintenance programs aiding the elderly, and all are operated with little financial support from the City of New York. The federal government alone is responsible for funding and administering Social Security; the State adds funds to the SSI payments that are principally financed and administered by the federal government; and the federal government finances food stamp benefits, although the municipal Department of Social Services is responsible for determining eligibility. However, municipal government has taken a more substantial role in three other programs that provide income-related support to the elderly.

The City of New York has adopted a policy of providing mass transit to senior citizens at a reduced price. To achieve this objective, it provides earmarked subsidy payments to the Transit Authority and private bus lines. In its 1984 fiscal year, the City provided $15.5 million for these purposes with the largest share ($13.8 million) for the Transit Authority.[8] These benefits are likely to be used almost exclusively by elderly residents without any activity limitation, for whom the expenditures represent an average annual subsidy of $20 per person.

Second, the City helps subsidize public housing projects in which many elderly live. The New York City Housing Authority operates housing units which were home to 171,323 households containing 490,088 individuals in 1983. These activities required expenditures of $707.8 million. Of these total expenses, 47 percent were covered by rents. The remainder was covered primarily through federal, State, and City subsidies.[9] This represents an estimated annual subsidy of nearly $2200 per household living in Housing Authority units. It is not known precisely how many of the Authority's tenants are over 65, but 27.6 percent of the families were headed by a person age 62 or more.[10] A reasonable estimate is that 80 percent of this group is over age 65. Assuming these 37,828 households receive a subsidy equal to the overall average, the program represented an annual subsidy to the city's elderly of nearly $83 million.

Finally, the City of New York helps many elderly through programs operated by the Human Resources Administration (HRA) and Department for the Aging. The HRA provides substantial resources for the elderly through 182 Senior Citizen Centers located throughout the five boroughs. Sixty-four of these are operated directly by HRA; the other 118 centers are operated by community groups under contracts from HRA. The programs of these centers vary, but in each case they provide at least one meal (lunch) and offer recreational activities during the day. On a typical day nearly 29,000 elderly persons attend these centers, and over 25,000 lunch at the centers. The costs of these centers were budgeted at $40.7 million in fiscal year 1984 with the bulk of the funds provided by the federal Social Services Block Grant Program.[11]

The New York City Department for the Aging (DFTA) was established in 1975 to provide a variety of services to the elderly. Given the important role of other agencies in providing cash assistance and medical care, the DFTA gives priority to other activities. Its programs are largely funded by the federal Older Americans Act

(OAA) and the New York State Community Services for the Elderly Act. In fiscal year 1984, the DFTA budget totaled $47.3 million.[12] The agency's largest program is nutrition services, which provides meals served at community centers and delivered to homes. The agency estimates that its centers serve approximately 24,000 elderly daily and that another 11,600 elderly are delivered meals at home. Assuming the HRA and DFTA programs do not duplicate each other, approximately 61,000 elderly New Yorkers receive a subsidized meal each day as a result of their combined efforts. However, both DFTA and HRA meal programs serve people over age 60, not just those 65 and over.

This combination of programs provides elderly New Yorkers with relatively generous minimum standards of living. Those with no or low Social Security benefits are provided incomes close to or exceeding the federal poverty threshold through SSI, and food stamps and other subsidies bring almost all the elderly above the poverty threshold. While not all who are eligible seek these benefits, and some with low incomes are disqualified because they have assets which exceed the strict limits for the SSI program, the elderly generally can secure minimally adequate incomes. This is not the case for other dependent groups in New York City, notably single-parent and other welfare families whose benefits are significantly below the appropriate federal poverty threshold.

This is not to argue that the federal poverty line is a suitable standard for the elderly or that income-maintenance benefits should not be raised above current levels. However, an equitable approach would be to provide suitable minimum standards for all in society, not just the elderly. The use of additional public resources to increase income maintenance benefits only for the elderly without increasing those for other groups in poverty would exacerbate existing inequities.

ACUTE MEDICAL CARE

Federal, state, and local governments provide a set of health care programs that assure access to medical care for virtually all the elderly. The largest and most significant of these is the federal Medicare program, which provides payments for both hospital care and physician services. Almost all (96 percent) of the elderly in New York City are enrolled in Medicare.

Medicare requires supplemental actions by state and local governments because some elderly do not qualify for its benefits and, more importantly, because it does not cover all medical care expenses. In the case of hospital care, the enrollee is responsible for an amount equal to the average cost of a day of hospital care ($356 in 1984), plus additional copayments for certain subsequent days of care. Medicare pays 80 percent of physician charges up to fee limits established by the program administrators. If physicians charge more than the allowed fees, the individual is responsible for 100 percent of the additional charge. Moreover, some items are not covered by Medicare. Prescription drugs, eye care, and dental care, for example, are completely excluded, and nursing home care is covered only up to 90 days and under relatively restrictive conditions. As a result of these exclusions and copayments, Medicare covers about 45 percent of all health care expenses for the elderly.[13]

To cope with the limitations in Medicare coverage, most middle- and upper-income elderly purchase supplemental insurance. It is estimated that nationwide about two-thirds of the elderly have some form of supplemental insurance.[14] The plan marketed by Blue Cross in the New York area cost approximately $350 annually in 1984 and covers many of the copayments required by Medicare. Due to the combination of Medicare and supplemental insurance, most middle- and upper-income elderly enjoy reasonable access to medical care.

For the elderly poor, the gaps in Medicare coverage can be filled by the Medicaid program. Medicaid pays for the hospital, physician, and other medical care costs not covered by Medicare. Medicaid is available to the elderly receiving SSI and those with slightly higher incomes. In 1983, fully 128,564 elderly individuals were enrolled in Medicaid in New York City.[15]

Despite the large enrollments in Medicare, Medicaid, and private-insurance plans, some elderly are not covered at all. For this group, the City guarantees access to health care through its Health and Hospitals Corporation. Its 11 acute-care hospitals, four neighborhood family care centers, and four skilled nursing facilities assure care to all who seek it. In addition, voluntary hospitals also care for some indigent elderly patients and receive partial payment for these services through the State's bad debt and charity care fund.

Given this extensive system for financing care, access to health

TABLE 10.6
Sources of Care for the Disabled Elderly, 1980

	Number	Percentage
Institutionalized	37,560	23.9%
Living in Community	119,431	76.1
Formal Source Only	17,795	11.3
Both Informal and Formal Sources	21,975	14.0
Informal Sources Only	75,720	48.2
No Reported Care	3,941	2.5
Total	156,991	100.0%

SOURCES: Estimates derived from Health Interview Survey and the 1980 Census of Population; see Note 1.

care has not been a major problem for New York City's elderly. Health costs, however, have been a serious problem, though for the health care system in general, not just for the elderly. Solutions to the problem of high cost, therefore, should be pursued keeping the whole system in mind. The State has adopted this approach and has been active in designing regulatory programs. These efforts and future options are discussed in Chapter 9.

LONG-TERM CARE

As is shown in Table 10.4, nearly 157,000 elderly New Yorkers suffer physical disability requiring extended or long-term care. Given the projected growth in the elderly population, and particularly its older members, the next four years will see this population increase. A number of public programs have been created to help the frail elderly, but a major current and future issue is how to meet these needs at a reasonable cost. There is significant evidence that current programs both leave some of those in need without adequate service and work for the others in ways that generate excessive public expenditures.

Current Programs. The overall pattern of care for the disabled elderly is summarized in Table 10.6. The most important sources of care are "informal," that is, from friends or relatives who receive no compensation. Fully 48 percent of the frail elderly received care only from informal sources, while another 14 percent used informal together with formal sources.

Heavy reliance on informal sources of care has both positive and

TABLE 10.7

Institutional Long-Term Care Facilities, New York City, 1983

	Total	Voluntary	Proprietary	Public
All Facilities				
Number of beds	39,424	16,945	20,045	2,434
Number of institutions	162	66	90	6
Hospitals with SNF beds				
Number of beds	3,401	1,698	—	1,703
Number of institutions	10	7	—	3
Nursing Homes				
Number of institutions	152	59	90	3
SNF beds only	82	15	65	2
HRF beds only	14	4	9	1
SNF & HRF beds	56	40	16	—
Number of beds	36,023	15,247	20,045	731
SNF	26,159	10,852	14,807	500
HRF	9,864	4,395	5,238	231

SOURCE: United Hospital Fund, *Health Facilities in Southern New York*, 1983 ed., Tables 111.1, 111.3–111.7.

negative aspects. The advantages are that informal care givers generally provide care of high quality with a degree of personal concern that is not matched by most paid care givers. In addition, the voluntary nature of informal care means it requires no public expenditures or outlays by the needy elderly. The disadvantages are that providing such care often places physical and emotional strains on the care givers, and it may involve economic sacrifices as well. Moreover, informal care should not be equated with adequate services. Stephen Crystal has recently summarized the limitations of informal care well.

Before generalizing about the strength of the "informal support system," however, it is important to understand clearly what it consists of. These and other studies show that a majority of all the care comes from spouses. Of the rest, the largest part comes from middle-aged daughters and daughters-in-law, much less from other relatives and very little from friends. Most care comes from relatives within the household. One observer has characterized the so-called "family support system" as a euphemism for female children and in-laws. The strain of care, particularly for relatives who hold jobs, can be extreme: studies report stress-related illnesses, job interruptions, depression, fatigue, fear of the consequences of further dependence, guilt, conflicting demands on time, and family strife. . . . It would be a mistake to believe that the "family support system" can be taken for granted or that it can pick up the slack from budget cuts. Further, many of the elderly, particularly those who now use long-term care programs, have neither spouse nor capable children. Since impairment is most frequent in the late 70s and 80s, it is not uncommon that the children of an impaired elderly are themselves aged, perhaps feeble. We need to be quite cautious about glib assumptions of the strength of informal supports.[16]

Formal sources of care are almost equally divided between institutional sources and community-based care. Institutional care is provided in two types of nursing homes: skilled nursing facilities (SNFs) and health-related facilities (HRFs). The former serve patients requiring care involving licensed nurses, while the latter serve patients who need some nursing care along with personal care. In 1983, New York City had 162 nursing homes with one or the other type of care. (See Table 10.7.) Ten of these facilities with 3401 beds were acute-care hospitals that included nursing home beds. In total, the 162 facilities included 29,560 SNF beds and 9864 HRF beds. A majority of these facilities are operated for profit, with most of the balance run by voluntary groups. Fully 92 percent of the nursing home beds are occupied by people over age 65.[17]

Expenditures for nursing home care totaled over $1150 million in 1984. Of this total, 93 percent was paid for under public programs, with 91 percent financed through Medicaid. Since few elderly have private, long-term care insurance, the remaining 7 percent of private payments is derived primarily from the savings of the elderly and their families.[18]

The disabled elderly who are not institutionalized receive formal home-care services supported by Medicare, Medicaid, and private sources. There are three general types of agencies providing formal home care in New York City. One group is "certified" home health agencies. These are public or nonprofit organizations certified as eligible for Medicare payments. These agencies are qualified and licensed to provide certain health-related services including nursing care, physical therapy, and occupational therapy. In addition, these agencies generally perform personal care services.

In 1983, there were 34 certified home health agencies in the city, 28 of which were sponsored by hospitals, and six were operated by community-based voluntary groups.[19] Of the more than 1.5 million visits they made, approximately 43 percent were by skilled nurses,

TABLE 10.8

Services Provided by Certified Home Health Agencies,
New York City, 1982

Type of Service	Cases	Visits
Skilled Nursing	135,067	667,447
Physical Therapy	23,638	255,982
Occupational Therapy	4,429	37,079
Speech Pathology	1,947	26,103
Medical Social Worker	10,977	29,606
Nutrition Service	170	261
Home Health Aide	18,177	528,455
Total (net)	135,067	1,544,933

SOURCE: Data prepared by the Bureau of HMO and Home Health Services, New York State Department of Health and presented in Tracy Revenson, "Home Health Care in New York City," Final Report under the Gerontological Society Research Fellowship, August 1984, Table 5.

34 percent were by home health aides, 17 percent by physical therapists, and the remainder by those who provided all other kinds of services (see Table 10.8). Since it is likely that all cases received some skilled nursing care, a reasonable estimate is that the net number of persons served is the number of such cases, or approximately 135,000. This indicates an average of less than five nursing visits and approximately 11 visits of all types per case. Such service levels suggest that certified home health agencies primarily reach

TABLE 10.9

New York City Human Resources Administration
Home Care Activities, 1984

	Number of Cases	Average Hours of Care per Week	Estimated Annual Expenditures[a]
Home Attendants	28,823	50	$345,776,000
Housekeepers	9,135	10[b]	21,676,000
Homemakers	845	17[b]	8,664,000
Total	38,803	N.A.	$376,116,000

SOURCE: Office of Home Care Services, Medical Assistance Program, Human Resources Administration, City of New York, "Summary Report, Home Care Activity," May 1984.

NOTE: N. A. means not applicable.

a. Annual expenditures are estimated based on quarterly disbursements for January through March, 1984.

b. Hours are for adult cases. Average hours for cases with children are 11.6 for housekeepers and 32.1 for homemakers.

persons who need care following an acute illness rather than those with chronic conditions requiring continuing assistance.

A second source of home care is agencies operated for a profit, "noncertified" organizations ineligible for Medicare reimbursement. They provide services similar to those of certified agencies but to persons who do not receive Medicare payments. A survey revealed 130 such agencies operating in New York City in 1983, but no data are available on the volume or type of services or the number of persons served.[20]

The third general type of home care agencies provide only personal care and homemaking services with Medicaid funding. There are 72 voluntary agencies providing home care services to Medicaid-eligible clients under contract with the New York City Human Resources Administration. These agencies served 38,803 clients in May of 1984 (see Table 10.9). Most receive services from home attendants which involve personal care primarily; about one-quarter of the caseload is served by homemakers who clean or cook but do not provide personal care and by housekeepers who clean, cook, and provide only incidental personal care. Most of the cases receiving homemaker services are families with children in which the mother is temporarily absent or disabled; the elderly are served primarily by home attendants, and persons over age 65 account for 76 percent of the caseload of home attendants.[21]

For clients assigned a home attendant, the annual cost averages nearly $12,000. This relatively high cost results from the large number of hours home attendants are assigned to their clients. The average case receives over 50 hours of home care each week. These intensive services are authorized because the clients tend to have multiple disabilities. The typical home attendant client is a woman in her late 70s living alone, suffering from three medical conditions of which one is a circulatory system disorder; she has only partial sight, sometimes suffers memory loss, and is physically unable to leave her apartment without assistance.[22]

Most of the Medicaid home-care clients are poor individuals who are receiving SSI payments. However, over 6100 of those who rely on home attendants or 21 percent of the total have somewhat higher incomes and are required to allocate all of their "surplus" (above income eligibility criteria) income towards the cost of services. The total annual sums they are expected to pay is about $7.6 million or 2 percent of total program expenditures.[23]

Current Problems. The provision of both institutional and community-based care is characterized by serious flaws. There is a shortage of nursing home care for New Yorkers, and the consequences of this shortage are borne disproportionately by a small but significant group of people with intense need of services. With respect to home care, the current programs restrict access largely to those poor enough to qualify for Medicaid and leave many others relying on inadequate arrangements for informal care.

It is not possible to estimate precisely the number of additional nursing home beds New York City should have, because widely accepted, objective standards for gauging need do not exist. However, a number of indicators suggest that a shortage of beds exists in New York City. Probably the most significant evidence is that the city has only 4.1 nursing home beds per 100 elderly compared to 5.9 nationwide.[24] Although some of New York City's elderly are cared for in suburban nursing homes close to their children, and although some other parts of the nation undoubtedly have nursing home beds which are used inappropriately, the size of the gap between New York City and other areas indicates a serious shortage. To reach the national rate, 44 percent more nursing home beds would have to be added in New York City.

Another indicator of a shortage of nursing home beds in New York City is the substantial number of patients in acute care hospitals waiting to be discharged to nursing homes. During a typical day in 1982, approximately 2000 individuals or 7 percent of New York City hospital patients were in the hospital *only* because they were waiting to be placed in some type of long-term care service.[25] Since the cost of a day of hospital care is approximately five times the cost of a day of nursing home care, this use of hospitals is inefficient. One estimate was made that the excess cost generated by patients awaiting placement was approximately $260 million in New York City in 1982, of which 56 percent was paid by Medicaid and 6 percent by Medicare.[26] More importantly, the frail elderly would be better served by a nursing home because it offers a more natural environment for long-term care, and superior rehabilitation and recreation services.

This problem does not affect equally all patients seeking nursing-home care; rather, the ability of nursing home administrators to select the patients they admit forces a relatively small group of patients with intense service needs to suffer most from the shortage of nursing home beds. Only 25 percent of all patients discharged from a hospital to a nursing home experience a wait.[27] For some who wait, the delay is relatively short and can be attributed to delays in determination of Medicaid eligibility; in contrast, those willing to pay for their care privately almost never are obliged to wait.

Those who suffer most are the approximately 3 percent of hospital patients seeking nursing home care who eventually must wait over 90 days to obtain a placement.[28] These patients account for about 50 percent of all of the alternate level of care days and costs. In addition to being eligible for Medicaid, these patients typically have extensive service needs and may have psychiatric and addiction problems. Since they are difficult to deal with, such patients are forced to wait the longest by nursing home administrators who can readily find less troublesome patients to admit. These admission patterns are reinforced by the Medicaid reimbursement policy which pays nursing homes an average daily rate regardless of the severity of the condition of patients actually admitted. In addition, there are allegations that some nursing homes practice racial discrimination by refusing to admit more than a limited number of patients who are black.[29]

It should be added that the shortage of nursing home beds is not an artificial one created merely by filling beds with people who do not need intensive care. While there is substantial evidence that this is a problem in many parts of the country, it is not the case in New York City where beds are limited in number.[30] A 1981 review of patients by the State Health Department found that only 700 patients or 1.8 percent did not meet all the requirements for institutional care, and most of these were individuals who needed care when admitted but whose condition improved.[31]

Problems with regard to community-based long-term care are reflected in the heavy reliance on often unsatisfactory informal arrangements and in the high cost of formal home care supported by Medicaid for those who qualify. The fact that nearly one-half of all disabled elderly, and over 63 percent of the frail elderly living in the community, rely exclusively on informal sources of care suggests there are serious obstacles to obtaining formal care. One of the most important barriers is financial. While the poorest of the elderly qualify for Medicaid assistance, others must rely on private resources which are often insufficient to purchase regular care for

TABLE 10.10

Weekly Hours of Home Attendant Care Authorized by New York City Human Resources Administration, 1984

	Number of Cases	Percentage Distribution
1–19 hours	389	1.4%
20–34	8,285	28.9
35–48	5,580	19.5
49–55	4,173	14.6
56–83	4,778	16.7
84–167	750	2.7
168	4,703	16.4
Total	28,685	100.0%

SOURCE: City of New York, Human Resources Administration, Medical Assistance Program, Office of Home Care Services, "Summary Report, Home Care Activity," May 1984.

their chronic conditions. In 1983, a single individual with an annual income below $4500 would qualify for Medicaid, but others had to devote all their "surplus" income (i.e., income above $4500) to paying for home care in order to receive Medicaid benefits. As stated earlier, about one-fifth of the home-attendant clients are in this surplus income category, but the small amounts they pay suggest their incomes are only slightly above the eligibility level. Most of the near-poor and others requiring long-term care, therefore, are prevented from receiving public aid to pay for formal care.

Adding to the difficulties in obtaining home care through Medicaid is the cumbersome administrative procedure for authorizing assistance. Persons seeking home care must demonstrate both that they are financially in need of Medicaid assistance and that they are medically in need of home care services. These two determinations are made separately by different units of the HRA. Applicants must go through two separate review procedures. The financial application is virtually identical to that required of all Medicaid applicants. It involves providing extensive documentation of income and assets. The review for medical necessity begins with a physician's recommendation for home care. The physician's assessment, submitted on a standard form to HRA, is followed by a social worker's review of the case and recommendation for a specific number of hours of care per week. The social worker's recommendation, based on interviews with the client and the client's physician, is then reviewed by a separate HRA panel to ensure that the recommended number of hours is appropriate. Because the medical determination is sometimes not initiated until after the financial review is under way or even completed, the combined process is often lengthy, requiring multiple visits to or by two divisions of HRA.

Those who successfully complete the eligibility process typically receive a relatively generous level of service. The maximum number of hours available is 168 per week. Nearly one of every six clients receives this level of service (see Table 10.10) either through a live-in attendant or two daily 12-hour shifts by different attendants. A slightly larger group (19 percent) receives eight or more hours of care per day, seven days a week. Another 15 percent receive at least seven hours of care each day per week; and one-fifth receive between five and seven hours of care each day. Only about 30 percent of the cases receive less than five hours of care per day, and nearly all of this group receive between four and five hours.

For those receiving care, a major difficulty is assuring reasonable standards. The HRA relies on private nonprofit agencies to provide services. Since HRA is generally the agency's sole source of funding, they are monitored by the HRA in terms of overhead costs and salary levels. The agencies are directly responsible for ensuring that the personnel they hire are adequately trained, arrive at the prescribed times, work the approved number of hours, perform their assigned tasks, and do not engage in inappropriate behavior while in their clients' home. This oversight is difficult to accomplish under circumstances in which relatively low-skilled individuals are working alone in over 28,000 separate locations. As a result, there are frequent complaints—both from clients complaining about how they are treated by those giving the care and by home attendants. The situation is described in a recent review by the Community Service Society.

Worker-client compatibility is a domain in which problems regularly occur, particularly among new cases. Although clients and workers are informed in advance of the nature of worker responsibilities, the guidelines are broad enough to allow for substantial differences in interpretation. Clients and workers, for example, may have quite different expectations about the effort to be devoted to house-cleaning, and the standards of cleanliness and neatness which should be met. Cultural differences are

TABLE 10.11

*Capacity for Conversion of Beds from Acute Care to Long-Term Care
at New York City Health and Hospitals Corporation Hospitals
Scheduled for Reconstruction*

	Bronx	Elmhurst	Kings	Queens	Total
Low-occupancy Beds[a]	180	170	317	255	922
Beds Occupied by Patients Awaiting Nursing-Home Placements[b]	44	69	45	45	238
Total Capacity for Conversion	224	239	362	328	1,125

SOURCES: Unpublished data from New York City Health and Hospitals Corporation. Figures for alternate level of care days are based on New York State Statewide Planning and Research Cooperative System (SPARCS) data files.

a. Low-occupancy beds are beds decertified since 1976 due to low occupancy and beds that could be decertified while maintaining a 90 percent occupancy rate.

b. Based on 1982 average experience.

sometimes an element in problems of client-worker relationships. Many current clients are of Eastern European origins while many home-care workers are recent newcomers from the Caribbean or Central America. In some cases, language is an issue. Even when both client and worker know some English, they may have difficulty understanding one another. . . . A predictable set of problems in worker performance does occur. Some clients have reason to complain that workers are absent, consistently late, or that they spend less time on the job than they should. Occasionally, workers are accused of theft. Sometimes clients complain with justification that they have been abused or mistreated by workers. (Similar complaints are made by workers.) In cases involving confused clients living alone, gross malfeasance has occurred. In some rare instances, presumably unknown to vendor agencies, clients have been without attendants for weeks. Such cases, of course, clearly invite questions about adequacy of supervision.[32]

POLICY OPTIONS

Policy initiatives to promote the welfare of the elderly are most appropriately focused on the problems of securing adequate long-term care for the frail elderly. Public programs relating to income maintenance and acute health care needs assure relatively generous minimum standards to the elderly; in contrast, the availability of long-term care appears to be limited and provided inefficiently.

Moreover, the numbers of frail elderly requiring long-term care will increase, making the current problems even more severe.

To improve the functioning of long-term care programs, municipal leaders can pursue two strategies. First, access to institutional care can be made easier and more equitable through an expansion of nursing home capacity and greater regulation of their admission policies. Second, access to community-based care can be improved through financing changes that rely less on means-tested eligibility criteria and shift towards a more universal form of social insurance. If implemented with proper restraints, both approaches could achieve broadened access without substantial increases in public expenditures.

INCREASING ACCESS TO INSTITUTIONAL CARE

Increasing access to nursing home care requires that more beds be provided and admission policies be changed. Expansion of nursing home capacity requires the creation of new or expanded facilities and raises the question of how many additional beds are needed. Currently planned construction is expected to increase capacity to 40,625 by 1990.[33] This would leave the city 15,499 beds below the number required to meet the current national ratio of beds to elderly residents.

However, there is little reason to believe the national ratio is a desirable standard. As noted earlier, numerous studies have shown there is widespread inappropriate use of nursing homes in other parts of the country. Instead, more defensible methods of assessing need lead to an estimate that as many as 7800 additional beds are needed. The Health Systems Agency of New York, the local health planning organization, has estimated that the need in New York City is well below those for specific age and sex groups in the entire nation. Their calculations indicate a need for between 41,178 and 48,416 beds in 1987, or between 553 and 7,791 beds higher than currently planned. The low figure is based on utilization rates below the current New York State average, and that average is low because of the shortage of beds. Therefore, an appropriate target is likely to be closer to the higher number.

The most efficient way to expand nursing home capacity is to convert hospital beds to nursing home beds. Although New York City has relatively fewer nursing home beds than the rest of the nation, it has relatively more acute care beds. In New York City, there are 5.3 hospital beds per 1000 population compared to 4.4 nationally and 4.0 in the rest of the State.[34] These excess beds are used daily to serve an estimated 2000 of the patients awaiting nursing home care, so conversion of these beds would create a more efficient balance in the availability of beds for acute and long-term care. The conversion of hospital beds to nursing home beds also reduces service costs if the conversions are done when a hospital is being reconstructed. In such a case, the entire scale of the part of the facility to be used to provide acute care can be reduced in size; fewer surgical suites and smaller laboratory facilities need to be built. It is the decrease in expensive, fixed-cost items that lead to lower construction and operating costs.

The City can play a major role in the conversion of hospital to nursing home beds. The HHC is planning to rebuild five of its acute care hospitals during the next 10 years.[35] Four of these hospitals (Queens Medical Center, Elmhurst Hospital, Bronx Medical and Health Center, and Kings County Medical Center) have large numbers of patients awaiting nursing home placements and are located in communities where neighboring hospitals also have substantial numbers of patients awaiting placements. In addition, these hospitals have lower-than-average occupancy rates and face increased competition for acute care patients in the future. Table 10.11 indicates that 1160 beds for acute care could be converted to long-term purposes at the four hospitals without affecting their ability to care for their current patients receiving acute care. These new nursing home beds would meet 63 percent of the city-wide backlog problem.

Moreover, since nursing home facilities cost less to build than those for acute care, the City would save a substantial amount in its capital budget over the next ten years. Other capital savings could be expected for the City since a decrease in patients awaiting placement would justify decreases in the number of acute care beds needed at some of the voluntary hospitals which also are planning reconstruction in the coming years.

Although the reduction of unneeded beds for acute care and the increase in nursing home beds normally should be considered as independent policy decisions, there are important political reasons for making the decisions together. Neighborhoods where public hospitals are located do not want the facilities to shrink in size because this action is seen as a service reduction and leads to a loss of jobs in the neighborhood. However, the simultaneous reduction of the number of beds for acute care and expansion of the number for long-term care result not in a service reduction but in a better targeting of public resources on the needs of the community. In addition, employment levels in most job categories are maintained.

The expansion of nursing home capacity should be accompanied by measures to strengthen public control over the admission practices of the homes. The objectives of these measures are to avoid admitting people who do not require institutional care and to establish priorities for the allocation of beds among those requiring institutionalization that eliminate racial discrimination and that do not give undue weight to the convenience of nursing home operators.

The danger of admitting patients who may not require institutionalization arises from the method of admitting so-called "private-pay" patients. For the majority of nursing home patients who are admitted after establishing Medicaid eligibility, the process requires a verification by the New York City Human Resources Administration that their health status requires the services of an ICF or a SNF. This review is based on a relatively detailed report submitted by the physician recommending nursing home care. Only after the report is reviewed and approved by State Health Department officials will Medicaid finance the patient's care. However, such verification is not required for patients not seeking Medicaid support at the time of their admission. Thus, the need for institutional care among patients initially willing to pay for this care from their own resources is not verified by a public agency.

The case for screening these private-pay patients is twofold. First, by occupying a bed required by others awaiting care in hospitals, these admissions sometimes cause inefficient and inequitable uses of publicly licensed facilities. Given the shortage of nursing home beds, this misuse is a public problem even though the immediate costs are borne privately. Second, most private-pay patients remain in this status only for a relatively short time. After being admitted and paying privately for their care for several weeks, many of these patients apply for Medicaid. With an average stay of about 500 days and average costs of $84 per diem, few nursing home patients are able to cover all their costs without eventually seeking support from Medicaid. Thus, the private-pay admission process becomes a way for those with some private resources to obtain priority in admissions. By requiring all nursing home admissions to be subject to the same review, regardless of payment status, it would be possible to avoid admitting patients who may not require nursing home care. However, even if all unnecessary admissions were avoided, a significant shortage of beds would remain for those who require care until the recommended expansion is accomplished. Even then, there will be competition for beds in tight supply.

Under present policies, scarce nursing home beds are allocated through a decentralized, ad hoc set of decisions by hospital discharge planners and, more importantly, nursing home administrators. As the previously noted figures indicate, this system works to the advantage of white patients with relatively less intense physical care needs and with relatively few behavioral or psychiatric problems. Yet other types of patients often are those in greatest need of care and most often are those who must wait in a hospital for the longest period of time. To promote both equity and efficiency, more centralized review and control over nursing home admissions are required.

Part of the source of bias in nursing home admission practices may be overcome by changes in State reimbursement policy now being designed. The State is planning to shift from paying nursing homes based on their average per diem costs to paying them on the basis of the costs of caring for patients according to the severity of their disabilities. If properly designed and implemented, this new system could reduce incentives to select patients with the least needs. However, other forms of discrimination and the desire to avoid certain types of behavioral problems are not likely to be counteracted fully by these financial arrangements. Thus greater public intervention in nursing home admissions is likely to be warranted even after the new payment system is put into effect.

Of the approximately 17,450 nursing home admissions each year, 80 percent are Medicaid and Medicare patients subject to public approval prior to admission.[36] The desirable changes would expand reviews of the necessity of care to *all* patients and establish admission priorities. The new criteria not only would involve medical necessity but would require certain patients who had awaited placement longer than others to be admitted first. The agency responsible for conducting the reviews and assigning priorities should be publicly accountable, but might include representatives of all interested constituencies, including hospital administrators, nursing home operators, and patient representatives.

IMPROVING ACCESS TO HOME CARE

Financial and administrative changes are required to deal with the current problems of community based long-term care. Changes in financing programs are needed to expand access to care and alleviate heavy burdens now borne by some families; changes in administrative arrangements are needed to handle the new financing arrangements and to ensure quality and appropriateness of services purchased with public funds.

The essential problem with Medicaid, the public program which finances most long-term care, is that its benefits are available on a basis that approaches an all or nothing policy. Patients with resources of their own, even relatively limited resources, are excluded from the program unless they impoverish themselves by transferring assets to relatives and/or spending all available discretionary income in partial payment for their care; in contrast, those sufficiently poor to qualify receive relatively generous benefits, including institutional care or full-time, live-in home care. To avoid the inequities of this system, it will be necessary to shift the financing of long-term care towards an insurance model. Many of the difficulties in financing long-term care could be overcome with a program of universal benefits for the elderly that provided payments for their care based on degree of disability. Eligibility would not be linked to income and assets.

At the federal level the major objection to relying on insurance and universal benefits is the additional public expenditure it would require. The added costs result primarily from the transfer of the financing of much of the care currently being provided by family and friends to the public. In addition, there is the potential for the availability of insurance benefits to generate new demand for care among those not now receiving it.

Two lines of argument suggest that the national concerns of added public expenditures might not be justified with respect to a social insurance program to support long-term care in New York City. First, a benefit program could be designed that avoids the danger that an insurance program will generate inappropriate new demand or will shift costs from private to public sources. Under an insurance program, benefits for long-term care would take the form either of cash payments to eligible individuals (or their families) to enable them to purchase care or payments to vendors who provide the services. The case for cash payments is that it encourages informal care by letting those for whom such care is available benefit financially. The drawback is that this arrangement could provide "windfall" economic gains, at taxpayer expense, to those who retain informal arrangements. Payments to those who provide care have the opposite drawback. While it prevents windfall gains to families caring for elderly relatives, it could encourage unnecessary use of services and the conversion of informal care arrangements to formal, paid arrangements.

Fortunately, approaches are available to cope with either type of problem. If the cash benefits are provided, then deductions could be made from the benefits to the elderly with available sources of informal care (such as a spouse in the home). These "in-kind" deductibles would be based on the assumption that the benefits can be reduced by an amount equal to the value of services an available family member could reasonably be expected to provide (for example, seven to 21 hours of care per week). If service payments are provided, then requiring copayments could limit unnecessary care. In particular, requiring a significant deduction would deter many families from dropping informal care. However, any copayment requirements should be income related to avoid hardship for the poor elderly.

Second, while even a well designed insurance program for long-term care is likely to require substantial additional tax financing at the national level, this is not necessarily true in New York City. The city deviates significantly from national norms in its high expenditures under Medicaid for long-term care due to relatively generous eligibility rules, the extensive home care benefits, and the significant backlog problem which finances long-term care in expensive hospital beds. Given the high current level of public expenditures, it should be possible to finance an insurance program with existing resources if present rules are altered.

The financial feasibility of relying on long-term care insurance is suggested by analysis comparing current public expenditures for long-term care with the projected costs of a social insurance program. Combined federal, State, and City spending under Medicaid and Medicare for institutional and home care for the elderly approached $1.4 billion in 1984 or approximately $1450 per elderly New York City resident. This consists of an estimated $984 million for nursing homes, $233 million for home attendants, and $161 million for providing alternative level of care days in a hospital.[37]

Could the combined spending under Medicare and Medicaid finance a long-term care insurance program? Estimating the gross cost of such a program would require information about the disability status of the elderly and about the costs of caring for varying disabilities. A variety of means for assessing disability have been developed, and some are used by state Medicaid programs to determine eligibility for nursing home benefits. They could be used in administering a long-term care program that would determine the amounts to be paid according to point scores. However, such data are not available for a broad segment of the population. In the absence of more relevant information, nine categories of disability based on HIS data can be identified (see Table 10.12). They are based on patterns of disability for people identified as having at least one of 11 different types of limitations on their activities.

Table 10.12 also describes a possible level of service that people in each category might require. The levels are arbitrary and require refinement, but they provide a basis for further analysis. The intensity of services required varies from one hour of in-home assistance for those requiring aid only in managing their household funds to 63 hours weekly (or institutionalization) for those with the most severe limitations. Using an average hourly cost of $5 yields approximate annual costs for each level of disability ranging from $260 to $16,380 annually.

Data from the census and HIS provide estimates of the number of New York City elderly likely to fall into each disability category. Combining the costs for each level of disability and the number of people with each type of disability yields an estimated gross cost for the program of $1.6 billion.

The gross cost would be reduced by the copayments required to design an effective program. Data on the income and family characteristics of the disabled elderly indicate that between $120 million and $140 million in copayments or "in kind" deductibles would be likely with a program including such features.[38] These bring the net cost of the social insurance program to under $1.5 billion or close to the current expenditure levels. The broader coverage with

TABLE 10.12
Illustrative Eligibility Categories, Benefit Levels, and Gross Cost for Long-Term Care Insurance

Degree of Disability	Possible Level of Service Required (weekly hours)	Projected Annual Cost per Beneficiary	Projected Number of Beneficiaries	Projected Total Annual Cost (in thousands)
Home Management Limitations Only				
Money Management Only	1	$260	479	$125
Chores Only or Shopping Only	4	1,040	9,095	9,459
Meal Preparation Only	14	3,640	5,624	20,471
Other Home Management Only	21	5,460	16,633	90,816
Physical Activity Limitations				
Going Outside Only	7	1,820	2,513	4,574
Walking Only	14	3,640	5,624	20,471
Walking and Some Home Management; Going Out and Some Home Management; Bathing Only; Bathing and Some Home Management; or Bathing and Walking or Going Out	28	7,280	32,788	238,697
Using Toilet, but not Eating and not Getting in/out of Bed; or Dressing, but not Eating and not Getting in/out of Bed	54	14,040	22,377	314,173
Getting in/out of Bed, but not Eating; or Eating	63 or institutionalization	16,380	55,749	913,169
Total	N.A.	N.A.	150,882	$1,611,954

SOURCES: Beneficiary estimates derived from the Health Interview Survey and the U.S. Census of Population, Public Use Microdata Sample, 1980. See note 1.

NOTE: N.A. means not applicable.

nearly similar levels of public funding is achieved by generating the copayments and by reallocating some of the Medicaid expenditures for very intensive services to somewhat less intense benefits for a larger number of beneficiaries.

Implementing such a demonstration program, on a citywide basis or for a major segment of the city, would require leadership from State and City officials to obtain necessary federal waivers and to reorganize affected agencies. But the potential benefits, both to the city and a broader national audience interested in testing an innovative and progressive model, make the effort worthwhile.[39]

Administrative changes also are necessary to maintain and enhance the quality of home care services. New financing rules that eliminated the detailed income documentation required for Medicaid eligibility also would eliminate many of the present delays and administrative problems. But improved mechanisms are still needed to monitor the quality of such care. Organizational mechanisms to review and audit the performance of home care agencies should be expanded beyond the current efforts of the HRA Office of Home Care.

SUMMARY

Relative to other groups in American society, the elderly are treated well by social welfare programs. Largely as a result of federal efforts, virtually all elderly in New York City are assured a minimally adequate income and most receive Social Security benefits that significantly exceed the federal poverty threshold. Moreover, through the combination of Medicaid and Medicare the elderly are provided the equivalent of national health insurance that eliminates financial obstacles to adequate medical care.

The principal remaining social welfare problem of the elderly is inadequate care for disabilities arising from chronic health problems. Long-term care for the frail elderly is now provided primarily by family and friends at great private cost and at levels that often are inadequate. A significant number of frail elderly receive long-term care through the Medicaid program, but these benefits are restricted to those who impoverish themselves. Moreover, a shortage of nursing-home beds limits the access of some groups of elderly to institutional care.

To overcome these problems the supply of nursing home beds should be expanded and new financing arrangements for long-term care should be tested. The expanded supply of nursing home beds should be created primarily through a planned program of conversions of acute care hospital beds to chronic care facilities. The Health and Hospitals Corporation can play a major role in this effort because it has facilities scheduled to be reconstructed that have relatively low occupancy rates. The HHC's construction funds could be a major means for expanding the supply of available nursing home care.

An imaginative and innovative group of municipal leaders, with State and federal cooperation, could launch a demonstration project to test new rules for the financing of long-term care. By combining new financing arrangements with greater public involvement in the allocation of available resources, it should prove possible to design a program that would broaden access to care, serve the elderly more equitably, and avoid new burdens on non-elderly taxpayers.

NOTES

1. The Health Interview Survey is an annual household survey which collects data concerning health status, health care utilization and socioeconomic/demographic characteristics from approximately 69,000 individuals nationwide. The survey data are described in National Center for Health Statistics, "Health Interview Survey Procedure, 1957–74," *Vital and Health Statistics*, PHS Publication No. (HRA) 75-1311, Health Resources Administration, Washington, D.C., 1975, or in any of the Series 10 reports of *Vital and Health Statistics*. The survey is designed to provide national estimates of the health status and health care utilization patterns of the civilian, non-institutionalized population. However, the households surveyed in New York City are a self-representing sample of New York households and allow disability rates specific to New York City to be calculated. The detailed subgroups for which disability rates were calculated were defined in terms of age, sex, income and living arrangements. In addition to the two sexes, the subgroups include five age groups (65–69, 70–74, 75–79, 80–84, 85 and over), three income groups (less than poverty threshold, from 100 percent to 200 percent of the poverty threshold, and more than twice the poverty threshold), and two living arrangements (alone or with another person). This combination of variables produced 60 separate subgroups ($2 \times 5 \times 3 \times 2$) for which separate disability rates were calculated. These rates were applied to actual numbers of elderly in each group as reported in the 1980 Census Microdata Public Use Sample computer tapes.

2. Unpublished data supplied by U.S. Social Security Administration.

3. Estimates reported in this and the next paragraph are authors' calculations based on data from the 1980 census public use microdata sample.

4. City of New York, Human Resources Administration, Office of Policy and Economic

Research, *New York City Social Report, Fourth Quarter 1983*, Publication RR-SOC-4-83 (April 1984), p. 5.

5. Total SSI expenditures are reported in New York State Department of Social Services, *1982 Annual Report Statistical Supplement*, Table 39. The share available to the elderly is estimated at 35 percent, based on the share of beneficiaries who are aged.

6. Office of Policy and Economic Research, *New York City Social Report*, op. cit.

7. Estimates based on data reported in New York State Department of Social Services, Division of Income Maintenance, "Characteristics of New York City Food Stamp Households, February–March 1981."

8. City of New York, *Comprehensive Annual Financial Report of the Comptroller for the Year Ended June 30, 1984*, Part II-C, p. 158.

9. New York City Housing Authority, *Annual Fiscal Report, Year Ending December 31, 1983*.

10. New York City Housing Authority, "Special Tabulation of Tenant Characteristics," January 1, 1984.

11. See City of New York, Human Resources Administration, Office of Service Planning, *Consolidated Services Plan Report for Federal Fiscal Years 1982–84*, September 1984.

12. *Comprehensive Annual Report of the Comptroller*, op. cit., p. 134.

13. Unpublished data from the U.S. Health Care Financing Administration cited in Karen Davis and Diane Rowland, *Financing Health and Long-Term Care for the Elderly*, Report to the Commonwealth Fund, July 1984, Table III-1.

14. Ibid., p. III-6.

15. Figures from the City of New York, Human Resources Administration, Office of Policy and Program Development, *Medicaid Data Report 1983 Year-End Summary*, June 1984, Table 2, and estimates of elderly in institutions based on City of New York, Human Resources Administration, Office of Policy and Program Development, *Characteristics of the Medicaid—Eligible Chronic Care Population*, October 1980.

16. Stephen Crystal, *America's Old Age Crisis* (New York: Basic Books, 1982), p. 80.

17. New York State Department of Health, "Annual Report of Residential Health Care Facilities, 1982" (June 1984).

18. Ibid.

19. Agency figures from New York State Council on Home Care Services, "Annual Report to the Governor and Legislature, April 1, 1982–March 31, 1983," April 1983, p. 29.

20. See Tracy Revenson, "Home Health Care in New York City," Final Report under the Gerentological Society Research Fellowship (August 1984), p. 13 and Table 4.

21. Age distribution based on unpublished data supplied by the New York City Human Resources Administration for the month of April, 1984.

22. Profile based on unpublished data supplied by New York City Human Resources Administration.

23. Surplus income data from City of New York, Human Resources Administration, Medical Assistance Program, Office of Home Care Services, "Summary Report, Home Care Activity," May 1984. Figures are annual estimates based on monthly figures for May.

24. New York City ratio based on data in Tables 10.1 and 10.7; United States ratios from William Scanlon and Margaret Sulvetta, *The Supply of Institutional Long-Term Care: Descriptive Analysis of Its Future Growth and Current State*, Report of the Project to Analyze Existing Long-Term Care Data, Volume 5 (Washington, D.C.: Urban Institute, no date).

25. New York City figures estimated based on statewide data in Jacob Andoh and Philip Vernon, *Alternate Care Patients: Profiles, Costs and Analysis, 1980–82*, Health Planning Information Monograph Series #3 (Albany, N.Y.: New York State Health Planning Commission, September 1984).

26. Authors' estimate based on statewide data in Andoh and Vernon, op. cit. and James

Lake and Anita Lay, *New York State Health Care Profile* (Albany, N.Y.: Hospital Education and Research Fund, 1983).

27. Andoh and Vernon, op. cit.

28. Ibid.

29. A Report by Friends and Relatives of Institutionalized Aged, Inc., *Racial Discrimination in New York City's Residential Health Care Facilities*, January 1984.

30. For national figures, see for example, Bruce C. Vladeck, *Unloving Care* (New York: Basic Books, 1980).

31. Data supplied by New York State Health Planning Commission based on their December 31, 1981 census.

32. Francis Caro, "Structure and Operations of New York City Human Resources Administration Home Care Programs," Draft, September 1984, pp. 33–34. See also, Office of the New York State Comptroller, "New York City Human Resources Administration Home Attendant Program," Report NYC-13-83, March 2, 1984.

33. Health Systems Agency of New York City, "Residential Health Care Facility Bed Need Methodology (709-3), Part II" (July 25, 1984) and unpublished data supplied by the agency.

34. American Hospital Association as cited in Lake and Lay, op. cit.

35. City of New York, Office of Management and Budget, *Ten Year Capital Plan*, April 1984.

36. New York State Department of Health, "Annual Report of Residential Health Care Facilities, 1982," op. cit.

37. Nursing home expenditures based on total spending of $1150 milllion with 93 percent publicly financed and 92 percent of that sum for the elderly; see note 17 above. Home attendant expenditures based on total spending of $376 million of which 76 percent is for the elderly; see Table 10.9 and note 21 above. Alternate level of care estimate based on total spending of $260 million, of which 62 percent is from Medicare and Medicaid; see note 25 above.

38. For details see Charles Brecher, James Knickman, and Ronald Vogel, "Local Implications of Alternate Policies for Financing Services to the Elderly," paper presented at the Sixth Annual Research Conference of the Association for Public Policy Analysis and Management, October 1984, pp. 22–23.

39. The demonstration proposed here is distinctly different from that of the national channeling demonstration recently completed in ten cities. The channeling demonstration tested two models. The first added a case management program feature to the existing financial and eligibility systems governing public support for long-term care. The second model allowed for the use of an expanded list of support services that are not currently funded by Medicare or Medicaid. In addition, some flexibility in the use of services by elderly who were not normally eligible for benefits was permitted as long as each channeling program kept within established budget limits. Neither model involved universal eligibility for long-term care services. See Linda Hamm, Thomas Kickham and Dolores Cutler, "Research Demonstrations and Evaluations" in Ronald Vogel and Hans Palmer, eds., *Long-Term Care: Perspectives from Research and Demonstrations* (Washington, D.C.: Health Care Financing Administration, 1983).

11

Criminal Justice

ESTER FUCHS AND
JOHN PALMER SMITH

To New Yorkers, from average citizen to mayor, crime is the most serious problem facing the city.[1] Underlying these attitudes is the reality of too much crime and too little punishment. Crime, in a word, pays. It also sells. In New York City's media markets, the public's demand for news about crime and new proposals to deal with it seemingly is insatiable. Politicians too often attempt to satisfy this demand without giving adequate thought to the problem and proposed solutions.

This chapter is intended to provide some frequently ignored and some previously unassembled information about crime and criminal justice in New York City. The first section describes recent trends in crime in New York City. The second section analyzes the workings of a series of public agencies, the criminal justice system, and identifies shortcomings both in agency performance and in knowledge about that performance. The third section examines the financing of the criminal justice system and its components. The final section identifies policies that might help fashion a better criminal justice system.

CRIME IN NEW YORK CITY

Confusion about crime, and what government should do about it, begins with a failure to understand its causes. Social scientists are divided over why crime occurs and how to prevent it. One group of analysts sees the causes of crime as grounded in the social and economic structure of society.[2] Accordingly, they view government policies that focus primarily on fighting crime as doomed to failure because they address the effects rather than the causes of crime. If, as this group believes, crime is a function of factors such as unemployment, income inequality, and deteriorating family structures, then government must address these problems in order to reduce crime.

A second group explains most crime with principles of economic rationality.[3] Stated simply, if crime pays, people will commit crime. According to this view, government policies that raise the cost of crime by increasing the likelihood of punishment will reduce crime most effectively.[4] Other analysts link the incidence of crime to demographic trends, particularly the age distribution of a population, because young people commit disproportionately large numbers of crime.[5] As they age, and if they are not replaced by cohorts of equal or larger size, crime will fall independently of government's response to it.

Whatever its causes, crime is an objective phenomenon that can be measured for its incidence and kind. Measuring crime is complicated, however, by myriad factors related to private and public reaction to crime. A large proportion of crimes are not reported by citizens, and the ratio of reported to actual crime varies according to the kind of crime. One determinant of citizens' propensity to report crime is their degree of confidence that the criminal justice system will do something abut it. A skeptical citizenry will report a lower share of crimes to the police. (Since unreported crimes cannot be solved, the failure to report crime contributes to the incidence of crime as well as to the difficulty in determining its incidence.) Assuming, however, that the share of actual to reported crime has not fluctuated significantly in recent years, it is possible to gain some understanding of changes in the level and nature of crime by examining available trend data on reported crimes.

TABLE 11.1
Reported Crime in New York City, 1975–84

	1975	1976	1977	1978	1979	1980	1981	1982	1983	1984	Percentage Change 1975–84
Part I Index Crimes[a]	582,090	658,172	610,069	570,380	621,119	710,205	726,826	689,019	622,877	600,216	3%
Non-economic Crimes	49,105	47,995	47,538	48,683	49,820	49,018	48,019	49,532	48,610	52,751	7
Murder and Manslaughter	1,690	1,647	1,580	1,530	1,741	1,821	1,838	1,673	1,622	1,450	-14
Rape	3,866	3,400	3,898	3,882	3,875	3,711	3,862	3,547	3,662	3,829	-1
Assault	43,549	42,948	42,060	43,271	44,204	43,486	43,832	42,799	43,326	47,472	9
Economic Crimes	532,985	610,177	562,531	521,697	571,299	661,187	677,294	641,000	574,267	547,465	3
Robbery	83,263	86,183	74,375	74,029	82,572	100,556	107,558	95,977	84,043	79,541	-4
Burglary	177,105	195,243	178,888	164,447	178,162	210,716	206,039	172,818	143,698	128,687	-27
Larceny	189,415	232,069	214,848	200,109	220,817	249,430	258,989	264,775	253,801	250,759	32
Motor Vehicle Theft	83,202	96,682	94,420	83,112	89,748	100,485	104,708	107,430	92,725	88,478	6
Part II Crimes[a]	N.A.	N.A.	126,369	144,343	141,159	133,477	149,459	163,283	182,382	199,157	58
Non-economic Crimes	N.A.	N.A.	70,674	89,502	98,392	93,528	102,032	110,787	120,489	134,367	90
Controlled Substances	N.A.	N.A.	24,230	26,992	28,656	27,952	22,653	24,641	31,748	37,325	54
Public Intoxication	N.A.	N.A.	34	378	252	27	63	64	4	2	-94
Liquor Law Violation	N.A.	N.A.	1,469	1,651	4,639	6,694	15,022	18,375	16,756	18,010	1,126
Driving While Intoxicated	N.A.	N.A.	2,980	2,820	2,651	2,433	2,376	3,632	5,622	7,631	156
Kidnapping	N.A.	N.A.	176	156	135	154	139	148	195	246	40
Sex Offenses	N.A.	N.A.	5,043	4,936	4,692	4,138	4,207	3,797	4,174	4,875	-3
Simple Assault	N.A.	N.A.	25,891	40,105	42,849	40,791	43,315	45,033	48,424	52,699	104
Family Offenses	N.A.	N.A.	1,039	431	298	279	371	533	474	402	-61
Arson	N.A.	N.A.	3,744	3,607	7,776	5,352	8,295	7,654	6,464	6,284	68
Dangerous Weapons	N.A.	N.A.	5,978	5,858	6,370	5,646	5,527	6,858	6,556	6,826	14
Coercion	N.A.	N.A.	90	2,568	74	62	64	52	72	67	-26

Economic Crimes	N.A.	N.A.	55,695	54,841	42,767	39,949	47,427	52,496	61,893	64,790	16
Bribery	N.A.	N.A.	283	280	223	172	191	168	249	323	14
Extortion	N.A.	N.A.	512	429	387	418	452	485	363	307	-40
Forgery and Counterfeiting	N.A.	N.A.	3,643	3,350	2,738	2,275	2,234	2,300	2,503	2,454	-33
Prostitution and Vice	N.A.	N.A.	6,809	9,992	10,478	8,992	10,372	6,494	14,987	17,671	160
Stolen Property	N.A.	N.A.	5,678	5,978	5,704	5,756	5,432	6,519	5,992	7,063	24
Fraud	N.A.	N.A.	33,090	27,612	16,198	16,267	23,627	30,916	33,028	32,957	0
Gambling	N.A.	N.A.	3,492	5,270	5,526	4,485	3,270	3,540	3,284	2,286	-35
Embezzlement	N.A.	N.A.	835	837	665	772	1,011	986	861	1,058	27
Possession of Burglary Tools	N.A.	N.A.	1,353	1,093	848	812	838	1,088	626	671	-50
All Other Offenses[a]	N.A.	N.A.	371,207	485,243	470,933	410,420	419,947	609,424	576,537	579,154	56%
Criminal Mischief	N.A.	N.A.	80,862	75,249	78,436	73,851	72,096	69,260	64,210	68,268	-16
Offenses Against Public Order	N.A.	N.A.	82	2,115	2,692	2,646	5,362	110	63	48	-41
Unauthorized Use Vehicle	N.A.	N.A.	1,220	1,428	1,485	1,477	1,533	1,521	1,574	1,972	62
Disorderly Conduct	N.A.	N.A.	46,695	36,734	36,445	34,309	37,794	50,335	60,907	71,197	52
Loitering	N.A.	N.A.	10,342	7,403	9,180	19,640	14,165	21,687	9,912	9,380	-9
All Other Offenses	N.A.	N.A.	232,006	362,314	342,695	278,497	288,997	466,511	439,871	428,289	85

SOURCES: Data for Part I offenses for 1975–82 and for Part II (including "All Other Offenses") for 1978–82 are from the State of New York, Division of Criminal Justice Services, *Crime and Justice Annual Report*, issues for 1975–1982; Data for Part I offenses for 1983 and 1984 and for Part II (including "All Other Offenses") for 1977, 1983, and 1984 are from the City of New York, Police Department, Office of Management Analysis, Crime Analysis Section.

Notes: N.A. means not available; percentage changes for all non–"index" crimes are for the 1977–84 period.

a. Part I "Index" Crimes is the designation given to those felonies reported to the New York City Police Department and in turn reported to the Federal Bureau of Investigation as a part of the Uniform Crime Reports (UCR). Part II Offenses are those felony and nonfelony crimes (including "All Other Offenses") reported to the Police Department and the Federal Bureau of Investigation as part of the Uniform Crime Reports, not classified as Index Crimes.

CRIME TRENDS IN NEW YORK CITY

Comprehensive data on crime nationally and in New York City are contained in Uniform Crime Reports compiled by the Federal Bureau of Investigation on the basis of information provided by local law enforcement agencies (the Police Department in the case of New York City). The data provide a basis for examining crime trends in New York City. (See Table 11.1.)[6]

Serious felony crimes, the so-called "Index" or Part I crimes, were 3 percent higher in 1984 than in 1975. The net increase, however, is less interesting than the trends during the 10-year period. Index crimes rose sharply in 1976, declined to below the 1975 level in 1977 and 1978, rose to a high of nearly 727,000 in the 1979–81 period, and then fell again in the 1982–84 period to about 600,000.

Part II crimes, which include less serious offenses than those in Part I, increased to a greater extent (58 percent) than Part One crimes. Only in 1981 did Part I and Part II crimes move in the same direction. In the 1980–84 period, Part II crimes rose steadily, largely because of increased numbers of crimes involving controlled substances (drugs), liquor law violations, simple assaults, prostitution and vice, and fraud. An even larger increase occurred in the third category involving lesser crimes. Crimes in the "All Other Offenses" category rose 56 percent between 1977 and 1984.

The distribution of Part I crimes between the primarily economic and noneconomic categories virtually was stable. The noneconomic crimes—murder, manslaughter, rape, and aggravated assault—accounted for 7 to 9 percent of Part I crimes throughout the 1975–84 period. Thus, trends in Part I crimes are driven by trends in the primarily economic crimes. As Table 11.1 shows, crimes for economic gain declined sharply (by about 130,000) in the 1981–84 period. Among the serious economic crimes, the shares of robbery and motor vehicle theft were essentially unchanged; the major changes involved burglary which fell 27 percent and larceny which rose 32 percent in the 1975–84 period.[7]

In contrast, about two-thirds of the Part II crimes in 1984 were noneconomic crimes. The largest percentage increase occurred in liquor law violations and simple assaults. Part II economic crimes declined from 1977 through 1980, but rose steadily thereafter. The net effect was an increase of 16 percent between 1977 and 1984.

The frequent shifts in the level of reported crime in New York City should not be ignored, but the general trends are encouraging. Serious felony crimes have declined notably since 1982, primarily because of falling numbers of economic crimes, burglary in particular. It is possible that a lower share of these crimes is being reported, but national studies suggest this is not the case.[8]

These trends do not neatly mesh with theories of the causes of crime. The city's youth are declining in number, but gradually and over a period that included both large increases (1978–81) and large declines (1981–84) in crime. The number of poor New Yorkers is rising, but crime—including economic crime—is falling. Crime trends running in counter-intuitive directions do not mean that crime is not related to demographic and economic variables, but the data suggest that other factors also are correlated with crime. Some believe anticrime programs focusing on career criminals have contributed to crime reduction by putting repeat offenders in jail. In addition, the decline may reflect the decision of many citizens to take self-protective actions. Illustrative of this trend are the results of a recent poll of New Yorkers. Of the respondents, 40 percent had put locks or alarms on windows, doors, or cars; 23 percent reported they were careful and alert when walking; 27 percent said they do not go out at night; and 4 percent carry a gun, knife, or mace.[9]

COMPARATIVE CRIME TRENDS

Another perspective on crime trends is to view New York City relative to other major cities in the United States. Table 11.2 ranks in descending order the 20 cities with the highest incidence of reported Index crimes per 100,000 population. Thus the top-ranked city in 1978, Phoenix, had the highest per capita crime rate. In 1978, New York City ranked seventeenth, its best comparative performance in the period. In 1979 and 1980, crime in New York City increased to the thirteenth and ninth highest per capita crime rates. In 1981 and 1982, New York City's comparative position improved slightly, but in 1983 and 1984 it returned to the ranking it held in 1981 as the city with the tenth highest per capita crime rate. Thus, although the number and per capita rate of crime have fallen recently in New York City, the improvements have been less than those in most other large cities.

TABLE 11.2
Per Capita Reported Crime in Major U.S. Cities, 1978–84

Rank	1978	1979	1980	1981	1982	1983	1984
1	Phoenix	Phoenix	Phoenix	St. Louis	Boston	Boston	Detroit
2	San Francisco	Dallas	St. Louis	Denver	Detroit	Detroit	Boston
3	Dallas	Boston	Boston	Dallas	Dallas	St. Louis	Dallas
4	St. Louis	Houston	Dallas	Seattle	Houston	Denver	Seattle
5	Boston	San Francisco	San Francisco	San Francisco	Denver	Dallas	Denver
6	Houston	St. Louis	Los Angeles	Detroit	Seattle	Los Angeles	Los Angeles
7	San Diego	Los Angeles	Seattle	Phoenix	Los Angeles	Kansas City	Houston
8	Seattle	New Orleans	Columbus	Kansas City	Washington	Houston	Chicago
9	Los Angeles	San Diego	NEW YORK CITY	Cleveland	San Francisco	San Francisco	Washington
10	Detroit	Columbus	New Orleans	NEW YORK CITY	Phoenix	Washington	NEW YORK CITY
11	Cleveland	Baltimore	Houston	Los Angeles	Cleveland	NEW YORK CITY	San Antonio
12	San Jose	Honolulu	Detroit	Washington	NEW YORK CITY	Baltimore	San Francisco
13	Columbus	NEW YORK CITY	Cleveland	Baltimore	Columbus	Phoenix	Phoenix
14	New Orleans	San Jose	Baltimore	Columbus	New Orleans	Cleveland	Baltimore
15	Baltimore	Washington	Washington	New Orleans	Baltimore	San Antonio	New Orleans
16	Honolulu	Detroit	San Jose	San Jose	San Jose	New Orleans	Cleveland
17	NEW YORK CITY	Cleveland	Honolulu	Jacksonville	San Antonio	Columbus	Columbus
18	Washington	Jacksonville	San Diego	Memphis	Memphis	Jacksonville	Memphis
19	San Antonio	San Antonio	Jacksonville	San Diego	Jacksonville	San Diego	San Diego
20	Jacksonville	Memphis	San Antonio	San Antonio	San Diego	Chicago	Jacksonville

SOURCE: New York Police Department.

NOTES: Rankings are of the most populous cities in the United States by decreasing magnitude of crime rate per 100,000 population for index crime offenses reported to the Federal Bureau of Investigation for the first six months of the respective years.

Crime rates are apparently correlated with city size. The ten cities with the highest per capita incidence of reported crime in 1984 include five of the six cities with populations over 1,000,000. They are Detroit, Los Angeles, Houston, Chicago, and New York. The sixth, the "city of brotherly love," Philadelphia, lives up to its name by not even appearing in Table 11.2. Three of the other five cities among the top ten with the worst crime rates are among the 20 largest American cities: Dallas, Washington, and Boston.

Many New Yorkers probably would be surprised to learn that serious crimes have declined in number in recent years and that people in several other large American cities experienced more crime. But New Yorkers also find little consolation in these figures; the fact remains that more than 600,000 serious crimes were reported in New York City in 1984, and many more were committed. These crimes were committed by a large criminal element within the population despite government's efforts to police, process, and punish them. How that criminal justice system functions, from crime to punishment, is the subject of the next section.

CRIME AND PUNISHMENT IN NEW YORK CITY

The city's criminal justice system is procedurally complex. This fact, coupled with the absence of useful data on what happens to defendants as they pass through and out of governmental agencies, makes analysis of the workings of the criminal justice system—and of options to improve it—quite difficult. This section describes the system in a way that would permit systematic analysis of its performance if more complete information were available. The section begins with the "activators" of the criminal justice system, criminals and the crimes they commit, and traces government's responses from policing to punishing criminals.

CRIME AND CRIMINALS

The previous discussion of crime trends in New York City was based primarily on the number of serious crimes *reported* to the police, but there is a substantial difference between reported and actual crime. It is also important to recognize that the number of persons committing crimes is lower than the number of committed

TABLE 11.3

Estimated Outcomes of Felony Arrests in New York City, 1983

	Number	Percentage
Felony Arrests	95,456	100%
Not Prosecuted	35,463	37
Plead or Found Guilty of Misdemeanor	34,524	36
Sentenced to City Jails	15,266	16
Other Punishments	19,258	20
Felony Indictments	25,469	27
Convicted	21,526	23
Sentenced to State Prisons	10,623	11
Sentenced to City Jails	4,618	5
Other Punishments	6,285	7
Other	3,943	4

SOURCE: See text and note 19.

crimes because some criminals commit more than one crime. Thus, examination of the criminal justice system in New York City begins with two important unknowns: the number of criminals and the number of crimes they commit. The latter may be estimated on the basis of national survey data; the only basis for estimating the former is an educated guess.

It is possible to obtain reliable data on committed as opposed to reported crime by conducting victimization surveys. The National Crime Survey measures the incidence of selected personal and household crimes and the rates at which people fail to report those crimes to the police.[10] This is done using national samples, but the sample size is too small to yield valid local estimates. However, by applying national reporting rates for various crimes to their distribution in New York City, the total number of serious crimes actually committed in the City may be estimated.[11] This methodology, using the base of 623,000 reported index crimes in 1983, suggests that approximately 1,664,000 felonies were committed in New York City in 1983.[12] (The 1983 base is used because 1984 data on crime reporting rates were not available.)

The number of criminals who committed serious crimes is a more speculative matter. Studies based on interviews with convicted criminals indicate their propensity to commit crimes more than once, but applying these results to the general criminal population is inappropriate because people sentenced to prison are more likely to have committed multiple crimes than the general criminal population.[13] However, these and related studies suggest strongly that a small share of criminals commits a disproportionately large share of crimes. (This interpretation of the distribution of the commission of crime underlies the City's attempts to target "career criminals" for special police and prosecutorial attention.) While it would be useful to know more about the distribution of criminal activity, it is not essential to estimate the probability that the commission of a serious crime will lead to punishment.

CRIMINALS AND POLICE

Police made approximately 95,000 felony arrests in 1983 (see Table 11.3). This yields a felony arrest rate of approximately 15 percent for reported felonies and 6 percent for committed felonies. However, in some cases one arrest solves more than one crime; in other cases, several people are arrested for committing the same crime. Police estimate clearance rates that take into account these phenomena, and in 1983 the clearance rate also was 15 percent of reported felonies.

The significance of felony arrest and clearance rates is hard to evaluate without knowledge about the number of criminals. If each criminal committed but one crime, then the felony arrest rate of 6 percent would certainly be judged inadequate by most citizens. But an unknown number of criminals commit a number of felonies before they are arrested, so the share of criminals who the police apprehend clearly is above 6 percent. Assuming an average of between two and ten felonies per criminal per year yields an estimated criminal population of between approximately 832,000 and 166,000 people. This suggests police arrest between 57 and 11 percent of the number of felons.

Police officers in New York City make, on average, few arrests. In 1983, the average was 4.2 felony arrests per uniformed employee year of effort—roughly one felony arrest every 12 weeks.[14] Police policy contributes to this low number because in New York City (and elsewhere) police officers do many things other than investigate crime. Perhaps the largest amount of police time is spent patrolling streets, usually in radio patrol cars. Available research indicates that deploying police in radio patrol cars does little to deter crime.[15] However, radio patrol cars enable police to respond relatively quickly to citizen requests for assistance through the 911 emergency response system. While many of these calls are unrelated to criminal activity, police officials increased the number of patrol cars dispatched in response to 911 calls by more than 20 percent over the 1978–83 period.[16] In 1984, Police Commissioner Benjamin Ward stated that he intended to assign a higher priority to crime fighting by putting more officers "on the street."

Another explanation for the low number of felony arrests per police officer is that other criminal justice agencies lack the capacity to handle a greatly increased number of cases. Evidence of this is found in jail overcrowding, which in 1983 led to the release of 613 persons being held in City correctional facilities under conditions which a federal judge found to be unconstitutional "cruel and unusual punishment."[17] Although most observers agree that the efficiency of the prosecutorial and judicial functions could be improved, there is a limit on the number of persons that can be arrested, prosecuted and, if convicted, jailed or imprisoned without significant investment of new resources. For example, if one-half of the approximately 100,000 annual felony arrests resulted in conviction and sentences averaging one year in prison, existing and planned space in City and State correctional facilities would be filled almost to capacity. This would leave almost no room in State prisons for felons convicted elsewhere in New York State and in City jails for misdemeanants or persons detained pending trial or sentencing.[18]

DEFENDANTS AND PROSECUTORS

A large number of people who are arrested for committing a felony are not indicted for that crime. Approximately 95,000 arrests of individuals were made in 1983, but there were only 25,000 felony indictments in that year. Note, however, that the 25,000 felony indictments include both individuals *and* charges due to the peculiar fashion in which indictments are counted. If two indictments apply to the same defendant, then each indictment is counted separately; if one indictment applies to two defendants, then each defendant is counted separately.

Most of the difference between the volume of felony arrests and the number of felony indictments can be related to the proscutors' "selective enforcement" policies. Prosecutors exercise significant discretion throughout the criminal justice process—at pretrial screening (booking), arraignment, and in presentation of cases to the grand jury. At pretrial screening, the prosecutor decides to dismiss a case or to seek criminal charges. At this time, the prosecutor also may decide to reduce the felony charges to misdemeanor charges.

At arraignment in Criminal Court, when a defense attorney is present, the prosecutor again may reduce a felony charge to a misdemeanor, may resolve the case through plea bargaining, or may decide to proceed to the grand jury for criminal indictment. If the grand jury votes an indictment, another arraignment is held. At this time, the prosecutor once again may seek to resolve the case through a plea-bargained agreement. If the case is not resolved at this stage, it will finally go to trial.

The District Attorneys and courts do not maintain sufficient records to make the outcomes of the exercise of prosecutorial discretion readily available, but the general patterns can be pieced together from periodic studies and the limited annual statistical reports.[19] Approximately 37 percent of those who are arrested are not prosecuted. Another 36 percent engage in plea bargaining and are convicted of a misdemeanor rather than the initial felony charge. The remaining 27 percent are indicted for felonies. The reasons for this seemingly large number of cases that are not prosecuted or are settled by plea bargaining are not well documented, but there appear to be several. Prosecutors may decide to dismiss or reject cases for prosecution because they believe there is insufficient evidence or that witnesses will be unwilling or unable to testify. The evidentiary problems may reflect poor police work. Discretionary decisions also may reflect the desire of prosecutors to build up their conviction records. Another reason is the limited capacity of the courts, which are backlogged, and of correctional facilities, which often are full. Under those conditions, there are strong practical incentives to avoid trials by allowing plea bargaining that results in both shorter time in court and shorter time in jail.

DEFENDANTS AND JURISTS

Relatively few of those who are prosecuted go without some form of punishment. The approximately 25,000 felony indictments in 1983 resulted in approximately 21,500 felony convictions. In other words, about 85 percent of those charged either plead or are found guilty; the remaining 15 percent have their charges dismissed, are acquitted, or have the charges dropped or consolidated for other reasons.[20] The felony convictions result largely from plea bargaining; about 90 percent of the convictions or 19,600 cases yielded guilty pleas as a result of such bargains.[21]

Of those found guilty of a crime as a result of a felony arrest, it is estimated that, at most, 54 percent are sentenced to jail or prison. This includes 71 percent of those guilty of a felony and 44 percent of those guilty of a misdemeanor.[22] Only 19 percent of those found guilty are sentenced to more than one year and go to State prison; the others sentenced to jail serve less than one year in City jails. The remaining 46 percent of those found guilty receive other sentences, including probation. However, some of these individuals may have spent time in a City jail while waiting for a court appearance or a trial.

To summarize, an unknown number of criminals committed an estimated 1,664,000 serious felonies in 1983. The police arrested 95,000 people for felonies. Approximately 56,000 of these people eventually were convicted of a crime. They received a variety of punishments ranging from imprisonment for terms over one year in State facilities (19 percent) to incarceration in the City's jails for under one year (35 percent), to other forms of punishment including probation (46 percent).

THE PROBABILITY OF PUNISHMENT

Many observers may find it tempting to conclude from the foregoing figures that criminal justice agencies fail to respond to serious crime in New York City adequately. The 10,600 criminals sentenced to State prison in 1983 seems a low number in a city where an estimated 1,664,000 felonies were committed that year. The fallacy in this conclusion is that it compares the number of *persons* sentenced with the number of felony *crimes* committed. This line of reasoning ignores the fact that the small number of persons sent to State prison committed a large number of the felonies. For repeat offenders, the probability of punishment is higher than the simple inference implies.

As noted previously, the criminal justice system does not report the information necessary to make precise estimates of the probability of being punished for committing serious crimes in New York

City. However, it is possible to obtain first approximations of the probabilities that someone who commits one or more felonies will be punished. A felony offender is subject to a probability of arrest (A) for any felony he or she commits, a probability of conviction after arrest (C), and a probability of being punished (probation, City jail or State prison) after conviction (P). Thus, the probability of being arrested, convicted and punished in a given manner is the product of these three probabilities or $A \times C \times P$. Estimates of the probabilities for each of these elements can be made from figures presented in the previous sections.

For example, in 1983 the probability that the commission of a felony would result in arrest was approximately 95,000 out of 1,664,000, or 5.7 percent (see Table 11.4); the probability of an arrest resulting in conviction for some crime, including plea-bargained misdemeanors, was approximately 56,050 out of 95,000 or about 95 percent; the probability of receiving some form of punishment on being convicted was 1.0, but the chances of being sentenced to jail were only 30,507 of 56,050 or 54 percent. Therefore, the combined probability of receiving some kind of punishment for committing a *single* felony is .034 (.057 × .59 × 1.0); the probability of going to jail for a single felony is .018; the probability of being sentenced to a State prison is .0054 or about one out of 200.

If a criminal committed more than one felony, what would be the probability of his or her being punished? The probability of being arrested can reasonably be assumed to increase with the number of felonies committed, probably at a uniform rate. Thus, while the probability of being arrested after committing one felony is only .057, the chance increases to .255 for five crimes, and .770 for 25 crimes. Assuming that a criminal committed as few as five felonies, his or her probability of being punished in any form was .168 (one chance out of six); the probability of being sent to jail was .082 or eight of 100, but being sent to State prison was .024 or less than three chances out of 100. High-rate offenders, someone who might have committed 25 felonies (a not extraordinary number for some criminals) would have an almost even chance (.454) of conviction and punishment of some type, a one-in-four chance (.247) of going to jail, and a 7 percent chance of being sent to State prison.

This analysis strongly suggests that crime pays for the majority of felony offenders in New York City. For relatively low-rate felony offenders, the probability of being arrested, convicted, and sen-

TABLE 11.4

Probabilities of Being Punished for Felony Offenses

Annual Felony Offenses S	Felony Arrest (A)	Probabilities			State Prison Sentence P2	A×C×P
		Any Conviction C1	Felony Conviction C2	Any Jail Sentence P1		
1	0.057	0.590	—	0.544		0.018
5	0.255	0.590	—	0.544		0.082
25	0.770	0.590	—	0.544		0.247
1	0.057	—	0.232	—	0.409	0.005
5	0.255	—	0.232	—	0.409	0.024
25	0.770	—	0.232	—	0.409	0.073

SOURCE: Authors' calculations based on data in Table 11.3.

tenced to State prison is so low that it is unlikely to play any significant role in deterring serious crimes. For the minority who are high-rate offenders, the probability of serving time in State prison is significantly higher, but the odds are still against it.

EXPENDITURES FOR CRIMINAL JUSTICE

Efforts to improve the performance of criminal justice agencies should be guided by an awareness of the requisite public expenditures. Surprisingly and unfortunately, there is no systematic collection of expenditures by the number of agencies involved. This section uses the limited available data to analyze public expenditures for criminal justice in terms of their distribution among three functions: policing, processing, and punishment. The first part includes activities of the three local police departments (the New York City Police Department, the Transit Authority Police, and the Housing Authority Police) and the Department of Investigations. The processing activities include the work of the five local district attorneys' offices, the Legal Aid Society, the criminal courts, and several other agencies. Punishment includes the work performed by the municipal correction and probation departments, as well as the services by State prisons to offenders from New York City. The source of funding for each of these functions is also examined.

USES OF CRIMINAL JUSTICE FUNDS

In fiscal year 1984, State and local expenditures for criminal justice agencies approached $2.1 billion (see Table 11.5). This excludes capital costs and debt service for the agencies, as well as most pension and fringe benefit expenditures for personnel working in these agencies. Fifty-seven percent of the expenditures were devoted to police agencies. The New York City Police Department accounted for $962 million of the $1,179 million total. However, as noted earlier, the police perform many activities not related directly to the prevention and investigation of crime. Undoubtedly, a large share of these police expenditures are not truly a part of the criminal justice system, but should be viewed as other service functions.

The second largest set of agencies are those punishing criminals. These activities account for nearly $650 million or 31 percent of

TABLE 11.5

Expenditures for Criminal Justice Agencies, Fiscal Year 1984
(millions of dollars)

	Amount	Percentage Distribution
Policing	$1,179.4	56.6%
NYC Police Department	961.6	46.1
NYC Transit Authority Police	162.7	7.8
NYC Housing Authority Police	51.6	2.5
NYC Department of Investigation	3.5	0.2
Processing	255.2	12.2
Court Expenditures	99.1	4.8
New York City Criminal Courts	32.4	1.6
Supreme Courts (Criminal Terms) in New York City[a]	66.7	3.2
District Attorneys	72.9	3.5
New York County	25.2	1.2
Bronx County	14.1	0.7
Kings County	20.6	1.0
Queens County	11.3	0.5
Richmond County	1.7	0.1
Legal Aid Society	34.0	1.6
NYC Criminal Justice Coordinating Council	15.0	0.7
NYC Department of Juvenile Justice	16.1	0.8
Office of Prosecution— Special Narcotics Court	4.3	0.2
Crime Prevention Injury Award	0.1	0.1
NYC Department of Probation	13.7	0.7
Punishing	649.7	31.2
NYC Department of Probation	13.7	0.7
NYC Department of Corrections	253.3	12.2
NYC Board of Correction	0.4	0.2
State Prison Expenditures Attributable to New York City[b]	382.3	18.3
Total	$2,084.3	100.%

SOURCES: All expenditures of the City of New York are as reported in *City of New York, Comprehensive Financial Report of the Comptroller for the Fiscal Year Ended June 30, 1984.* State prison expenditures attributable to New York City are derived from the budgeted expenditures of the New York State Department of Corrections as reported in State of New York, *Executive Budget, Fiscal Year 1984.* Estimated criminal justice expenditures of the State courts in New York City are derived from the budgeted expenditures for the State of New York, Unified Court System as provided by the Office of Court Administration.

a. These figures are estimates of criminal justice expenditures by the State-funded courts in New York City, which assume that 55 percent of all State Supreme Court expenditures were devoted to criminal cases during the 1978–82 period and, subsequent to 1982, that 66 percent of State Supreme Court expenditures were devoted to criminal cases.

b. These figures are estimates of the costs of incarcerating in State correctional facilities those persons convicted of felonies in New York City. These estimates were derived by multiplying the average annual share of admissions to State prison that originated in New York City (67 percent of the statewide total over the 1978–83 period) by the budgeted expenditures for the State Department of Corrections.

the total. The largest item ($382 million) is the expenditures of State prisons related to the incarceration of felons from New York City. Most of the remaining expenditures are for City-operated jails and other activities of the New York City Department of Corrections.

The processing of defendants was allocated over $255 million or 12 percent of the total. Just under $100 million was spent for the operation of the two criminal court systems—New York City Criminal Courts and the criminal units of the State Supreme Court. The five district attorneys spent a total of nearly $73 million. The Legal Aid Society was given $34 million, primarily to defend the indigent. Together, the judges, prosecutors, and public defenders account for $206 million or four-fifths of the total for processing. Other agencies include the Department of Probations and the Department of Juvenile Justice.

The current pattern of spending results from recent shifts in the allocations of funds among the functions and agencies. Table 11.6 shows the trends in expenditures in constant (1978) dollars. Total, real operating expenditures rose 9 percent in the 1978–84 period, but the entire increase is accounted for by a sharp rise in spending between 1981 and 1984.

Although total spending for criminal justice was increased, expenditures for the police were decreased 9 percent in the 1978–84 period. This reduced the police share of total expenditures from 68 percent in 1978 to 57 percent in 1984. The New York City Police Department's spending declined 11 percent, more than the overall decrease. Spending for the Police Department fell more than spending for the other police agencies.

In contrast, the constant dollar sums spent on processing criminal defendants rose 34 percent. District Attorney's offices and courts experienced large gains in resources, as did the Legal Aid Society. Spending fell for the Department of Probation, which prepares presentencing reports, and for the City's Criminal Justice Coordinating Council.

Correctional services showed the largest increase in operating costs during the 1978–84 period, rising 51 percent in constant dollars. The City's Department of Corrections spent 52 percent more, and the costs to the State of imprisoning New York City's criminals rose 55 percent. In summary, then, spending priorities shifted towards punishing and processing, and away from policing. This

TABLE 11.6

Uses of Criminal Justice Funds in New York City, 1978–84

(millions of constant 1978 dollars)

	1978	1979	1980	1981	1982	1983	1984	Percentage Change 1978–84 %
EXPENDITURES[a]	$1,229.6	$1,123.3	$1,135.1	$1,072.6	$1,138.3	$1,233.7	$1,340.8	9%
Policing	830.8	729.3	722.4	663.0	688.1	710.7	758.7	−9
NYC Police Department	692.0	602.3	595.2	546.6	566.6	581.0	618.6	−11
NYC Transit Authority Police	101.2	96.7	98.1	90.2	92.6	97.6	104.7	3
NYC Housing Authority Police	35.4	28.3	27.1	24.3	26.9	29.8	33.2	−6
NYC Department of Investigation	2.2	2.0	1.9	1.8	2.1	2.2	2.3	2
Processing	122.4	121.9	132.5	132.3	152.2	166.4	164.2	34
NYC Criminal Justice Coordinating Council	13.4	10.9	11.2	12.6	14.9	9.5	9.6	−28
NYC Department of Juvenile Justice	N.A.	N.A.	9.0	9.1	10.5	10.7	10.4	N.A.
District Attorneys								
New York County	11.2	12.2	12.8	12.3	13.6	14.9	16.2	45
Bronx County	6.5	6.6	6.8	6.7	7.4	8.1	9.1	40
Kings County	10.5	10.8	10.8	10.5	11.6	12.4	13.3	26
Queens County	4.7	4.5	5.0	5.0	5.8	6.3	7.3	55
Richmond County	0.8	0.7	0.8	0.8	0.9	0.9	1.1	37

Office of Prosecution—							
Special Narcotics Court	1.6	1.7	1.6	1.6	2.3	2.6	2.8	73
Legal Aid Society	16.5	17.1	17.1	16.2	17.6	23.4	21.9	33
Crime Prevention Injury Award	0.1	0.1	0.1	0.1	0.1	0.1	0.1	-36
NYC Department of Probation	10.3	8.5	8.6	7.5	7.5	8.1	8.8	-14
Court Expenditures							
New York City Criminal Courts	16.5	17.0	17.9	19.7	21.1	28.4	20.8	26
Supreme Courts (Criminal Terms) in New York City[b]	30.3	31.6	30.8	30.3	39.1	41.1	42.9	42
Punishing	276.5	272.1	280.2	277.4	298.0	356.6	417.9	51
NYC Department of Probation	10.3	8.5	8.6	7.5	7.5	8.1	8.8	-14
NYC Department of Corrections	107.2	110.0	122.0	121.2	133.4	145.9	162.9	52
NYC Board of Corrections	0.3	0.4	0.3	0.2	0.3	0.3	0.3	-14
Total State Prison Expenditures Attributable to New York City[c]	158.7	153.2	149.4	148.4	156.8	202.3	245.9	55

SOURCES: All expenditures of the City of New York are as reported in the annual reports of the City Comptroller for the respective City fiscal years; State prison expenditures attributable to New York City are derived from the budgeted expenditures of the New York State Department of Corrections as reported in the New York State Executive Budget for the respective State fiscal years; estimated criminal justice expenditures of the State courts in New York City are derived from the budgeted expenditures for the State of New York, Unified Court System as provided by the Office of Court Administration.

a. Expenditures are in constant dollar (Fiscal Year 1978 = 100) terms and are based on changes in the Consumer Price Index (CPI-U) for New York-Northeastern New Jersey as reported by the Bureau of Labor Statistics.

b. These figures are estimates of criminal justice expenditures by the State-funded courts in New York City which assume that 55 percent of all State Supreme Court expenditures were devoted to criminal cases during the 1978–82 period and, subsequent to 1982, that 66 percent of State Supreme Court expenditures were devoted to criminal cases.

c. These figures are estimates of the costs of incarcerating those persons convicted of felonies in New York City in State correctional facilities. These estimates were derived by multiplying the average annual share of admissions to State prison that originated in New York City (67 percent of the statewide total over the 1978–83 period) by the budgeted expenditures for the State Department of Corrections for the respective fiscal years.

trend was consistent throughout the period, both when real spending for criminal justice was falling and, more recently, as expenditures rose. Part of the explanation for these trends is changes in the sources of funds for criminal justice services in New York City.

SOURCES OF CRIMINAL JUSTICE FUNDS

The major source of financing for criminal justice is local government. The City contributed 77 percent of total operating expenditures in 1984 (see Table 11.7). However, the State of New York has played an increasingly important role in financing local criminal justice services. Indeed, the growth in total real spending between 1978 and 1984 resulted entirely from an 88 percent increase in spending from State funds that compensated for a 3 percent decline in City support.

Part of the explanation for the decline in financing local criminal justice services on the part of the City, particularly between 1978 and 1981, is that the City still was recovering from the fiscal crisis. Police expenditures, which represent the major use of City funds, were restricted by the City's larger fiscal problems. In fact, the 9 percent decline in real Police Department spending was less than the 13 percent decline in real City spending over the 1978–84 period.[23]

Criminal justice processing also is largely a City responsibility, but the State's role has grown substantially, due to its assumption of local court costs in the 1978–80 period. City spending for processing, reflecting the State's judicial assumption, was decreased 14 percent overall but was increased in the 1981–84 period.

Where the City had to increase spending for punishment, its costs have gone up rapidly. The combination of rising numbers of jail inmates and federal judicial mandates to reduce overcrowding in City jails caused the City to increase the budget for correctional facilities by 46 percent in the 1978–84 period. The State's contribution, which is made through its prison system incarcerating New York City felons, was increased 55 percent. Unlike the processing function, where the State's entry into financing New York City criminal justice services was delayed until it assumed financial responsibility for local courts, New York State long has had a large share of its prison inmates from New York City. In 1983, that share was 71 percent, and was rising.

TABLE 11.7

Sources of Criminal Justice Funds in New York City, 1978–84

(millions of constant 1978 dollars)

	1978	1979	1980	1981	1982	1983	1984	Percentage Change 1978–84
Total Expenditures[a]	$1,230.2	$1,123.6	$1,135.3	$1,073.1	$1,139.0	$1,234.2	$1,340.3	9%
City of New York	1,065.6	946.1	949.5	874.7	922.1	962.4	1,031.4	−3
State of New York	164.6	177.5	185.8	198.4	216.9	271.8	308.9	88
Policing	831.3	729.7	722.7	663.3	688.5	710.9	758.7	−9
City of New York	831.3	729.7	722.7	663.3	688.5	710.9	758.7	−9
Processing	122.4	121.9	132.5	132.4	152.5	166.7	163.7	34
City of New York	116.5	97.6	96.0	82.4	92.4	97.2	100.7	−14
State of New York	5.9	24.3	36.5	50.0	60.1	69.5	63.0	968
Punishing	276.5	272.0	280.1	277.4	298.0	356.6	417.9	51
City of New York	117.8	118.8	130.8	129.0	141.2	154.3	172.0	46
State of New York	158.7	153.2	149.3	148.4	156.8	202.3	245.9	55

SOURCE: See Table 11.6

a. Expenditures adjusted by the Consumer Price Index for All Urban Consumers (CPI-U) for the New York-Northeastern New Jersey area.

POLICY OPTIONS

The previous sections provide some basic information about the workings and cost of the criminal justice system that can serve as a basis for identifying options to improve its performance. Specifically, the steps in the process of administering justice that warrant attention are the apprehension of criminals by the police, the prosecution by district attorneys of those arrested, and the nature of punishment for those convicted.

ARRESTING MORE CRIMINALS

The felony arrest and clearance rates of 15 percent suggest that for only this relatively small fraction of serious crimes is someone arrested. However, as noted earlier, there is good reason to believe the people arrested for these crimes account for a significantly larger share of the crimes committed. Many of those eventually convicted admitted that they had committed multiple offense (albeit to researchers, not to judges). It is likely that more than 15 percent of the active felons are apprehended by the police.

Nevertheless, the share of criminals arrested is probably below the public's expectations. How can more criminals be arrested? The possible strategies include expanding the volume of police activities and concentrating more police resources on apprehending those who commit serious crimes. The first approach is frequently recommended in the form of hiring more police officers. But without other policy changes, this strategy is relatively inefficient and ineffective. The average police officer costs approximately $50,000 including salary and fringe benefits and arrests approximately 4.2 felons annually. In other words, if the current pattern of police activities is sustained, the direct costs of a felony arrest would be about $12,000. Using this estimate, it would cost $2.7 billion and require nearly 126,000 additional officers to increase the arrest rate from 15 percent to 51 percent and thus bring the odds in favor of being arrested rather than not for committing felonies. The approach could be ineffective as well as inefficient; if other elements of the criminal justice system were not expanded or reinforced, these additional arrests probably would result in large percentages of those arrested not being prosecuted and, without more expansion of jail capacity, most of those arrested not going to jail.

A more desirable approach is to concentrate present and additional police resources on arresting felons, and particularly multiple offenders. Improved strategies for policing in New York City are not difficult to identify, however difficult they have been to implement. As noted, most police officers in New York City devote most of their time to activities that have little to do with the prevention or investigation of crimes and the apprehension of criminals. However much New Yorkers may be comforted by the arrival of a policeman to help when they have locked themselves out of their own homes or to wait with them for the ambulance to arrive in a medical emergency, such uses of scarce police resources are not consistent with New Yorkers' perceptions about the seriousness of the crime problem.

Police officials should redeploy uniformed personnel to maximize the amount of time devoted to their primary mission. Specifically, the current shift in deployment away from overwhelming reliance on radio patrol cars and toward alternative types of patrol, including foot patrols, should be accelerated. To minimize the impact of these changes in the uses of patrol cars on noncrime-related emergencies, police officials should implement an expanded "one-officer patrol car" strategy. Police efforts, in cooperation with the district attorneys, to target their crime-fighting resources on multiple felony offenders, the so-called "career criminal program," also should be accelerated. Apprehension of repeat offenders may be the single most effective means of reducing the overall incidence of serious crimes in the city.[24] Relatively less emphasis should be placed on so-called "victimless" crimes.

PROSECUTING MORE CRIMINALS

Whether or not more criminals are arrested, there is substantial room to improve the rate at which those arrested are prosecuted. At present, approximately 37 percent of those arrested for felonies are not prosecuted at all and only 27 percent are prosecuted for felonies. The reasons for this substantial discontinuity in the criminal justice system have not been examined carefully. However, a 1979 study of cases that were rejected and dismissed found that the two major reasons were evidence problems and witness problems.[25] Together, these factors accounted for about seven of every ten cases of this type. More careful analysis of these problems could lead to initiatives to aid prosecutors in their effort to bring criminals to trial successfully.

It should be noted that those grand juries indict for felonies very likely will be convicted. Thus, the problems in prosecuting criminals are related more to securing adequate evidence and the cooperation of witnesses than to the reluctance of juries to find people guilty.

While problems with evidence and witness cooperation are the major obstacles to effective prosecution, there are numerous ways in which the processing of defendants is made inefficient. A 1982 report by a State Advisory Commission (the Liman Commission) proposed changing the method currently used to select juries (voir-dire) by adopting the system used in federal court which gives judges the primary responsibility to pick juries and limits the number of challenges that lawyers can make. This system takes less time, is less expensive, and would free judges for more cases. The Liman Commission found that nearly 40 percent of trial time is consumed by lawyers selecting juries. Voir-dire time actually exceeded trial time in 20 percent of the cases surveyed. This proposal has been supported by the Mayor and the Governor, but was not enacted by the State legislature.[26]

Another proposal would change the method of case disposition. Currently, a single case can come before several judges before it is sent to trial. It would be more efficient to change to an individual calendar system so that each case would be placed on the docket of a single judge from start to finish.[27] This would eliminate much of the delay caused by lawyers dealing with different judges, and it would make judges more accountable for their productivity.

Finally, processing would be more efficient if grand-jury indictments were not required (except in cases where secrecy is essential). The federal Supreme Court does not require states to maintain grand juries and one-half the states have abandoned the system. Prosecutors should bring felony charges directly to a judge.[28] Such open hearings would save time and money and make the district attorneys more accountable for felonies they choose not to indict.

Sending More Felons to Prison. Present policies lead to a maximum of 54 percent of those initially arrested for a felony and subsequently convicted of a crime going to jail or prison. Of this group, less than 35 percent are sentenced to more than one year in prison (refer to Table 11.3). Many observers suggest that more convicted criminals should be sent to prison and that the length of sentences should be increased. Such plans are believed to have the dual effects of deterring crime by increasing the likelihood of stern punishment and preventing crime by incapacitating for long periods those who are likely to commit additional crimes.

While both the arguments for stiffer penalties are questionable, the practical obstacles to pursuing these policies have been limited by prison capacity and the high cost of adding prison spaces. However, the City and State have begun a combined $1 billion program to expand jail and prison capacity by 14,000 beds. The planned 40 percent expansion of the City's jails to increase capacity from 10,000 to 14,000 beds is estimated to cost more than $300 million; the planned 9000 cell expansion of the State prison system's capacity to 40,000 cells is estimated to cost more than $700 million.[29]

The number of additional felons who can be sentenced to jail and prison due to the new cells will depend on sentencing policies. Obviously, longer sentences will lead to fewer people being incarcerated. Since the minimum sentence in State prisons is one year, no more than 9000 felons can be assigned to these new facilities; the figure will probably be smaller. Moreover, if past patterns are followed, about 70 percent will be filled by felons from New York City. Among those serving sentences in City jails, the average stay is 49 days. If this remains constant (and no new cells are used by those awaiting trial), the new City cells could accommodate about 28,800 offenders annually. Thus, under current sentencing practices, the new jail and prison capacity will handle a maximum of 35,100 new offenders. This would more than double the number of offenders now incarcerated and permit virtually every person convicted to be sentenced to jail or prison. However, for the reasons noted, the actual additional capacity available for sentenced offenders may be substantially smaller.

The new jail and prison capacity creates an opportunity to think strategically about how to use it. To what extent should more offenders be imprisoned and to what extent should sentences be made longer? Systematically developing answers to these questions is beyond the scope of this chapter, but the appropriate answer is likely to be a combination of longer sentences for multiple offenders and shorter sentences for others. In addition, an optimal sentencing policy is likely to include a range of alternatives to incarcerations. The number of persons punished through probation, community service sentencing, victim restitution and other means could be increased significantly at costs well below those of building and operating new jail and prison cells.

CONCLUSION

There are numerous opportunities to improve the system of criminal justice in New York City. The police can concentrate more on arresting multiple offenders, the district attorneys can cooperate more with police and citizens in order to prosecute more of those arrested, and the planned additional jail capacity provides judges an opportunity to revise sentencing policies. But to work effectively, the actions taken require improved coordination among the agencies involved. The Department of Corrections' new jails can be filled with more convicted criminals or with more people experiencing delays in their trials, depending on the behavior of judges. The police can arrest more people only to have them released due to policies adopted by district attorneys. The district attorneys, in turn, can prosecute more cases, but find that fewer people are sentenced to jail or prison because of decisions by judges and the Probation Department.

A mechanism to coordinate the approaches of the various criminal justice agencies could improve their efficiency and effectiveness. At present, the mayor's Criminal Justice Coordinator is supposed to perform such a role, but has no legal authority to control others involved. The most effective source of control may be the mayor's budgetary authority. City revenues fund over three-quarters of all criminal justice expenditures, including virtually the entire budget of the police agencies, the district attorneys, and the Department of Corrections. Coordination with the governor also would be helpful, but the mayor's authority is extensive. Instead of struggling to avoid responsibility for the criminal justice system, political leaders could agree on strategies to improve current practice and ensure that sufficient funds are allocated to support these policies.

NOTES

1. Forty-one percent of the respondents to a *New York Times* poll cited crime as the most important problem facing New York City. See *The New York Times*, "New York City Survey," January 10, 1985; see also Josh Barbanel, "Koch Recommends Stiffer Penalties and More Prisons," *The New York Times*, February 15, 1985, p. A1.

2. See, for example, Charles Silberman, *Criminal Violence, Criminal Justice* (New York: Random House, 1980); Robert K. Merton, "Social Structure and Anomie" in his *Social Theory and Social Structure* (New York: Free Press, 1968); Richard Cloward and Lloyd Ohlin, *Delinquency and Opportunity* (New York: The Free Press, 1960); David Abrahmsen, *The Psychology of Crime* (New York: Columbia University Press, 1972).

3. See, for example, Isaac Ehrlich, "Participation in Illegitimate Activities: A Theoretical and Empirical Investigation," *Journal of Political Economy*, Vol. 81, No. 3 (May/June 1973), pp. 521–565; Alfred Blumstein, Jacqueline Cohen, and Daniel Nagin, eds., *Deterrence and Incapacitation: Estimating the Effects of Criminal Sanctions on Crime Rates* (Washington, D.C.: National Academy of Science, 1978); and James Q. Wilson and Barbara Boland, "Crime," in William Gorham and Nathan Glazer, eds., *The Urban Predicament* (Washington, D.C.: Urban Institute, 1976), pp. 179–230.

4. For a summary of the literature estimating effects of deterrence and an articulation of this approach, see James Q. Wilson, *Thinking About Crime* (New York: Basic Books, 1983).

5. See, for example, Marvin E. Wolfgang, Robert M. Figlio, and Thorsten Sellin, *Delinquency in a Birth Cohort* (Chicago: University of Chicago Press, 1972); Llad Phillips, Harold L. Votey, Jr., and Darold Maxwell, "Crime, Youth, and the Labor Market," *Journal of Political Economy*, Vol. 80, No. 3 (May/June 1972), pp. 491–504.

6. Uniform Crime Reports of the Federal Bureau of Investigation distinguish between Part I or "Index" crimes and Part II crimes. This distinction is necessitated by variation among the 50 states in the definition of crimes and the need for consistency inherent in the Bureau's centralized data collection and dissemination effort. The seriousness of all Part I crimes is evident; they include murder and manslaughter, rape, assault (aggravated as opposed to simple), robbery, burglary, larceny, and motor-vehicle theft. The range of crimes included under the Bureau's Part II crimes, however, is very broad. Serious Part II crimes (at least to the authors) are mingled with obviously less serious crimes. Serious Part II crimes include kidnapping, driving while intoxicated, or arson; less-serious Part II crimes include criminal mischief, offenses against the public order, unauthorized vehicular use, disorderly conduct, loitering, and an "all other offenses" category.

The data in Table 11.1 exclude from the Bureau's Part II category the least-serious crimes (those ranging from criminal mischief to "all others") and show those in a third category called "All Other Offenses." This permits separate analysis of what the authors consider serious crime in New York City. Readers still may object to the differentiation between serious crimes and less-serious crimes implied by retaining the distinction between Part I and Part II crimes, but the detailed information by offenses is provided for those who would reorder further the Uniformed Crime Report data.

Table 11.1 presents the federal crime data, distinguishing between noneconomic and economic crimes. Criminologists argue about the meaning and content of such categories (and others, like crimes against property and crimes against persons); the classifications employed in Table 11.1 are necessarily judgmental. The classification of kidnapping and arson is illustrative. Despite their classification in Table 11.1 as noneconomic crimes, some (unknown) share of each is motivated by pecuniary gain rather than emotion. Again, the detail is shown so that readers with different judgments may reinterpret Table 11.1.

7. The Uniform Crime Reports define burglary as the unlawful entry of a structure to

commit a felony or theft. The use of force to gain entry is not required to classify an offense as burglary. Larceny is the unlawful taking of property from the possession or constructive possession of another in which no use of force, violence, or fraud occurs. It includes crimes such as shoplifting, purse-snatching, theft from motor vehicles, theft of motor vehicle parts and accessories, and bicycle thefts.

8. The National Crime Survey indicates that reporting rates remained relatively constant over the 1973–1983 period. See U.S. Department of Justice, Bureau of Justice Statistics, "Criminal Victimization in the United States" (NCJ-90541), September 1983.

9. *The New York Times*, "New York City Survey," op. cit.

10. U.S. Department of Justice, Bureau of Justice Statistics, *Report to the Nation on Crime and Justice: The Data* (hereinafter, BJS *Report to the Nation*), p. 6. National Crime Survey data are collected through interviews conducted at six-month intervals with the occupants of approximately 60,000 households representing some 135,000 persons. This survey is based on a national sample that is representative of the population of the United States ages 12 and over.

11. The equation for the unknown occurrence of each type of crime is specified as follows:

$$\frac{\text{average reporting rate}}{100} = \frac{\text{number of crimes reported}}{X}$$

The average reporting rate for murder (which is not reported by the National Crime Survey but is reported by the Federal Bureau of Investigation from police reports and by the National Center for Health Statistics from death certificates) is assumed to be 1.0 since it is widely believed that almost all murders are reported to the police.

12. Both the National Crime Survey and the Federal Bureau of Investigation's Uniform Crime Reports (which are based on police records of reported crime) indicate that the incidence of serious crime is substantially higher in metropolitan areas than in suburban or rural areas. However, the estimates of the number of serious crimes in New York City are based on *national* rates of crime victimization, which almost certainly are lower than the actual victimization rates in New York City. Assuming that the rate of crimes reported to the police in New York City in 1983 was not higher than the national average for that year, there is little reason to believe that the actual incidence of serious crime in New York City was lower than the 1,664,000 estimated.

13. On this issue, see Jan M. Chaiken and Marcia R. Chaiken, *Varieties of Criminal Behavior* (Santa Monica, Cal.: The Rand Corporation, August, 1982), p. v; see also Mark A. Peterson and Harriet Braiker with Suzanne M. Polich, *Who Commits Crimes: A Survey of Prison Inmates* (Cambridge, Mass.: Oelgeschlager, Gunn & Main, 1981).

14. For a comparative analysis of police performance in two other cities, see Thomas A. Reppetto, "The Influence of Police Organizational Style on Crime Control Effectiveness," *Journal of Police Science and Administration*, Vol. 3, No. 3 (1975), pp. 274–279. For each of these two cities, Reppetto reports measures of (UCR Index) arrests per officer per year which are roughly comparable to the measure of felony arrests per uniformed year of effort in New York City.

15. The point of view that police patrol has little effect on crime gained currency from the research in Kansas City and elsewhere which found no significant differences between different types of police patrol and the occurrence of crime. For a summary of the research findings from the Kansas City studies, see George Kelling et al., *The Kansas City Preventive Patrol Experiment: A Summary Report* (Washington, D.C.: The Police Foundation, 1974).

16. The number of patrol cars dispatched increased 21.7 percent from 2,540,000 in fiscal year 1978 to 3,092,000 in fiscal year 1983. See City of New York, *The Mayor's Management Report*, end-of-fiscal-year issues for 1979 and 1983.

17. Diane Steelman, "New York City Jail Crisis: Causes, Costs and Solutions," The Correctional Association of New York, December 1984.

18. The City's current jail expansion program is designed to expand capacity to approx-

imately 14,000 by 1989, and the State plans to increase the capacity of its prisons to approximately 40,000 over the next several years.

19. The outcomes shown in Table 11.3 were estimated from multiple sources using different reporting units and should be interpreted as only approximations of the general pattern. The number of felony indictments and their outcomes is from New York State, Division of Criminal Justice Services, *Crime and Justice Annual Report*, 1983 edition. The reader is again reminded that while arrest figures are numbers of people, indictment figures are people and/or charges against people. The estimate of the number of people who plead or are found guilty of misdemeanors is based on a study of the disposition of a single set of felony cases in Manhattan in 1979; see Barbara Boland, *The Prosecution of Felony Arrests* (Washington, D.C.: Bureau of Justice Statistics, 1983). She found that 59 percent of felony cases resulted in convictions of either felony or misdemeanor charges. Since it is reported that felony convictions are 23 percent of felony arrests, we estimate that the remaining 36 percent of convictions are accounted for by misdemeanor pleas or trials.

20. Felony outcome data from *Crime and Justice Annual Report*, op. cit.

21. Ibid.

22. The number of persons sentenced to jail for felony convictions is from ibid. The number of persons sentenced to jail for a misdemeanor plea after a felony arrest is based on the estimated total number of persons sentenced to City jails (19,884) in 1983 minus the number of convicted felons sentenced to City jails (4618). The number of persons sentenced to City jails during the year was estimated based on the fact that the average daily number of sentenced inmates was 2669 and their average length of stay was 49 days. See City of New York, Office of Operations, *The Mayor's Management Report*, end of fiscal year 1983.

23. Citywide trends in spending are described in Chapter 6 in this volume.

24. Research indicates that most felony offenders commit crimes at fairly low rates while a few commit crimes at high rates. See Peter Greenwood, *Selective Incapacitation* (Santa Monica, Cal.: The Rand Corporation, August 1982). This study reported that one-half of the convicted robbers in California, Michigan, and Texas each committed five or fewer robberies per year, and one-half of the convicted burglars each committed 5.5 or fewer burglaries per year. However, 10 percent of the convicted robbers each committed 87 or more robberies per year, and 10 percent of the convicted burglars each committed 232 or more burglaries per year.

25. Barbara Boland, op. cit.

26. *Recommendations to the Governor Regarding the Administration of the Criminal Justice System*, The New York State Executive Advisory Commission on the Administration of Justice, Arthur Liman, Chairman, November 22, 1982.

27. "Winners in the Crime Wars," *The New York Times*, May 9, 1983.

28. "Do We Need Grand Juries?" *The New York Times*, February 18, 1985, p. A16.

29. Josh Barbanel, op. cit.

12

Housing

GEORGE STERNLIEB AND
DAVID LISTOKIN

The city's housing supply plays an important role in shaping its future. The availability of housing not only determines how many and what types of people will live in the city, it also shapes the course of economic development. Business location decisions are linked to judgments about the availability and costs of a labor force with a wide range of skills. If a local area cannot house adequate numbers of both high- and low-skilled workers at affordable costs, then firms will question the desirability of locating or retaining operations in that city.

This connection between housing and economic development is evident in New York City. The old law tenements of Manhattan were a response to nineteenth-century business needs for worker housing near the sweatshops; the art deco apartment buildings of the Bronx reflect the capacity of the subway lines to make the outer boroughs available as a home to a new middle class that commuted to Manhattan's central business district. More recently, the suburbanization has spread to outlying counties of the New York region. The older suburbs, both within the city and immediately adjacent, have become nearly stable in population size; the outer ring is now dominant as a new home for middle management. Long Island's Nassau County, adjacent to New York, lost 7.4 percent of its population from 1970 to 1980, but Suffolk, farther to the east, gained 14 percent. Westchester County's stable population size contrasts with Rockland County's growing inhabitants.[1] The same dispersion to the outer ring is evident in New Jersey.

The 1980 census and more recent data point to an increasing dependence on commuters to fill the requirements of the city's new economy. The number of commuters increased 46,000 from 1970 to 1980, contrasting with the 271,000 decline in city residents holding jobs in New York City. As of 1980, over 700,000 persons commuted to jobs in New York City—most of them to Manhattan.[2] Since 1980, the trend probably has accelerated. Reviewing divergent trends in payroll employment and resident employment, the Regional Commissioner of the U.S. Bureau of Labor Statistics said in 1984: "The sharp discontinuity in the intercensal period suggests that the changes in the commuter data from the 1970 Census to the 1980 Census probably underestimate the growing role of commuters in the city's economy in recent years."[3]

Over time, this reliance on commuters affects corporate decisions on the type and scale of activities to locate in the city. If New York City is defined as a residence only for the poor who cannot afford to leave it and the rich who can afford isolation from it, then enterprises requiring people in the middle will be dependent upon those who live outside of New York City. Given the increasing cost,

TABLE 12.1

Change in New York City Housing Supply, 1941–83

	Additions		Losses		
	New Units Completed	Conversions	Units Demolished	Conversions	Net Change
1941–50	165,590	56,918	52,369	23,441	+ 146,698
1951–60	323,330	56,567	121,865	15,587	+ 242,445
1961–70	348,045	37,911	100,269	13,878	+ 271,809
1971–80	165,828	28,696	101,794	9,142	+ 83,588
1981–83	25,061	11,906	23,530	3,311	+ 10,126

SOURCE: City of New York, Department of City Planning, *New Housing in New York City 1981–83* (January 1985), p. 24.

NOTE: These figures understate the level of rehabilitation activity because they report changes as indicated by Certificates of Occupancy and many rehabilitation programs do not affect these tallies.

TABLE 12.2

Permits Issued for New Housing Units,
New York City and Rest of New York State, 1960–84

	New York City		Rest of New York State	
	Total	Percentage Publicly Assisted	Total	Percentage Publicly Assisted
1960	46,792	20.7%	45,887	1.7%
1961	70,606	29.4	47,023	3.3
1962	70,686	28.3	51,072	2.0
1963	49,898	23.2	53,560	4.6
1964	20,594	31.1	54,839	2.3
1965	25,715	45.4	65,455	4.3
1966	23,142	53.5	52,278	2.8
1967	22,174	49.6	54,829	2.2
1968	22,062	55.3	58,898	6.7
1969	17,031	50.6	53,264	5.6
1970	22,365	68.9	46,466	22.0
1971	32,254	65.1	70,979	18.9
1972	36,061	51.3	75,221	16.2
1973	22,417	66.1	57,053	7.9
1974	15,743	27.7	35,894	3.8
1975	3,810	20.6	28,813	4.0
1976	5,434	3.7	27,936	3.4
1977	7,639	20.8	33,972	9.9
1978	11,096	23.7	32,655	13.8
1979	14,524	5.5	25,318	15.6
1980	7,800	16.8	19,004	16.5
1981	11,060	21.9	18,790	14.5
1982	7,760	N.A.	17,520	N.A.
1983	11,758	N.A.	24,271	N.A.
1984	11,566	N.A.	29,105	N.A.

SOURCE: New York State Division of Housing and Community Renewal, unpublished data.

NOTE: N.A. means not available; publicly assisted housing includes federal, State, and City direct assistance programs but excludes units receiving only tax incentives.

time, and uncertainty of commuting, a narrowing set of economic functions eventually will be left to the city. A balanced mix of housing and the demographic elements it shelters do not guarantee a balanced mix of economic enterprise, but they are an essential condition.

To be economically successful in the longer-run, the city must meet two distinct types of housing needs. One group of low- and moderate-income people, the "shelter society," requires the basics of adequate physical housing. Members of a second, more affluent group, the "post-shelter society," want housing to serve also as a symbol of prestige and a vehicle for capital accumulation. The primary consideration in choosing a dwelling for these people is not whether one can afford the investment, but whether it is retrievable at a profit. For the young members of this group location close to core areas of jobs and consumption is an equally key concern.

The distinction between the shelter and post-shelter societies parallels the split between the old New York City, with its industrial-worker base, and the new one of the affluent office worker. The scale of the latter has been much exaggerated by media that offer them as prototypes of the New Yorker. They are the gentrifiers, the loft residents, the occupants of the new, high-cost residential facilities in the city. In their youth they are willing to compromise on housing standards, capable of doubling and tripling up in prestige neighborhoods, but their long-term goal is ownership and amenity. If they cannot achieve this within the city, they will move outside of it—and take their essential skills as well. These decisions will take place against a backdrop of significant change in the pace and composition of the city's housing production.

TRENDS IN HOUSING SUPPLY

Housing nationally is dependent on the economic cycle. Within any two years, there can be more than two million housing starts, followed by a halving of that figure.[4] New York City's housing record bears all of the problems of the national pattern with accentuated stigmata of its own. One of the latter is a lack of new housing starts without parallel in the city's history. The long-term trends, unlike those of the nation, clearly are down.

After wartime shortages that limited the increase in the city's housing stock from 1941 through 1950 to under 150,000 units, a burst of activity yielded an increase of more than one-half million units in the following 20 years (see Table 12.1). This contrasts with the decade of the 1970s, which saw the construction of only about 84,000 units. The increases from 1981 through 1983 were at an even slower rate, and 80 percent were attributable to conversion rather than new construction. In earlier periods new construction dominated growth in the housing supply.

Rehabilitation is a necessary but insufficient way to increase the housing supply in New York City. It is essential in coping with a housing stock whose average age is over half a century.[5] But it cannot cope with the obsolescence that characterizes much of the city's housing. New construction is essential, but it is the sharply declining component of housing activities.

The decline in the annual production of new housing in New York City is indicated in Table 12.2. In the early 1960s, new housing starts exceeded 70,000 units each year (equalling between 3 and 4 percent of the national total). It was reduced to less than a third of that level by the end of the decade. While between 32,000 and 36,000 units annually were started in the peak national years of 1971 and 1972, this production accounted for only 1.5 percent of the national total—a market share less by half. Starts reached an all-time low in the 1975–77 period, when new housing construction ranged between only 3800 and 7600 units annually. There was more local housing construction in the midst of the Great Depression.[6] While there has been some increase in activity in subsequent years, production was still a modest 8000 to 12,000 units annually in the early 1980s. New York City, in which more than 3 percent of the families in the United States live, thus has the dubious distinction of currently generating barely one-half of 1 percent of new housing starts. In New York City, it takes four years to create as many new units as were added to the stock in any one year in the early 1960s, while current production nationally exceeds those base years.[7]

Certainly, suburbanization and regional demographic and job shifts account for part of the decline in new housing starts. But the balance of New York State, which also is affected by these changes, has been less seriously affected than New York City. Housing permits in the rest of the state were better than half their 1960 level in 1984; for New York City, the 1984 rate was only one-quarter the 1960 figure. While the rest of the state's record may be poor, the city's is far worse.

A large part of the city's dismal performance results from the near cutoff of funds for publicly assisted units. In 1971, assistance for 21,000 housing units was extended, accounting for two-thirds of the citywide total. In contrast, less than 2500 units or under 22 percent of the total were publicly assisted in 1981. The private sector in recent years shows some signs of increasing its financing of new housing, though it is barely at one-fifth of the production

TABLE 12.3

Permits Issued for Publicly Assisted New Housing Units, New York State and New York City, 1960–81

	Total		Public Housing[a]		Federal Middle Income[b]		State and City Middle Income[c]		Federal Section 8[d]	
	New York State	New York City	New York State	New York City	New York State	New York City	New York State	New York City	New York State	New York City
1960–64	75,476	68,455	29,056	25,356	1,950	834	44,470	42,265	—	—
1965–69	68,223	55,860	18,312	11,864	8,287	4,286	41,624	39,710	—	—
1970–74	115,784	74,097	21,564	12,095	16,991	8,944	77,229	53,058	—	—
1975–79	19,912	6,007	2,190	873	100	0	922	830	16,700	4,304
1980	4,436	1,307	310	266	0	0	0	0	4,126	1,041
1981	5,147	2,424	1,072	600	0	0	0	0	4,075	1,824
Total	288,978	208,150	72,504	51,054	27,328	14,064	164,245	135,863	24,901	7,169

SOURCE: New York State Division of Housing and Community Renewal, unpublished data.

a. Federal and State-assisted low-income housing operated by local public-housing authorities.

b. Federal assistance with no State involvement.

c. State- and City-assisted middle-income housing with or without federal involvement.

d. Section 8 new construction only.

TABLE 12.4

New Dwelling Units Completed in New York City, 1921–83
(in thousands)

Period	Total	Public[a]	Private[b]
1921–30	762.3	0.5	761.8
1931–40	207.3	13.8	193.5
1941–50	165.6	66.1	99.5
1951–60	323.3	125.8	197.5
1961–70	348.0	175.7	172.3
1971–80	165.8	111.5	54.3
1981	8.7	3.9	4.8
1982	7.3	3.7	3.6
1983	9.1	N.A.	N.A.

SOURCES: City of New York, Department of City Planning publications: *Housing Data-base—Public and Publicly Aided Housing* (August 1983), *New Housing in New York City 1983* (January 1985); and *New Dwelling Units Completed*, annual series.

NOTES: N.A. means not available.

     a. Includes public housing (units built or operated by the New York City Housing Authority) and publicly assisted housing (units insured, subsidized and in other ways aided by the municipal, State or federal governments).

     b. The private unit figures were obtained by subtracting the publicly assisted housing units from the total housing unit production. It should be noted, however, that the total housing unit production series and the publicly aided housing production series are dissimilar in their reporting base. The former reports a unit as "completed" upon the issuance of its final Certificate of Occupancy; the latter indicates a unit is "completed" if it is reported as such by the respective local/state federal housing agency. It is possible for the public agencies to report a housing unit as "completed" before a final Certificate of Occupancy is issued.

level a generation ago. The decline in public support accounts for most of the decline in new housing.

The increasing difficulties of New York City's job market during the early 1970s had their equivalent in housing. In the former, there was little notice of the relative decline of the private sector and its replacement by governmental and publicly supported jobs. In the latter, private housing production fell by between 60 and 80 percent with publicly assisted housing starts filling the gap. In both cases, the harsh realities became evident when the capacity to fund public sector efforts disappeared.

Table 12.3 contrasts the dependence of the state and the city on publicly assisted housing. With less than one-half of the state's population, New York City in the 1960s secured nearly three-quarters of all the public housing units, roughly one-half of the federal middle-income units, and nearly all of the more than 80,000 state and city middle-income units. All three sources subsequently were drastically reduced. The surviving federal Section 8 program found the rest of the state in a much more active or, perhaps better, qualifying role than New York City. A statewide total of 25,000 units was supported under this program by 1981, but less than 30 percent were started in New York City.

Other sources reveal a similar trend of diminished new housing production in New York City due to declining public subsidies for housing. The dramatic change in completed new housing units (as opposed to the earlier figures for housing permits) is illustrative (see Table 12.4). In the 1920s, over 750,000 new units were completed in the City, almost exclusively by the private sector. The depression of the 1930s saw completions drop to roughly 210,000 units; the war years and difficult recovery of the early postwar period saw a further decline in the 1940s to approximately 165,000 units. Production increased to almost 325,000 completed units in the 1950s and just below 350,000 units in the 1960s—decades of increased public housing assistance. In the 1970s, completion of publicly aided housing continued at the same pace, accounting for 115,000 units, but total production plummeted to 165,000 due to less private construction. In the 1980s, diminished public subsidies suggest that even less new housing will be constructed unless private sources begin to build it.

The change in the characteristics of new housing is described in Table 12.5. In recent years, nearly one-half of the City's new housing was built in Manhattan, the bulk of it in large-scale configurations and nearly all south of 96th Street. Roughly another quarter of the total starts were in Staten Island, typically in smaller buildings. Little new housing was started in the other three boroughs. In 1984, for example, the housing starts in the Bronx, Brooklyn, and Queens combined were barely one-half the total a dozen years before in *any one* of those boroughs.

New York's housing configurations are unlike those of the rest of the nation. In 1984, permits for one-family units accounted for under 11 percent of the total locally, compared to 54 percent nationwide.[8] Two- to four-family units are of minuscule importance nationally, but they represented 27 percent of New York City's new units. Large-scale structures, those with five or more units, represent nearly two-thirds of the total locally. The national constituency that generally prefers home ownership in one-family houses

TABLE 12.5

Permits Issued for New Housing Units by Borough and Building Type, New York City, 1970–84

	1970	1971	1972	1973	1974	1975	1976	1977	1978	1979	1980	1981	1982	1983	1984
Manhattan	3,826	8,468	15,818	7,887	10,812	424	1,707	3,106	5,938	8,464	4,406	5,275	2,830	5,487	4,190
One Family	—	—	1	—	—	—	—	1	1	—	3	11	—	—	—
2–4 Family	5	—	4	—	2	—	—	—	3	16	4	—	2	4	3
5+ Family	3,821	8,468	15,813	7,887	10,810	424	1,707	3,105	5,934	8,448	4,399	5,264	2,828	5,483	4,187
Bronx	6,282	5,369	2,759	3,390	285	322	316	983	535	486	312	873	466	731	712
One Family	21	32	10	33	29	3	4	5	10	8	—	44	45	112	120
2–4 Family	340	297	270	306	256	146	216	181	141	83	34	128	67	72	93
5+ Family	5,921	5,040	2,479	3,051	—	173	96	797	384	395	278	701	354	547	499
Brooklyn	5,083	4,939	7,239	4,369	1,728	595	485	723	824	1,442	680	1,674	1,631	1,624	1,450
One Family	29	45	128	1	3	5	6	10	37	13	27	19	194	463	276
2–4 Family	582	638	568	613	393	326	323	286	233	205	200	183	348	518	392
5+ Family	4,472	4,256	6,543	3,755	1,332	264	156	427	554	1,224	453	1,472	1,089	543	782
Queens	2,858	7,942	3,243	3,384	1,282	1,032	663	805	1,529	1,214	1,048	1,763	1,025	1,326	2,020
One Family	200	151	86	81	73	92	54	59	42	55	38	49	61	128	65
2–4 Family	1,176	1,383	1,181	908	521	762	512	349	436	457	887	1,449	456	633	646
5+ Family	1,482	6,408	1,976	2,395	688	178	97	397	1,051	702	123	265	508	565	1,309
Richmond	2,841	4,071	4,504	2,739	1,636	1,437	2,263	2,022	2,270	2,918	1,354	1,475	1,697	2,690	3,194
One Family	1,088	1,121	1,045	737	608	812	1,215	1,155	1,452	2,000	732	561	739	649	787
2–4 Family	1,106	1,586	2,350	1,580	451	489	662	664	668	695	526	587	624	1,424	2,032
5+ Family	647	1,364	1,109	422	577	136	386	203	150	223	96	327	334	617	375
Total	20,890	30,789	33,563	21,769	15,743	3,810	5,434	7,639	11,096	14,524	7,800	11,060	7,649	11,858	11,566
One Family	1,388	1,349	1,270	852	713	912	1,279	1,230	1,542	2,076	800	684	1,039	1,352	1,248
2–4 Family	3,209	3,904	4,373	3,407	1,623	1,723	1,713	1,480	1,481	1,456	1,651	2,347	1,497	2,651	3,166
5+ Family	16,343	25,536	27,920	17,510	13,407	1,175	2,442	4,929	8,073	10,992	5,349	8,029	5,113	7,755	7,152

SOURCE: New York State, Division of Housing and Community Renewal, Construction Activity in New York State, Based on Building Permits Issued, 1970–84 annual series.

NOTE: Totals do not correspond to those in Table 12.2 because of differences in reporting procedures.

TABLE 12.6

New York Regional Housing and Office Market, 1980–84

	1980	1981	1982	1983	1984
Housing Market					
Total Units (Number)	28,883	29,801	27,447	44,965	35,000
Location (percentage)					
New York City	24%	22%	23%	24%	20%
Long Island	13	15	11	11	13
New Jersey	44	41	49	50	54
Northern Suburbs	19	22	17	15	13
Office Market					
Total Construction					
(millions of square feet)	17.8	19.5	18.7	22.5	21.0
Location (percentage)					
New York City	44%	32%	32%	30%	20%
Long Island	3	6	11	4	11
New Jersey	38	43	40	45	50
Northern Suburbs	15	19	17	21	19

SOURCE: Landauer Associates, "New York Metropolitan Area Market," *Development Review and Outlook* (Washington, D.C.: Urban Land Institute, 1984), pp. 253, 257, and unpublished data supplied by F. W. Dodge, Inc.

is largely ignored by the housing industry in New York City. Indeed, in all of the United States in 1983, only 191,000 privately financed, unsubsidized, unfurnished apartments were completed in buildings of five units or more. The bulk of these were in the South and West; only 16 percent were rented at $500 or more, the base (but not for long) for rents in new New York City units.[9]

The eye of the Manhattan visitor is captured by the tall residential towers, but more modest buildings are becoming apparent. The proportionate number of two- to four-family houses has been increased to more than one in five of the city's new units. These buildings that arise in Brooklyn and Staten Island are a hybrid, combining the tax virtues of home ownership and the advantages of rental operation outside the strictures imposed by rent control.

From one point of view, the construction of two- to four-family buildings indicates the potential of the housing market if the City could reduce its regulatory strictures. Two- to four-family homes are the major "success story" of the outer boroughs. They provide new rental housing at prices competitive with those of suburbia. A less positive view is that such units are made possible only if the contractor does not adhere to the building code (particularly in constructing illegal three-family apartments) as well as by substantial subsidization through underassessment. Nevertheless, there may be something to be learned from their growing popularity.

While housing starts increased slightly during 1984, the level barely exceeded 10,000 units a year, well below the attrition through abandonment. Without a renewal of the private housing industry within the city, the filtering process that previously improved at least the physical characteristics of the city's low- and moderate-income housing will be halted—abruptly.

In essence, current housing policies fail to result in an adequate supply of housing. The city's new business functions, and hence its future economic vitality, increasingly depend on people who do not live within it. As a result, jobs are following residences. As shown in Table 12.6, New York City's share of the region's new housing and office construction has slipped markedly in the early 1980s. This is particularly the case when measured against New Jersey. The northern counties of that state have two-and-one-half times as many dwelling units being constructed within them as does New York City. Ultimately, the new population housed within those dwelling units will be complemented by job growth, and at a loss to New York City.

MUNICIPAL HOUSING PROGRAMS

No city in the United States has a longer or more comprehensive involvement in housing than New York. New York has been a pioneer, inspiring other central cities and setting the pattern for many federal-housing programs. Notable examples include the tenement-house laws of the nineteenth century, public housing begun in the early twentieth century, and today's rehabilitation of housing.

New York's first housing law dates from 1648, when the municipal government regulated chimney construction and ordered that "hogs and goats be pastured only in fenced areas."[10] In response to the squalor of nineteenth-century slums, Tenement House Acts were legislated in 1867 and 1901; these were followed by Multiple Dwelling Laws in 1929, 1955, and subsequent years.

But regulation was only part of the municipal role. In 1920, New York State permitted cities to abate real estate taxes on newly constructed housing. The City of New York applied this incentive to its fullest capacity. In a decade, over 750,000 housing units were built and over $300 million in property taxes abated. The 1920s also witnessed the start of Limited Dividend Companies (LDCs), providing low-income housing with the assistance of financing below the market rate and partial exemption from real estate taxes. The LDCs constructed over 10,000 housing units, mainly in the late 1920s and early 1930s.

Of even greater import were the public housing projects first authorized in New York City in 1934, three years before the federal public housing program was enacted. New York City's first public housing venture was a 135-unit project built on the lower east side in 1936. A half century later, the New York City Housing Authority encompasses 2800 buildings containing 174,000 units. The Housing Authority provides shelter to over 480,000 people, a population larger than that of the city of Buffalo.[11]

In the 1950s and 1960s, New York City took full advantage of newly available State and federal funds for housing construction. As a result, Mitchell-Lama and State- and City-sponsored housing efforts led to the erection of 120,000 rental and cooperative housing units; State Redevelopment Corporation housing created 12,000 units; numerous federal programs such as Title I and Section 207 built 64,000 units; and Section 608 subsidized 28,000 units.[12] These initiatives were followed by federal efforts in the 1970s, such as Section 8 which assisted the construction of over 11,000 new units.

The numerous housing programs from 1928 to 1982 resulted in over 500,000 housing units being built and another 57,000 units rehabilitated with public assistance.[13] Yet, most of what has been described is history. The major housing programs of yesteryear, such as Public Housing, Mitchell-Lama, and Section 8, either no longer exist or are merely maintaining what was built in the past. The housing theme today is modest effort and making the most of the limited available funds.

This more modest activity is reflected in the City's current housing activities. The operating budget of the Department of Housing Preservation and Development (HPD) for fiscal year 1985 was approximately $418 million or roughly 2 percent of all municipal operating expenditures.[14] Moreover, most of HPD expenditures are financed by federal aid rather than locally generated funds. While the HPD budget does not include revenues foregone through tax abatement programs, it still is a relatively modest level of commitment.

The City's current housing programs emphasize rehabilitation as

TABLE 12.7
Major New York City Housing Programs

Program	Description		1978	1979	1980	1981	1982	1983	1984	(Plan) 1985	1985 CDBG Funding (millions)
							Activity (Fiscal Year)				
I. *LOAN/GUARANTEE/OTHER SUBSIDY PROGRAMS*											
Article 8-A	Offers rehabilitation loans at 3 percent interest and 20-year terms to owners of multiple dwellings occupied by lower-income tenants ($5,000)	Units Rehabilitated	1,472	2,700	4,869	6,640	7,230	7,398	7,613	7,895	N.A.
		Loans Closed ($ Million)	$1.5	$4.6	$8.9	$13.0	$15.4	$15.3	$15.9	$16.6	$15.5
Participation Loan	Offers a 1 percent interest loan in combination with privately financed market-cost mortgage money to finance repairs/renovations on deteriorating multiple dwellings ($8,000–$10,000).	Units Rehabilitated	392	776	1,904	3,322	3,321	3,571	2,793	2,400	N.A.
		Loans Closed ($ Million)	$2.5	$11.4	$30.3	$53.9	$54.8	$61.1	$52.2	$48.0	$24.0
Neighborhood Preservation	NPP provides a range of rehabilitation services in selected neighborhoods.	Mortgage Commitments ($ million)	$ 9.2	$14.9	$24.3	$31.7	$38.6	$55.1	$39.5	$36.0	$ 3.2
		Units Repaired	4,726	4,703	5,668	8,937	10,650	13,043	11,584	10,200	N.A.
Section 8	Provides significant subsidy for multifamily new construction and rehabilitation (federal subsidy).	New Construction	1,897	2,799	778	1,537	2,208	1,738	1,362	1,000	N.A.
		Substantial Rehabilitation	851	1,920	3,275	3,967	1,281	3,477	967	500	N.A.
		Moderate Rehabilitation	N.A.	N.A.	N.A.	N.A.	N.A.	2,317	2,882	161	N.A.
Other	Small Home Improvement Programs (SHIP) provides loan fund applied by Neighborhood Housing Services (NHS); Home Improvement Program (HIP) provides improvement loans; Real Estate Mortgage Insurance Corporation (REMIC) insures rehabilitation/refinancing mortgage loans.	HIP Units	N.A.	N.A.	N.A.	N.A.	418	914	1,461	N.A.	N.A.
		REMIC Units	1,252	1,383	1,370	2,608	403	N.A.	N.A.	N.A.	$11.7

II. REAL ESTATE TAX EXEMPTION/ABATEMENT

Program	Description	Metric									
J-51	Provides a 12-year *exemption* from taxation on an increase in assessed valuation resulting from alterations and also permits *abatement* of real-estate tax equaling 90 percent of the certified reasonable costs.	Applications Approved ($ Million)	$71.4	$79.2	$122.3	$154.9	$152.3	$121.7	$66.4	N.A.	N.A.
		Units Approved	48,161	41,251	73,808	73,705	73,087	83,296	60,330	N.A.	N.A.
Section 421	Provides for an 8- to 10-year phase-in of property taxes resulting from the construction of new residential units. $421(a) applies to multiple dwellings, and $421(b) to one- and two-family homes.	$421(a)—Units	2,690	2,346	3,679	5,778	1,449	3,852	2,678	N.A.	N.A.
		$421(b)—Units	N.A.	122	723	1,020	1,236	1,492	1,565	N.A.	N.A.

III. CARETAKER FUNCTIONS

Program	Description	Metric									
Article 7-A	Provides for court-appointed administrators to manage multiple dwellings where the owners have been unable/unwilling to provide essential services/maintenance.	Units	N.A.	N.A.	N.A.	N.A.	1,839	1,200	1,159	1,200	N.A.
		Financial Assistance ($000)	N.A.	N.A.	N.A.	$ 832	$ 575	$ 621	$ 800	$ 1.4
Demolition and Sealing	Removes the danger and blighting influence of open, vacant buildings through demolition and sealing.	Buildings Demolished	1,455	1,888	2,235	2,065	1,974	1,532	1,456	1,500	$18.8
		Buildings Sealed	4,795	5,293	6,454	5,962	4,226	2,656	2,342	3,250	N.A.
Emergency Repair	Makes/provides emergency repairs/services where serious violations exist that the property owner refused to correct.	Repairs Completed	20,450	21,762	26,329	38,186	37,503	17,321	13,348	15,000	$ 6.2
In-Rem Central Management	The city manages, maintains, and eventually disposes of properties acquired for non-payment of real-estate taxes.	Total Buildings	N.A.	8,593	9,106	8,417	7,809	9,083	9,983	10,110	$91.2
		Total Units	N.A.	100,995	101,352	76,361	76,162	88,466	91,457	95,267	N.A.
In-Rem Alternative (Community) Management	There are numerous efforts to foster community/tenant/other private-interest management, and ultimately ownership of the in-rem stock. Examples include the Tenant Interim Lease (TIL) program, Community Management Program (CMP), and Private Ownership and Management Program (POMP).	Total Buildings	81	708	635	647	523	488	507	527	$33.3
		Total Units	1,664	7,377	14,969	14,787	12,464	11,457	11,643	11,172	N.A.

SOURCE: City of New York, *The Mayor's Management Report* 1978; City of New York, *City Fiscal Year 1985 Community Development Program*; City of New York, *Housing Database—Public and Publicly Aided Housing*, August 1983.

NOTE: N.A. means not applicable or information not available.

opposed to new construction and also concentrate on a caretaker's role for the marginal housing stock (see Table 12.7). The latter is exemplified by the maintenance of *in rem* structures, buildings taken by the City for nonpayment of taxes. Nearly one-half of the federal funds provided to HPD under the Community Development Block Grant (CDBG) program in 1985 were devoted to maintaining *in rem* inventory. Such activity represents fully one-third of the total HPD budget. The City's caretaker role is manifested in other ways, ranging from the appointment of receivers on almost 1200 units in 1984, to making almost 14,000 emergency repairs and to sealing or demolishing almost 4000 deteriorated buildings in the same year.

In the City's rehabilitation programs, there is an evolving substitution of modest for more significant rehabilitation. For example, nearly 4000 units were substantially rehabilitated under the Section 8 program in 1981. By 1984, the figure dropped to 967 units, but another nearly 2900 units benefited from moderate rehabilitation under the program. But this increase in moderate rehabilitation is a poor substitute for the demise of other federal programs. Present upscale city housing activity is nearly exclusively financed by Section 421 and J-51 tax abatement programs. The J-51 program exceeds all of the other rehabilitation efforts under the aegis of HPD. The Section 421 programs resulted in 35 percent of all housing starts in 1982 and 45 percent in 1983 (refer to Tables 12.5 and 12.7).

The City faces abrupt declines in the federal funding for housing construction. Yet, there is no clear municipal housing policy to replace the federal efforts. In the words of the Executive Director of the Settlement Housing Fund,

This year [1984], New York will receive funds from the federal government for the following: about 125 units of public housing; a few hundred units of Section 202 housing for the elderly; 10 or so mixed-income rental housing developments for perhaps 1,000 units. . . . 900 units of Section 8 moderate rehabilitation; 3,000 or so units of moderate rehabilitation . . . grants with vouchers to go with some of them; only 589 units of Section 8 for existing housing; Section 235 interest-rate subsidies for about 500 units . . . .

Pointing out that New York State, through its grant program, will provide relatively small subsidies, she concluded, "If all goes well, we will have 4,000 units of rehabilitation or new construction, and another 600 units of assistance for existing housing."[15] In a city of more than 2.5 million housing units, that is a modest figure indeed. And even this level will be reduced by additional federal cutbacks.

HOUSING FUTURES

Most American cities have few alternative economic activities to replace those they are losing. The loss of economic activities may be accelerated or slowed by local policy, but the negative direction is obvious and seemingly unavoidable. New York is different. Its economy has the potential for long-run vitality, but the challenges of optimizing the relationship between its residents and its economic activities are substantial. New York has a choice of futures, and housing policy will be important in defining the one that is decided upon.

FUTURE HOUSING DEMAND

Forecasts of housing demand require estimates both of the number of residents and of their "headship rates," that is, the number of households that will be formed among people in specific age and sex categories. Nationally, from World War II until 1980 headship rates increased dramatically. By 1980, however, the increases in real housing costs, the decline in real housing buying power, and widespread declining confidence in the future caused the rate of new household formation to drop. Thus, while earlier national Census Bureau forecasts for the first four years of the 1980s suggested the formation of 1.7 million new households, the actual number was 1.3 million.[16] The divorce rate, a key influence on the extent of household formation, had been rising for many years, but even it declined in the face of the economic uncertainty of the early 1980s.[17]

The trends in New York City were somewhat different. From a housing point of view, New York City's population decline of approximately 800,000 people from 1970 to 1980 was nearly offset by the decline in household size. The population loss was more than

10 percent; the household loss was less than 2 percent or just 50,000.[18]

As a result, New York City is characterized by a relatively small average household size. In 1980, New York City's average household size was 2.54 persons, approximately 10 percent below that of the nation.[19] In 1984, the median number of persons per rental unit in the city was 1.89; for owner households, it was 2.41. Nearly one-half of the city's total housing was occupied by one- and two-person households. Density levels had fallen to roughly two rooms per person. Within rent-controlled housing, sheltering the city's oldest and longest-term residents, there were only 0.413 persons per room.[20]

The second parameter to be considered in viewing the future is the anticipated size, by age category, of the population. For New York City, the predictions of population size vary substantially. The New York State Division of Housing and Community Renewal, for example, in its demand forecasts anticipates an increase in New York City's population of about 19 percent and an increase in households of 36 percent during the 1980s.[21] It is unique in this estimate; most other analysts do not foresee such substantial growth. The New York State Department of Commerce projects a 1990 population in New York City within a few thousand of the 1980 figure.[22] Current Census Bureau forecasts indicate stabilization after the city's substantial population loss during the 1970s and are generally in accord with those presented by Emanuel Tobier in Chapter 2 of this volume.[23]

Utilizing the New York State Department of Commerce forecast of population by age and assuming a continuation of the headship rates within New York City as of 1980, yields a projection of no change in the number of households between 1980 and 1990. Applying the same assumptions to the estimates in Chapter 2 suggests a slight decline in the number of households from 1980 to 1990.

The character of the city's housing future depends upon changes in buying power as well as population size. There has been a long, sad, negative relationship of income (and with it the ability to buy housing) and minority status. Unless this relationship is broken, the decline projected by Tobier for non-Hispanic whites in the 18–54 and 55–64 age categories is particularly ominous. It suggests a serious reduction in the ability of city residents to pay rent or to buy a house.

The large and possibly growing share of the city's population dependent on public assistance will face the greatest difficulty in securing affordable housing because their purchasing power is so meager. This population includes over 900,000 people who receive public assistance and another group of over 200,000 aged and disabled who receive Supplemental Security Income. Only 43,172 welfare families were living in public housing in 1984.[24] Even allowing for some illegal "doubling up" in public housing, and taking into account the growing number of people living in City-owned *in rem* units, it remains true that the private market provides shelter for most welfare households.

The gap between the costs of private housing and welfare purchasing power is enormous. The rents permitted by government to welfare recipients are below even the *current maintenance* costs of typical accommodations, with no allowance for any other charges. In 1983, for example, 68 percent of families receiving public assistance and living in private housing in New York City received the maximum State shelter allowance. The average allowance paid to four-person households was $202 monthly; for one person it was $143 monthly. The overall average was $173 monthly.[25] At the same time, federally established Fair Market Rents (FMR) set as guidelines for the Section 8 existing housing program were at least twice as high. For example, the FMR was $311 for a studio apartment, $372 for a one-bedroom unit, $436 for a two-bedroom unit, $540 for a three-bedroom unit, and $599 for a four-bedroom unit.[26]

HOUSING THE POOR: HOMELESS PEOPLE
AND ABANDONED HOUSING

The enormous gap between the housing purchasing power of many city residents and the operating costs of private housing has led to the dual phenomenon of people without homes and housing abandoned by owners. Both of these problems are insoluble without significant expansion of the housing supply and increases in the resources available to support housing for the poor, but a well-managed municipal program to deal with abandoned or *in rem* housing can help.

Homeless People. There are no definitive data on the number of homeless people. Advocates of their cause suggest that 1 percent

TABLE 12.8

New York City In Rem Housing Inventory and Management, Fiscal Years 1979–85

	Fiscal Year						
	1979	1980	1981	1982	1983	1984	1985 (Plan)
	INVENTORY PROFILE						
Buildings							
Central[a]	8,593	9,106	8,417	7,809	9,083	9,983	10,110
Alternative[b]	708	635	647	523	488	507	527
Total	9,301	9,741	9,064	8,332	9,571	10,490	10,637
Occupied Buildings							
Central	4,347	3,801	4,928	4,582	3,430	4,190	4,407
Alternative	708	635	647	523	488	507	527
Total	5,055	4,436	5,575	5,105	3,918	4,697	4,934
Total Units							
Central[c]	100,995	101,352	76,361	76,162	88,466	91,457	95,267
Alternative[c]	7,377	14,969	14,787	12,464	11,457	11,643	11,172
Total	108,372	116,321	91,148	88,626	99,923	103,100	106,439
Units in Occupied Buildings							
Central	52,144	39,933	47,386	44,674	31,756	34,471	39,439
Alternative[c]	7,377	14,969	14,787	12,464	11,457	11,643	11,172
Total	59,521	54,902	62,173	57,138	43,213	46,114	50,611
Occupied Units							
Central	31,875	24,269	23,184	25,370	26,739	29,601	34,067
Alternative[c]	7,377	14,969	14,787	12,464	11,457	11,643	11,172
Total	39,252	39,238	37,971	37,834	38,196	41,244	45,239

MANAGEMENT PROFILE

Alternative Management						
Percentage of Buildings[d]	6.6%	14.3%	15.9%	14.0%	12.5%	10.8%
Percentage of Units[e]	15.7%	33.3%	34.4%	30.1%	28.0%	26.1%
Percentage Occupancy[f]						
Central	61.0%	61.0%	80.0%	81.0%	84.0%	86.0%
Alternative	N.A.	N.A.	N.A.	N.A.	N.A.	N.A.
Percentage Rent Collection[g]						
Central	30.0%	N.A.	N.A.	N.A.	N.A.	85.0%
Alternative	N.A.	N.A.	N.A.	N.A.	N.A.	90.0%
Sales (Buildings/Units)						
Central	0/0	380/ 878	236/3,040	376/2,276	720/4,124	419/2,247
Alternative	100/2,400	37/ 589	50/1,630	112/2,263	104/3,049	73/1,935
Total	100/2,400	417/1,469	286/4,670	488/4,539	824/7,173	492/4,182
Program Cost (CDBG Funded)						
Central ($ Million)	N.A.	N.A.	N.A.	N.A.	N.A.	$ 76.9
Alternative ($ Million)	N.A.	N.A.	N.A.	N.A.	N.A.	$ 32.2
Total	N.A.	N.A.	N.A.	N.A.	N.A.	$108.1

10.7%	
22.8%	
86.0%	
N.A.	
85.0%	
90.0%	
493/2,182	
106/2,779	
599/4,961	
$ 91.2	
$ 33.3	
$124.5	

SOURCES: City of New York, Office of Operations, *The Mayor's Management Report*, annual series; City of New York, *The In Rem Housing Program*, annual series; City of New York, *Community Development Program*, Fiscal Year 1985; and unpublished data supplied by the New York City Department of Housing Preservation and Development.

NOTES: N.A. means not available or not applicable.

a. Central (city management); b. alternative (community group, tenant, private real estate) management; c. assumes all units under alternative management are in occupied buildings which are fully occupied; d. percentage of occupied city-owned buildings under alternative management. e. percentage of occupied city-owned units under alternative management. City-supplied data; f. percentage of units in occupied buildings which are occupied (central management only); g. percentage of owed rents collected.

of the nation's population fits this description, while others have suggested a far smaller number. In New York City, a nightly average of more than 5000 people received lodging in municipal shelters in the fourth quarter of 1983; this was up 38 percent and 72 percent, respectively, from one and two years earlier. The equivalent figure in the fall of 1984 was approaching 20,000.[27] The number of persons in shelters, of course, does not indicate the number of people who are homeless. A walk through the city's bus terminals, public comfort facilities, and railroad stations (to say nothing of countless hallways) would provide some indication of the true number.

The responsibility of the City to provide emergency aid in the face of temporary necessity is long established. The provision of emergency housing was budgeted over $200 million in fiscal year 1985, more than 20 times the amount just three years earlier. The costs per person sheltered are in excess of $10,000 annually.[28] The results are, at best, a holding operation yielding inferior shelter and frequent scandal. The fear among City officials is that providing decent accommodations will create a permanent and continually growing group of shelter-dependent individuals. Their needs could absorb even more of the City's budget.

Abandoned Housing. A substantial part of New York City's housing stock is abandoned; it receives no maintenance from the landlord. But only a fraction of this abandonment is evident in tax delinquency and *in rem* proceedings by the City. Some owners whose interest in their buildings' operations has ended may keep their tax payments up to date because of the speculative value of even the stripped lot. In order to become officially recognized as abandoned, a building must be tax delinquent for a significant period of time and have been moved into a vesting procedure by the City. The latter process is generally initiated after a so-called "tax sweep," a thorough investigation of tax delinquency for a large area within a borough. If this is not done frequently, there may be buildings which should be *in rem* but are not. The number of buildings *in rem*, therefore, depends upon whether the City moves to make functional reality a legal and statistical one.

The number of functionally abandoned buildings is far larger than the number that have been taken over by the City. However, statistical information is available only on the housing in the legal domain. As shown in Table 12.8, *in rem* housing has included approximately 8000 to 10,000 buildings since 1979. Slightly less than one-half the buildings are occupied. These buildings include approximately 100,000 units; again, one-half are in occupied buildings. In recent years, the City has pursued a policy of relocating tenants out of poorer buildings or those nearly vacant in order to facilitate management, reduce costs, and provide a higher level of housing amenity. This policy is reflected in the rising ratios of occupied to total buildings from 1979 through 1985.

By 1985, there were approximately 45,000 occupied units operated by the City. The *in rem* occupied units comprise about 2 percent of the city's total rental housing and about one-quarter of the units under all public housing programs. This is *the* new housing program for the very poor. While the average gross income of families living in public housing in 1984 was close to $10,000, the *in rem* equivalent was about 70 percent of that level.[29]

Tax-delinquent properties are conventionally viewed as temporary aberrants; financial distress, marital discord, or other personal fiscal tragedies cause a building to pass into municipal ownership. According to this view, municipal involvement should be short-lived. Abandoned bicycles and automobiles are auctioned off by the police; the equivalent holds for buildings. The municipal role is merely to bridge the gap from one private owner to another. The only operating issue is the time until an auction can be arranged.

Such long-held concepts tend to have a life of their own, extending into periods when they no longer are appropriate. The *in rem* phenomenon in New York City is not a temporary phenomenon, but a fact of life best dealt with by professional organization rather than "pick up" expedience. The City has moved in this direction. It has explored numerous forms of tenant management, including non-profit groups, private realty firms, and partnerships between them. The tenant-consolidation efforts and increased rent collections within *in rem* buildings are solid accomplishments resulting from these efforts.

Yet by 1984, only 507 of the 10,490 *in rem* buildings were under some form of management other than direct City operation. Those tended to be larger, occupied buildings; thus, alternate management efforts accounted for over one-quarter of all occupied *in rem* units. The nonprofit groups involved in alternate management have a mixed record. Some have achieved notable success; others have not. In addition, the best buildings and those most suitable to non-profit operations often are the ones taken out of the municipally managed inventory. This is evident in the relatively large size of the buildings under alternative management. Unfortunately, the relative success of the alternative forms of management is obscured by the claims of their partisans. An evaluation of the several years of experience is needed.

In addition, the *in rem* program as a whole deserves review. The City's reason for adopting a procedure of taking buildings after one year (rather than three) of tax delinquency before beginning *in rem* proceedings was the belief that tax delinquency constituted inexpensive borrowing by owners. It was thought that after a long period of tax delinquency, the private holder of property typically abandoned the structure in the face of the accumulated debt on it. There also was the hope that if the City took buildings earlier, they would be in better condition and easier to maintain. While this may be true, there has not been a significant study of how well the present process works.

Tax Abatements and Exemptions. The controversy over the use of local tax abatements and exemptions to promote construction and renovation of housing for the middle class provides insights into the conflict between meeting the needs of the "post-shelter" segment of the population and meeting the shelter needs of the less fortunate. Enacted in 1955, the J-51 program provided long-term tax abatements on assessments and exemptions on the value of new improvements to owners who rehabilitated multifamily housing (and later to convert nonresidential buildings to residential use). It was originally intended to induce owners of cold-water tenements to upgrade their buildings, and it succeeded admirably in that goal. By 1980, such dwelling units had been reduced to a handful.[30] However, the program has become an important means to upgrade middle-income and luxury units as well.

The very success and widespread use of tax abatements led to growing opposition. How could the City forego taxes for the benefit of the affluent, while the less fortunate suffered? Moreover, many of the conversions of loft buildings to residential purposes required the displacement of industrial jobs that were available to the poor and near-poor. Due to these objections, the program was circumscribed in terms of its area application in 1982, and a ceiling of

$38,000 in total value per unit was imposed in 1983. While there are exceptions to these rules, they can be made only at the discretion of the Housing Commissioner rather than as "of right." Given the cost of construction in New York, as well as the uncertainties of rehabilitation generally, the stipulation that any project whose cost exceeds $38,000 per unit loses its tax exemption is particularly limiting. Despite some exceptions for moderately rehabilitated units in which most of the tenants remain in occupancy and for some publicly financed efforts, tax abatement is little used now.

Yet, studies have indicated that in a fiscal sense, the City can benefit by housing the affluent even at the cost of foregoing real estate taxes. The diversity of the New York City tax system, coupled with the relatively low utilization of municipal services by the tenants typically housed in units built with J-51 funds, yields a net fiscal gain.[31] The opposing arguments, however, have strong political appeal. The program's greatest potential has been in the conversion of nonresidential facilities into apartments. But the structures involved are symbols of the old economy of the city. They have a strong constituency, and the J-51 program threatens them. The jobs that are left in the old industrial areas may be shrinking in numbers, but they are substantial in absolute scale; moreover, there is little on the horzion to replace them for current job holders. Would the generation of wealth, of ratables, and of ancillary service jobs through broader conversion efforts more than offset the displacement of current industrial jobs? And even if it did, is this reason to sacrifice the job of the sewing machine operator or warehouse worker who may not find an equivalent job? The popular answers to these rhetorical questions are to hold on to the old as long as possible, even at the risk of inhibiting the city's economic growth. From a housing perspective, however, the fastest way to increase New York City's supply and to create more competitive pressure to lower prices would be to allow the conversion of lofts to apartments in Manhattan and in the other boroughs.

Another example of the political restrictions on efforts to reconcile the needs of the future economy, the post-shelter society, with those of current residents still living in the shelter society is the controversy over the extension of the 421(a) program, which was established in July 1971. As administered by the New York City Department of Housing Preservation and Development, it provided partial tax exemptions for the construction of new residential units.

TABLE 12.9

Filings for Conversions from Rental to Ownership, New York City,
1981–84

	Cooperatives		Condominiums		Total	
	Buildings	**Units**	**Buildings**	**Units**	**Buildings**	**Units**
1981	472	37,619	15	1,470	487	39,089
1982	407	33,222	45	5,073	452	38,295
1983	330	32,991	35	4,696	365	37,687
1984	277	20,801	32	12,502	309	33,303
Total	1,486	124,633	127	23,741	1,613	148,374

SOURCE: Conversion filings, New York State Attorney General's Office.

NOTE: Because of a backlog in filings, this table does not accurately indicate changes in trends. The data represent filings for conversion as opposed to completed conversions. Finally, the 1984 condominium-conversion figure (units) is relatively high because it includes the conversion of the very large Parkchester development.

Tax exemption was granted during construction and the first two years of occupancy and then declined gradually over a ten-year period. There were no income limits for tenants; however, a maximum initial rent, reflecting the tax savings, was established and approved by the City. All units were regulated by the Rent Stabilization Association and thus subject to limitations on rent increases. At the end of the tax-exemption period, however, the units were to be freed from rent regulations.

The City made a commitment, and substantial investments were made by developers. Most of the multifamily housing constructed in the city within the last ten years has benefited from the program. One may quarrel with the lack of limitations and with any of a variety of other provisions, but what is most crucial—and harmful for the future—is that the City reneged on its commitment. Rather than permitting the units to become part of the open market at the end of the tax abatement period, the City imposed continuing rent regulation for occupied units. In addition, the areas in which future benefits are available have been restricted.

The merits of the new rules are much debated. Current estimates of the savings due to the foregone taxes are approximately $4 per square foot in terms of first-year rents. For example, a 1000 square-foot apartment would produce savings of approximately $333 a month. But is this savings to tenants or merely windfalls for the developer? Since housing policy is made in a factual and research vacuum in New York City, no one knows.

The substantive rights or wrongs of this issue are less consequential than the implications for decisions by potential private investors. Housing is a long-term investment. The rules of the game of ownership and management are subject to the vagaries of the market, and these are substantial enough to make real estate a high-risk investment. When, however, to these risks are added a local government's tendency to renege on commitments, the issue becomes not why there is so little rental housing constructed in the city but rather why any is constructed.

Conversions to Cooperatives and Condominiums. Condominium and cooperative conversion in New York City was begun in the 1970s. The scale, however, was small compared with things to come. According to the federal Department of Housing and Urban Development, the proportion of all rental housing in New York City converted during the 1970s was less then 1 percent.[32] Since this figure included offering plans, some of which did not succeed, the actual count was somewhat less.

The inflationary pattern of the early 1980s, coupled with the changing economics of rental housing within the city, caused an enormous boost in conversions. As shown in Table 12.9, from 1981 through 1984, there were filings on almost 1500 buildings, with some 125,000 housing units, for conversion to cooperatives. During the same years condominium conversion, earlier relatively rare, grew rapidly; the owners of nearly 130 buildings with more than 24,000 units filed conversion plans.

However, the filing of a conversion plan does not indicate the level of marketing. It is not known how many of the nominally "owned" units actually are rented. There is evidence, however, from newspaper offerings that the purchase of condominium units, both nationally and in New York City, is increasingly within the purview of small-scale speculators. They hold them as rental units with tax advantages and also hope for future appreciation. In any case, from 1981 through 1984, owners of between 5 and 6 percent of the city's total rental housing stock filed for conversion.

The shift from rental to ownership is not unique to New York, but the scale of the phenomenon is unrivaled. The State and City either purposefully—or, more probably, inadvertently—have fostered this market choice. Statewide, condominium owners pay an average of one-third less property tax than do owners of single-family homes of comparable market value.[33] Similarly, those who rent individually owned units in a free market have an advantage over owners who operate stabilized or controlled rental buildings. This advantage is accentuated by the possibilities of condominium values rising while property values are held down by rent regulation in the conventional structures.

The assessment discrepancy derives from a 1964 State law requiring that condominium buildings be assessed as though they were a rental apartment house. Though each apartment is a separate tax lot, the sales price of individual units cannot be used as a measure of market value of the building or as a basis of reassessment. While there have been efforts to rectify the situation, they have been discouraged by the protests of owners. Due to this State law, the City is losing a significant amount of potential tax revenue. Even $1000 in tax per unit, assuming that the filings of 1981–84 period were to be successful, suggests an additional annual flow in excess of a $100 million to the City. The precise division of this additional tax between the owners of structures that are converted and their eventual occupants cannot be determined. However, to the extent individual owners are affected, current income tax laws oblige the federal government to indirectly subsidize approximately 40 percent of the potential new City tax revenue.

The growing use of conversions in the city represents an adaptation of New York's high density housing stock to the ownership incentives built into high marginal rates of taxation and long-term inflation. Without ownership opportunities, higher-income residents would be driven from the city in order to accomplish their objectives. The large difference between housing values in rented and owned apartments indicates the appeal of the latter. Another measure of the value of ownership is the large profits typically made by tenants in residence at the time of conversion who promptly sell their newly acquired property. Similarly, landlord buyouts of tenants during conversions are at levels not even dreamed of by the advocates of displacement allowances for the victims of governmentally inspired renewal efforts.

Is this a process which should be encouraged to continue in its own market-driven fashion with relatively low levels of participation by tenants required for noneviction conversion plans? The rise of a stable, upscale homeowner group within the city is a primary goal of most other American municipalities. In New York, however, judging from the variety of bills proposed to impede this process, it is a feared outcome. These proposals epitomize the near paranoia characterizing housing development in New York City.

CONCLUSION

The conflicts between the old and the new, the rich and the poor, those inside the system and those outside of it, are among the few constants of New York City history. Their resolution, although often inefficient and costly, has been successful enough to yield the extraordinary artifact which is New York. New York City has gone through and largely surmounted the changes from an industrial to a postindustrial city. What is different in the current era, however, is the renewed challenge of alternative locations for economic activity.

In order to maintain and enhance its economic base, the City requires a more aggressive and more productive housing policy. New York historically supported unique housing ventures. There has been substantial experience gained even in the ten years of near housing blight that followed the fiscal crisis. The shelter mechanisms do not have to be invented; the market is presently waiting for more housing, but it will not wait forever. The missing ingredient is political will and local financial commitment in the wake of federal retreat from housing subsidy.

It is politically difficult in a city with many poor people to endorse housing for the more fortunate. In this context, there is not merely effective opposition to direct displacement (i.e., construction on sites presently occupied by low-income individuals); increasingly, criticism and effective opposition are based on the concept of secondary displacement. The new fear limiting construction is that while a project may not directly displace the poor, its completion may enhance real estate values nearby and make these buildings too costly for the current neighborhood residents. In 1983–84, for example, Lincoln-West, a project that would have generated 4000 housing units over the railroad yards on Manhattan's West Side, was stopped as the political consequence of the fear of secondary displacement.

If housing is to be produced to complement the city's economic base, that housing must secure broader political backing than is presently the case. Substantial forces stand in the way of this. The insiders, both owners and residents in the city, are doing well as a function of the rarity of new development. The undervalued and underassessed rent-controlled, rent-stabilized stock subsidizes tenants and owners. The subletting phenomenon is an open scandal, with housing aspirants being exploited in a fashion that drives many away. It is difficult to conceive of a more successful mechanism to minimize housing production—and perhaps maximize the present values of some of those who already have a piece of the action—than the New York City housing system. However, the system may become self-defeating. A city reduced only to the few who can afford to partake of expensive housing will, in turn, find its economic functions similarly circumscribed. The ultimate losers will be not only the real estate stakeholders, but the more modest job aspirants in the city as well.

NOTES

1. U.S. Department of Commerce, Bureau of the Census, *Characteristics of the Population, 1980—Number of Inhabitants: New York* (Washington, D.C.: United States Government Printing Office, February 1982).

2. U.S. Department of Commerce, Bureau of the Census, *Characteristics of the Population, 1980: New York* (Washington, D.C.: United States Government Printing Office, August 1982).

3. Samuel M. Ehrenhalt, "Challenges of the Changing Economy of New York City," 1984. Paper presented at the 17th Annual Institute sponsored by the New York City Council on Economic Education, New York City, 1984, p. 4.

4. U.S. Department of Commerce, Bureau of the Census, *Construction Reports* (Washington, D.C.: United States Government Printing Office, Series C20).

5. Michael A. Stegman, *The Dynamics of Rental Housing in New York City* (New Brunswick, N.J.: Center for Urban Policy Research, 1982).

6. City of New York, *New Dwelling Units Completed 1972* (New York City: Department of City Planning, 1972), p. 5.

7. U.S. Department of Commerce, Bureau of the Census, *Historical Statistics of the United States, Colonial Times to 1970, Part II* (Washington, D.C.: United States Government Printing Office, 1975).

8. U.S. Department of Commerce, Bureau of the Census, *Housing Units Authorized by Building Permits and Public Contracts* (Washington, D.C.: United States Government Printing Office, November 1984). This is the source for national figures in this paragraph.

9. Bureau of the Census, *Current Housing Reports, Characteristics of Apartments Completed in 1983* (Washington, D.C.: United States Government Printing Office, 1984).

10. The historical material in this section is derived from the Citizen's Housing and Planning Council, *Housing in New York City—A Chronology* (New York: The Council, 1965).

11. *The New York Times,* June 25, 1984.

12. See City of New York, *Housing Database—Public and Publicly Aided Housing* (New York City Department of City Planning, August 1983), pp. 4–5.

13. Ibid., pp. 42–43.

14. City of New York, *Adopted Budget Fiscal Year 1985—Expense Revenue, Capital,* 1984. It should be noted that the $418 million does not include the New York City Housing Authority or other housing-related agencies such as the Buildings Department, City Planning Department and Landmarks Preservation Commission.

15. Carol Lamberg, "Public Tools to Enhance Affordability," in New York City Housing Partnership, Inc., *New Homes for New York Neighborhoods* (New York: Housing Partnership, October 15, 1984), p. 150.

16. U.S. Department of Commerce, Bureau of the Census, *Projections of U.S. Household Formation 1980–85* (Washington, D.C.: United States Government Printing Office, August 1979); U.S. Department of Commerce, Bureau of the Census, *Patterns of Household Formation in the United States for 1980–83* (Washington, D.C.: United States Government Printing Office, March 1984).

17. U.S. Department of Commerce, Bureau of the Census, *Statistical Abstract of the United States, 1984* (Washington, D.C.: United States Government Printing Office, 1982).

18. U.S. Department of Commerce, Bureau of the Census, *Characteristics of the Population: General Population Characteristics, New York, 1980* (Washington, D.C.: United States Government Printing Office, 1982).

19. U.S. Department of Commerce, Bureau of the Census, *Census of Population, U.S. National Summary 1980* (Washington, D.C.: United States Government Printing Office, 1982).

20. New York State Division of Housing and Community Renewal, *An Analysis of the Housing Needs of New York State* (New York: Division of Housing and Community Research, April 1984).

21. Ibid., pp. 4–20.

22. New York State Department of Commerce, *Preliminary Official Population Projections,* March 4, 1983.

23. U.S. Department of Commerce, Bureau of the Census, *Estimates of the Population of New York Counties and Metropolitan Areas, July 1, 1981 and 1982* (Washington, D.C.: United States Government Printing Office, 1984).

24. New York City Housing Authority, *Tenant Data as of January 1, 1984.*

25. City of New York, Human Resources Administration, *New York City Social Report,* First Quarter, 1983 (April 1984).

26. *Federal Register,* Vol. 49, No. 27 (February 8, 1984), p. 4894.

27. "Why They Have No Homes," *Progressive,* Vol. 49, No. 3 (March 1985), p. 26.

28. City of New York, Human Resources Administration, *New York City Social Report,* Fourth Quarter, 1984 (1985).

29. Michael A. Stegman, *Housing in New York: Study of a City, 1984* (New York: New York City Department of Housing Preservation and Development, February 1985).

30. U.S. Department of Commerce, Bureau of the Census, *Detailed Housing Characteristics: New York, 1980* (Washington, D.C.: United States Government Printing Office, December 1983).

31. See George Sternlieb, et al., *Tax Subsidies and Housing Investment* (New Brunswick, N.J.: Center for Urban Policy Research, 1976); Kristina Ford, *Housing Policy and the Urban Middle Class* (New York: Citizens' Housing and Planning Council, 1978).

32. U.S. Department of Housing and Urban Development, *The Conversion of Rental Housing Condominiums and Cooperatives* (Washington, D.C.: United States Government Printing Office, 1980).

33. Alan S. Oser, "Residential Tax Inequities Growing," *The New York Times,* November 4, 1984, Sec. 8, p. 1.

13

Sanitation

JOHN A. KAISER

Ten years ago, few, if any, New Yorkers would have predicted that their Sanitation Department would provide important examples of ways to improve the productivity and quality of municipal services. However, changes in the way the Department collects refuse serve as a model for enhancing other labor-intensive public services. Yet, despite this record of accomplishment, the Department faces serious problems whose resolution will require the concerted efforts of the next administration. The efficiency and effectiveness of street cleaning should be improved. Even more important is the need for elected officials of the City of New York to adopt and implement a comprehensive plan for waste disposal. If this is not done in a timely fashion, New York City residents will incur serious financial and environmental costs.

This chapter begins with a brief description of the Sanitation Department that provides information essential to analysis of its major functions. The next three sections examine each of the agencies' major functions: refuse collection, street cleaning, and waste disposal. In each case, recent trends are described and an agenda for further improvement is identified.

OVERVIEW OF THE DEPARTMENT

The Sanitation Department is responsible for residential and institutional refuse collection, street cleaning, snow removal, waste disposal, and ancillary cleaning services such as lot cleaning. To provide these services, the Department was allocated over $396 million in fiscal year 1985. It employed approximately 8000 uniformed sanitationmen and 3600 civilians (see Table 13.1).

The Department is organized into functional bureaus. The Bureau of Cleaning and Collections (BCC), with a complement of approximately 6950 uniformed and 500 civilian personnel, is responsible for collecting abut 14,000 tons of refuse daily and cleaning 6000 miles of streets. The Bureau also is responsible for snow removal and salting streets during winter storms. It is organized into 11 regions that are subdivided into districts coincident with the City's 59 Community Districts. All collection and most cleaning services are decentralized, with a distinct work force and set of equipment operating out of a district garage under the direction of a District Superintendent.

The Bureau of Waste Disposal disposes of over 7,000,000 tons of refuse each year. The Bureau has approximately 1000 employees who are assigned to four landfills, three municipal incinerators, and nine marine transfer stations. Closely associated with this Bureau is the Office of Resource Recovery and Waste Disposal Planning. This group is charged with developing energy-producing, resource recovery plants to replace the city's diminishing landfill capacity.

The Sanitation Department's equipment, including refuse collection trucks, mechanical brooms used to clean streets, and landfill vehicles used in waste disposal, is maintained by the Bureau of Motor Equipment. The Bureau's 1160 civilian mechanics and other personnel are assigned to the 59 district garages, five borough shops, and a large central repair shop.

The largest of several smaller, specialized units are the Bureau of Building Maintenance and the Office of Community Services. The latter coordinates special services such as cleanup campaigns, lot cleaning, and festivals with neighborhood groups.

Throughout the past ten years the Bureau of Cleaning and Collections has accounted for most of the Department's personnel. The Bureau employed over two-thirds of the workers in 1985. However, its share of manpower has declined from over 77 percent in 1974,

TABLE 13.1

Allocation of Resources in the Sanitation Department, Fiscal Years 1974–85

	1974	1975	1976	1977	1978	1979	1980	1981	1982	1983	1984	1985
Operating Expenditures (000)	$241,600	$268,000	$239,900	$243,600	$301,347	$282,557	$298,792	$310,566	$336,332	$386,435	$411,308	$396,388
Constant (1974) Dollars	241,600	245,646	207,886	198,210	227,776	191,954	178,810	168,511	171,861	191,304	195,303	180,505
Capital Expenditures (000)	33,400	61,700	52,870	37,628	43,995	40,400	54,675	43,051	94,460	123,260	132,975	167,795
Constant (1974) Dollars	33,400	56,554	45,815	30,617	33,254	27,446	32,720	23,359	48,268	61,268	63,141	76,409
Total Employees	15,029	14,384	12,722	12,153	12,030	11,811	10,928	11,684	11,811	11,598	11,198	11,600
Uniformed	12,231	11,824	10,130	9,772	9,472	8,808	8,235	8,397	8,386	8,171	7,633	8,018
Civilian	2,798	2,560	2,592	2,381	2,558	3,003	2,693	3,287	3,425	3,427	3,565	3,582
Cleaning and Collection	11,609	11,317	9,516	8,953	8,822	8,856	8,149	8,270	8,193	7,982	7,443	7,854
Uniformed	11,251	11,012	9,238	8,772	8,497	8,224	7,760	7,747	7,707	7,520	6,954	7,365
Civilian	358	305	278	181	325	632	389	523	486	462	489	489
Waste Disposal	1,438	1,346	1,249	1,118	1,087	1,014	819	989	993	968	1,028	1,028
Uniformed	680	652	563	502	476	368	273	323	359	340	371	371
Civilian	758	694	686	616	602	646	546	666	634	628	657	657
Vehicle Maintenance	Combined with Support and Other Missions		966	966	1,013	1,073	1,110	1,238	1,180	1,147	1,152	1,162
Uniformed			37	37	36	4	2	6	5	4	5	3
Civilian			929	929	977	1,069	1,108	1,232	1,175	1,143	1,147	1,159
Enforcement, Derelict Vehicles	Combined with Support and Other Missions		130	179	195	152	156	164	289	303	372	372
Uniformed			125	173	188	144	145	143	91	88	91	91
Civilian			5	6	7	8	11	21	198	215	281	281
Support and Other Missions	1,982	1,721	861	937	822	716	694	1,023	1,156	1,198	1,203	1,184
Uniformed	300	160	N.A.	288	175	68	53	178	224	219	212	188
Civilian	1,682	1,561	N.A.	649	647	648	639	845	932	979	991	996

SOURCES: Unpublished data from Department of Sanitation for fiscal years 1974 and 1975; City of New York, *Mayor's Management Reports* for fiscal years 1976 through 1985. All data are actual except fiscal year 1985, which are as budgeted. Constant dollar calculations are based on the Consumer Price Index for urban areas with an estimated rate of inflation in fiscal year 1985 of 4.3 percent. Budget figures exclude pensions, fringe benefits, and debt service.

NOTE: N.A. means not available.

reflecting both a reduction in cleaning services and productivity gains in refuse collection. Operational changes in the collection service during this period are probably the most extensive of any municipal service during the past six years, and its record of successes and failures is particularly instructive.

REFUSE COLLECTION

The history of refuse collection is one of a steep decline in service quality due to severe budget cuts in 1975 followed by service improvements due to progressively more successful productivity improvements. Even greater gains are possible in the future, provided the pursuit of innovation does not lag with improvements in City finances.

SERVICE DECLINE

In fiscal year 1974, the BCC was assigned 11,609 employees including 11,251 uniformed workers. This was the largest number of employees in recent history because the fiscal crisis forced significant resource reductions. Between fiscal years 1974 and 1981 the Department's constant dollar budget fell by nearly one-third. Manpower losses were nearly as severe. Total agency employment fell over 27 percent from the 1974 high of 15,029 to a 1980 low of 10,928. Manpower assigned to cleaning and collection services declined even more precipitously. The BCC's staff dropped about 30 percent from the 1974 high of 11,609 to a 1980 low of 8149.

The Department's leadership responded to resource reductions by reducing the frequency of scheduled refuse collections. In 1974 the Department collected refuse an average of 3.6 times per week. Fully 39 percent of the city's residential and institutional buildings received six weekly collections. By 1976 the citywide average collection frequency fell to 2.5 times per week, and in that year 90 percent of the buildings received only two or three weekly collections.[1] The 27 percent cut in average frequency of collection was nearly proportional to the cut in BCC manpower.

However, the strategy of responding to resource cuts with less-frequent collections backfired in several ways. New Yorkers did not significantly reduce the amount of refuse they generated, so nearly the same volume had to be collected in fewer trips. But the Sanitationmen retained their unwritten quota of the amount of refuse they would collect in a work day, that is, two truck loads. So, the only source of savings was reduced travel time, and the result was a large volume of refuse left uncollected at the end of the scheduled workday. In 1975 only 0.4 percent of the refuse scheduled for collection was left uncollected at the end of an average day; by 1978 the backlog had reached 8.4 percent of all scheduled collections (see Table 13.2).

The deterioration in refuse collection service was intensified by other decisions related to the fiscal crisis. The Department's vehicle-maintenance and other support personnel were cut 13 percent in 1975. The shortage of capital funds led to a failure to replace vehicles. The average age of collection trucks rose from 4.2 years in 1974 to 6.4 years in 1979, and the percentage of trucks out of service at any given time rose from 12 percent to 43 percent. With more vehicles down, available vehicles were double shifted; this caused night-time collections to rise from 4.6 percent of the total in 1974 to 28.8 percent in 1979. As more trucks were double shifted, the maintenance force grew increasingly incapable of repairing the wear and tear caused by overworking the equipment. Overtime costs also rose as the need for night-time collections, special backlog runs, and delays due to vehicle breakdowns made rational scheduling impossible.

In addition, morale among the uniformed employees fell. They bore the brunt of criticism for poor service, and their personal lives became chaotic as days off, weekends, and nights were increasingly sacrificed to pick up the backlog of refuse. The increased time at work was made more unpleasant because budget cuts eliminated even minimal maintenance and repair of garages, vehicle repair facilities, and the workers' locker rooms. Refuse collection became a nightmare for workers as well as managers.

MANAGERIAL RESPONSE

The traditional municipal response to "crises" analogous to the deterioration in refuse collection services evident in the late 1970s had been simply to channel funds towards the problem in sufficient quantity to relieve pent-up pressures and restore service to a politically acceptable level. The fiscal crisis prevented this response.

TABLE 13.2
Refuse Collection Performance Indicators, Fiscal Years 1974–85

	1974	1975	1976	1977	1978	1979	1980	1981	1982	1983	1984	1985
Tons Collected (000)	3,500[a]	3,475[a]	3,458	3,426	3,471	3,470	3,325	3,183	3,217	3,320	3,420	3,431
PAR Index (Average)[b]	N.A.	N.A.	N.A.	N.A.	N.A.	N.A.	63.2	66.2	71.7	74.7	80.0	94.7
Percentage Collections at Night	4.6%	5.1%	14.2%	14.5%	20.9%	28.8%	14.1%	8.7%	8.8%	9.8%	13.5%	9.5%
Percentage of Daily Loads Uncollected in Normal Weeks	0.9%	0.4%	4.4%	4.6%	8.4%	6.1%	3.0%	2.6%	1.3%	5.4%	3.0%	2.5%
Average Loads Uncollected End of Normal Weeks	N.A.	N.A.	N.A.	N.A.	83	26	5	0	0	25	0	0
End of Holiday Weeks	N.A.	N.A.	N.A.	58	25	192	107	54	5	39	1	0
Percentage of Required Trucks Out of Service	N.A.	N.A.	9.0%	10.0%	20.2%	22.6%	3.1%	0.0%	0.0%	0.2%	0.1%	0.0%
Percentage of Total Trucks Out of Service	12.5%	23.1%	32.1%	31.5%	43.6%	42.7%	22.8%	N.A.	N.A.	19.1%	19.6%	19.0%
Average Age of Trucks (Years)	4.2	4.9	5.2	6.0	5.5	6.4	4.5	3.5	3.0	4.0	4.0	N.A.

SOURCES: Department of Sanitation for fiscal years 1974 and 1975; City of New York, *Mayor's Management Reports* for fiscal years 1976 through 1985. Figures for 1985 are as planned; all other years are actual performance.

NOTES: N.A. means not available.

  a. Approximate figures, since weighing scales at disposal points were inoperable for portions of the year.

  b. PAR Index was substantially revised after fiscal year 1979, making comparisons with prior years invalid.

Instead, a turnaround had to be generated internally by the Department. The decline in services eventually was reversed through a targeted expansion of resources for equipment and maintenance and, more importantly, by improving collection productivity.

New Resources for Equipment and Maintenance. Despite the small size of City capital budgets in the years after 1975, the deterioration in sanitation services was severe enough to generate a policy decision in 1977 to replace the collection fleet within five years and thereafter to maintain a seven-year replacement cycle. This would result in a stable average fleet age of between 3.5 and 4.0 years. The first vehicles ordered were 200 standard 20-cubic yard, rear-loading trucks whose design essentially had been unchanged for over two decades. Their arrival, beginning in January 1979, was an important first step in the improvement of refuse collection.

The second initiative was the development of a more systematic maintenance program. This primarily involved an intradepartmental reorganization, but also required expanded staffing.

The most significant administrative step was the separation of the Bureau of Motor Equipment (BME) from the BCC in 1979. Prior to that, the Deputy Commissioner in charge of BME reported directly to the Department's First Deputy Commissioner, who was also director of the BCC. During the extended periods of equipment shortages and collection backlogs, this administrative arrangement contributed to the deterioration of the collection fleet. The Director of BME could not hold back equipment for necessary maintenance because he was under pressure from the First Deputy Commissioner to keep vehicles on the street regardless of the consequences for the equipment's longevity. The reorganization in 1979 meant that the BME Director, now reporting directly to the Commissioner, was able to institute a firmer maintenance policy. As the new trucks began arriving in 1979, a preventive maintenance program was enforced strictly.

In addition, a single, senior manager was made responsible for daily repair and maintenance of collection and cleaning equipment in the district garages. Priorities for major repairs were established, outside contracts were let to reduce the accumulated maintenance backlog, and finally, a labor/management committee was established to channel employee experience and insight into the administration of the Bureau.

The maintenance reforms went beyond administrative changes. Fifty new mechanics were hired in 1978 and another sixty in 1979. These positions were funded in part by savings resulting from the civilianization of 32 of the 36 uniformed positions in BME and in part by a reduction in overtime.

The results of these measures were evident in increased vehicle availability. The percentage of required vehicles available for service rose from an average of 77 percent in 1978 to 100 percent in 1980. Night collections declined from 29 percent to less than 9 percent of the total. While the new equipment contributed to these gains, improved maintenance also permitted older trucks to perform well. During 1980, for example, the average downtime rate for new trucks was 16.4 percent, while that for old trucks was 18.1 percent.[2] The increased care given to the older equipment was worth the effort.

The Department estimated that the maintenance policy reforms resulted in annual savings during 1979 and 1980 of $4.5 million in reduced BME overtime, $7.1 million in reduced spare part purchases due to better inventory management, $4.6 million in reduced differential pay for night collections, and $2.8 million from converting vehicles to diesel fuels. The net savings to the City, after deducting $2.5 million for additional civilian clerks and mechanics, was $16.5 million.[3]

Increased Productivity. Perhaps the best-known element of the strategy to improve collection services was a series of productivity measures culminating in two-man crews as the standard in most of the city. However, the so-called "gainsharing" reform was only one of several productivity initiatives. These efforts were designed largely by a combined civilian and uniformed analytical unit, the Office of Program Evaluation and Control. It integrated the talent and experience of uniformed officers with those of more academically oriented civilian managers and statistical specialists. Moreover, the Office reported to the Department's senior career officer rather than the Commissioner or another civilian manager. Its success reflects the increasing capacity of diverse groups within the Department to work together.

Efforts to improve collection productivity began in 1978 with the Route Extension Program. This initial attempt represented a "crack-the-whip" approach. A team of 40 foremen was created to implement the program. They selected one district, and for four to six weeks they pressured that district's work force to extend route lengths and thus achieve a 10 to 15 percent improvement in productivity. Foremen would ride on each collection truck to demonstrate efficiencies, monitor the number and length of work breaks, and attempt to generate a more productive work ethic.

This early effort was characterized by two serious flaws: It offered no incentive for sanitationmen to cooperate, and it defined the collection problem as being due essentially to worker apathy. Managerial failures, including inefficient route structures, inappropriate equipment, manpower imbalances, and delays in disposal activities, were not addressed by the Route Extension Program. Not surprisingly, shortly after the team of foremen moved to the next district, old work practices of sanitationmen reemerged; the short-term productivity gains of from 10 to 15 percent dwindled to permanent improvements of less than 5 percent.

As the Route Extension Program entered its second year, the Department made a new attempt to improve collection productivity. Revisions to the New York City Charter adopted in 1975 required several major departments, including Sanitation, to reorganize their functional units along common boundaries. Spurred by these coterminality requirements, the Department contracted with a consultant to redesign its collection routes. The effort yielded an extensive package of planning documents, route books, and officers' manuals for each district. The program was implemented with the assistance of a team of foremen from the Route Extension Program. Moreover, sanitation officers were drawn into the route restructuring process. They were trained not only to use, but to modify, the route system as needs changed in their sections and districts. This experience proved to be useful preparation for later, more ambitious programs.

In terms of productivity, the initial route restructuring effort was successful only in the sense that it avoided declines that otherwise might have accompanied coterminality. For many years prior to the fiscal crisis, the City's three-man crews had collected slightly less than ten tons per crew daily. After the route restructuring, the averages rose slightly to almost 11 tons per crew or about 3.6 tons per man day.[4] However, the Sanitation Department's performance was still well below that of other cities. Surveys showed that most large municipal refuse collection operations averaged over four tons per man day. For example, Los Angeles averaged 6.9, Baltimore and Dallas averaged 5.0, Cleveland averaged 4.6, and Philadelphia averaged 3.9 tons per man day.[5] Private collection firms reported even higher results.

Departmental leaders recognized that significant further improvements in productivity would require fundamental changes in the way refuse was collected in New York City. One opportunity for such reform was to use larger (higher capacity) collection trucks. The larger trucks would improve productivity by either reducing the number of trips a crew had to make to disposal points (an incinerator, marine transfer station or landfill) or by permitting the crew to carry more refuse to the disposal point in the same number of trips.

The potential impact of larger trucks derived from prevailing work patterns among sanitationmen. With few exceptions, crews followed an unwritten practice of collecting two loads per day, a morning load and an afternoon load, each followed by a disposal trip. In densely populated neighborhoods, where trucks can be filled quickly, sanitationmen slowed the pace of their work so that the second dump trip ended about 15 minutes before wash-up time. In these neighborhoods larger trucks would permit the collection of more refuse in the same time period and with the same number of disposal trips. In less populated neighborhoods, trucks were filled only partially by the time it was necessary to make the afternoon dump trip and return to the garage by wash-up time. In these neighborhoods, large trucks could eliminate one disposal trip and permit more garbage to be disposed of in a single daily trip.

The first step towards using larger trucks was taken in 1980. Instead of standard trucks of 20 cubic yards, new ones were acquired with a capacity of 25 cubic yards for use in Manhattan on an experimental basis. Their introduction increased tonnage per man day from 3.6 to 4.3.[6] Acquisition of the new trucks continued until approximately 300 were in the fleet by 1982. This is the maximum number of trucks of this design that can be used effectively in the city. Additional vehicles of this size, but with greater compaction power and thus load capacity, were ordered in 1984 for replacement purposes.

A second opportunity for fundamental reform was to reduce crew sizes. While it could be argued that three men are needed to load refuse along dense routes with many multifamily buildings, it seemed clear that one or two men are sufficient along routes serving mostly single-family homes. In these areas three-man crews were a highly inefficient use of scarce manpower.

Recognizing this, Departmental leaders proposed to use high-capacity, side-loading, two-man trucks in less densely populated areas. Design factors such as dual drive controls, low entry cabs, and loading hoppers located directly behind the cab could make it possible for drivers to load also. Moreover, the higher capacity of these trucks would eliminate the need for a second dump trip. The time saved through the elimination of a second dump trip, as well as the work-saving design features, would allow a two-man side loader to provide the same amount of collection service as a three-man rear loader. The result, in theory, would be a one-third reduction in direct personnel costs.

To implement this plan, the City ordered side loading trucks in February of 1980. The new vehicles were scheduled to arrive in the fall of 1980. To pave the way for this innovation, the Department proposed that sanitationmen working on side-loading vehicles in two-man crews receive a share of the savings generated by the program. A productivity savings fund would be established for each of the 59 districts. While a large share of the fund would be paid to the men working the trucks, all members of the district team, including clerks, would receive some payment in recognition of the contribution of support staff to the work done on the street.

The sanitationmen's union initially opposed the proposed arrangement. Faced with continued intransigence on the part of the union, the City solicited proposals in March from private carters for refuse collection in up to three districts on an experimental basis. Faced with this threat, the sanitationmen's union agreed to negotiations in July, 1980.

In the ensuing discussions, union officials made it clear that the City's proposal of differentiated bonuses would cause them problems because the majority of the members collected refuse and were not anxious to share their productivity bonus with those not "on the street." As a result, the proposal was modified so that only those sanitationmen who manned the new collection trucks would benefit. With this issue resolved, negotiations turned to the issue of what share of the productivity savings would be paid to sanitation men and what share would be reserved for the City. Unable to resolve this issue, both sides agreed to submit the issue to arbitration. An arbitrator's decision in December, 1980 resolved this issue and provided the basis for the initial use of the new trucks.

Under terms of the arbitration decision, each crew member on a two-man truck would receive a nonpensionable payment of $11 for each such shift worked as long as the the one-for-one replacement for rear loaders was maintained. After two years, the payments would become pensionable. The City agreed to postpone for at least two years its proposal to experiment with private residential refuse collection. A three-man panel was established to settle disagreements during the implementation of the decision. One of its first tasks was to assist in the equitable definition and monitoring of the one-for-one replacement aspect of the decision. A set of weekly targets based on historic performance records for each district was developed as a basis of comparison for the two-man truck crews.

Following this agreement, 250 side-loading trucks were put in service in seven districts between January and June of 1981. These vehicles served about 20 percent of all collection routes in the city. The "gain-sharing" arrangement yielded the City a net saving of 24 percent in collection personnel costs in the districts affected.[7] A second group of 247 side loaders began arriving in February 1982 and was deployed in six more districts. This raised to 40 percent the share of collection routes served by two-man crews. Savings to the City reached an annual rate of $7.7 million in the fall of 1982.[8]

The relatively smooth transition to two-man crews in 13 of the City's sanitation districts was aided by the establishment of labor-management committees in each of the district garages. Consistent with the earlier experience in the BME maintenance shops, these committees often were the source of valuable insight and goodwill. They helped restructure routes, facilitated the transfer of men freed by the reduction in crew size, planned the most efficient departure points for dump trips, and suggested numerous adjustments for improved truck performance that eventually were incorporated into design specifications for the second order of side loaders.

As experience with the new equipment and bonus payments became more widespread, workers in the 46 districts not affected by the agreement began to urge their union representatives to explore the extension of the gainsharing plan throughout the city. An agreement was ratified by the union in May 1983 under which two-man crews would become the standard in all districts regardless of the collection equipment in use. The shift differential would be $12.50 for those working on trucks with a capacity of 20 cubic yards, and the payment for members of two-man crews working on those with a capacity of 25 cubic yards was increased to $15 per shift. The one-for-one replacement criteria was retained, and work began immediately to develop targets for the newly affected districts. Complete conversion to two-man crews was projected to save the City $37 million after bonus payments and expenses.[9]

Implementation of the new agreement was to begin as soon as the production target and personnel transfer planning could be completed and to continue at the rate of four districts per month until all districts were transformed by July, 1984. This schedule was not met. By January of 1984 only 19 of the 46 districts had been switched to two-man trucks, and two that did were returned to three-man crews because of consistent failure to meet the production targets. The Department attributed these problems to the use of existing equipment not specifically designed for two-man crews, poor field supervision in some areas, and occasional local resistance to the one-for-one replacement requirement. By January 1985, these problems were overcome, and 58 of the 59 districts were converted to two-man crews.

The Department measures its progress in collection productivity with the Productivity Analysis Reporting (PAR) index. The PAR index was developed in 1978 to measure collection productivity in 225 separate sections of the City. Local factors, such as density, garage location, and dumping requirements, were considered in order to create targets for each section that indicate comparable success regardless of location. While there have been month-to-month fluctuations, the PAR index has improved steadily. As shown in Table 13.2, the average score rose from 63.2 in 1980 to 80.0 in 1984. A score of 94.7 is forecast for 1985. With 25 cubic yard trucks operating in 11 districts and two-man crews becoming standard throughout the city, the Department feels that the maximum score of 100 is within reach. When this is achieved, it will be time for the standards built into the PAR index to be revised.

FUTURE DIRECTIONS

Since the time of poor performance in the late 1970s, the Sanitation Department has made substantial progress in improving its collection service. However, there is still room for improvement. At least six specific reforms can be identified: containerization, relay dumping, schedule revisions, new equipment, expanded gainsharing, and civilianization.

Containerization. Containerization is a method of refuse collection which uses three types of specially designed trucks to empty or remove refuse containers of up to 30 cubic yards mechanically. The containers are used to remove 11 percent of the city's refuse.[10] The vehicles serving containers are operated by either one or two men and are far more efficient than even a two-man crew working a 25-cubic yard truck. A reasonable estimate is that each additional bulk container truck of the largest type could replace three conventional trucks. In other words, containerization can roughly triple collection productivity.

In light of its great potential, expanded containerization should be a high priority for the department. A suitable goal is to increase the share of refuse collected in this manner from 11 to 20 percent. This can be accomplished by encouraging the use of containers, and aiding departmental clients with large facilities to find suitable storage locations. The containers could best be used for buildings operated by the Housing Authority, the Board of Education, other institutions, and large apartment buildings.

Relay Dumping. Relay dumping is a technique for improving productivity by reducing the man-hours required for disposal time. With this process, the driver of an empty truck meets a collection crew with a full truck at a predetermined time and place along its route, exchanges trucks with the crew, and drives the full truck to a disposal point while the collection crew continues along its route. Savings result because only one person, rather than the entire collection crew, spends time on the disposal trip. Obviously, potential savings are greatest in areas farthest from disposal points.

This approach has not been followed in the past primarily because of a lack of available equipment. However, the recent revitalization of the collection fleet has made available enough equipment to begin experiments with relay dumping. These demonstrations should be implemented in districts in which routes involve long disposal trips. If each crew in these districts spends approximately four man-hours per day on disposal trips, this time could be halved using relays. Every three crews using relays would save the equivalent of a full man day or approximately $32,000 annually.

Rescheduling. Sanitationmen work according to a schedule intended to match available manpower in each district to a workload which varies throughout the week depending on collection cycles. To achieve this match as well as to provide each worker with a contractually guaranteed number of two- and three-day weekends, days off are assigned in a staggered fashion that was last revised in the early 1970s.

However, collection frequencies throughout the city have changed since then, and so has the distribution of collection demand because of shifts in population. These changes have resulted in a mismatch between the supply of manpower and service requirements on different days of the week. In general, the Department needs more men to work early in the week and fewer at the end of the week. The Department, with union participation, should revise the work schedules. The cost would be minimal, and it could save up to $2 million annually.

New Equipment. The Department should continue to work with manufacturers to develop labor-saving vehicles optimally matched to the conditions of New York City. Specifically, the City needs a high-capacity (25-cubic yard and above), rear-loading collection vehicle with a small turning radius for use on narrow and congested streets. Another high priority for equipment development is improved vehicles to facilitate expansion of containerization.

Gainsharing Extension. Financial incentives should be extended to officers, clerks, and mechanics who make documented contributions to improve productivity. Field officers are uniquely positioned to initiate innovative scheduling and other operational techniques that would reduce manpower requirements. Savings from such efforts should be shared with those who are instrumental in designing them. Similarly, productivity savings achieved by means of improved planning and operations throughout each district should be shared by the officers and clerks in the district who develop them. In the maintenance area, garage and maintenance workers who achieve measurable savings also should benefit from a gainsharing policy directed at rewarding, and thus stimulating, their efforts.

Civilianization. Since 1977, the Department has replaced 745 uniformed personnel with lower-paid civilians for an annual savings of more than $7.5 million. Civilianized positions included headquarters clerks and some field clerks, mechanics, technical workers in the Bureau of Waste Disposal, and most of the Sanitation Police force. The City Comptroller has recommended that the civilianization program be extended to the remaining 143 district and borough clerks and to 279 special duty Sanitationmen in district garages.[11]

The Department's response is that civilianization has reached the point of diminishing returns. A scheduled civilianization of 98 positions during 1982 was cancelled after internal analysis indicated that it was not likely to yield net savings. The jobs were located in garages and were filled by Sanitationmen who served as "jacks-of-all-trades" to fill in as needed for both uniformed and other workers. To civilianize these positions would leave uncovered tasks that would have to be filled by additional uniformed workers.

The case against civilianizing the 143 clerical positions is less straightforward. The experience in placing civilians in these jobs has been mixed. When clerks perform staff responsibilities in borough and headquarters offices, civilianization has worked well. However, civilian clericals are less effective than uniformed sanitationmen when their duties involve them in field operations. Some advantage may remain for further civilianization of clerical personnel.

The civilianization issue highlights another problem within the Department, the need to develop better defined career paths for both Sanitationmen and civilians. With a view towards developing senior management, the Department should move personnel between key uniformed and civilian positions. This happens now only in an ad hoc manner. A well-defined and better publicized career system could improve the motivation of younger workers and add to their capacity to assume higher level responsibilities.

STREET CLEANING

The most visible and esthetically distasteful effect of the fiscal crisis was the deterioration of street cleanliness. The Department's street cleaning force was reduced from 2500 in 1975 to 800 in 1976 and remained at that level until 1982. (See Table 13.3.) During this period fewer than 500 men actually worked to clean the streets on any given day. Whereas 100,000 man-days were devoted to mechanical sweeping in 1974, the figure decreased to 55,000 in 1979. Manual sweeping plunged from 120,000 man-days to virtually zero during the same period.[12]

Street cleanliness is measured with a monitoring system called Scorecard. Each month, teams from the Mayor's Office of Operations inspect a sample of streets in each district. Before the service reductions of the mid-1970s, Scorecard levels were about 70 percent, meaning that more than seven of every ten streets were judged to be "acceptably clean." Qualifications for this rating are stringent, and a citywide average of 70 percent was considered a reasonable performance level. Average annual Scorecard ratings declined an average of five points per year from their high point early in 1976, to a low of 53 percent in 1980.

Street cleanliness ratings have been making a slow comeback since 1980, rising to nearly 65 percent in 1984 and projected to exceed that figure in 1985. This improvement is attributed to increased staffing, new and better maintained equipment, and stronger enforcement of sanitary codes.

MANPOWER INCREASES

The congestion endemic to Manhattan, many areas of Brooklyn, and parts of the other boroughs necessitates a large manual cleaning force and other special-purpose cleaning teams in addition to standard mechanical brooms. Even where mechanical brooms are used, a few illegally parked cars may cut their effectiveness in half because of the wide, semicircular detours required to steer around these obstacles. It was not surprising, therefore, that cleanliness ratings plummeted when virtually all nonmechanical cleaning was eliminated in 1976. The 800 men assigned to mechanical brooms were not cut during the fiscal crisis, although maintenance problems reduced the number of brooms actually in use on any given day.

The steady decline in street cleanliness caused largely by the near elimination of manual cleaners caused the Department to seek increases in these positions. This request was granted in 1981, when 456 manual cleaners were added to the existing complement

TABLE 13.3

Street Cleaning Performance Indicators, Fiscal Years 1975–85

	1975	1976	1977	1978	1979	1980	1981	1982	1983	1984	1985
Uniformed Cleaners[a]	2,500	800	800	800	800	800	800	1,256	1,200	1,350	1,750
Percentage of Streets Rated Acceptably Clean	71.3%	72.0%	68.1%	63.1%	55.7%	53.0%	57.5%	62.0%	62.9%	64.9%	65.3%
Total Broom Routes	N.A.	N.A.	61,474[b]	55,263[b]	52,858	68,063	66,946	73,312	73,661	76,607	79,293
Percentage Completed	N.A.	81.0%	69.0%	53.7%	71.0%[c]	81.0%[c]	93.5%[c]	90.4%	93.0%	93.0%	93.0%
Percentage of Required Sweepers Out of Service[d]	N.A.	13.0%	17.0%	29.2%	25.4%	1.8%	0.0%	0.9%	0.4%	0.0%	0.0%
Average Age of Sweepers (Years)	N.A.	N.A.	6.1	6.8	7.5	5.8	6.5	5.1	4.4	5.0	N.A.

SOURCES: See Table 13.2.

NOTES: N.A. means not available.

a. Approximate yearly averages. The authorized strength of the Clean Team has fluctuated within a broad range. See text.

b. Approximate number based on curb miles assigned, the reporting unit in use prior to fiscal year 1979.

c. Refers to completed alternate side parking routes only.

d. Required Sweepers is the number of sweepers needed to complete all peak day assigned routes.

of 800 men assigned to mechanical brooms. However, 456 men do not go far in cleaning New York City's streets. Since roughly one-third of all sanitationmen do not work on a given day due to vacations, sickness, and other time off, an increase of 456 manual cleaners yielded an average of only five manual sweepers in each of the 59 districts. Since the demand for street cleaning varies from district to district, with high-congestion, commercial districts leading the way, the Department confronted difficult resource allocation decisions.

In making these decisions, the Department faced the danger of becoming a political prisoner of the Scorecard system. Under this system, the percentage of streets rated "acceptably clean" is the measure most widely used to evaluate cleaning performance. But the many grades of filth and cleanliness on either side of the magic dividing line known as "acceptably clean" are blurred by the reporting system. This means, in practical terms, that large numbers of manual sweepers could be assigned to the busiest areas of Lower Manhattan and significantly increase street cleanliness. However, so much littering occurs in these areas that relatively few streets might be consistently rated "acceptably clean." The small improvement in the percentage of streets so rated would reflect neither the effort expended nor the objective improvements. In other words, the Department could assign manpower where it was most needed but receive little credit under the Scorecard evaluation system.

However, allocating available cleaners to districts with low congestion in Staten Island, Eastern Queens, and the Northern Bronx, known as the "Golden Crescent," promised significantly higher Scorecard ratings. The dirtiest streets in these areas are close to being rated acceptably clean, which means that major improvements in district Scorecard ratings could be achieved with a lower allocation of manpower than in, for example, lower Manhattan. Since the computation of the citywide Scorecard average is based on district ratings weighted according to curb miles in the district, and since the districts in the "Golden Crescent" are the largest in the city, the effect of achieving improvements that are easier to realize in these areas would be magnified further in their effect on the citywide figure. To its credit, the Department resisted the temptation to deploy added cleaners to the "Golden Crescent." New cleaners were assigned to the dirtiest districts of the city, subject to the political necessity of increasing cleaning service at least to some extent in each of the boroughs.

Since its creation in July 1981, the "Clean Team," as manual cleaners have come to be known, has faced repeated uncertainty. The Clean Team was increased from 456 to 555 men in July 1982, but in November 1982 it was cut to 288 men due to delays in the expansion of the two-man truck program and projected fiscal constraints. The group was to be eliminated under the City's January 1983 gap-closing plan, but predicted dire effects on street cleanliness saved it. The Clean Team was returned to its original number of 456 in July 1983, increased to 550 in the spring of 1984, and was projected to grow to 950 in fiscal year 1985. The combined manual and mechanical broom cleaning force of 1750 was expected to raise the average Scorecard to above 69 percent in 1985. Some City officials believe a target of 2000 cleaners is desirable and that this would restore Scorecard ratings to the level of 72 percent where they stood before the fiscal crisis.

This is a worthwhile goal for the next administration. At least 72 percent of the streets in a great city should be "acceptably clean." The costs of realizing this goal are relatively modest. Past experience suggests approximately 75 manual cleaners are required to increase the average Scorecard one percentage point. Thus, an additional 225 cleaners could restore the city's street cleanliness to the earlier, more desirable level. The annual cost of these new workers is less than $10 million.

EQUIPMENT MAINTENANCE

In 1978, the mechanical broom fleet experienced the same problems of delayed maintenance and replacement afflicting the collections fleet. The equipment continued to age, and older brooms were cannibalized to keep more serviceable vehicles on the street for as many hours as possible. Eventually, many of these brooms succumbed to excessive wear and tear, until only 70 percent of the required brooms were available on a given day. In fact, the situation was worse than this figure indicates, because some brooms were unable to complete their routes due to breakdowns and others operated at less than full effectiveness due to defective brushes or other parts.

Beginning in 1980, the Department withheld sweepers for necessary repairs and preventive maintenance. The most serviceable vehicles were completely overhauled, and one-third of the fleet was replaced. The vehicle replacement program coupled with improved maintenance ended the problem of having insufficient brooms available. For example, the percentage of required sweepers out of service fell from 29 percent in 1978 to none in 1981. Similarly, the percentage of routes completed rose from 54 percent in 1978 to over 93 percent in 1981.

In addition to replacing and maintaining the conventional fleet of sweepers, the Department has experimented with new, labor-saving equipment. In the past, Motorized Litter Patrols (MLP) typically consisted of two men using a standard collection truck. The Department has acquired 200 smaller trucks that can be manned by a single worker and still service all but the most bulky debris. This step, plus revision of MLP routes to take advantage of alternate side parking and other relevant factors, resulted in a 10 percent increase in MLP productivity.[13] In light of this success, further purchases of the smaller, one-man trucks have been authorized.

The next major step to improve street cleanliness should be a citywide revision of street-cleaning schedules. Current schedules include cleaning of residential areas two or three times weekly, and this may be excessive for some neighborhoods. Selective reduction in the frequency with which each street is swept coupled with improved route structures might permit a 10 percent reduction in cleaning personnel without noticeable changes in street cleanliness.

The principal obstacle to revised street cleaning schedules is that it requires simultaneous changes in alternate side parking regulations. The Transportation Department is responsible for setting these rules and for posting them. Since the regulations are marked on permanent metal signs, the Department of Transportation has not been anxious to revise them. Perhaps more importantly, the Department would have to engage in negotiations with community groups over the modifications, a process which requires considerable time and effort. Nevertheless, revision of alternate side parking rules is critical to productivity gains in street cleaning, and a citywide review is overdue.

ENFORCEMENT

Enforcement of municipal laws relating to sanitation was not always perceived as closely related to street cleanliness. Historically, the uniformed Sanitation Police were concerned primarily with issuing summonses for alternate side parking violations. When that function was transferred to the Transportation Department in 1978, Sanitation enforcement concentrated on violations of the local Health and Administrative Codes. State legislation permitting officers to mail violation notices to building owners, and the transfer of most such cases from the Criminal Court to the Environmental Control Board greatly facilitated the issuance and processing of Sanitation summonses.

The number of sanitary violation notices rose steadily from 62,000 in 1978 to almost 400,000 in 1983, and is projected to exceed 560,000 in 1985. In 1981, revenue per ticket averaged $15, making the 120-man Sanitation Police force almost self-funding. Civilian Sanitation Enforcement Agents, 54 of them, were introduced in 1982 in an effort to reduce personnel costs, expand enforcement, and spur the uniformed officers towards improved productivity. By January 1983, their number had risen to 153, including civilianization of over 70 uniformed positions. By September 1983, some 206 civilian agents were issuing an average of 14.4 summonses per day, slightly short of the target of 15 per day.[14]

Assuming the expanded enforcement team reaches it productivity target, this still would not be a large enough effort for effective enforcement. A complement of 250 personnel issuing 15 summonses daily would reach 3750 violations. But a recent study revealed that approximately 51,000 violations occur daily.[15] While currently targeted levels of enforcement should reduce this illegal and antisocial behavior, significant reductions will require an even greater effort.

A useful complement to enforcement efforts are commercially supported education campaigns which use television, radio, and other media to promote public responsibility for the cleanliness of the city. Littering begets more littering. Publicity programs such as those sponsored by the group, We Care About New York, and by the New York City Partnership help overcome this pattern. A combination of marketing and regulation can ease the difficult problems the Department faces in deterring littering.

NEW OPTIONS

Most of the recent improvements in street cleanliness result from devoting more resources to the problem rather than developing new approaches that increase productivity. One explanation for the apparent difficulty in increasing the productivity of cleaners is that they feel like "second-class" citizens within the Department and the larger municipal bureaucracy. This perception arises in part from the frequency with which Clean Team staff levels are cut in response to citywide budgetary shortfalls. Perhaps equally important is the higher pay, through gainsharing, available to other departmental workers. As the policy of two-man crews and associated productivity bonuses spread throughout the department, assignment to the cleaning force has become relatively less desirable than collection duty.

A suitable cure for low morale among the sweepers is to design an incentive pay plan. A plan based on curb miles swept per day above historic averages seems feasible. Analysis and experimentation could determine reasonable targets which would trigger bonuses for their successful completion. For mechanical sweepers this would require revision of alternate side parking rules, but this should be done in any case. As experience with the collection force indicates, direct financial incentives are an effective way to improve productivity.

In summary, four options can be applied to improve street-cleaning services. First, the number of men assigned to street cleaning should be increased to 2000 and a high priority should be given to maintaining this level even if the budgetary climate worsens. Second, alternate side parking rules should be revised to facilitate extension of cleaning routes and reductions of service for some areas. Third, efforts to reduce littering and other code violations generating filth should be intensified including the issuance of more summonses and expansion of educational campaigns. Finally, a financial incentive plan for the cleaning force should be developed as a means of improving their productivity.

WASTE DISPOSAL

The dwindling capacity of the City to dispose of the more than 26,000 tons of refuse collected every day is one of the most important problems facing the next administration. It is like a time bomb ticking away. Its eventual consequences have few currently visible manifestations. If nothing is done, little effect will be perceived by the public for a number of years. When the smaller Brooklyn and Queens landfills are closed in 1986, refuse still will be collected and removed with no appreciable service deterioration, although costs will increase due to longer disposal trips to Fresh Kills, the City's last landfill. But in a little more than a decade, when Fresh Kills will be filled up, there simply will be no place to put the 20,000 tons of refuse per day not burned in remaining incinerators or shipped out of state. That is when the time bomb goes off.

BACKGROUND

At the start of the 1970s the City relied on a multifaceted, refuse-disposal system that included:

- 11 municipal incinerators burning about 9000 tons per day;
- 9 marine transfer stations serving Fresh Kills, a huge 3000-acre landfill on Staten Island;
- 8 landfills in The Bronx, Brooklyn, Queens, and Staten Island which received refuse by truck;
- extensive transport by private carters to dumps in New Jersey which handled about 5000 tons per day.

Thousands of private incinerators in institutions and large apartment buildings relieved some of the demand on the system for both collection and disposal.

Since then, the disposal system has been reduced at an alarming rate. Federal environment legislation required either the overhaul of all municipal incinerators to comply with clean-air standards or their closure. After reviewing the remaining useful life and engineering characteristics of each facility, the City decided that only three of its 11 incinerators should be upgraded. Eight municipal incinerators with a combined daily capacity of 6200 tons were closed. After the retrofitting of pollution control devices, the remaining three are able to handle a maximum of only 2800 tons per day. The same air quality legislation required the closing of all but the most modern private incinerators in the city, putting additional pressure on municipal collection and disposal services.

While there were eight landfills in the city as recently as 1974, there are now four. Because they reached or exceeded their capacities, the Pelham, Idlewilde, South Avenue, and Brookfield facilities with a combined capacity of 3300 tons per day were all closed by 1979. Of the remaining four, two are scheduled to become part of Gateway National Seashore in December 1985. These include Brooklyn's large Fountain Avenue landfill, which presently receives 40 percent of the daily refuse disposed of by the Department, or 8000 tons daily. A third, smaller landfill, Edgemere on the Rockaway Peninsula, is also scheduled to close because it has reached its originally designated capacity. Thus by 1986, the City probably will depend entirely on the Fresh Kills landfill to receive 18,000 tons of refuse per day plus incinerator residue. This material will be delivered via a barge system and long truck hauls over the Verrazzano Bridge. Furthermore, ever-tightening restrictions placed by the State of New Jersey on the importation of out-of-state garbage seriously threaten to halt the disposal of 3000 tons per day in that state by private carters. If this occurs, the additional amount also will end up in Fresh Kills.

The prognosis for the disposal system is troubling. All landfill capacity will be exhausted by the year 2000, assuming a continued ability to export some refuse to New Jersey. The approach of this date will be accompanied by increasing labor costs due to long dump trips and difficulty in handling refuse at Fresh Kills as the grades steepen. If the City fails to develop new alternatives, officials probably will solve the problem by reopening or creating new landfills throughout the city at sites already deemed unsuitable because of their location in residential areas, dedication as parkland, or danger of severe environmental deterioration. The risks to public health and environmental deterioration caused by such measures are unknown, but certainly they are substantial.

THE CURRENT STRATEGY

In order to avoid the dire consequences of exhausted acceptable landfill and no alternative disposal means, the City has extended the life of the present facilities and developed a new resource recovery network. The aforementioned retrofitting of three incinerators resulted in a combined capacity for 2800 tons per day of pollution-free incineration. The closing of the Pelham landfill in The Bronx and the Hamilton Avenue incinerator in Brooklyn was accompanied by construction of two new marine transfer stations to facilitate the removal of refuse from those areas to Fresh Kills.

Simultaneously, the unloading capacity at Fresh Kills was expanded.

During 1982, a plan to extend the maximum useful life of Fresh Kills landfill was developed. The plan allows more efficient use of Fresh Kills in the near term and extends its use for residue and nonburnable refuse after resource recovery plants are constructed. The City also has requested extensions from the federal and State governments of the scheduled closing dates for the Fountain Avenue and Edgemere landfills. These extensions would help bridge the lapse in time between landfill closures and the opening dates for recovery plants.

Passage of the New York State Returnable Beverage Container law in 1982 was expected to reduce daily refuse in the city by up to 1000 tons. Early in 1984 the Department estimated that between 30 and 50 percent of the 8 billion containers sold in New York State each year were being recycled, but the exact impact on refuse totals in New York City could not be estimated.[16]

All of these measures will help extend the time before landfill capacity is exhausted. But the second, and more important, element in the current strategy is the creation of a network of resource recovery plants, facilities which burn refuse under environmentally acceptable standards while simultaneously generating marketable energy.

The first step towards this goal was the creation in 1978 of the Office of Resource Recovery and Waste Disposal Planning. This was followed by exploratory talks with possible consumers of energy generated at resource recovery plants including the Port Authority of New York and New Jersey, The Power Authority of the State of New York, and Con Edison. The discussions with Con Edison led to the development of a draft proposal in 1980 for the City's first resource recovery plant—a barge-fed incinerator with a capacity of 3000 tons per day located at the site of the old Brooklyn Navy Yard. Constructed and operated by a private firm, the facility would generate steam and electricity for sale to Con Edison.

The City's initial plan was to construct this plant before moving further on the seven other plants needed to complete the citywide network. Municipal leaders believed that many of the problems in developing resource recovery plants in New York would be ironed out with the first one, and that the succeeding plants would move ahead smoothly.

Subsequent events changed these tactics. The proposed Navy Yard plant fell behind schedule for several reasons including community opposition based on environmental issues. In addition, concentration on a single plant in Brooklyn gave rise to the feeling among some in that borough that they were being singled out for a heavier burden than other areas of the city. Some also suspected that once the Navy Yard project was approved, other projects might go unbuilt, leaving the Navy Yard area with the City's only recovery plant.

These factors led the Department in 1983 to begin developing a citywide plan for a network of resource recovery facilities together with implementation schedules and a review of options. The report was completed in April of 1984. In addition to completion of the Navy Yard plant by 1988, the report recommended a three-stage program to construct seven additional plants.[17] First, three plants with a combined capacity of 6400 tons per day would be ready for operation by 1990. They would be located in the Inwood section of Manhattan, Hunts Point in the Bronx, and Spring Creek in Brooklyn. Next, two additional plants with a combined capacity of 4250 tons per day would be built for operation in 1993. They would be located at College Point in Queens and at the west end of Canal Street in Manhattan as part of the Westway development. Finally, in 1996 two more plants with a combined capacity of 4200 tons per day would be opened. They would be located in Maspeth in Queens and Arthur Kill in Staten Island. The recommended plan also called for a citywide program for the recycling of high-grade office paper, corrugated paper, newspaper, and glass.

Three features of the plan make it attractive. First, it provides for the distribution of plants among all boroughs of the City. This reduces the need to haul refuse over long distances and distributes equitably the inconveniences caused by the plants. Indeed, the seven recommended sites (in addition to the Navy Yard) were selected after an analysis of almost 50 possible sites. Consideration was given to remoteness from residential areas, proximity to waterways for the transportation of refuse and residue, road access, stack height limitations, and land ownership and availability.

Second, the phasing in of the eight resource recovery plants reduces contract management and financing burdens for the City. Phasing in the plants also allows the Department to take advantage of technological progress made during the next decade in the design of the later facilities.

Finally, the plan recognizes and makes provision for the need for landfill sites even after all plants are operating. At that time there will still be up to 55_ tons per day of unburnable refuse that will have to be placed at landfill sites. The recommended schedule of plant openings permits the capacity of the Fresh Kills landfill to be extended well into the next century and thus serve as a site for disposal of this remaining refuse.

Perhaps equally important in making the case for the network of resource recovery plants is the fact that the Department's review of options found no other approach that provided a long-term solution. The most feasible alternative to resource recovery plants is to open new landfill sites. Three are identified in the report: a new site near Co-op City in the Bronx, a former landfill site in Ferry Point Park, and a site on Arthur Kill, the proposed location for the eighth recovery plant. However, opening of these new areas would give the City only ten additional years of landfill capacity (assuming the Navy Yard plant is opened). In the year 2012 the City still would run out of places to put its refuse.

Undoubtedly, other alternatives involving new landfill sites could be devised. But they all represent short-term approaches involving severe environmental hardships for nearby residents and substantial costs for all local taxpayers. A new landfill approach would sharply increase on-street hauling costs and would require substantial capital costs to prepare new sites to meet federal and State sanitary regulations.

Given the attractions of a network of resource recovery plants and the disadvantages of the alternatives, why is there delay in implementing the proposed plan? The most significant obstacle is the potential danger from toxic dioxin which some fear will be produced by the plants. Studies show that no measurable amounts of the most serious form of dioxin are formed when refuse is incinerated at the normal operating temperature of the proposed plants.[18] But critics claim that too little is known about dioxin and its formation, and that its toxicity is so potent that present measurement methods fail to detect levels that, though small, are dangerous nonetheless.

In response to these concerns the Board of Estimate commissioned a study of possible risks. The results indicate that the Navy Yard plant would increase cancer rates between 0.24 and 5.9 cases per million people, assuming exposure for 70 years to plant emissions at the point of maximum concentration.[19] Considering the unlikely nature of the assumptions, and the current cancer rate of 250,000 per million people, the plant's emissions should not be a serious health concern.

No decision can be completely free from risk, but construction of the resource recovery plant network appears justified. Studies support the safety claims of the plant proponents. Given the absence of generally accepted scientific evidence showing the production of dioxin by these plants at levels dangerous to surrounding communities, elected officials can responsibly move ahead. Should subsequent evidence indicate that the plants are dangerous, they could be shut, although at a financial loss. But the risk of such financial loss due to presently unknown health dangers seems slim. The next administration should move expeditiously, but cautiously, to construct a network of resource recovery plants that will serve New Yorkers well into the future.

CONCLUSION

The unanticipated success of the Sanitation Department in improving refuse collection through greater productivity can serve as an example of the possibilities inherent in imaginative managerial approaches. But this success was preceded and accompanied by less fruitful efforts and also demonstrates that municipal leaders must be willing to try several forms of innovation in order to find those that are truly effective.

The Department's success in refuse collection is considerable but incomplete. More remains to be accomplished in improving collection productivity and in improving other services for which the Department is responsible.

With respect to refuse collection, the new administration's agenda should include extension of successful efforts as well as experimentation with untried ones. Effective innovations that can be expanded include (1) containerization, which can be extended to new sites; (2) gainsharing, which can be extended to officers and other workers besides sanitationmen working on trucks; and (3) civilianization, which should be extended to additional clerical jobs. Untried ideas which warrant experimentation include relay dumping, a revised work schedule, and new high-capacity vehicles for use in congested neighborhoods.

The methods of cleaning the streets remain almost unaffected by the successful innovations in refuse collection. Recent improvements in street cleanliness result almost entirely from the addition of more resources; the new administration should target street cleaning for productivity improvements. These gains can be achieved through extension of the gainsharing concept to cleaning personnel, route extensions accompanied by revised alternate side of the street parking regulations, and efforts to change citizen behavior including stricter code enforcement and enhanced educational campaigns through mass media.

Finally, perhaps the most critical challenge with regard to sanitation success is the development of a waste disposal system that can serve New Yorkers beyond the tenure of the next administration. Mindful of potential unknown risks, municipal leaders should begin to construct the proposed network of resource recovery plants. Its three stages permit appropriate revisions, and new evidence may warrant further changes, but unless action is taken soon the next generation of New Yorkers may face an unprecedented waste disposal crisis.

NOTES

1. New York City Department of Sanitation, *A Third Anniversary Report to the Mayor,* September 1981.

2. Unpublished internal analysis by the Department of Sanitation.

3. New York City Department of Sanitation, Bureau of Motor Equipment, *Productivity Gains Through Labor/Management Cooperation,* July, 1983.

4. *New York City Department of Sanitation Rerouting Project Final Report* (New York: Ecodata, Inc., December 30, 1980), pp. 76–78, and subsequent internal departmental analyses.

5. Author's survey conducted for the Sanitation Department, Fall, 1980.

6. Unpublished figures from the Department.

7. New York City Department of Sanitation, *A Third Anniversary Report to the Mayor,* September, 1981. One-third of the collection manpower was reduced at a savings of $12.5 million. Approximately $3.5 million was paid as bonuses, leaving $9.0 million as savings.

8. City of New York, Office of Operations, *The Mayor's Management Report,* September 1982, p. 74.

9. City of New York, Office of Operations, *The Mayor's Management Report,* January 1984, p. 71.

10. Unpublished figure from the Department.

11. City of New York, Office of the Comptroller, *Department of Sanitation, Bureau of Cleaning and Collection, Deployment of Uniformed Personnel,* Audit Report #3201, November 3, 1983.

12. "New York City Sanitation: Staging a Comeback," *Waste Age* (November 1981), pp. 22–30.

13. Unpublished figure from the Department.

14. City of New York, Office of Operations, *The Mayor's Management Report*, September 1983, p. 91.

15. Unpublished results of a survey performed in 1982 for the Department of Sanitation by the New York City Office of Operations.

16. "Officials Find New York's Bottle Law is Reducing Litter, Especially Upstate," *The New York Times*, May 7, 1984, p. B-1.

17. New York City Department of Sanitation, *The Waste Disposal Problem in New York City: A Proposal for Action*, April 1984. This was a preliminary planning report to the Board of Estimate in response to the resolution (Calendar No. 87) adopted by the Board on June 16, 1983.

18. Such studies are cited in "Incinerate New York Garbage," *The New York Times*, August 20, 1983, p. A-20.

19. *Assessment of Potential Public Health Impacts Associated with Predicted Emissions of Polychlorinated Dibenzo-Dioxins and Polychlorinated Dibenzo-Furans from the Brooklyn Navy Yard Resource Recovery Facility*, a study prepared by Fred C. Hart Associates, Inc. for the Department of Sanitation, August 17, 1984.

14

Mass Transit

ROSS SANDLER

The mass transit system serving the New York region is essential to its economy. Without it the region could not sustain an employment base of its current scale and character. Two important policy implications may be derived from this fact. First, for the long-run, a healthy and growing economy requires that mass transit be maintained at least at minimally acceptable standards. Second, the public subsidies required to maintain the system can be reduced if paid ridership can be increased beyond the minimum level dictated by the imperatives of employment commutation. Attracting more than the minimally essential ridership requires policies aimed at achieving more than minimally acceptable standards of service.

This chapter considers the policy implications of the New York region's dependence on mass transit. The first section explains the nature of this unavoidable reliance on subways, buses, and commuter rail lines. The second section reviews the policies developed to maintain adequate services. The final section identifies actions that could be taken to make the system more attractive and thus increase ridership beyond the minimum levels of economic necessity.

TABLE 14.1
Hub-Bound Travel on a Fall Weekday, 1982

Transportation Mode	Number of People	Percentage
Public Transportation	2,139,783	68.1%
Rail Rapid Transit	1,631,730	52.0
Subways	1,534,260	
PATH	97,470	
Suburban Rail	204,863	6.5
Intercity Rail	8,992	.3
Express Bus	148,193	4.7
Local Bus	101,718	3.2
Private Transportation		
(Auto, Taxi, Truck)	1,000,395	31.9
Total	3,140,178	100.0%

SOURCE: New York Metropolitan Transportation Council, "Hub-Bound Travel 1982," May 1984.

TABLE 14.2
Total Weekday Usage of Public Transportation in the Tristate Region, 1970–83
(ridership in thousands)

Year	Ridership	Percentage Change
1970	9,165.6	—
1971	8,940.3	−2.4%
1972	8,449.1	−5.5
1973	8,133.3	−3.7
1974	8,270.8	1.7
1975	7,946.5	−3.9
1976	7,401.9	−6.9
1977	7,258.0	−1.9
1978	7,388.2	1.8
1979	7,616.1	3.1
1980	7,421.1	−2.5
1981	7,315.8	−1.4
1982	7,182.8	−1.8
1983	7,351.9	2.4
Change	−1,813.7	−19.8%

SOURCE: New York Metropolitan Transportation Council, "Regional Transportation Status," October 1984.

DEPENDENCE ON MASS TRANSIT

The central business district or "hub" of the New York region, defined as Manhattan south of 60th Street, is the base for approximately 2,030,000.[1] While some of these workers walk to their jobs, the vast majority commute. In addition, numerous other people enter the hub to conduct business with those based in the area as well as to shop and see the sights. On a typical weekday over 3.1 million people enter the hub. (See Table 14.1.)

Of those entering the hub, the vast majority (68 percent) rely on public transportation. Within the public transportation sector, subways are the most important part accounting for 72 percent of the volume and 49 percent of all trips. In the peak morning hours, when most of the travel is work related, public transportation moves 88 percent of the commuters.[2] Overall, private transportation, consisting of autos, taxis, and trucks, accounts for 32 percent of the trips into the central business district.

The New York region, and New York City in particular, is unique in this heavy reliance on mass transit. With 8 percent of the nation's population, the New York region contributes to the national total approximately one-quarter of all public transit trips, one-third of all such passenger miles, and two-thirds of all public rail passenger rides. The number of persons in the region who use public transit to commute to work dwarfs the number in other large cities.[3]

Despite the wide area that public transit covers in the New York region, long-term trends have increased the use of the auto, while use of the major mass transit facilities has declined. As Table 14.2 shows, one out of five riders stopped using public transit in the 1970–83 period. Nearly all of this decline occurred in the 1970–77 period, coterminous with decline in the New York City economy. Between 1977 and 1983, ridership increased slightly because of an upturn of two percent in 1983.

New York City's subway and bus systems, which account for nine out of ten riders on the region's public transit system, are responsible for the overall decline (see Table 14.3). Subway ridership declined 21 percent in the 1970–84 period, and bus ridership fell 30 percent. Ridership on the Long Island Railroad, after declining in the early 1970s, rebounded 8 percent in the 1970–83 period. A similar though less pronounced pattern of decline and growth is evident in passengers on Metro North, which drew 18 percent more customers from New York City's northern suburbs in the 1970–84 period. The PATH system, which connects New Jersey to the World Trade Center and Pennsylvania Station, enjoyed a 41 percent increase in passengers.

TABLE 14.3

Revenue Passengers by Public Transportation System,
1970–84

(in millions)

Year	Subway	Bus[a]	PATH	LIRR	Metro North[b]
1970	1,262.3	888.3	39.0	70.1	40.7
1971	1,201.6	878.2	38.9	69.6	38.6
1972	1,149.2	821.5	40.3	59.8	37.8
1973	1,105.4	815.2	30.0	57.0	36.9
1974	1,104.6	846.3	37.8	58.1	39.7
1975	1,058.3	810.6	38.3	59.0	39.3
1976	1,013.3	724.5	40.7	59.7	39.8
1977	1,002.9	711.3	40.7	61.3	41.2
1978	1,047.6	702.7	41.8	64.2	43.6
1979	1,081.9	723.1	44.3	69.0	46.8
1980	1,014.1	678.5	35.9	70.4	48.6
1981	1,018.3	628.4	47.9	71.2	48.6
1982	994.9	606.8	53.0	71.4	47.7
1983	1,011.2	617.8	54.9	73.3	40.5
1984[c]	1,003.6	N.A.	54.9	76.0	47.9
Percentage Change	−20.5%	−30.5%	+40.8%	+8.4%	+17.7%

SOURCE: New York Metropolitan Transportation Council "Regional Transportation Status," October 1984.

NOTES: N.A. means not available.

a. Includes bus operations of the New York City Transit Authority and private bus companies licensed by New York City; percentage change is based on 1970–83 period.

b. 1983 totals affected by a six-week strike.

c. Data for 1984 supplied by the respective agencies. Private bus data unavailable; TA buses fell 6.2 percent in 1984 to 490.9 million.

The declining use of the city's subway and bus systems is linked to three factors. First, the economic decline during the 1969–77 period reduced the number of jobs in the central city. Since commutation to work is the principal reason for mass transit ridership, fewer jobs meant fewer riders. Total trips to the central business district fell over 11 percent between 1970 and 1977; this was reflected disproportionately in subway ridership which fell more than 20 percent in the same period (see Table 14.3). Second, a greater share of the remaining jobs, and the new jobs of the post-1977 economic recovery, went to non-New York City residents. These commuters rely primarily on suburban rail systems rather than local buses or subways for their public transportation. The growing role of suburbanites in filling central city jobs is related to the favorable ridership trends on the Long Island Railroad, Metro North, and the PATH lines.

Finally, there is a long-term trend in favor of the auto as a means of transportation. For many people its door-to-door convenience and its privacy and relative comfort make the auto preferable to mass transit. The share of Manhattan commuters entering by auto gradually has risen since 1970. Only in the years when there was a gasoline shortage, 1974 and 1979, did the proportion of hub-bound trips made by auto diminish (see Table 14.4). By 1982, over 1,000,000 people or 32 percent of the total entering the hub came by car. This was an 8 percent increase from 1977. Of the increase in people entering the Manhattan hub since the beginning of the recent economic recovery, nearly 40 percent used autos. On a typical weekday in 1983, over 1.6 million motor vehicles crossed to and from Manhattan over 20 bridges and tunnels. Of these, 88 percent either were autos or taxis.[4] The auto travelers' preference for privacy was evident; fully 63 percent of all entering vehicles carried a single occupant during the morning rush hours.[5]

Since 1979, the historic long-term trends of declining use of public transit and increasing use of motor vehicles have become even more pronounced. Traffic over Manhattan crossings has increased 12.1 percent in six years (an annual growth rate of 2 percent), while citywide subway use has fallen 7.8 percent and bus use 23 percent (see Table 14.5). The increasing use of autos exceeds the historic annual growth rates for auto travel to and from Manhattan experienced since the 1950s.[6]

Given the growing role of suburban commuters in the New York

TABLE 14.4

Number of Persons Entering the Manhattan Central Business District Daily by Means of Transportation, 1970–82
(in thousands)

Year	Subway	PATH	Rail	Ferry	Roosevelt Island Tram	Bus	Auto	Total	Auto as a Percentage of Total
1970	1,774	69	176	34	—	255	925	3,233	28.6%
1971	1,720	69	172	36	—	256	926	3,179	29.1
1972	1,602	71	170	33	—	244	920	3,040	30.3
1973	1,586	66	168	31	—	232	941	3,024	31.1
1974	1,593	70	170	30	—	230	884	2,977	29.7
1975	1,610	69	171	31	—	232	885	3,008	29.8
1976	1,478	72	179	26	—	220	877	2,852	30.7
1977	1,414	73	189	26	3	233	924	2,862	32.3
1978	1,416	74	195	27	4	228	926	2,870	32.3
1979	1,467	79	212	24	4	246	914	2,946	31.0
1980	1,499	80	218	29	4	253	930	3,013	30.9
1981	1,527	87	218	25	4	243	970	3,074	31.5
1982	1,535	97	214	39	4	250	1,001	3,140	31.9

SOURCE: New York Metropolitan Transportation Council, "Hub-Bound Travel, 1982," May 1984.

TABLE 14.5

Recent Changes in Auto Use to and from Manhattan Compared to Citywide Subway and Bus Use, 1979–84

Year	Auto Use — Total Manhattan Crossings — Daily Traffic Volume	Percentage Change	T.A. Ridership (in millions) — Subway[a]	Percentage Change	Bus	Percentage Change
1979	1,455,112	—	1,081.9	—	638.2	—
1980	1,499,344	3.0%	1,014.1	-6.3%	590.8	-7.4%
1981	1,540,683	2.7	1,018.3	0.4	535.1	-9.4
1982	1,573,012	2.1	994.9	-2.3	512.8	-4.2
1983	1,608.979	2.3	1,011.2	1.6	523.8	2.1
1984	1,640,691	2.0	1,003.6	-.8	490.9	-6.2
Total Change	185,579	12.8%	-78.3	-7.2%	-147.3	-23.1%

SOURCES: New York Metropolitan Transportation Council, "Regional Transportation Status" (October 1984); New York City Department of Transportation, "Manhattan River Crossings, 1983," p. 56; data for 1984 from Metropolitan Transportation Authority and Department of Transportation.

a. Includes Staten Island Rapid Transit Operating Authority.

TABLE 14.6

Capacity of River Crossings to Manhattan, 1983

Facility	Hourly Capacity (Passenger Car Equivalents)		Actual Volume as a Share of Capacity	
	A.M.	P.M.	A.M.	P.M.
Battery Tunnel	4,170	3,920	90%	97%
Brooklyn Bridge	4,700	4,320	100	96
Manhattan Bridge	4,810	4,650	95	88
Williamsburg Bridge	3,810	4,510	100	90
Queens-Midtown Tunnel	4,170	4,170	91	75
Queensborough Bridge	6,250	5,590	100	94
Triborough Bridge	4,080	4,080	88	89
Willis Avenue Bridge	—	5,430	—	96
Third Avenue Bridge	6,260	—	88	—
Madison Avenue Bridge	2,130	1,680	67	82
145th Street Bridge	1,640	1,560	69	91
Macombs Dam Bridge	2,170	2,030	85	76
Washington Bridge	2,170	3,130	62	76
Alexander Hamilton Bridge	6,260	6,260	98	91
University Heights Bridge	1,830	1,550	86	88
Broadway Bridge	1,910	1,820	86	80
Henry Hudson Bridge	3,060	3,060	77	63
George Washington Bridge	12,180	12,400	95	94
Lincoln Tunnel	5,280	5,400	100	100
Holland Tunnel	2,610	2,830	100	100
Total	79,400	78,390	92	90

SOURCE: New York City Department of Transportation, "Manhattan River Crossings, 1983," pp. 26–27.

City economy and their apparent preference for the automobile, it is likely that auto use will increase in the future. But there are limits on the potential use of autos because of the central business district's congestion; most trips to Manhattan will have to be made by mass transit and probably by the subway and bus systems. Congestion on highway bridges and downtown streets places an effective limit on the number of entering autos, and the current volume appears to be close to that limit.

Bridges and tunnels to Manhattan currently are used to near capacity. (See Table 14.6.) During the morning rush hours, 8 percent of total capacity remains available on all bridges. Most (14 out of 19) in-bound lanes on bridges and tunnels operate near full capacity. Street space is similarly near capacity. Vehicles accumulate in the Manhattan hub throughout the day, reaching a maximum at

1 P.M. when 182,000 vehicles are present.[7] Vehicles in motion, a measure of the vehicles actually in use, reaches its peak in midtown at about 2 P.M. when about 8800 vehicles are in motion. It is this relatively small number of vehicles that produces massive congestion. Midtown congestion at the peak hours, about which so much is written, actually involves somewhat fewer (7000 to 8500) vehicles in motion. The New York Department of Transportation projects that a continuation of recent trends will produce, by 1990, daily congestion on New York City's streets and highways at the same level as was experienced during the 1980 transit strike.[8]

Current levels of congestion already are limiting the growth in auto use. During rush hours, when bridge and highways are near capacity, there has been little increase in auto volume; the growth in auto use in recent years has primarily been during the "shoulder" periods from 10 A.M. to 4 P.M. and from 7 P.M. to 1 A.M. Auto trips during these hours could increase even further, but limitations are evident. During part of the shoulder periods, there is increased congestion approaching that of rush hours. For example, recent waiting times at the Holland and Lincoln tunnels at 10 A.M. are comparable to or greater than those between the 7 and 8 A.M. rush hour just a few years earlier.[9] Perhaps equally significant, there are limits to the number of job holders who can commute during shoulder periods. Much of the business conducted in Manhattan offices requires personal interactions; people must be in their offices when others are in their offices, and this limits potential for staggered hours and other efforts to avoid rush hour travel.

Adding new bridges and tunnels would improve capacity relatively little. As Table 14.6 shows, the Queens-Midtown Tunnel is able to carry 4170 passenger cars per hour, a capacity which with the average occupancy is the equivalent of about 6700 passengers. Three to four subway trains handle a passenger load of comparable size. The Regional Plan Association makes the point more dramatically. It calculates that replacing Long Island Railroad service to Manhattan with automobile facilities would require six-and-one-half new tunnels the size of Queens-Midtown, 600 miles of new lanes on freeways in Queens and Nassau, and about 18 city blocks of six-story parking garages in Manhattan.[10]

In sum, the nature of the New York economy requires over 3.1 million people to enter its central business district each weekday. If the economy grows, this number also will grow. A greater share

TABLE 14.7

Metropolitan Transportation Authority Capital Needs, 1987–93

	State of Good Repair	Normal Replacement	New Initiatives	Total
Subways and Buses	$7,339.1	$3,954.4	$2,544.6	$13,838.1
LIRR	306.4	227.6	1,474.0	2,008.0
Metro North	563.6	287.6	325.0	1,176.2
Total	$8,209.1	$4,469.6	$4,343.6	$17,022.3

SOURCE: Metropolitan Transportation Authority, "Update of the MTA Staff Report on Capital Revitalization 1984–1993," April 16, 1984. Figures are in current dollars based on assumed annual inflation rates of 6 percent.

of these trips may be made by auto, but a mass transit system will be required to meet the bulk of this travel demand under any foreseeable circumstances. If it does not meet this demand adequately, the local economy will be threatened.

RECENT MASS TRANSIT POLICIES

The evolution of current mass transit policies can best be traced from the creation of the Metropolitan Transportation Authority (MTA) in 1967. The MTA was established by the State legislature as a regional body to assume control over the subways and buses operated by the New York City Transit Authority, the commuter railroads operated by the Long Island Rail Road, the New York Central Railroad, and the New Haven Railroad, and the facilities of the Triborough Bridge and Tunnel Authority. Shortly after its creation, the MTA adopted expansionary policies predicated on continued growth in the local economy and the desirability of increasing mass transit ridership. Its "new routes" program included a Second Avenue subway line, a new tunnel from Manhattan at 63rd Street to Queens, and the extension of additional lines in Queens. These objectives dominated transit planning until the fiscal crisis of 1975.

The fiscal stringencies of the mid-1970s led to revised MTA priorities. Most new construction was abandoned or delayed, and capital funds were shifted to operating purposes to promote the new priority of "saving the fare." The capstone of that effort was the "Beame Shuffle" by which Congress permitted the City, at the request of

Mayor Abraham D. Beame, to use $281 million in federal capital grants as operating subsidies between 1975 and 1978.[11] Work on the 63rd Street tunnel and the Archer Avenue extension in Jamaica, Queens, was continued, without, unfortunately, a plan to connect either line usefully to the system. Partly completed work on the Second Avenue subway was entombed.

Efforts to maintain a low fare in this period of fiscal austerity led to policies of deferred maintenance and reduced service. Transit Authority (TA) employment was cut by 5300 or 11 percent between 1975 and 1978.[12] Throughout the 1970s, the MTA spent only one-fifth of what was needed annually as capital replenishment.[13]

By the late 1970s, the policy of deferred maintenance was resulting in breakdowns and delays, and the service reductions added to overcrowding. In 1981, the MTA, in the face of the crises, adopted a new set of policies for capital spending aimed at restoring the system to a state of good repair. This objective was first articulated in a November 1980 staff report that identified ten-year capital needs of $17.4 billion in 1980 dollars.[14] Following the report, the MTA approved on September 25, 1981 a five-year capital program. Covering 1982–86, the program initially embraced $7.2 billion for rehabilitation and improvements including $5.7 billion for the New York City Transit Authority and $683 and $684 million, respectively, for the Long Island Rail Road and Metro North Commuter Railroad. With the avilability of additional funding, the five-year program was increased to $8.5 billion in 1983.

The new capital program in 1981 broke down the MTA's previous almost exclusive reliance on intergovernment grants by using financing techniques drawn from the private sector. The MTA persuaded Congress to allow it to sell depreciation on publicly owned buses and rail cars to private companies, which could then use the tax credits. This financing scheme will produce about $500 million over five years. The MTA negotiated loans at favorable interest rates from the Japanese and Canadian governments to finance its subway-car purchases, providing savings of $200 million. The MTA proposed to sell $2 billion in bonds backed by future fare revenues and State subsidies and obtained investment-grade ratings for the bonds. Finally, the MTA was able to convince the State legislature to increase tax financing through enactment of regional taxes in the MTA's service area. As a result, by 1982 the MTA was spending capital funds five times greater than the annual rate in the 1970s.

In June 1984, the MTA made its first adjustment in the 1982–80 capital program.[15] The amended capital program included an expanded statement of objectives that emphasized the reestablishment and maintenance of reliable operations on existing buses and subways and the long-term survival of that system. Innovative improvements or items designed to provide a more comfortable environment for passengers were downgraded. Consistent with these objectives and also in response to an increasing number of derailments, the MTA allocated an additional $200 million to track reconstruction, funds obtained largely by diverting $188 million from station modernization. As for the vestigial construction of new routes, the revised plan set a tightly restricted agenda. To the extent that a viable interim operation could be accomplished, the routes under construction would be brought to an orderly conclusion. That objective largely underlay the MTA's controversial decision in late 1984 to select the least costly option for connecting the 63rd Street tunnel to existing Queens subway lines despite the fact that, of the alternatives studied, that connection produced the fewest benefits in attracting riders or extending the system.

In 1984, a new MTA management team also focused attention on increasing their control over Transit Authority supervisors, most of whom were protected by both civil service rules and unions.[16] With City, and later State political leaders' support, the MTA leadership removed the twin protection as a measure to gain control over operations and promote effective use of capital funds.

The MTA filed a second amendment to the capital program in January 1985 which, among other changes, increased spending for subway car overhaul and deferred $231 million in yard rehabilitation work.[17] One significant innovation included in the amended plan was the introduction of an automated fare collection system. The first phase of the system is to be completed in 1986. The Transit Authority plans to issue magnetically coded passes to employees, school children, and other pass holders, and install "swipe readers" on one or more turnstiles in each station. Passholders will be able to slide the pass through a special slot on top of the turnstile to gain entry. This and other operational changes will permit the Transit Authority to close the slam gates, a reform the MTA estimates will save $8 million annually in fare beating.

The most striking fact about the MTA's capital program is that it simply ends in 1986. There is no approved continuation program;

neither work items nor funding beyond 1986 have been approved. However, the MTA estimated capital needs for the 1987–93 period (see Table 14.7). These estimates are derived primarily from the continuing objectives of restoring the system to a state of good repair and providing normal replacement of equipment, with limited provision in the later years for new initiatives which provide greater efficiencies in existing service or provide greater service to meet increased passenger demands. Specifically, the MTA projects $17 billion of needs through 1993 beyond needs already funded in the five-year plan ending in 1986. Of this total, over $8.2 billion, or 48 percent, is to achieve a state of good repair, nearly $4.5 billion, or over 26 percent, is for normal replacement, and the remaining $4.3 billion, or less than one-quarter, is for new initiatives.

What can be said of the MTA goals? Returning the system to a condition of good repair, given the condition of the subways, remains an apt and realistic goal. Perfect for 1980, the phrase conveyed the desperateness of the maintenance crises produced by prior policies and compelled attention to the disastrous financial situation of mass transit. It remains appropriate for the 1990s because the system has fallen so far behind.

What is lacking in the MTA's programs is a strategic plan for the region's mass transit system. What will be the size and shape of the services offered? How will changes in travel needs be accommodated? The MTA, created in large measure to provide regional guidance, never performed that function. Because of this failure, the State legislature in 1983 enacted legislation directing the MTA to commence strategic planning.[18] In October 1984, the MTA released its first set of plans covering the 1985–89 period. The plan is to be updated annually.

The new strategic plan and the capital plan do not relate one to another. The capital plan seeks primarily to rehabilitate and modernize the existing system. The strategic plan seeks to manage that system better. But what should the system be?

Without such a comprehensive plan, the MTA is unable either to reduce or expand service. The attempt to close the little-used Franklin Avenue shuttle is illustrative. In 1982, the Transit Authority sought to take advantage of the near collapse of the embankment supporting that shuttle (which serves about 14,000 persons per weekday) as a means of ending service. The Authority was able to show that, by substituting bus service, it could avoid an estimated $40 to $60 million capital expenditure. The community, quickly realizing the Transit Authority had no overall plan or standards for reaching such decisions, successfully argued that the Transit Authority's decision to close the Franklin Avenue shuttle was arbitrary.[19] The reverse situation occurred in 1984, when opposition from parts of Queens helped stifle expansion of subway service that would have utilized the 63rd Street tunnel. New rail service would have benefited nearly 150,000 residents of Queens and Nassau counties. Yet, residents had so little confidence in the MTA's plans and ability to provide reliable service they were unwilling to accept the short-term inconvenience that expansion of rail service would have entailed.

The MTA has begun to try to meet its planning needs. In January 1985, a chief planner was appointed to a top position reporting directly to the chairman. The crucial planning issues involve questions of growth and consolidation. As one transportation planner has written:

Rationally considered, the dichotomy between reconstruction and new construction should not exist; there should be only one criterion: what is the payoff from the investment? And there should be a long-term development plan, including reconstruction, abandonment and new construction.[20]

STRATEGIES FOR THE FUTURE

In thinking about a comprehensive strategy for mass-transit services, New York's leaders can draw lessons from the example of the Paris Metro. That system opened in 1900, four years ahead of the New York City subway, and suffered many of the same problems of deterioration and obsolescence. In 1963, about 40 percent of the Metro's subway cars were more than 35 years old; 35 percent of its buses were purchased before 1939.[21] In contrast to New York City's subway, the Paris Metro has been almost totally rebuilt since 1963. Today, Paris boasts a subway system it should be the long-term goal of New York City to approximate.

The Regie Autonome des Transports Parisiens (RATP), the French governmental corporation which runs the Paris Metro, rebuilt the subway system in three overlapping phases.[22] First, the

RATP emphasized raising the level and quality of subway service. It replaced its entire fleet of subway cars, added trains, and increased the size of its cars; the results were greater reliability, cleaner and quieter trains, reduced waiting time, and roomier conditions. The RATP completely renovated one-third of the system's 360 stations, added 600 escalators, and relighted platforms dramatically. Stations near the Louvre and the Rodin Museum, as well as others, became famous for their works of art and civilized ambiance. These stations are not aberrations but the product of planned effort to make the Paris Metro attractive.

In the next phase, which began roughly ten years after the development plan was begun, the RATP emphasized an aggressive marketing program designed to attract more customers, no longer a laughable proposition given the service enhancements achieved in the first phase. It automated fare collection, allowing passengers to use monthly passes in place of single fares. (Two million passengers now possess a monthly pass.) The RATP sponsored shows, dancing, music, and sports information in the Metro, and advertised Metro use as "chic." But better service and marketing did not exhaust the strategies to increase ridership. The French government taxed employers directly for Metro expenses, giving employees in return the right to purchase a monthly pass at reduced rates.

In the last and current phase, the RATP with other French transportation corporations has coordinated regional commuter rail services with the Paris Metro. The Réseau Express Régional (RER), roughly equivalent to our commuter lines, provides three main trunk lines through Paris but with multiple stops and subway connections. A suburban tram line is to be completed in 1988 to connect suburbs in the north of Paris and, with an extended Metro line, will improve suburban connections to the center of Paris. New RER and Metro stations are to be built with interconnected bus terminals and parking lots to facilitate transfers.

The modernization of the Metro has enabled it to increase productivity by reducing subway personnel as well as increasing ridership. The RATP's 40,000 employees do the work 55,000 employees did earlier, and the system has over 2.2 billion riders, up 30 percent since 1974. The program is now in its twenty-second year and will continue into the 1990s. The MTA is only in its fourth year of renovation, but it is not too early to learn from the Paris experience.

What are the implications for mass transit in New York City?

Three general approaches appear justified: to plan comprehensively for combined subway and commuter rail lines, to develop financing arrangements that encourage ridership, and to reduce congestion to facilitate bus service. While the first two draw from the French experience, the third derives primarily from innovations tested in New York City.

PLANNING FOR CHANGING TRANSIT NEEDS

As noted earlier, the post-1980 goals of the MTA essentially involve restoring its systems to good order. Restoring an old system to good order in a changing city is not responsive to current or future needs. Some sections of the city are underserved; others are overserved. To meet the challenge of increasing riders in a world of finite resources, the system will have to expand in certain areas and contract in others.

There are significant unmet transit needs within the MTA service area. These include service to large sections of Queens which, again, have been left without the prospect of rail service because of the collapse of the "new routes" program and the subsequent decision to make only limited use of the 63rd Street tunnel. The need for the Second Avenue line to serve the upper East Side and Wall Street is great. Expanded service on the West Side of Manhattan is required to meet predictable new travel demands arising from development of the Penn Central yards and Convention Center.[23] Public transit to the region's airports remains unsatisfactory. Outside the MTA service area, major needs also exist which affect the MTA and New York City. Greatly increased trans-Hudson auto traffic has sparked interest in reestablishing ferry service from Hoboken to lower Manhattan and spurred electrification of the Morris and Essex Line and other expansion plans by New Jersey Transit.

The planning functions being performed by various agencies, including the MTA, are balkanized, uneven, uncoordinated and, most important, unfocused on regional objectives. The private, nonprofit Regional Plan Association (RPA), virtually alone, views transit from a regional perspective. The RPA's efforts are designed to increase ridership by improving service. The RPA plans emphasize more speed and less crowding, goals designed to attract riders from autos. To accomplish these goals, the RPA advocates selective closing of stations (up to 30 out of 436), increasing distances be-

TABLE 14.8

Tristate Region Public Transportation Operating Expenses, Revenues,
and Subsidies, 1970–83
(millions of dollars)

Year	Expenditures	Revenues	Subsidies	
			Amount	Percentage of Expenditures
1970	$1,157.4	$1,051.5	$105.8	9.1%
1971	1,305.5	1,057.5	247.0	19.0
1972	1,393.1	1,108.0	287.6	20.6
1973	1,507.1	1,103.4	403.8	26.8
1974	1,723.3	1,149.9	574.7	33.3
1975	1,906.6	1,232.3	674.4	35.4
1976	1,933.3	1,312.5	620.9	32.1
1977	1,947.4	1,354.9	592.6	30.4
1978	2,176.9	1,394.2	782.7	36.0
1979	2,417.7	1,477.8	939.8	38.9
1980	2,703.6	1,620.1	1,083.6	40.1
1981	3,127.6	1,913.0	1,214.6	38.8
1982	3,322.1	2,007.9	1,313.1	39.5
1983	3,524.7	2,071.4	1,453.3	41.2
Percentage Change	204.5%	97.0%	1,272.3%	—

SOURCE: New York Metropolitan Transportation Council, "Regional Transportation Status," October 1984.

tween stations on proposed routes, and redesigning existing and new routes to eliminate duplicative rail service. The RPA plan includes substantial new route construction (as much as 37 new miles) coupled with route elimination (as much as 26 miles). The RPA is not alone in calling for route elimination as a necessary step in overall service improvement.[24]

In sum, the region's transportation networks require a regional perspective within planning organizations and a process to identify the system that will best serve the needs of the local economy. No such process now exists. Its absence hinders the credibility and financial viability of the MTA, and will eventually endanger the growth prospects for the regional economy.

NEW FINANCING MECHANISMS

Plans for enhanced services will require large sums of money. As noted earlier, the MTA needs $17 billion simply to continue its

existing capital program through 1993. If the present plan is inadequate, how could additional financing be obtained?

The ability of the MTA to raise capital is far greater than previously thought. From 1972 to 1981, the MTA's entire capital budget for both rehabilitation and construction of new routes averaged
less than $300 million annually in 1980 dollars, and there were only
two important sources of capital funds: federal and state grants.
During the 1970s, MTA management ascertained available federal
and State grants, and then tailored its capital expenditures to match
that amount. This behavior undermined the MTA's ability to raise
funds, let alone plan for the future. Repeating that approach, by
considering only the existence of currently planned financing, in-
vites similar problems.

The recent history is a lesson in diversity. Current MTA operating budgets benefit from toll surpluses; taxes on oil company
receipts and other specific business activities; sales taxes; direct
appropriations from the City, State, and federal governments
(though the future of the last source is in doubt); and special appropriations for engineering, police, and transportation of senior
citizens and school children.

What has not been altered during this period of enhanced financing is the concept that transit fares should be related directly
to transit use. The result is that government already has become a
major purchaser of transit services. As shown in Table 14.8, government subsidies have grown from 19 percent of all expenditures
for public transportation in 1971 to over 41 percent in 1983. In
1985, fare revenues will cover less than half of the Transit Authority's expenses.[25] If ridership continues its long-term trend, down,
subsidies will grow in both absolute and relative terms.

It is time, following the Paris model, to revolutionize financing
by integrating transit use and employee benefits. Over 2,000,000
Parisians possess a monthly pass, the *carte d'orange*, which makes
them pass holders, not single-trip purchasers of service. The economic and transportation implications of this reform are unmistak-
able. Because pass holders do not pay each time they use the
Metro, they use it more frequently. They also can link bus and
subway trips. As ridership increases, the system becomes more
efficient.

The key to financing an improved, not simply restored, subway and bus system is to turn as many potential customers as possible into transit pass holders, so their incentive to use public transit will increase. The MTA, City, and State need to design a system whereby employers are taxed and, in return, receive monthly transit passes for their employees. Purchases of passes (and of individual tokens) would augment the basic employer-financed pass.

In Paris, the tax-pass system has worked well. Employers with nine or more employees are taxed to subsidize the reduced price. Employers in Paris pay a tax of 2 percent of wages, those in the inner ring of suburbs 1.7 percent, and those in the Paris exurbs, 1.2 percent. Those holding passes account for 60 percent of RATP use.

There has been support in New York City for an employment tax to subsidize transit. In 1984, a study by the Permanent Citizens Advisory Committee (PCAC) to the MTA endorsed a payroll tax and demonstrated that a carefully designed payroll tax would not be regressive. The PCAC advocated an exemption from taxation at the bottom rather than the top, the effect of which would exempt a high proportion of businesses in the region and avoid a regressive impact.[26]

Studies by the Department of City Planning also indicate advantages of a payroll tax. The amount that could be raised is large: a 1 percent tax in the MTA region would produce about $850 million based upon 1982 wages. The tax also meets standards of equity based upon a geographical test; that is, the economic burden on a county basis equals the commutation benefits.[27]

Taxes dedicated to transit successfully enacted by the State legislature in the last five years have been regional in nature and, for the most part, applied to businesses. A regional payroll tax tied to reduced prices to employees for passes possesses these attributes. As a regional tax, the plan would be administered by the State, just as the State administers other specialized taxes. In addition, because the distribution of income among all transit users is very similar to that of all workers, the benefits and burdens are matched.[28]

There are those who believe employer taxes will be counterproductive. They prefer subsidies from taxes on other forms of transportation, primarily taxes on auto use by increasing tolls, parking taxes, registration fees, and the like. But these sources, consistently advocated by many groups, have proven less politically acceptable than business taxes. Nonetheless, such auto use charges and taxes could supplement the proposed regional payroll tax.

REDUCING CONGESTION FOR BUSES

Critical as a modern subway system is to the future of New York City, the importance of buses—and means of improving such service—deserves attention. Buses, it is easy to forget, still serve about 600 million riders annually in New York City, about 60 percent of the number using the subway. While the failures of the subway system attract more attention, those of the bus system, at least as measured by ridership, have been greater. As Table 14.4 showed, bus ridership dropped nearly one-third in the 1970–83 period.

More bus rides are convenience trips than are subway rides, prompted by choice rather than necessity. Most bus riders use the service for short journeys. Without minimizing the problems of safety, poor design, and overcrowding on some bus routes, the primary problem bus service faces is slow service; the primary reason for slow service is competition with cars and taxis for limited space in the city's streets. Thus, there is a simple means available to the City of New York, which controls the use of its streets, to speed bus travel—regulation.

Since the late 1970s the City has rationed the use of street space in the most dense parts of Manhattan to the advantage of bus services in a series of initiatives discussed below. The most immediate way of improving bus service in the city is to expand regulatory efforts, particularly on those public thoroughfares where volume and congestion are high. If the City could accomplish this, it could increase bus ridership substantially by making faster and thus more efficient transportation possible.

In 1971, the City established the contraflow bus and taxi lane on the Long Island Expressway leading to the Midtown Tunnel. That special lane saves 20 minutes each day for 340 buses carrying 17,000 passengers.[29] Building on this success, the New York City Department of Transportation began in 1977 to develop bus lanes in the middle of Manhattan.

In 1978, the City's first midtown effort established an exclusive contraflow bus lane on Second Avenue that allowed buses to move more quickly from 57th Street to the Queensborough Bridge during the afternoon rush period; it saves ten minutes a day for 10,000 passengers. In 1979, the City established a crosstown corridor on 49th and 50th Streets between Third and Seventh avenues. The corridor is open to buses, taxis, and local deliveries by commercial vehicles on weekdays from 11 A.M. to 4 P.M. This saves 10,000 crosstown bus passengers seven minutes a day, and cuts taxi times and commercial delivery times.

In May 1981, the City embarked on a larger experiment, exclusive bus lanes on Madison Avenue between 42nd and 59th Streets. The regulations, operative from 2 P.M. to 7 P.M. on weekdays, save 27,000 riders up to 20 minutes. Notable is that usage of both local and express buses has increased since the Madison Avenue bus lanes opened. Local bus ridership has risen 17 percent and express bus ridership 13 percent.

In 1982, the City established "red zone" bus lanes at 11 locations, covering 12 miles of midtown and downtown streets. Such "red zone" lanes prohibit standing of all vehicles in the right-hand lane, which is devoted instead to buses and right-turning vehicles. Violators are subject to fine and towing charges of at least $100. By 1984, some 4000 buses carrying nearly 180,000 riders traveled 20 percent faster than before.

The evidence is clear. Regulation of vehicular usage on the city's streets saves time and attracts riders. More should be done. Dedicated bus lanes with carrying capacity approaching the levels of rail systems are possible in mid-Manhattan. Designation of 49th Street as a two-way street open to buses only would speed midtown traffic and better link midtown to the Convention Center via 11th Avenue. Similar benefits could be provided on 42nd Street. Even greater potential exists by making First Avenue an exclusive bus way from the top of Manhattan to Wall Street. These initiatives would permit huge numbers of people to be transported quickly, reliably, and safely on the city's buses.

CONCLUSION

Without a good public transit system, the growth of the New York City economy will be threatened. This fact alone should spur public officials to greater efforts to ensure that the system is well planned and financed. While the MTA is a State agency, City officials can make an important contribution to improved service. Most notably, they can build on past successes in regulating the city's streets to speed bus travel. Their ability to affect subway service is less, but still substantial. The mayor's representatives on the MTA Board, while not a majority, are a visible minority that can express New York City's needs in concerted fashion.

Present MTA plans for restoring the city's subways are inadequate in conception. The recreation of the Paris Metro provides a model approach that should be considered in New York City. The first priority is to improve services in the existing system, but that should be a first step in a larger plan that would reconfigure the system to meet the region's transportation needs.

To help finance an expanded, modernized heavy rail system, the relationship of the fare to MTA finances should be reconsidered. In the past, tactics have focused narrowly on obtaining more and more subsidy to support fewer and fewer riders. The goal in the future should be more riders and less direct subsidy. The key to accomplishing this is, once again, to follow the Paris example by instituting a direct tax on the city's businesses to help support the system—and in return making the city's workers "owners" of the system by providing them a pass entitling "free" use. By separating payment from ridership, greater use will be realized; with greater use will come greater efficiency—not just for the subways but for the city's streets as well.

This plan presupposes service improvements, however. Present MTA leadership, now in possession of the control over its supervisors they believed essential to better service, should begin to demonstrate service improvements. The large sums being spent on subway improvements for new cars, better rails, and more comfortable stations should be sufficient to make the improvements visible.

If the first steps of service improvement are not achieved soon, then the city will be consigned to an expensive, second-rate subway system that will require more and more subsidy to service fewer and fewer riders. Inevitably, congestion will grow at street level, making the movement of people above ground harder and more expensive. That is a blueprint for economic decline.

NOTES

1. Regina B. Armstrong and N. David Miller, "Employment in the Manhattan CBD and Back-Office Locational Decisions," *City Almanac*, Volume 18, Numbers 1–2 (1985), p.4.

2. New York Metropolitan Council, "Journey to Work by Means of Transportation and Carpooling," March 1984.

3. New York Metropolitan Transportation Council, "Transit Ridership Effects of Journey to Work Changes," February 1984, p. 23.

4. New York City Department of Transportation, "Manhattan River Crossings 1983," no date, pp. 2, 56.

5. Ibid., p. 18.

6. Ibid., pp. 46–48.

7. New York City Department of Transportation, "Recent Trends in Traffic Volumes and Transit Ridership," February 1985, p. 12.

8. Ibid., p. 3.

9. Port Authority of New York and New Jersey, "Trans-Hudson Transportation Issues," January 13, 1984.

10. Regional Plan Association, "Funding Transit Deficits," November 1984, pp. 17–18.

11. New York City Department of City Planning, "A New Direction in Transit," December 1978, pp. XII-15-22.

12. Regional Plan Association, op. cit., pp. 4–5.

13. Metropolitan Transportation Authority, "Update of the MTA Staff Report on Capital Revitalization 1984–93," April 16, 1984, p. II-A-2.

14. Metropolitan Transportation Authority, "Staff Report on Capital Revitalization for the 1980s and Beyond," November 25, 1980.

15. Metropolitan Transportation Authority, "Amendment to the Capital Program as Submitted to the MTA Capital Program Review Board," June 15, 1984.

16. A clear statement of this priority is found in New York City Transit Authority, "Strategic Plan 1985–89," December 1984, pp. 15–17.

17. Metropolitan Transportation Authority, "Amendment to the Capital Program of the MTA," January 28, 1985.

18. 1983 N.Y. Sess. Law Ch. 427, Article 1269-d.

19. Steven M. Jurow and Ross Sandler, "Should We Scuttle the Shuttle?" *New York Affairs*, Volume 7, Number 3 (1982), pp. 43–50.

20. Boris Pushkarev, "Consolidated Growth: A Long-Term Transit Development Program," *New York Affairs*, Volume 7, Number 3 (1982), p. 51.

21. Information from remarks of Pierre Weil, former president of the RATP at the Conference on New York City Public Transit, December 16, 1982.

22. The RATP is state owned, and is chartered to operate the Paris Metro, the Paris and suburban bus system, and (jointly with the French Railways) the Regional Rapid Transit System. Facts concerning the rehabilitation of the RATP are reported in the annual *Plan d'Entreprise*. Much of the material in this section is based upon reports and presentations by Philippe Essig, Director General of the RATP, and Michel Gerard, RATP Director of Development, presented at the conference Metropolis, Paris, October 1984.

23. Sigurd Grava, "West Side Transportation Story," *New York Affairs*, Volume 7, Number 3 (1982), p. 79.

24. Edward S. Seeley, Jr., "Mass Transit," in Charles Brecher and Raymond D. Horton, eds., *Setting Municipal Priorities, 1982* (New York: Russell Sage Foundation, 1981), p. 394.

25. Transit Authority, "1985 Operating Budget Proposal," revised November 9, 1984.

26. Permanent Citizens Advisory Committee to the MTA, "Comparative Burdens of Alternative Revenue Sources for the Metropolitan Transportation Authority," November 1984.

27. New York City Department of Planning, "Alternative Financing for MTA Transit Operations," November 1984, and "Geographic Equity in Transit Financing, November 1984.

28. Regional Plan Association, "Funding Transit Deficits," November 1984, p. 14.

29. The figures on the City's bus-lane experiments are from periodic reports by the New York City Department of Transportation. See, for example, its "Priority Bus Treatments," March 1984.

INDEX

Adoption. *See* Foster care
Agency for Child Development (ACD), 133, 217–218, 219
Aid to Families with Dependent Children (AFDC), 213
  benefits under, 216–217
  creation of, 64
  eligibility for, 67–68, 129, 216–217
  expansion of, 64–66
  federal aid to, 120, 123, 124, 126, 129, 132–133
  Medicaid and, 287, 288
  number of persons receiving, Table 2.7 (p. 66), Table 7.4 (p. 216)
Automobile traffic, 447
  increases in, 447–451

Bald, Margaret, 229
Beame, Mayor Abraham D., 187, 453
Berne, Robert, 11–12, 113
Block grants. *See* Operating grants
Board of Education, 11, 129, 137, 159, 175, 197
  dropout rate and, 264
Board of Estimate, 178, 227
  capital budgeting and, 140, 141
  day care and, 218
Board of Higher Education, 175
Brecher, Charles, 13–14
Bridges
  capital spending for, 151, 158, 162–163, 167
  traffic on, 450–451
Bureau of Building Maintenance, 413
Bureau of Cleaning and Collection (BCC), 413–415
Bureau of Cooperative Educational Services (BOCES), 248
Bureau of Motor Equipment, 413
  maintenance programs of, 418–419
Bureau of Waste Disposal, 413
Bus system, 445, 447
  improving, 462–463, 464
  lanes for, 462–463

ridership on, 462, 463

Capital financing
  general obligation debt, 144–147
  sources of, 144–150
Capital grants, 121
  federal aid for, 133, 136
Capital spending, 7–8
  bridges and, 151, 158, 162–163, 167
  budgeting process for, 140–144
  commitments for, Table 5.1 (p. 142), Table 5.4 (p. 150)
  corrections and, 157, 158–159, 163, 166–167
  direction of, 140
  economic development and, 157, 161
  financing of, 7–8
  fire facilities and, 155, 159, 162, 167
  funding sources for, Table 5.2 (p. 143)
  hospitals and, 155, 158, 163, 167, Table 9.11 (p. 303), 304
  housing programs and, 157, 160–161
  implementation of, 163–167
  increases in, 157–161
  parks and, 156–157, 160, 162, 167
  planned and actual, Table 5.5 (p. 164), Table 5.6 (p. 165)
  police facilities and, 155, 159, 162, 167
  potential reductions in, 161–163
  priorities for, 150–151, 157–158
  sanitation facilities and, 155, 159, 162
  schools and, 156, 159–160, 162, 167
  sewers and, 153–154, 160, 162, 167
  streets and, 153, 158, 161–162, 167
  uniformed service vehicles and, 155–156, 158, 162
  waste disposal and, 154–155, 158, 162
  water distribution and, 152–153, 161
  water pollution control and, 154, 159, 163
  water supply and, 151–152, 158, 162, 167
Carter, President Jimmy, 121, 126
Categorical aid, 124–125, 128–129, 137
Census Bureau, 56
Child abuse and neglect, 10, 222

467

Child abuse and neglect (*Continued*)
  failure to provide services and, 224–225
  incidence of, 210–211
  investigation of, 224–225
Children in New York City
  characteristics of, Table 7.1 (p. 209), 208
  homelessness and, 211–213
  number of, 208
  poverty and, 208–213
Children's services
  child abuse and, 10
  day care and, 10, 217–222
  family support services and, 222–225
  foster care and, 10, 226–228
  future policy directions for, 228–231
  income maintenance and, 9–10, 214–217
  spending for, 207–208, Table 7.2 (p. 212)
  teenage pregnancy and, 10
City Council, budgeting process and, 140, 141
City Planning Commission, 129
  capital budgeting and, 140, 141, 160
City University of New York (CUNY)
  employment by, 175, 176
  State aid to, 5, 89, 107
Collective bargaining, 192
  structural characteristics of, 178–180, 181
Commercial occupancy tax, 40
Community development, federal aid for, 121, 122, 129, 131, 137
Community Development Block Grant program (CDBG), 121, 122, 129, 131, 137, 396
Community school districts
  characteristics of, Table 8.3 (pp. 240–241), 242, Table 8.4 (p. 244), 245
  inequalities among, 245–246
  low-income, 242–245
  poverty and education status in, Table 8.4 (p. 242)
  redefining boundaries of, 246–247
Community Service Society, 338
Commuters, 383–384
Comprehensive Employment and Training Act (CETA), 121–122, 125–126, 129, 130
Consolidated Edison, 149, 437
Consumer Price Index, 47
  growth of in 20 metropolitan areas, Table 1.7 (p. 33), 34
Consumer services, 26
Corporate headquarters complex, 17, 26
  economic growth and, 27

employment in, 50–51
Corporate income tax, 39–40
Corrections, capital spending for, 157
Council on Fiscal and Economic Priorities (COFEP), 99, 103–104
Crime. *See also* Felonies
  actual numbers of, 359–360
  career criminals, 357, 360–361, 375
  causes of, 353, 357
  comparative trends in, Table 11.2 (p. 358), 357–359
  felonies, 356, 360
  reported, 353, Table 11.1 (pp. 354–355), 359
  trends in, 356–357
Criminal Justice Coordinator, 378
Criminal justice expenditures
  by agency, Table 11.5 (p. 368), 367–373
  sources of, Table 11.7 (p. 372), 373
Crystal, Stephen, 331
Cuomo, Governor Mario, 96, 103–104

Day care, 7, 10, 213
  after-school, 221
  characteristics of those using, 218
  eligibility for, 218
  estimated need for, Table 7.5 (p. 220), 219–221
  expansion and integration of, 230
  funding for, 217–218
  Head Start program and, 217–218, 219
  income segregation and, 221–222
  Limited Purchase of Services agreements, 221
  private, 218–219, 221–222, 230
  quality of, 221
  unmet need for, 219–221
Department for the Aging (DFTA), 129, 133
  programs of, 327–328
Department of City Planning, 461
Department of Corrections, 378
  employment by, 176, 177, 198
  expenditures for, 369
Department of Finance, 190
Department of General Social Services (GSS), 222
Department of Juvenile Justice, 369
Department of Health, 13
  child health programs of, 309
  communicable diseases and, 308, 311
  data collection and, 310–311
  future role of, 309–312, 313

health care standards and, 311
  mission of, 307–309
  prevention services and, 311
  school health programs and, 312
Department of Housing Preservation and
  Development (HPD), 393, 396
Department of Investigations, 367
Department of Personnel, 178
  creation of, 191–192
  demise of, 192–193
Department of Probation, 369, 378
Department of Social Services, 129, 326
Department of Transportation, 167, 451,
  462
Deputy Mayor for Policy, 142
Doolittle, Fred C., 6
Drennan, Matthew, 3, 4, 81

Economic development, capital spending
  for, 157, 161
Economic performance
  local revenues and, Table 1.8 (p. 35)
  projections for, 46–51, Table 1.14 (p. 47)
Education levels
  adult, 242, Table 8.4 (p. 243)
  college graduates, Table 2.15 (p. 76)
  earnings and, Table 2.16 (p. 77)
  employment and, 73–75
  sex and ethnic group, Table 2.14 (p. 75)
Education services. See also Private schools,
  Public schools
  capital spending for, 156
  federal aid for, 129, 133, 137
  financing for, 11–12, 235
  spending for, 11
  State aid to, 6, 11, 113, 115, Table 8.10
  (p. 252)
Elderly population
  characteristics of, Table 10.5 (p. 323)
  disabilities of, 321–324, 330
  household types of, 318–319
  size of, Table 10.1 (p. 317)
Elderly services, 13–14, 316–318
  acute medical care, 328–330
  long-term for chronic disabilities, 13–14,
  330–339
  income maintenance programs for, 324–
  328
  Medicaid and, 329
  Medicare and, 328–329
Emergency Jobs Act of 1983, 122, 131, 133

Emergency Medical Service (EMS), 298,
  304, 313
Employment
  education levels and, 73–75
  health care workers and, 280–281
  labor market discrimination in, 75–78
  metropolitan areas and, Table 1.3 (p. 29),
  28
  projected changes in by sector, Table 1.15
  (p. 49)
  real output and, Table 1.1 (p. 25), 24–26
Employment and training programs, 125–
  126, 129
  federal aid for, 130–131, 137
Employment growth, 4, 25–26, 28, 35, 48,
  81
  during recessions, 28–33, Table 1.4
  (p. 30)
Employment-to-population ratios, Table 2.10
  (p. 70), Table 2.11 (p. 72), Table 2.12
  (p. 73), Table 2.13 (p. 74)
  for men, 71
  for teenagers, 71
  for women, 71–72
  trends in, 72–73
Entitlement grants, 120, 122, 136
Erie County, 108
Export industries, 26
  employment in, 27, 51

Family income, Table 2.3 (p. 57)
  drop in, 59
  earners in family and, Table 2.9 (p. 69),
  71
Family support services, 213
  availability of, 222–223
  early warning mechanism and, 223
  failure of, 224–225
  fragmentation of, 223–224
  recommended changes in, 230–231
Family structure, changes in, 62–71
Federal aid
  changes in welfare programs, 123–124
  cuts in Reagan's first term, 121–123
  debate over, 134–135
  general revenue sharing, 130–133, 136,
  137
  grant programs, 119–121
  impact of cuts in, 128–130, 136–137
  in real terms, Table 4.2 (p. 120), 121
  proposed changes in, Table 4.6 (p. 134),
  135–136

Federal aid (*Continued*)
    recent policy, 119–121
    reductions in, 6–7, 102, 118–119
    States' role in, 124–126
    to New York City, Table 4.4 (p. 127)
    to New York City agencies, Table 4.5 (p. 128), 129
    to State and local governments, Table 4.1 (p. 119)
Federal Housing Administration, 144
Felonies, 15
    arrest clearance rates for, 361–362, 374
    estimated outcomes of arrests for, Table 11.3 (p. 360)
    increasing arrests for, 374–375
    number of arrests for, 361–362, 364
    number of convictions for, 363–364
    number of indictments for, 362–363, 375–376
    probability of punishment for, Table 11.4 (p. 366), 364–367, 376–378
    sentencing policies for, 377–378
Female-headed single-parent families, 5
    children in, 208, 239
    day care and, 218
    growth in, 63–65, 82
    poverty of, 65, 82, 239
Finance Commissioner, 44
Finance Control Board, 1–7
    capital budgeting and, 141
Financial Plan 1985–1989, 91
Fire Department, 151, 175, 197
    capital spending for, 155
Food stamps program, 64, 68, 120, 124, 216
    elderly population and, 326, 328
Foster care and adoption, 10, 213, 222
    costs of, 227–228
    discharge objectives for, Table 7.6 (p. 225), 226, 227
    follow-up services for, 227
    payment system for, 228
    Program Assessment System (PAS) for, 227
    program closings and, 227
    standards of care for, 226–227
    recommended changes in, 231
    trends in, Table 7.7 (p. 225), 226
Fuchs, Ester, 15–16

Generally Accepted Accounting Principles (GAAP), 97–99, 100, 105–106
General obligation bonds, 7

rating of, 145
    sales of, 145–147
Goods production, 26, 27
Green, Cynthia, 6
Gross National Product, 46

Hartman, James, 7–8
Head Start program, 217–218, 219
Health and Hospitals Corporation (HHC), 13, 14, 137, 144, 155, 213, 341
    ambulance services of, 298
    ambulatory care services of, 297, 299–301
    capital spending for, Table 9.11 (p. 303), 304
    creation of, 294
    elderly population and, 329, 349
    emergency room services of, 295–297, 299–301
    employment by, 175, 176, 282
    financial independence of, 302–304
    hospital occupancy rates and, 301
    improvements by, 301–304
    leadership in City planning by, 306–307
    market share of hospitals in, Table 9.9 (p. 300), 299–301
    mental health services of, 297–298
    physical rehabilitation services of, 297–298
    recommendations for future, 304–307
    relationship with affiliates of, 305–306
    responsibilities of, 294–301
    subsidization of, Table 9.10 (p. 302)
Health care, 278
    employment in, 280–282
    expenditures for, 281–282
    intergovernmental constraints and, 282–285
Health Interview Surveys (HIS), 321, 346
Health Maintenance Organizations (HMOs), 12, 292–293
Health status
    communicable diseases and, 278–280
    death rates and, 278–280
    indicators of, Table 9.1 (p. 279), 278
    infant mortality and, 278–280
Health Systems Agency of New York, 340
Hennepin County, Minnesota, 222
Homeless
    families, 211–213
    housing programs for, 399–402
Home care services
    agencies providing, 332–334

expenditures for, 334
homemaker services and, 334
quality of, 348
Home Relief (HR) program, 66, 213
federal aid to, 132
Medicaid and, 287, 288
Horton, Raymond D., 8–9
Hospitals
capital spending for, 155
expenses per admission to, Table 9.3 (p. 281), 283
general care, Table 9.2 (p. 281)
Medicaid eligibility limitations and, 290–292
profits and losses of, Table 9.4 (p. 284), 283–285
State rate regulation policies and, 283–285
Housing and Vacancy Survey, 61
Housing Authority, 157
police, 367
programs for elderly of, 327
size of, 393
State aid to, 89
Housing construction, 16–17
incentives for middle-class, 17
publicly subsidized, 16
starts in, Table 12.2 (p. 384), 385–388, Table 12.5 (p. 390), 389
Housing Development Corporation, 161
Housing Finance Agency, 93
Housing programs, 150, Table 12.7 (pp. 394–395)
capital spending for, 157, 160–161
federal aid to, 131–132, 396
for elderly, 327
for homeless, 399–402
J-51 abatements, 396, 404–405
LDCs and, 393
Mitchell-Lama, 393
publicly assisted, 386–389, 399
rehabilitation, 385–386, 392, 393–397
Section 8, 389, 393, 396, 399
Section 207, 393
Section 421, 396, 405–407
Section 608, 393
tax abatements for, 392–393, 396, 404–407
Title I, 393
Housing supply
changes in, Table 12.1 (p. 383)
configurations of, 389–392

conversions in, Table 12.9 (p. 406), 407–409
future needs for, 397–399
market for, Table 12.6 (p. 391)
needs in, 384–385
trends in, 385–392
Human resource management, 8
productivity and, 8–9
Human Resources Administration (HRA), 129
day care programs and, 217–221
eligibility procedures and, 217, 229
employment by, 175, 176
family support services of, 222–223
foster care and, 227
home attendant care and, Table 10.10 (p. 337), 338, 348
programs for elderly of, 327–328, 334
Human Rights Commission, 129
Human Services Overburden Aid (HSOA) program, 288–289
Human Services Overburden Law, 133

Income levels, 3, 4, 60
declines in, 54–55, 61
ethnic divisions of, Table 2.5 (p. 59), 61
Income maintenance programs, 213. *See also* Aid to Families with Dependent Children, Home Relief
benefits under, 214–217, 229
Lower Level Living Standard and, 214–216, 229
federal poverty threshold and, 214–216
minimum standards for, 214–217
number receiving, Table 7.4 (p. 216)
Income taxes, 38–39
Industrial Development Bonds (IDB), 149
Inflation, 34–35
Infrastructure investment, 1, 7, 139, 150
amount of, 141, Table 5.1 (p. 142)
In rem housing, 17, 399
amount of, 402–403
inventory of, Table 12.8 (pp. 400–401)
management of, 403–404
tax delinquency and, 403–404

Jails
capacity of, 377–378
capital spending for, 157
overcrowding in, 362, 372
Jewish Hospital and Medical Center of Brooklyn, 283

Job Training Partnership Act (JTPA), 126, 129, 130
Joint Economic Commitee of Congress, 139

Kaiser, John, 18
Knickman, James, 13–14
Koch, Mayor Edward I., 147, 160, 184, 187, 193, 194

Landfills, 18, 158, 413, 435–436
    Fresh Kills, 435, 436–437, 439
Legal Aid Society, 367, 369
Levy, Reynold, 229
Liman Commission, 376
Limited Dividend Companies, 393
Limited Purchase of Services (LPOS) agreements, 221–222
Lindsay, Mayor John V., 186, 187, 192
Listokin, David, 16–17
Local industries, 26
Local revenues, 3
    forecast for, Table 1.16 (p. 50)
    of New York and 20 largest cities, Table 1.10 (p. 37)
    output and, Table 1.8 (p. 35)
    shifts in sources of, 38–39
Local tax burden
    changes in large cities, Table 1.9 (p. 36)
    reduction of, 37–38
Long Island Railroad, 445, 447, 451, 453
Long-term care programs, 13–14, 112, 222
    current for elderly, 330–335
    informal, 330–332, 348
    institutional facilities for, Table 10.7 (p. 331), Table 10.11 (p. 339)
    insurance-type financing of, 344–348
    formal, 332–335
    Medicaid and, 287–289, 337–338
    obstacles to obtaining, 336–338
    sources of, Table 10.6 (p. 330)
    standards for, 338–339, 348
Long Term Care Medicaid Takeover Act (LTCMTA), 112, 289
Lutheran Medical Center Health Care Plus program, 293–294

Management Service, 187
Mass transit
    bus service, 462–463, 464
    dependence on, 444–452
    employer tax for, 461–462
    fares on, 460–461

federal aid for, 102
financing of, 459–462
necessity for, 19, 443
operating expenses, revenues and subsidies for, Table 14.8 (p. 459)
pass system for, 19, 460–461
reduced fares for elderly, 326–327
revenue by system, Table 14.3 (p. 446)
ridership of, 443, Table 14.1 (p. 444), 445, Table 14.4 (p. 448), 447
subsidies for, 443, 460, 461–462
unmet needs for, 458
Mayor's Commission on Human Services Reorganization, 223
Mayor's Management Advisory Board, 187
Mayor's Management Report, 187
Mayor's Task Force on Child Abuse, 224
McCormick, Mary, 186, 187–188
Medicaid financing, 277
Medicaid Reform Act of 1984, 292–293
Medicaid services, 64, 68, 211, 213
    beneficiaries of, 287–288
    delivery systems for, 292–294
    elderly population and, 329
    eligibility for, 12–13, Table 9.6 (p. 286), 287–289
    expanding eligibility for, 289–292
    expenditures for, 286–289
    federal aid for, 102, 120, 123, 124, 126, 132–133, 136, 137
    HMOs and, 12
    home care and, 14
    limitations of eligibility for, 290–292
    prepaid delivery systems for, 293–294
    programs of, 12
    State aid to, 5, 6, 88–89, 91, 110
Medicare services, 13
    limitations of, 329
Mental health programs, 6, 297–298, 304
    State aid to, 113, 115
Metro North Commuter Railroad, 445, 447, 453
Metropolitan Transportation Authority (MTA), 19, 142, 193–194
    capital needs of, Table 14.7 (p. 452), 455
    capital program of, 453–455
    creation of, 452
    deferred maintenance and, 453
    fares and, 460–461, 464
    financing of, 453–454, 459–462, 464
    Permanent Citizens Advisory Committee to, 461

policies during fiscal crisis, 452–453
reduced services and, 453
State aid to, 89
strategic planning, 455–456
taxes for, 461–462, 464
Migration patterns, 56
Municipal Assistance Corporation (MAC), 107, 144
Municipal taxes, elasticity of, Table 1.11 (p. 39), 39–40
Municipal wage policies, 177–178
adjustments to, 181
allocation policies, 180–182, 200
arbitration and, 183–184
collective bargaining and, 177–181, 183–184, 186, 194
future, 184–185
gainsharing and, 182, 200, 201
managerial pay and, 194
parity rules and, 180, 182
past, 178–180
pay relationships, Table 6.3 (p. 179), 180–181
productivity and, 200, 201
progressivity rule and, 181, 182
real salaries, Table 6.4 (p. 181), 194, 200
real wage policies, 182–183
since 1984, 183–184
Municipal work force, 2
by agency, Table 6.2 (p. 174), 175
distribution of, 175–176, 177, 197–198
expenditures and employment, Table 6.1 (p. 172), 173
future employment policies for, 176–177
mayoral elections and, 173
past staffing policies for, 171–173
quality of, 185, 193–194, 196–197, 198–199
real spending for, 173
size of, 173, 176–177, 194, 195–197
staffing levels of, Table 6.6 (p. 195), Table 6.7 (p. 196), 197
staffing policies for, 171–177, 195–198
Municipal work force productivity, 170, 185
future development options for, 193–194, 197, 198–199
future management options for, 190–191, 199–200
gainsharing and, 199–200
improvements in, Table 6.5 (p. 188)
past development policies, 191–193
past management policies, 186–190

Productivity and Management Improvements and, 189–190, 194
Productivity-COLA program, 186
Program to Eliminate the Gap and, 189, 190
programs for, 186–190

Nassau County, 383.
National Crime Survey, 360
National economic assumptions, Table 1.13 (p. 46)
National Governors' Association, 126
Nehemiah and New York City Partnership, 157
Netzer, Dick, 40
New Jersey, 383
New York City Citizens Budget Commission, 99
New York City economy
change in major sectors of, Table 1.2 (p. 26), 27
federal aid to, Table 4.4 (p. 127)
New York City Partnership, 433
New York City Tax Commission, 43–44
New York Prospective Hospital Reimbursement Methodology (NYPHRM), 283–285
New York Public Interest Research Group (NYPIRG), 41, 43–44
New York State aid
amount of, Table 3.1 (p. 88), Table 3.2 (p. 90), Table 3.3 (p. 92)
availability of, 91–101, 104–105
categorical, 88–89, 110, 113
City's dependence on, 87–91, 113–114
expectations for, 91, 113–115
functional mix of, 110–112
"gap-closing," 89
general revenue sharing, 110–112
increases in, 5–6
indirect, 89, 107–108
local assistance appropriations of, Table 3.6 (p. 109), Table 3.7 (p. 110)
Medicaid, 88–89, 110–112, 113, 115, 288–289
other localities and, 108–110
outlook for, 100–107, 113–115
New York State Community Services for the Elderly Act, 328
New York State Department of Commerce, 398
New York State Department of Social Services, 224, 225, 288

New York State Division of Housing and Community Renewal, 398

New York State finances
borrowing practices of, 98–99, 105–107
expenditure policy of, 104–105
financial condition of, 92–93
financial reporting of, 97–99, 105–107
projected revenues and expenditures, Table 3.5 (p. 101), 100–102
spending for local aid and direct operations, Table 3.4 (p. 95)
spending priorities of, 94–97, 104–105
tax policy of, 93–94, 102–104

New York State Redevelopment Corporation, 393

New York State Task Force on Equity and Excellence in Education, 250, 260

Niagara Falls, 108

Nursing homes, 14
admissions policies of, 336, 342–344
expanding capacity of, Table 10.11 (p. 339), 340–342, 349
expenditures for, 332
Medicaid payments to, 336
number of, Table 10.7 (p. 331)
"private-pay" patients and, 342–343
shortage of beds in, 335–336, 348

Office of Community Services, 413
Office of Economic Development, 129
Office of Management and Budget, 142
Office of Operations, 187
Office of Program Evaluation and Control, 419
Office of Resource Recovery and Waste Disposal Planning, 413, 437
Older Americans Act, 327–328
Operating grants, 120–121
appropriations for, Table 4.3 (p. 124)
cuts in, 125

Paris Metro, 456–457, 464
Parks, capital spending for, 156–157, 160, 162, 167
PATH system, 445, 447
Personal income
below poverty level, 35
growth in, 35
in New York City, 34–35
per capita, Table 1.6 (p. 32)
Personal income tax, 38–39, 51
Plea bargaining, 363

Police Department, 175
capital spending for, 155
employment by, 175–176
expenditures for, 367
Police services, 16
felony arrests and, 361–362
Poor population, 3
children in, 239
increase in, 4–5, 59–61, 68, 82
Population. See also School age population
changes in, Table 2.1 (p. 55)
changes in by age and ethnic group, Table 2.2 (p. 56), 57, Table 2.18 (p. 80), 79–82
declines in, 56–58, 79, 397–398
employment ratio by race, sex and age, Table 2.10 (p. 70), 71
income and ethnic group, Table 2.5 (p. 59)
income group and family type, Table 2.6 (p. 62)
projections for, 78–82
Population loss, 4, 9, 17, 54, 56–58, 79
Port Authority of New York and New Jersey, 161, 437
Poverty level
definitions of, 67
incomes below, 35, 59–61
Power Authority of the State of New York, 437
Private education, 236, 244
characteristics of, 267–268
enrollment in, Table 8.17 (p. 265), Table 8.18 (p. 266), 267, Table 8.19 (p. 269), 268, 271
minority enrollment in, 267, 268
Private education financing
constitutionality of public funding for, 268–270
impact of tax deductions for, 270–273
public funding for, 12, 268–270
Productivity and Management Improvements (PMIs), 189–190, 194
Program to Eliminate the Gap (PEG), productivity and, 189–190
Property taxes, 3–4, 38, 51
assessment policy for, 45, 51
classification system of, 42
condominiums and, 407–408
elasticity of, 40
interclass inequities of, 41–46
"reform" of, 40–41
Public school financing, 235, 247

approved operating expenses (AOE) and, 248–253
capital spending for, 156, 159–160
compared to New York State, 249–250, 273–274
constitutionality of, 258
equity and, 256–261
federal aid for, 254, 274
impact of public funding for private schools on, 271–273, 274–275
local aid for, Table 8.11 (p. 252), Table 8.12 (p. 254), 255–256
property value per pupil and, Table 8.13 (p. 257), 259–260
revenues for, Table 8.9 (p. 251), Table 8.11 (p. 253), 253–256
State aid for, Table 8.10 (p. 252), 253, 254–255, 258–261, 274
Public school performance
attendance and, Table 8.14 (p. 259), 274
dropout rate and, Table 8.16 (p. 263), 264–266, 274
reading achievement test scores and, Table 8.15 (p. 260), 262–264, 274
Public schools
enrollment in, Table 8.2 (p. 237), Table 8.19 (p. 269)
equity in, 256–261
expenditures for, 247–253, 273–274
performance of, 235–236
school-age population and, 235, 236–247
Public service employment (PSE), 121–122, 126

Queens-Midtown Tunnel, 451

Reagan, President Ronald, 6, 118, 121–123, 126
Real Estate Board of New York, 44–45
Real output and employment, Table 1.1 (p. 25)
Refuse collection
civilianization of, 427, 440
containerization and, 425, 440
crew sizes and, 421–422
equipment for, 421, 426
future directions for, 424–427, 440
gainsharing and, 423–424, 426, 440
increased productivity in, 419–424
managerial responses to, 416–419
performance indicators of, Table 13.2 (p. 417)
relay dumping and, 425–426, 440
rescheduling and, 426
Route Extension Program and, 419–420
service decline in, 415–416
side-loading trucks for, 422
Regie Autonome des Transports Parisiens (RATP), 456–457, 461
Regional Plan Association, 451
mass transit recommendations of, 458–459
Rent Stabilization Association, 406
Resource recovery plants, 8, 18, 162, 167, 413, 437–440, 441
Revenue bonds, 7
Rochester, 109–110
Rockland County, 383

Sandler, Ross, 19
Sanitation Department, 8, 9, 175
allocation of resources in, Table 13.1 (p. 414)
bureaus of, 413–415
capital spending for, 155
employment by, 413
future directions for, 424–427
gainsharing agreements of, 18, 423–424, 426
improved performance of, 18
overview of, 413–415
PAR index, 424
police, 432–433
refuse collection, 415–427, 440
street cleaning, 427–434, 441
waste disposal, 434–440, 441
Sales taxes, 38–39
School-age population
composition of, Table 8.1 (p. 236), 238–242
decline in, 237–238
Sencer, Commissioner of Health David, 310–311
Senior-citizen centers, 7
Setting Municipal Priorities, 1982, 229
Settlement Housing Fund, 396
Sewers, capital spending for, 153–154, 160, 162
63rd Street tunnel, 453, 454, 456, 458
Smith, John Palmer, 15–16
Social Security, 13
elderly population and, 324–325, 328

Social Services Block Grant program, 217–218, 327

Special Deputy Comptroller's Office, 107

Special Services for Children (SSC) agency, 222, 223, 231
  negligence of child abuse of, 224

Stafford, Walter, 4, 5

State Charter Revision Commission, 187, 192–193

Stavisky-Goodman law, 255–256

Sternlieb, George, 16–17

Street cleaning
  Clean Team for, 431, 434
  enforcement for, 432–433, 441
  equipment maintenance for, 431–432
  littering and, 433
  manpower for, 427–431, 434
  options for, 433–434, 441
  performance indicators for, Table 13.3 (p. 429)
  Scorecard system for monitoring, 428, 430–431

Streets, capital spending for, 153, 158, 161–162, 167

Subway ridership, 445

Suffolk County, 110, 383

Supplemental Security Income (SSI), 13, 107
  elderly population and, 325–326, 328
  Medicaid and, 287, 288, 290

Supplemental State Targeted Assistance Program, 112

Surface Transportation Assistance Act of 1982, 122

Syracuse, 109–110

Tax revolt, 103, 121

Teenage pregnancy and parenthood, 10
  consequences of, 211

Third water tunnel, 143, 151–152, 158, 161, 167

Tobier, Emanuel, 4, 5, 197, 398

Tobis, David, 9–10

Transit Authority (TA), 19, 193–194, 327
  automated fare collection and, 454
  employment by, 453
  fare beating and, 454

fare revenues of, 460
federal aid for, 133
Franklin Avenue shuttle and, 455–456

Transit Authority Police, expenditures for, 367

Tunnels, traffic in, 450–451

Unemployment
  in 30 largest cities, Table 1.5 (p. 31)
  rate of, 3, 33, 46

Uniformed service vehicles, capital spending for, 155–156

Unincorporated business tax, 39–40

United Hospital Fund, 12
  City Hospital Visiting Committee of, 298

Urban Development Corporation, 93

Wagner, Mayor Robert F., Jr., 192

Ward, Police Commissioner Benjamin, 362

Waste disposal
  capital spending for, 154–155
  current strategies for, 436–440
  landfills and, 435–436, 439, 441
  reductions in capacity for, 435–436
  resource recovery plants and, 437–440, 441

Waste disposal plants, 7, 143, 144, 413
  financing for, 149–150, 162, 167

Wastewater treatment facilities, 121, 133

Water and Sewer Authority, 7

Water and sewer revenue bonds, 144, 168
  first offering of, 147–148

Water Board, 147

Water distribution, capital spending for, 152–153

Water Finance Authority, 147, 149

Water pollution control, capital spending for, 154, 159, 163

Water supply, capital spending for, 151–152, 157

We Care About New York, 433

Welfare, 5
  shelter allowances of, 399
  State aid to, 6

Westchester County, 383

Yonkers, 108–109